100 beards
edition two

the contemporary cult of the hirsute:
a documentary

Jonathan Daniel Pryce

GarconJon.com
www.JonathanDanielPryce.com
100beards.tumblr.com

This second edition first published by
Polwarth Publishing LLP
25 Polwarth Crescent
Edinburgh EH11 1HR
&
PPLLP London

www.polwarthpublishing.com

ISBN 978-0-9574356-4-3

British Library Cataloguing-in-Publication Data
A catalogue record for this book is available from the British Library

Designed by Martin Belk
Printed and bound by Martin's the Printers, Berwick Upon Tweed
http://martins-the-printers.co.uk/

Thank you to everyone who continues to support this project.

Special thanks to Nick Bain, Martin Belk, Thomas Haywood, Laura Kidd, Olivier Joly, Jeremy Langmead, Dan Larson, Daniel Peters, Jennifer Pryce, Rob Pryce and Dan Rookwood for making it possible for me to reach day 200. Most of all, to all the men in this book — without their participation and superb facial hair, we'd be left with blank faces and pages.

— JDP

100beards.tumblr.com

foreword

Beards grew back. And then they grew some more...

Not so long ago, a book or a blog documenting beards would have been seen as an ironic and mischievous wink at the pogonophiles of a bygone era. We would have laughed at the frisky, bristly man trying out the karma sutra positions in the 1970s edition of *The Joy of Sex*, the old barber shop posters of men with lustrous side-partings and goatees to match, and the bushy-faced TV presenters of yesteryear such as Bill Oddie, David Bellamy and, er, Rolf Harris.

But something changed. Facial hair was no longer shaved, but embraced. Unlikely characters such as Brian Blessed and Prince Michael of Kent suddenly found themselves at the centre of one the decade's biggest male trends. And we're not talking 'polite designer stubble,' but full-on fuzz – as championed by folk bands like Mumford & Sons and Fleet Foxes.

Theories as to why a new generation of men came to re-embrace facial hair abound, and there's a soupcon of truth to all of them: after the slick, slippery and shaved years that led up to the economic crisis, men began to yearn a return to a pastoral idyll of crafts, folk music and farm-to-table food. That, or a beard was a symbol that showed your disgruntlement with the superficial, consumer-savvy, UKIP-friendly society that surrounded you. Or, merely, it's a simple face stamp of virility, masculinity and adventure — a beard, after all, has been worn as a badge of honour by pioneers throughout history.

Today, adventures and ideas travel around the globe in microseconds. We use the Web, as opposed to Siberian huskies, to whisk us to new domains and far-flung territories. Blogs such as Jonathan's – where this book of beards originated – spreads the word for us. Hirsute of chin or not, to explore and examine how other men are choosing to grow and wear their beards across the streets of London and beyond is a cultural treat, and so much more polite than staring up-close at a stranger's beard yourself — an action which could easily be misconstrued as impolite. Happily, Jonathan has taken that risk for us.

Of course, perhaps there is no hidden context to growing a beard at all — *perhaps* it's just 'easier,' 'low-maintenance...' Perhaps, as in my case, it's just half a face less to worry about each morning. A beard, after all, can hide a multitude of sins, and chins.

Jeremy Langmead
Editor in Chief, Mr Porter

100 beards
edition two

the contemporary cult of the hirsute:
a documentary

Jonathan Daniel Pryce

Over the past few years, the beard has re-emerged as the ultimate accessory for the modern gentleman. By Summer 2012, this 21st century incarnation of masculinity, once again, demanded documentation. As a style photographer, I'm fascinated by the emergence of trends so every day for 100 days I photographed a new beard on the streets of London. From big and bushy to trendy and trimmed, I found men spanning three generations who all joined the contemporary cult of the hirsute.

From July 1st to October 8th 2012, the *100 BEARDS, 100 DAYS* project received enthusiastic international support. Because of this phenomenal response, I've decided to continue my documentation of bearded men. Beginning in January 2013 I took my 101st portrait. The journey now encompasses 200 men, bound together in this second collection. Readers share it with friends around the world, the press continues to produce features, and bloggers champion their favourite images - it seems appreciation of the beard is far from over.

JDP

GarconJon.com
www.JonathanDanielPryce.com
100beards.tumblr.com

100 beards
edition two

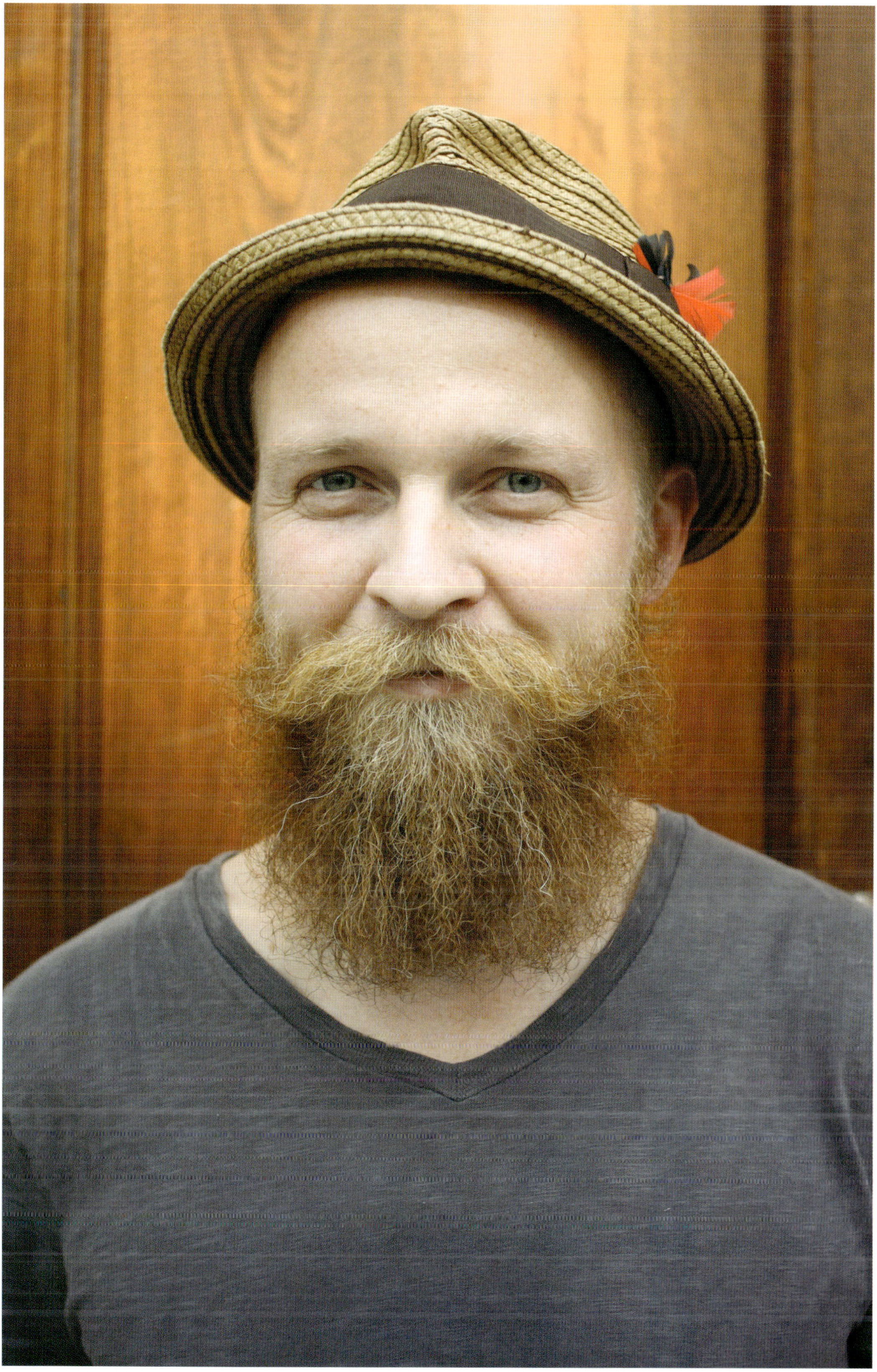

1 • Ben: Charing Cross Road, London

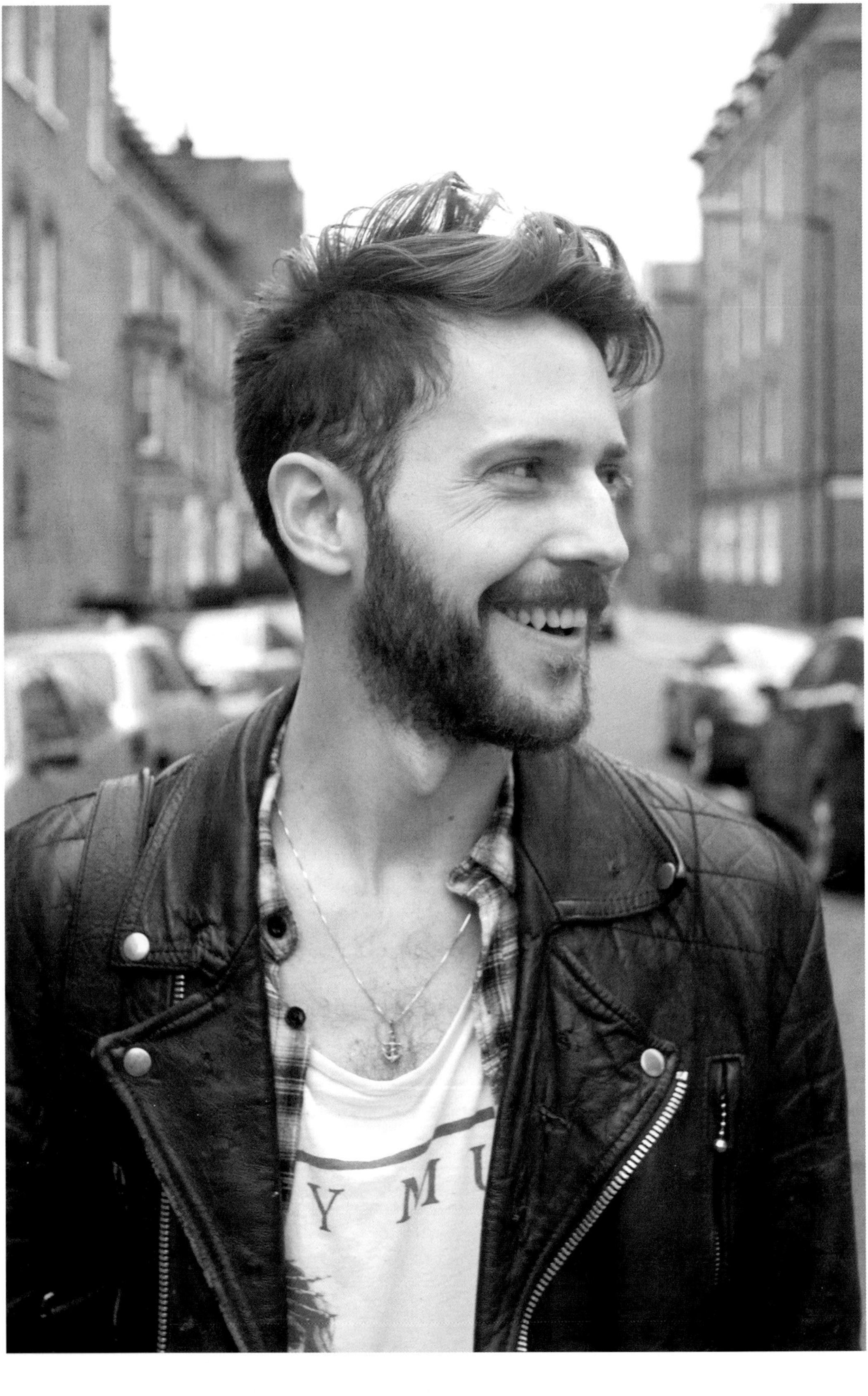

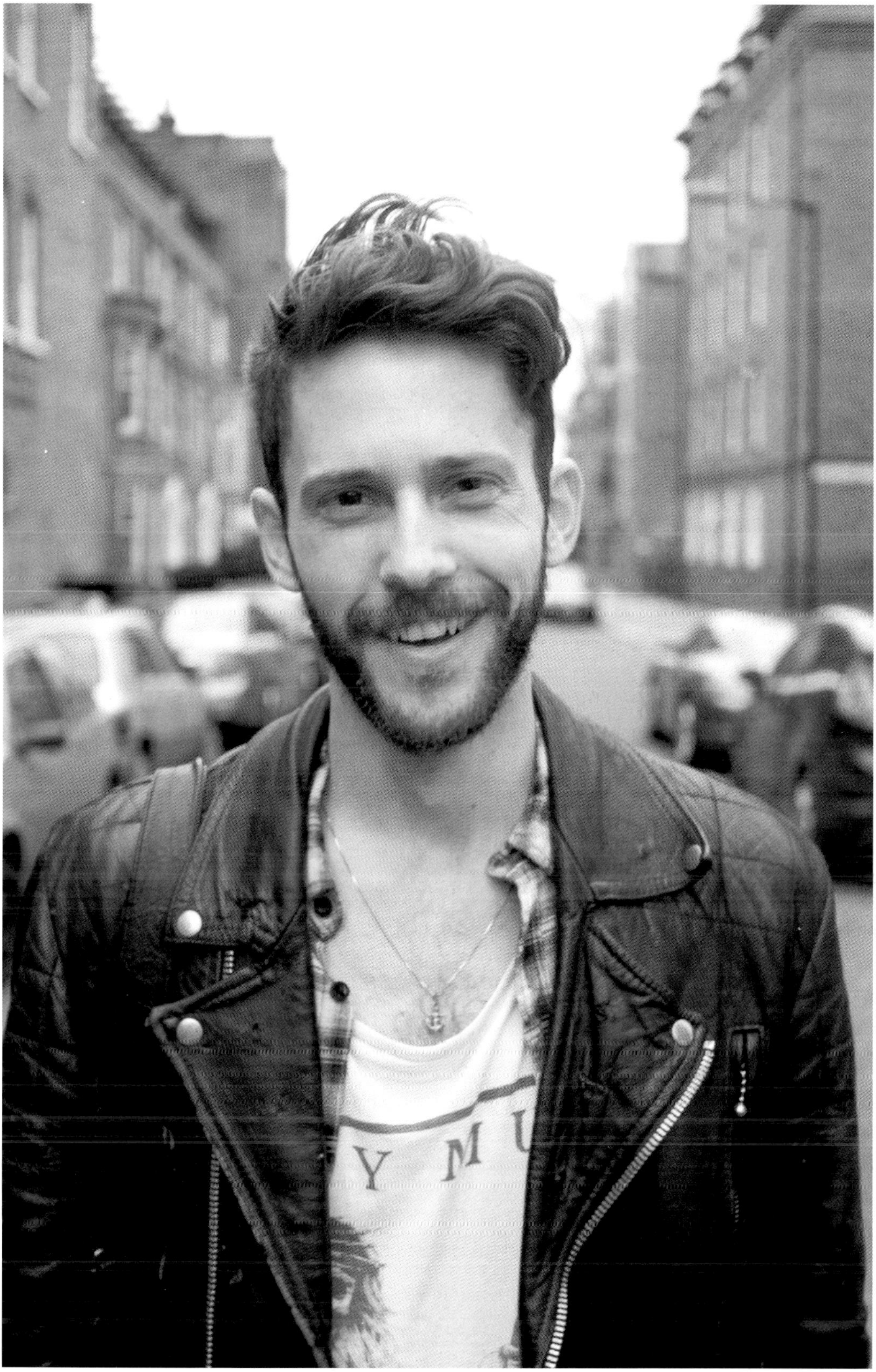

2 • Gregory: Swanfield St, London

Being of Mediterranean origin and growing up in the sub-continent, I had to conform to society by not being allowed to grow my facial hair. Having broken from the traditional construction of my original community, I have nurtured my beard as a seductive representation of masculine identity. I would now feel incomplete without my beard.

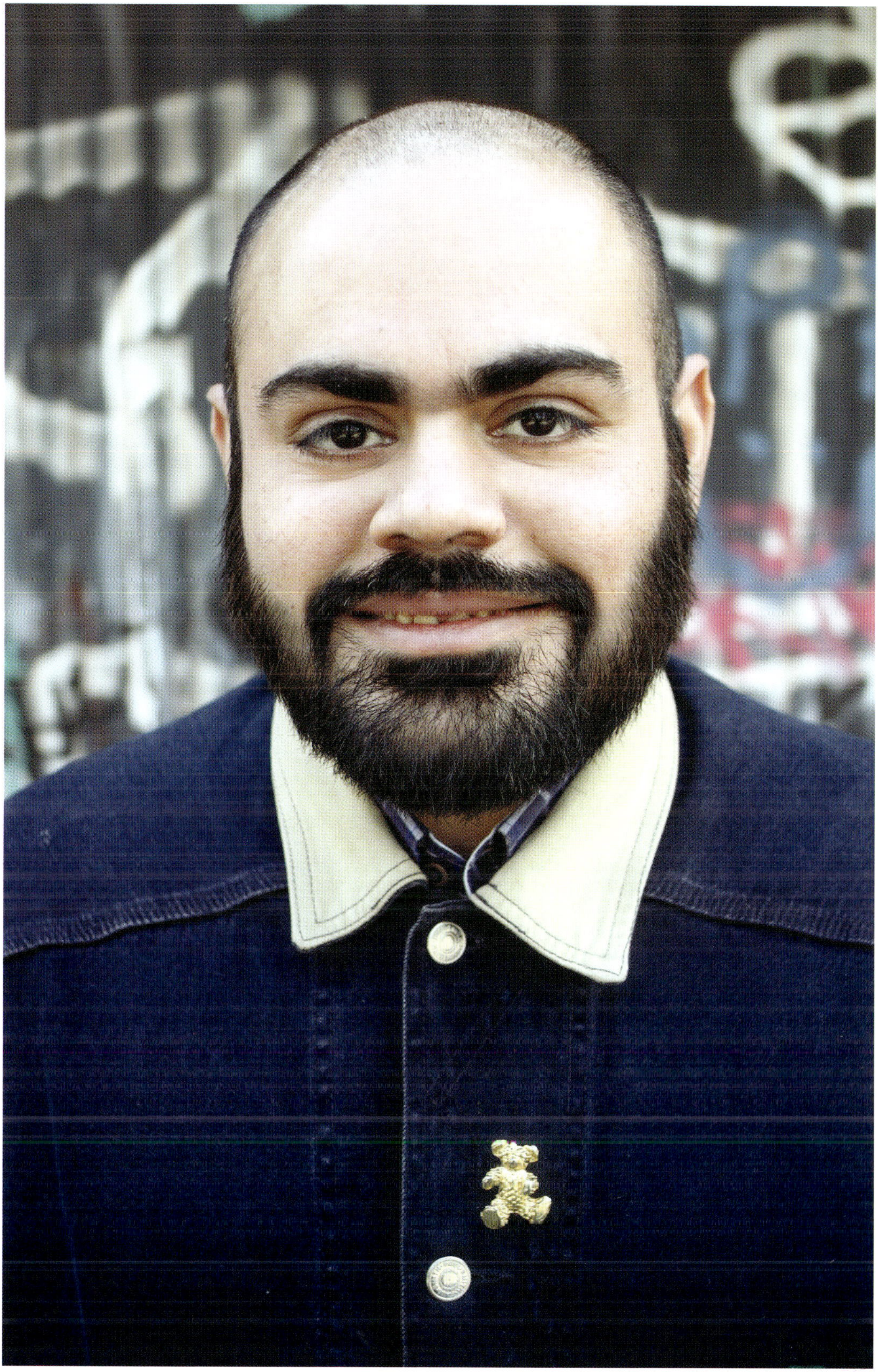

3 • Hormazd: Brick Lane, London

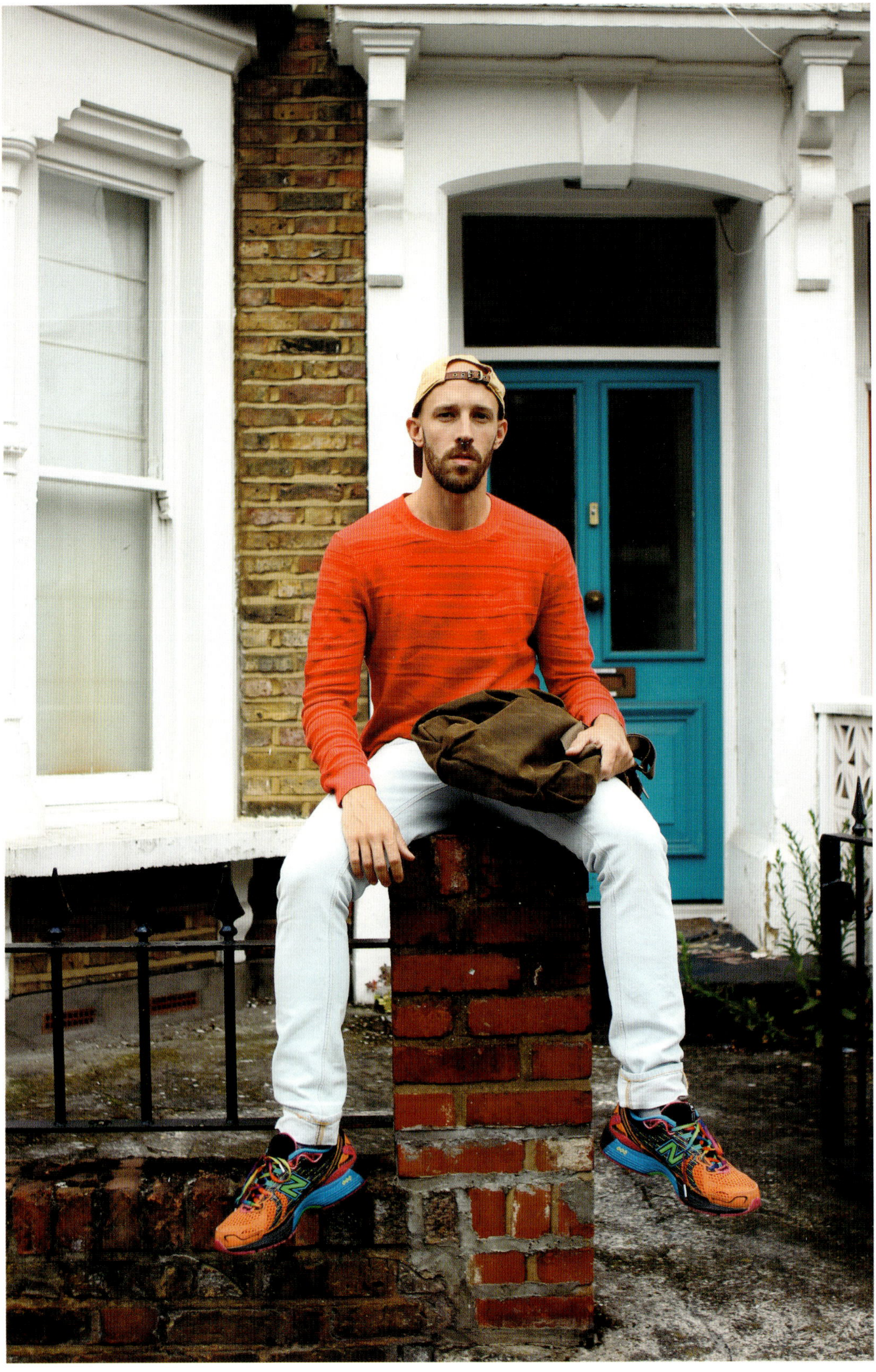

4 • Darren: Whitby Street, London

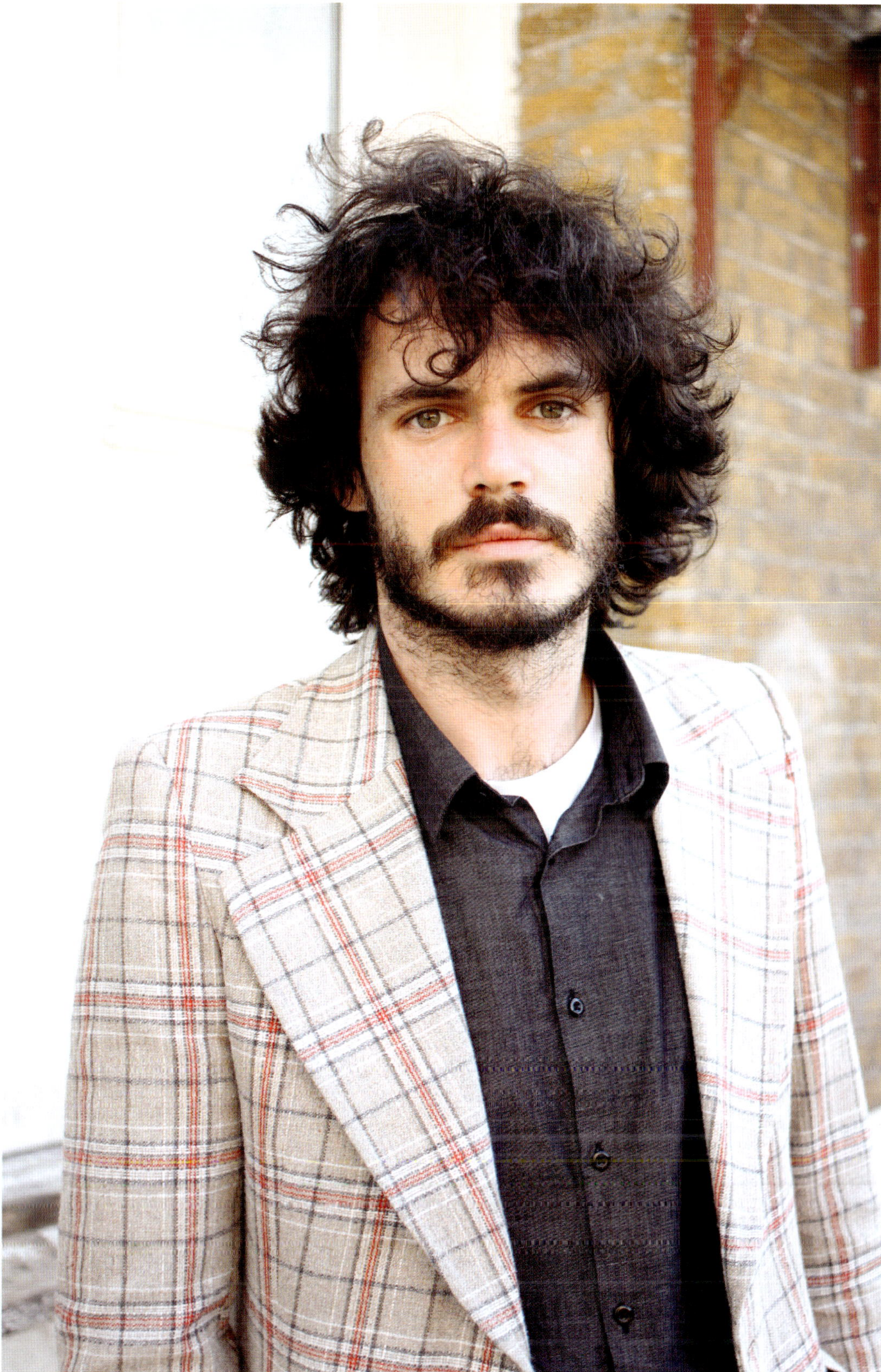

5 • David: Rivington St, London

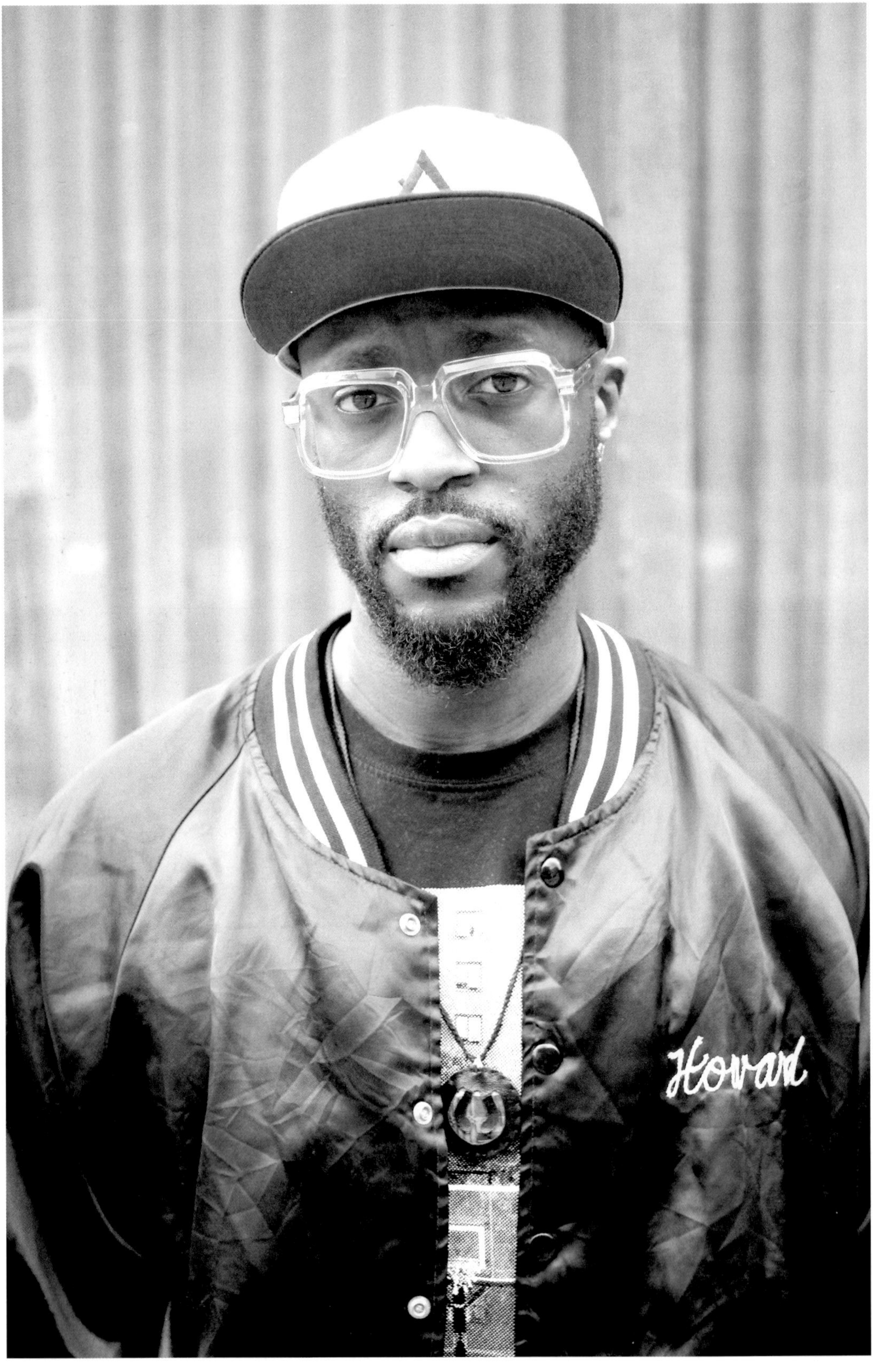

6 • Gabriel: Ebor Street, London

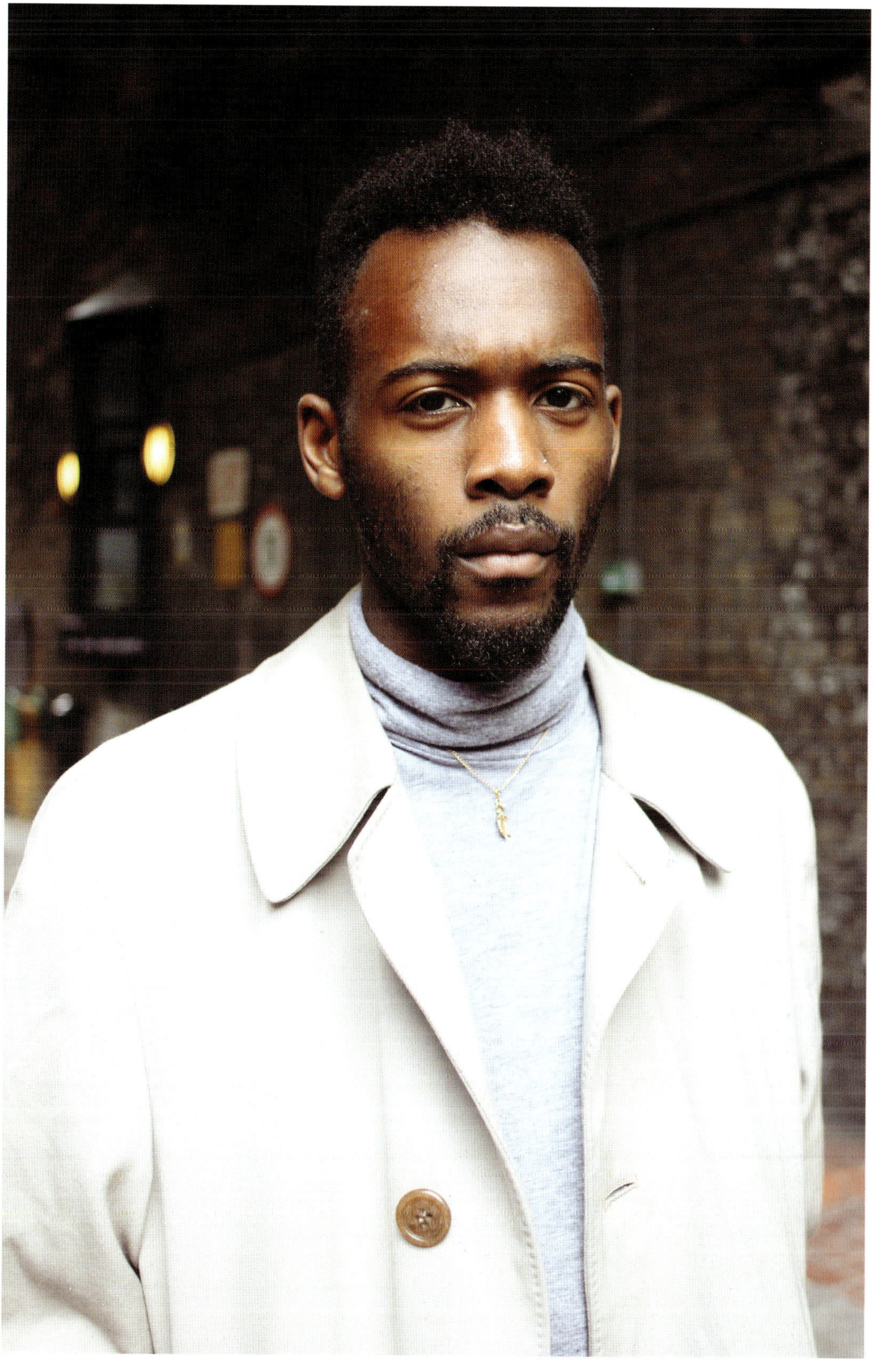

7 • Kamanii: Neal St, London

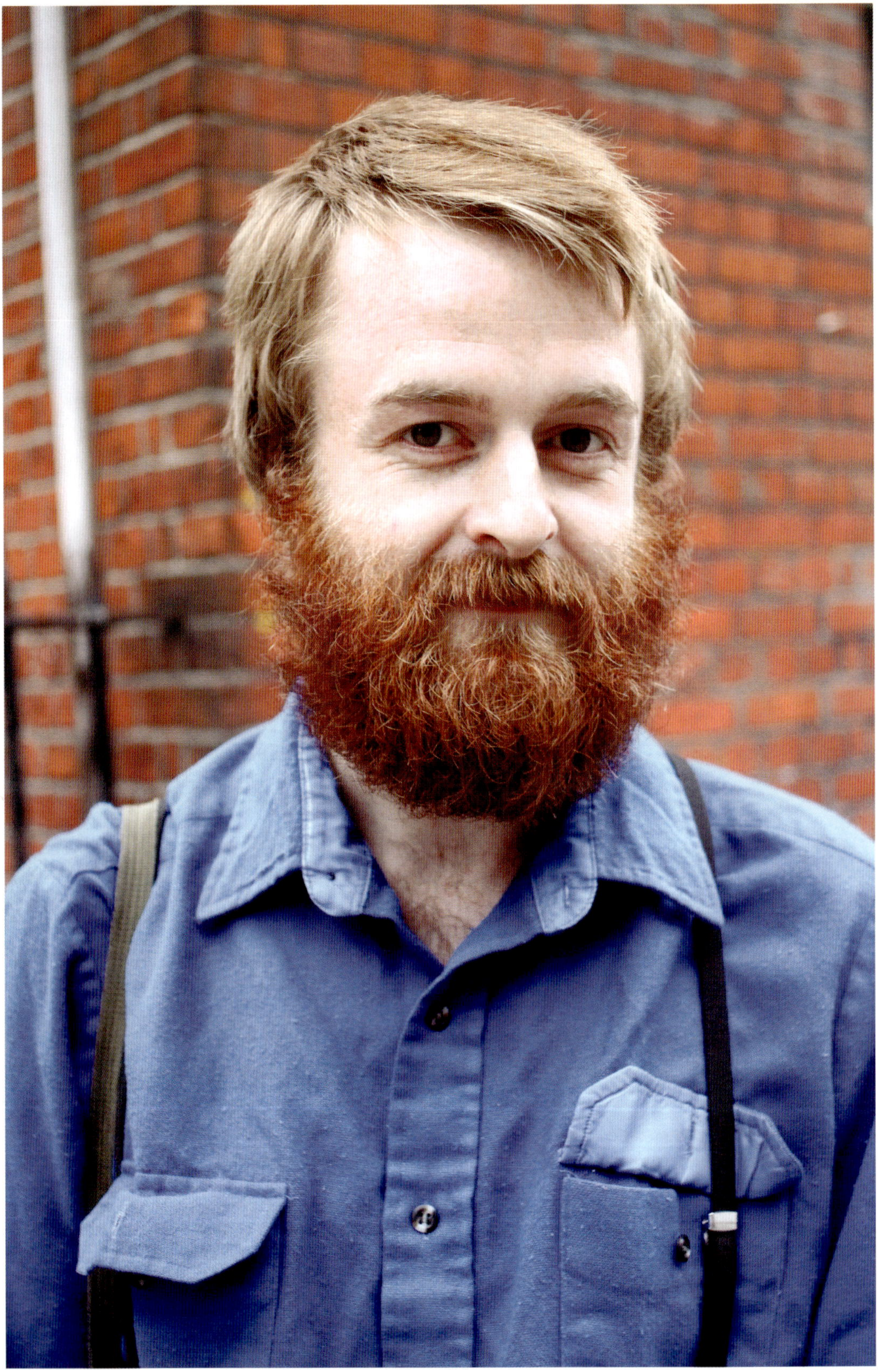

8 • Sean: Arnold Circus, London

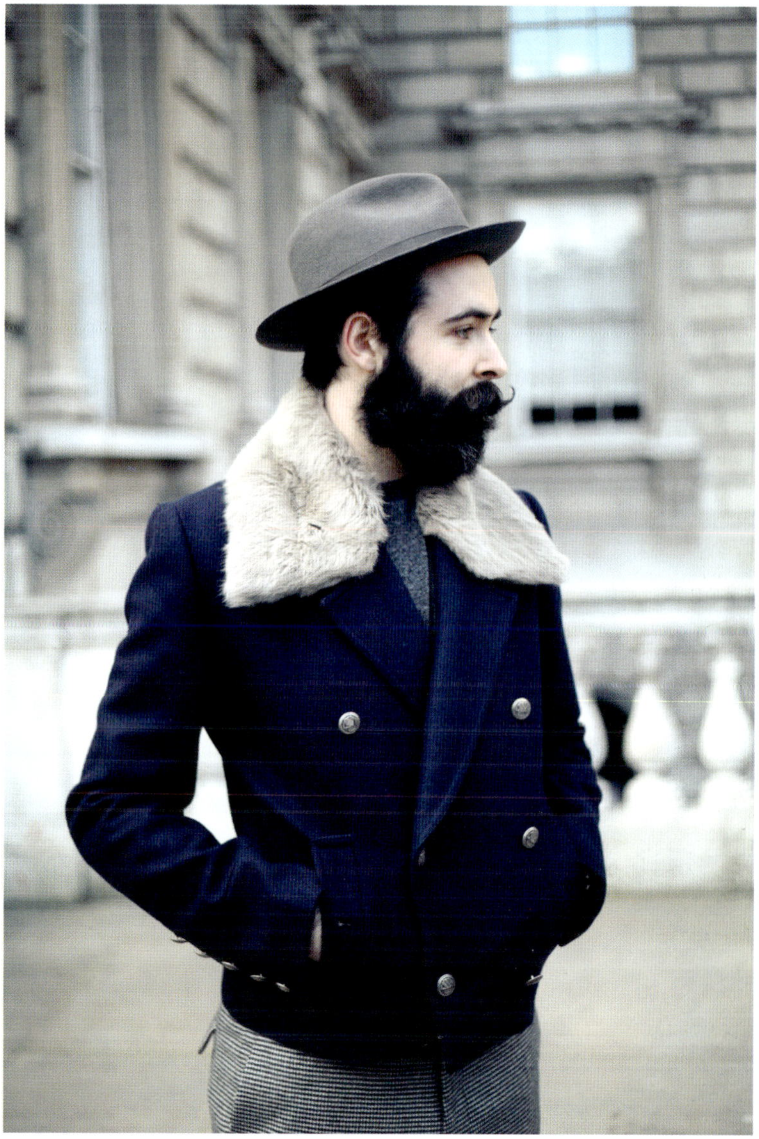

There's something quite comforting about having a beard. It gives you calm and confidence. I've received plenty of attention from girls, photographers and men who're curious to know how I look after it — not a day that goes by without talk of my beard. It's a massive labour of love, but I wouldn't have it any other way. I think beards have become popular because they're a very natural expression for men. For me it's a chance to rebel and that rebellious spirit has been apparent in all sorts of cultural environments.

9 • Chris: Somerset House, London

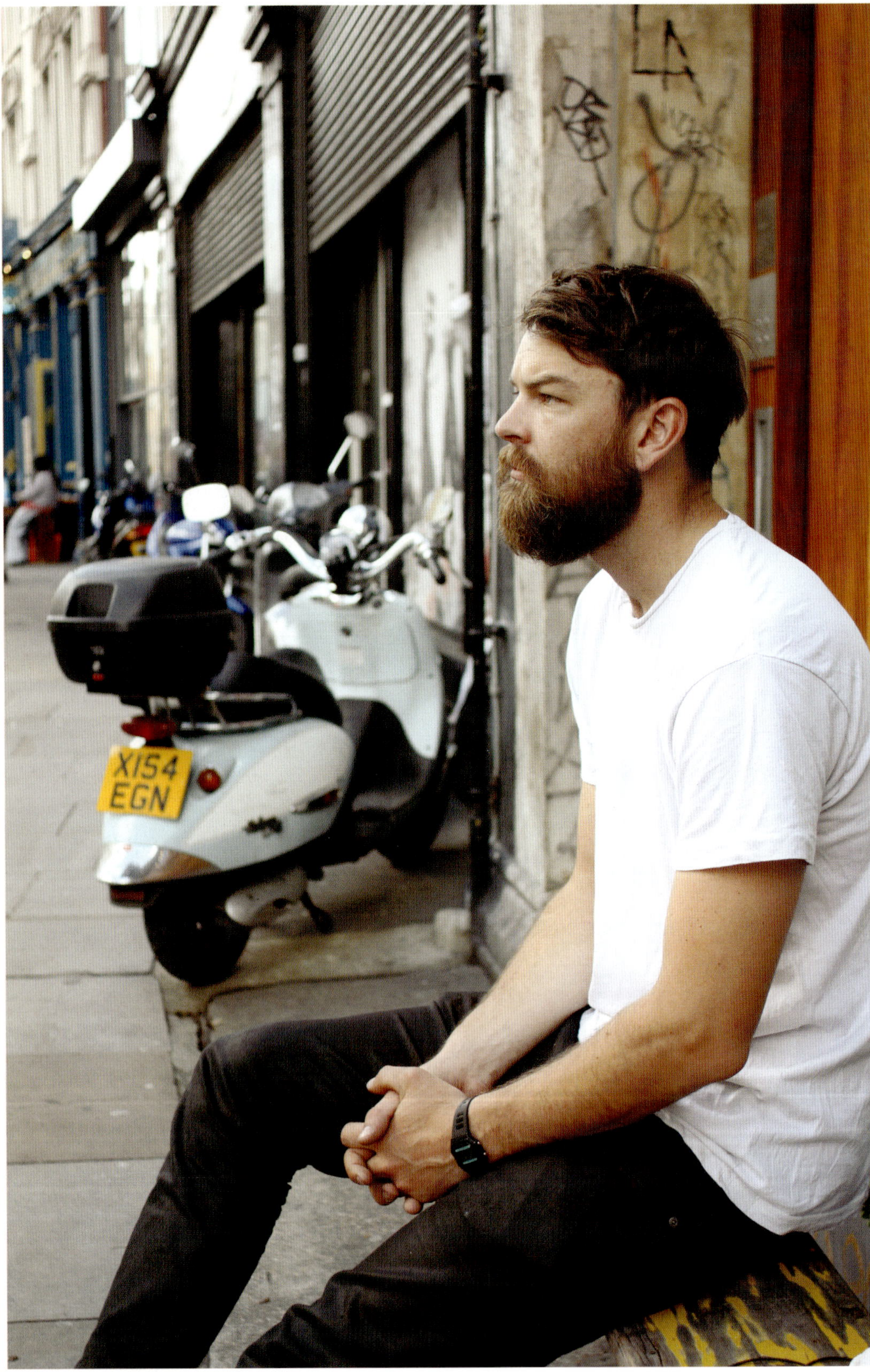

10 • James: Shoreditch High Street, London

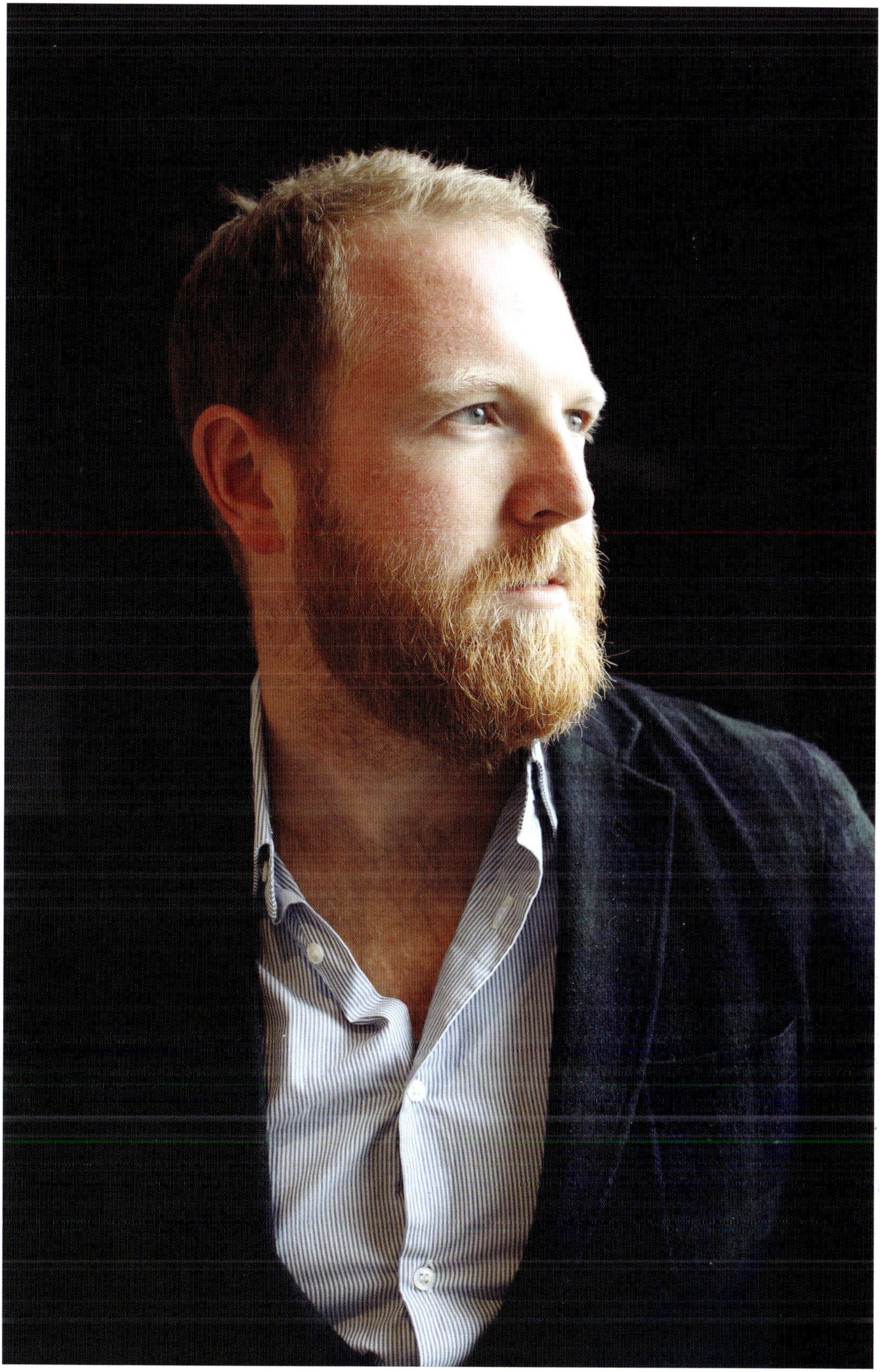

11 • Charlie: London Bridge Street, London

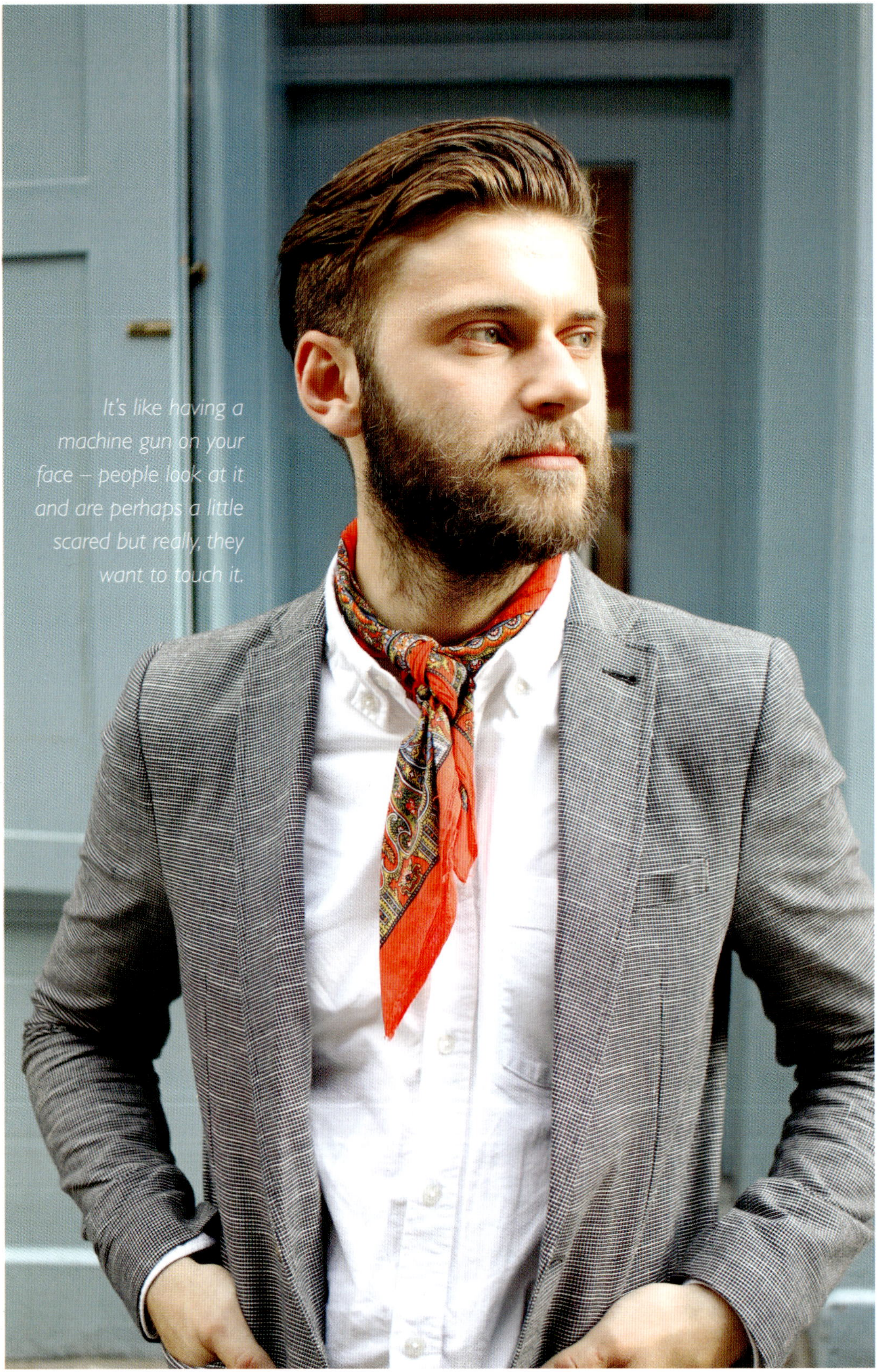

Terry: Earlham Street, London

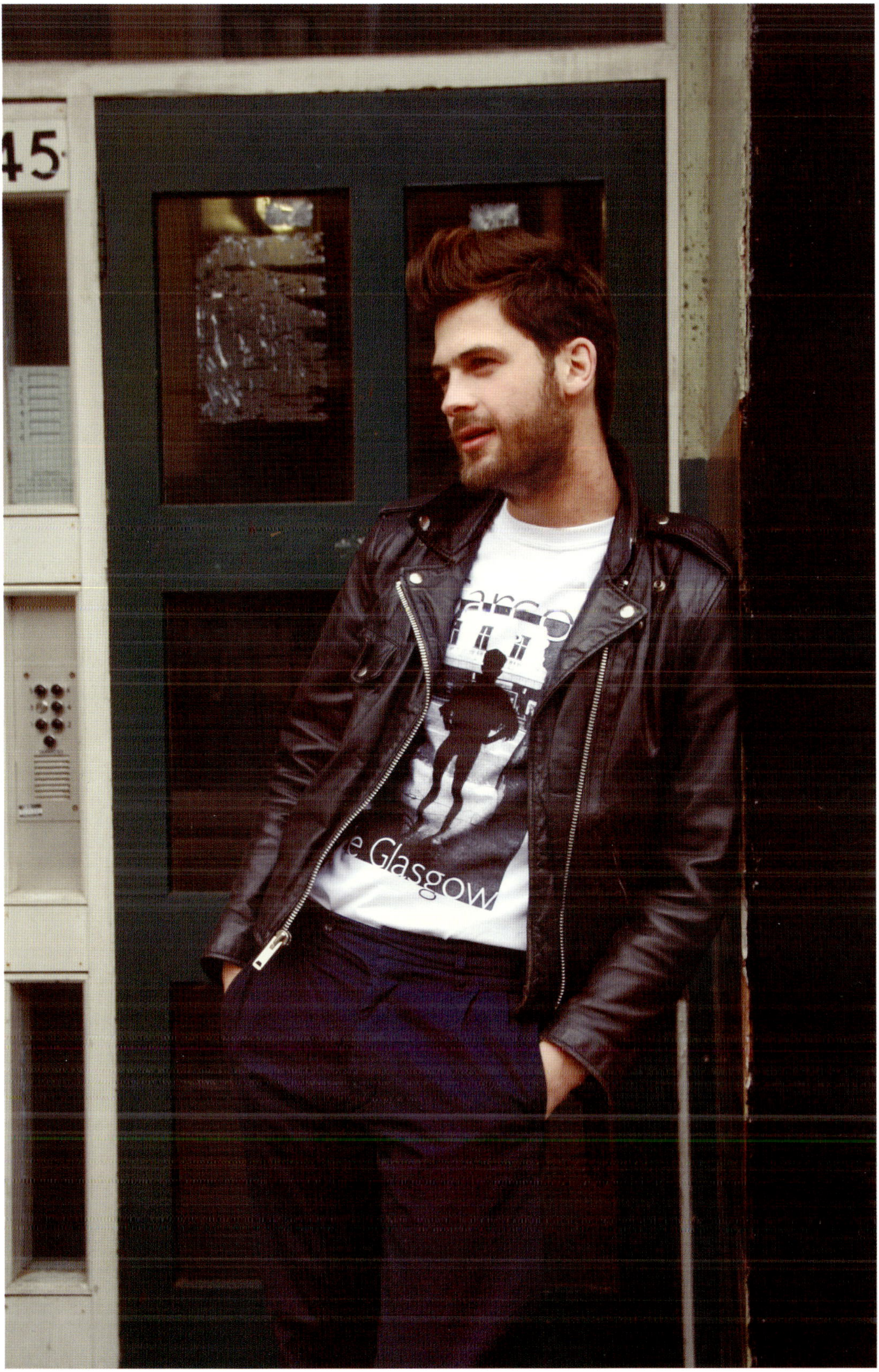

13 • Julian: Great Queen Street, London

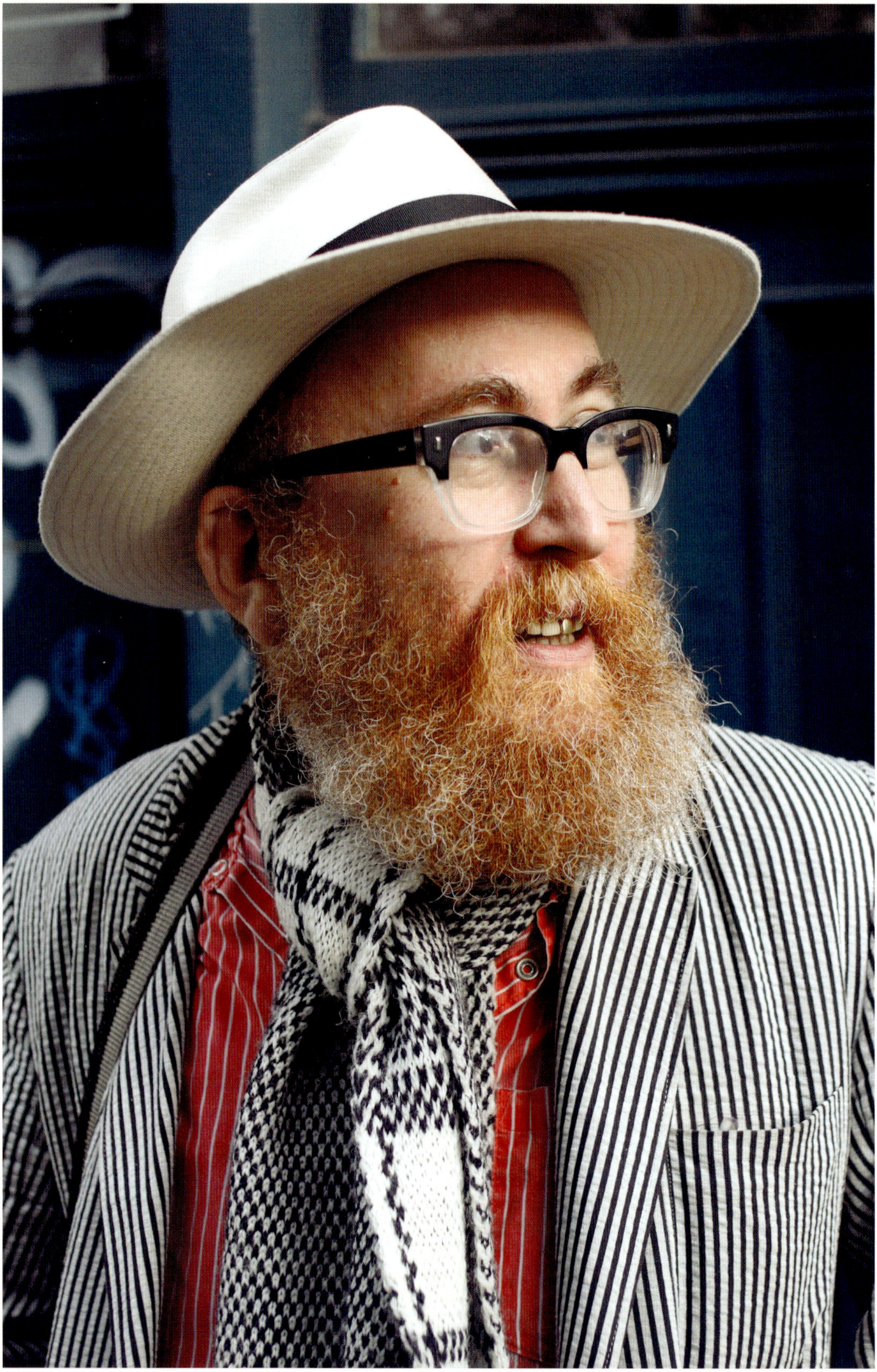

14 • Nicholas: Columbia Road, London

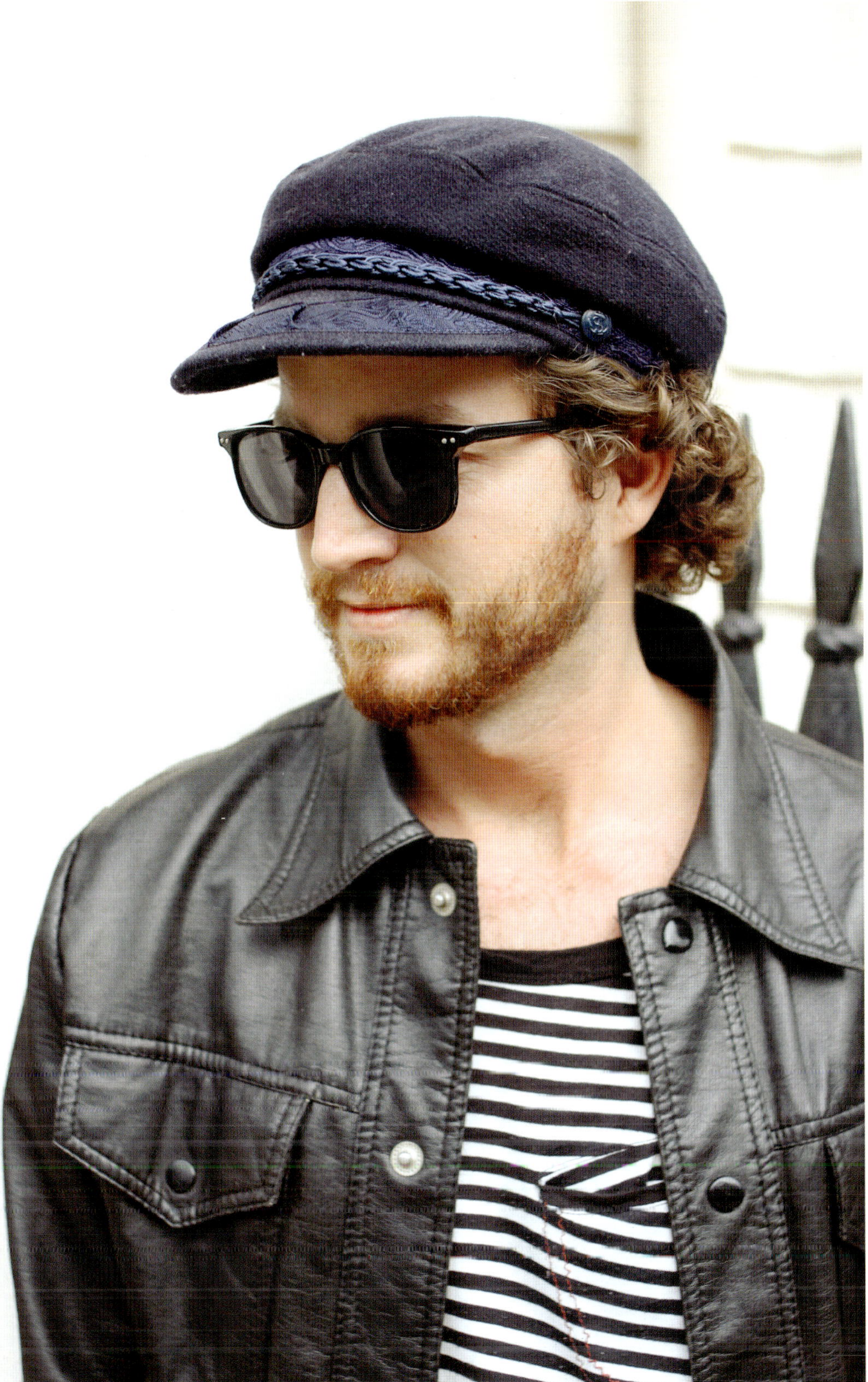

15 • Aaron: Regent St, London

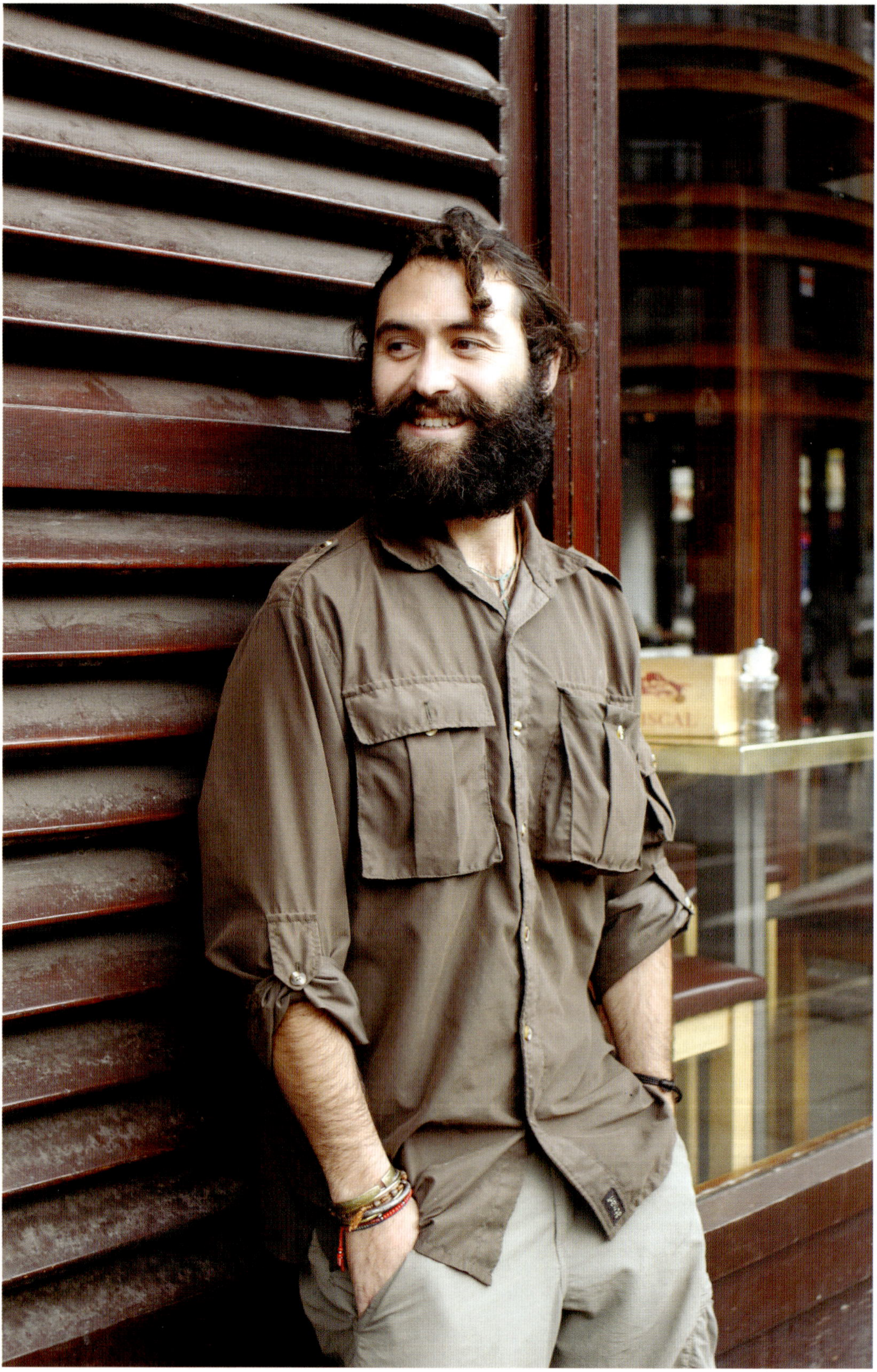

16 • Carlos: Cannon St, London

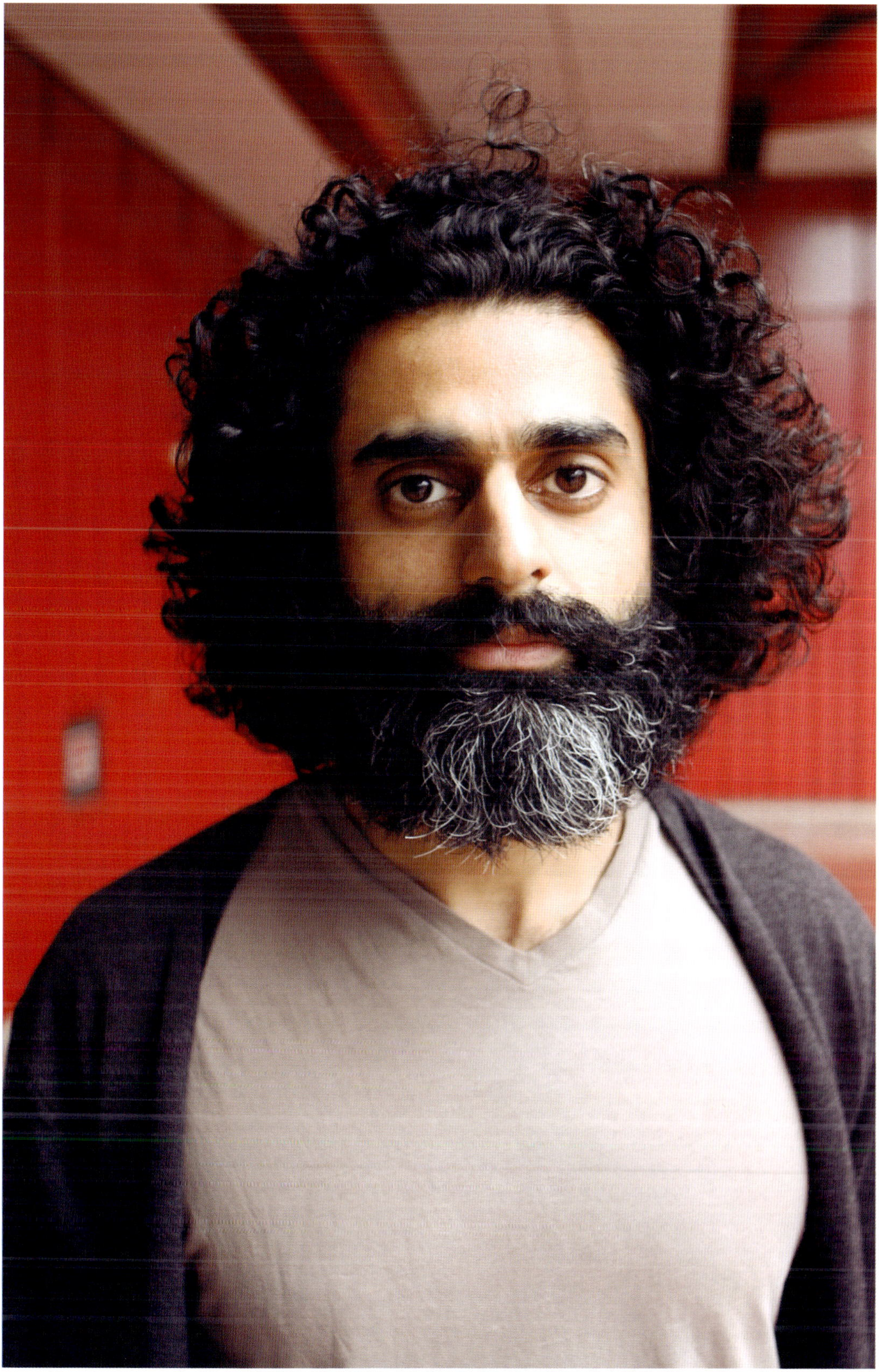

17 • Ali: British Library, London

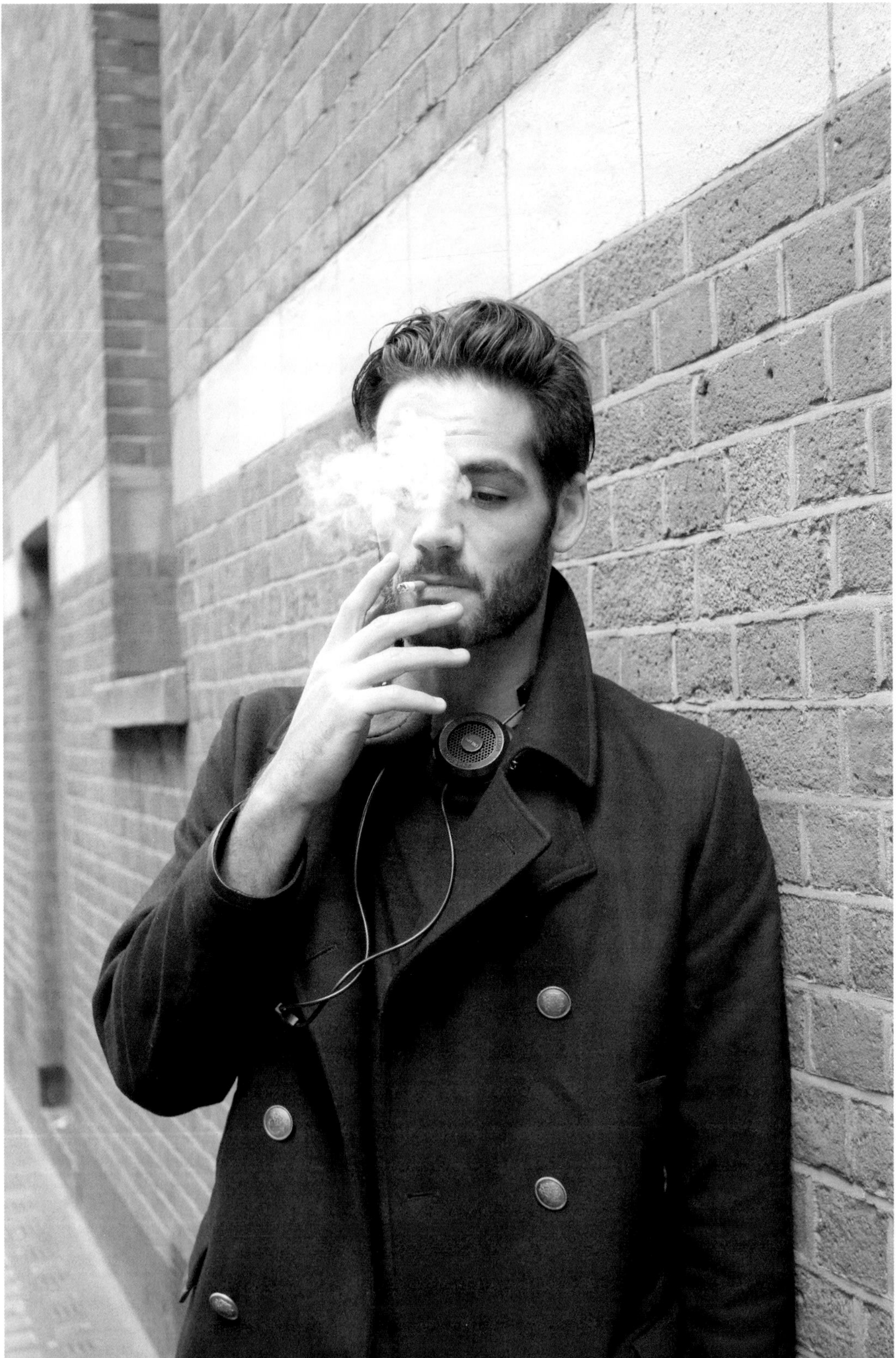

18 • James: Greek St, London

"For me it's all about getting just the right amount of facial hair. Too much and it can look untidy but stubble has the potential to look super suave and super sexy..."

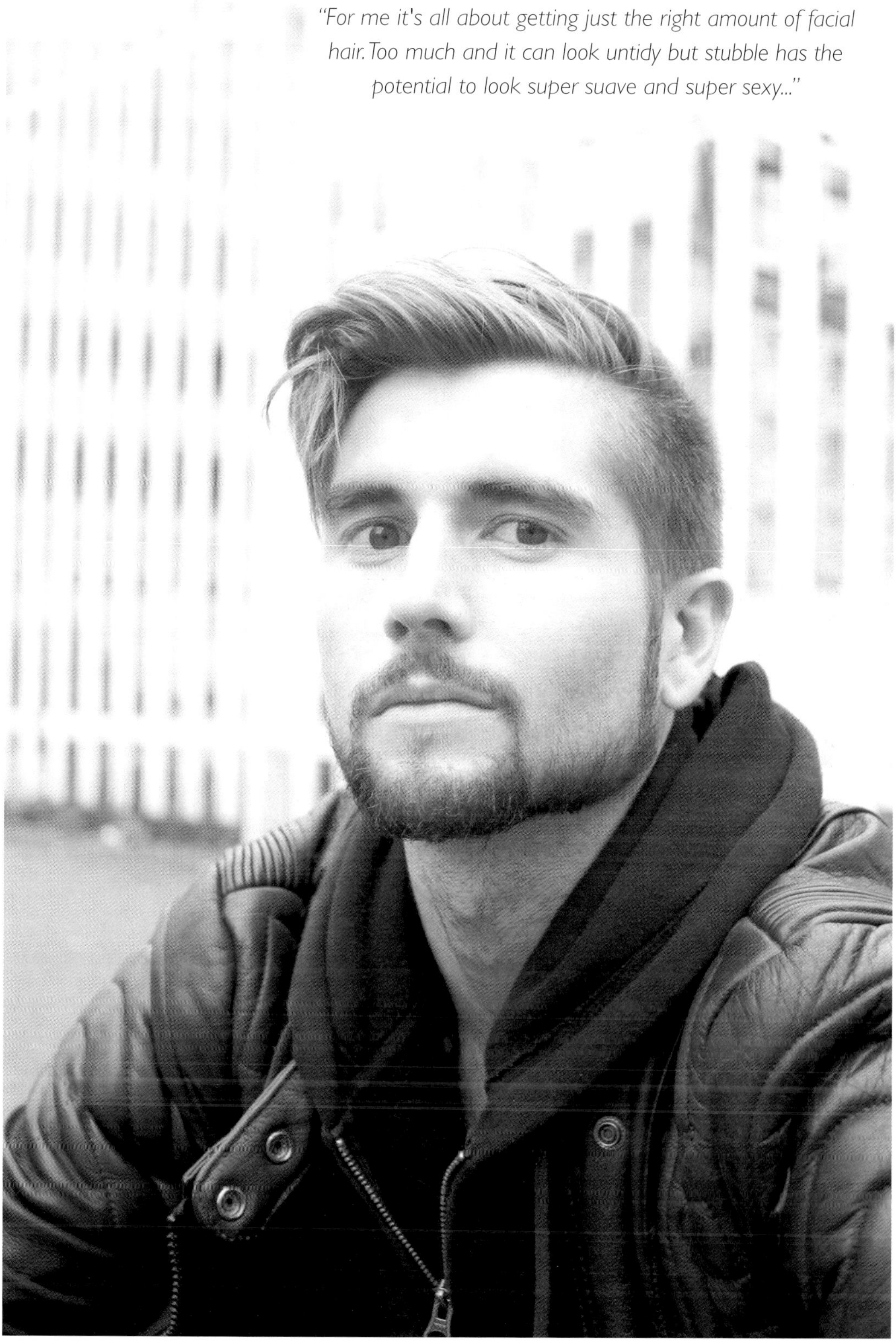

19 • Michael: Leonard Street, London

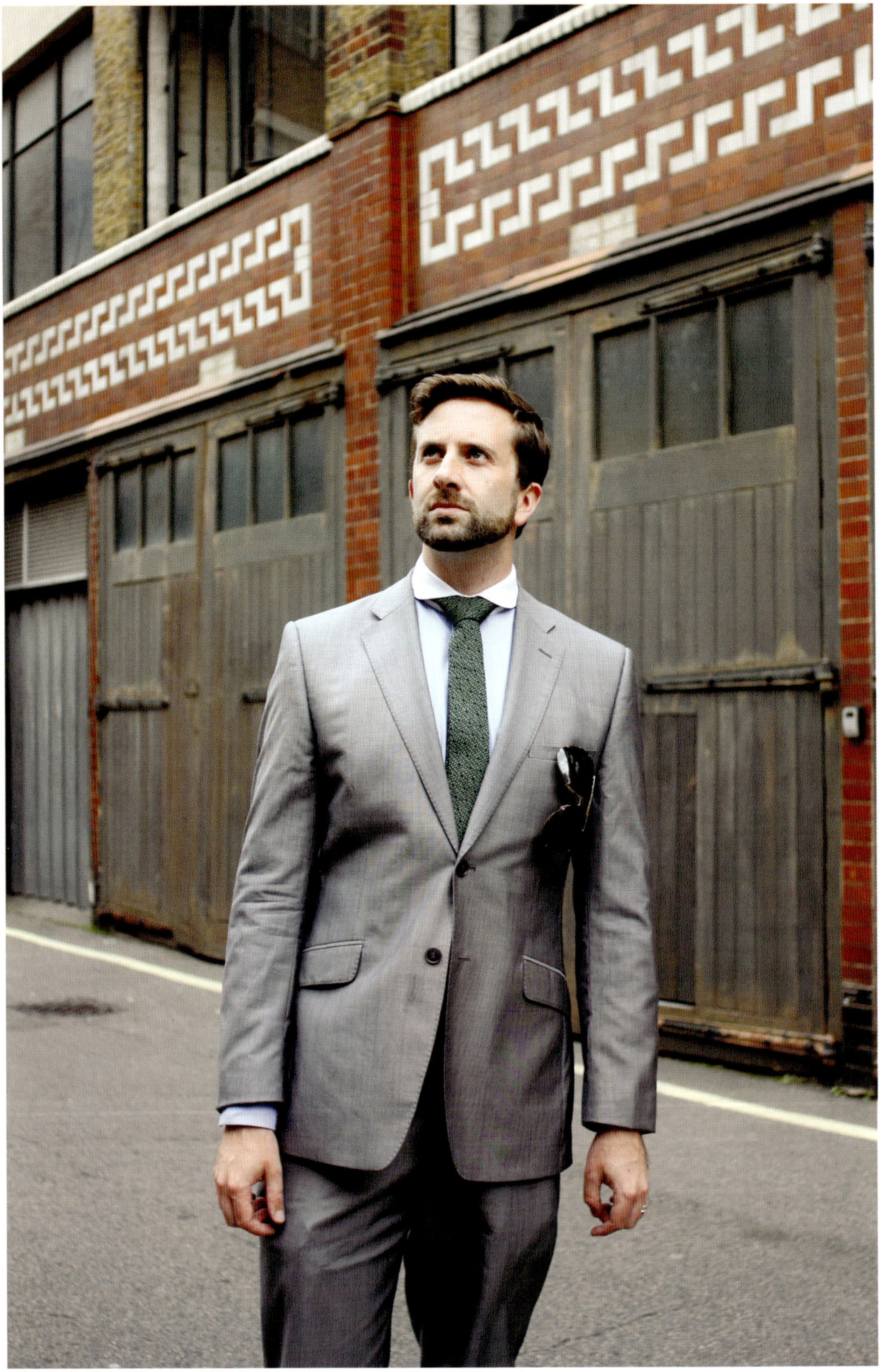

20 • Nick: Wells Mews, London

Having a beard over the last 7 years has become such an integral part of who I am, that being clean-shaven feels alien to me — it's strange to obsess about something that can be grown back within two weeks, but I had genuine trepidation when shaving off my beard for 'Movember.' I barely recognised who was looking back in my mirror. A beard can be quite tribal: they give access to a distinct club that is singularly masculine, and that may be why they're so popular these days. I can surmise and ask questions about beard theory but all I know is I don't feel like the same person clean shaven. Having a cold face doesn't suit me.

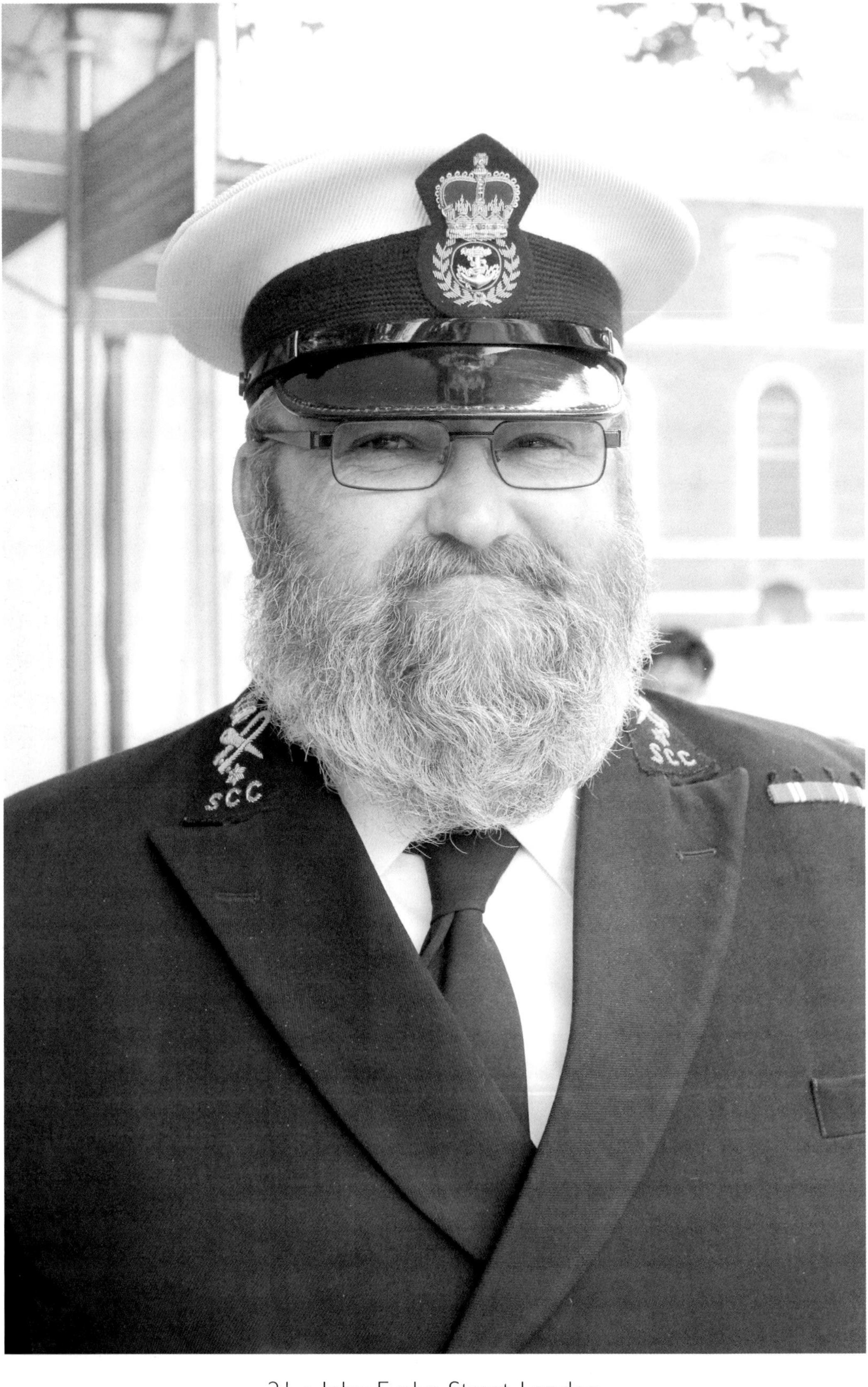

21 • John: Evelyn Street, London

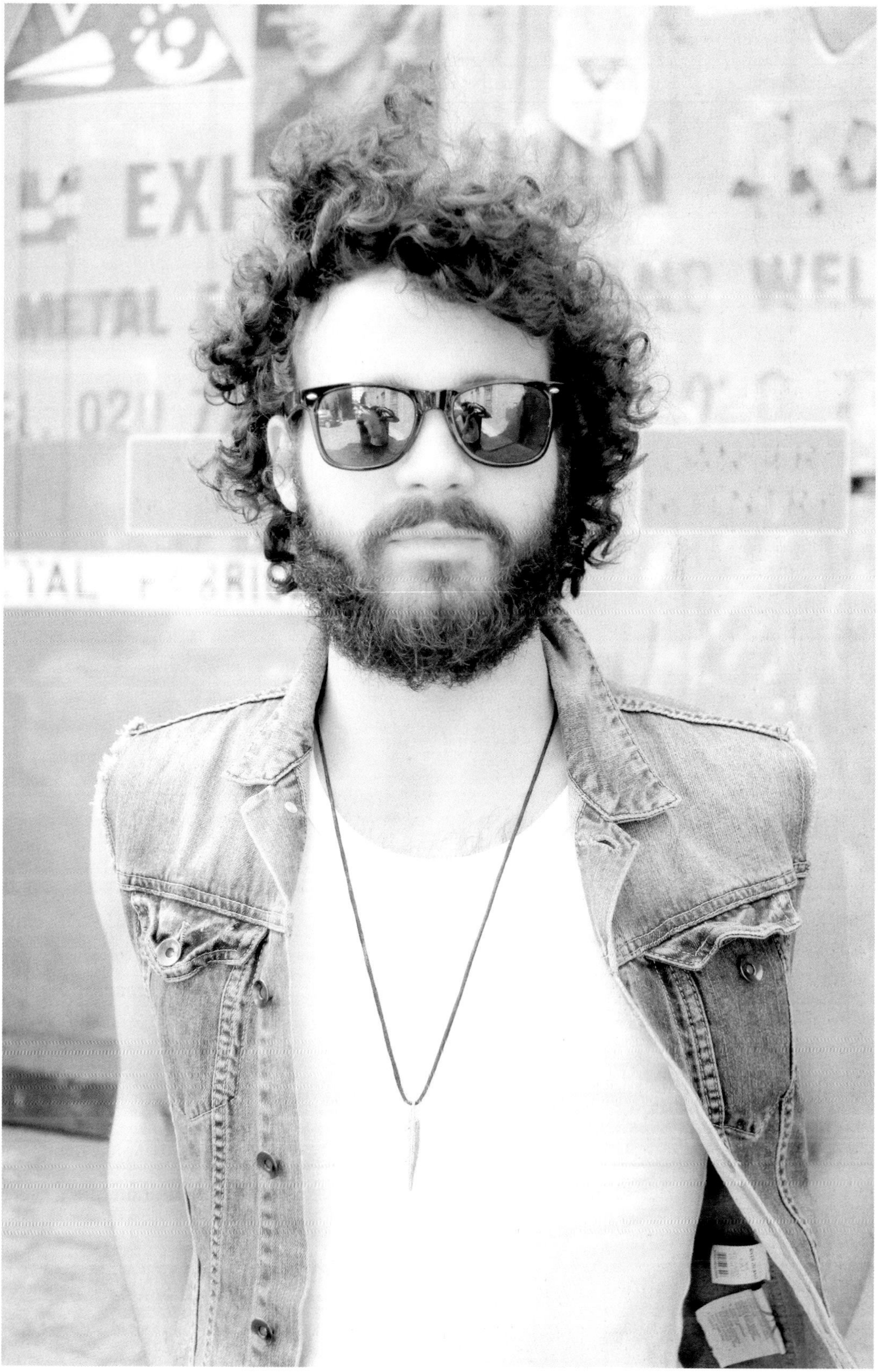

22 • Mads: French Place, London

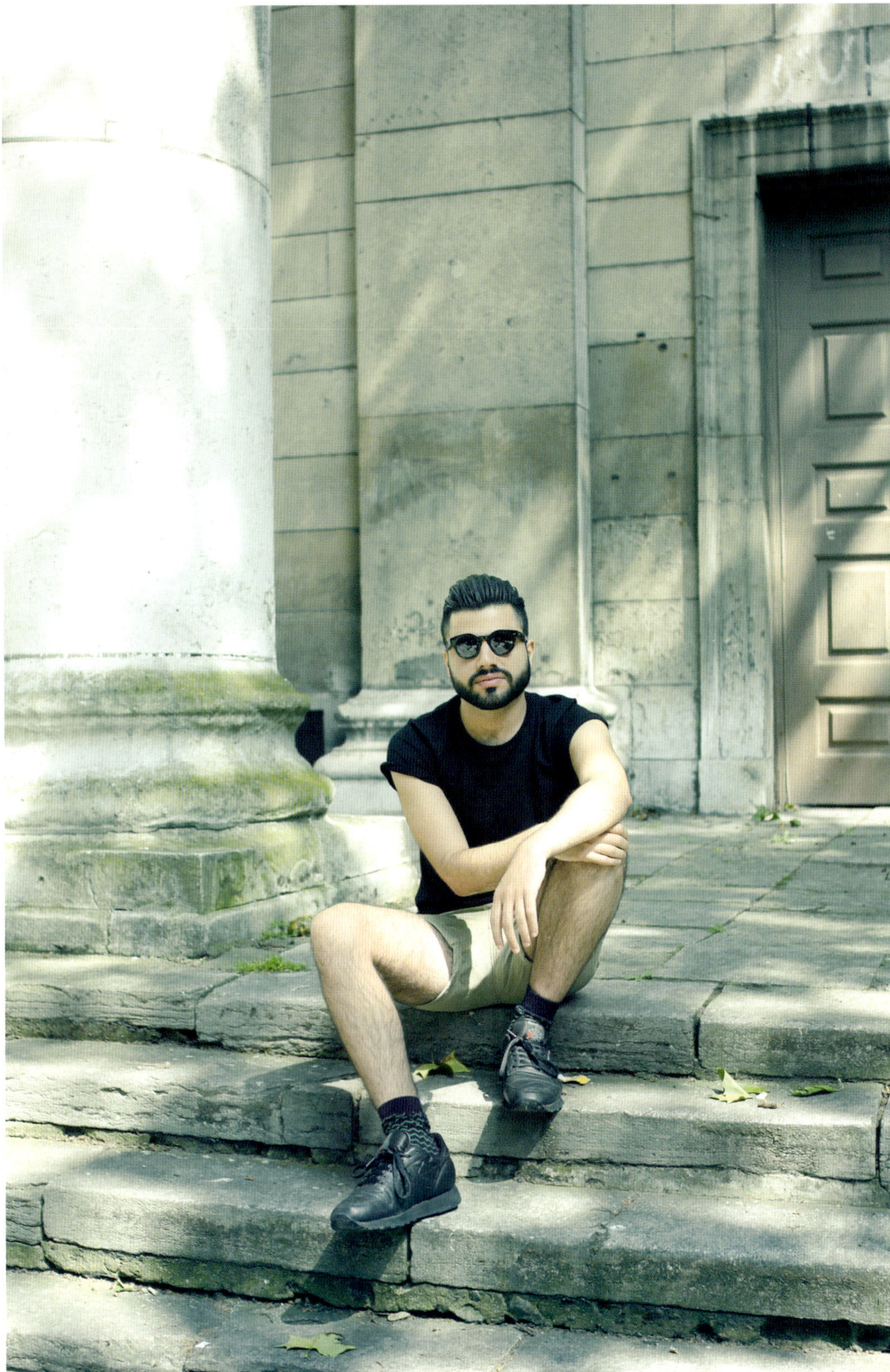

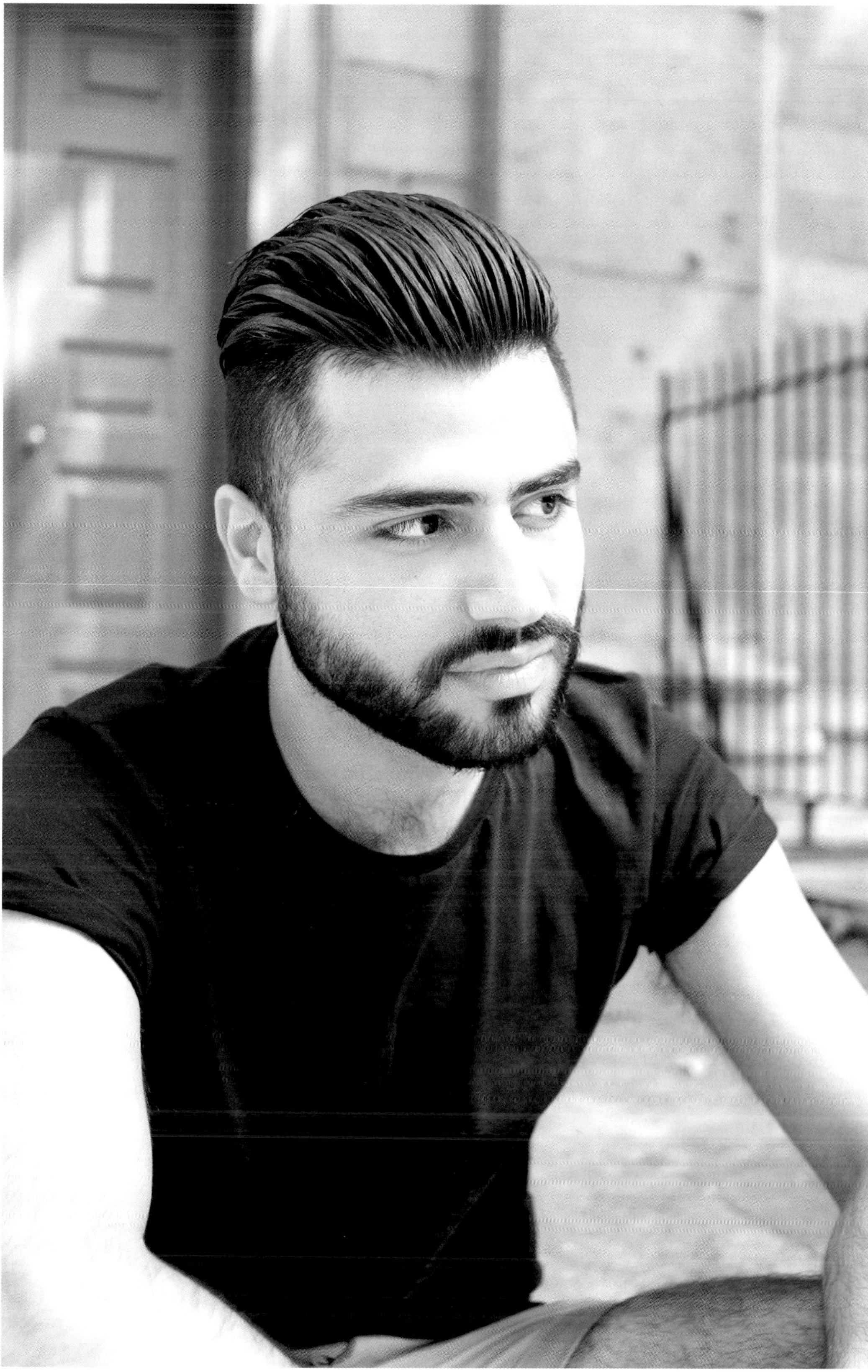

23 • George: Shoreditch Church, London

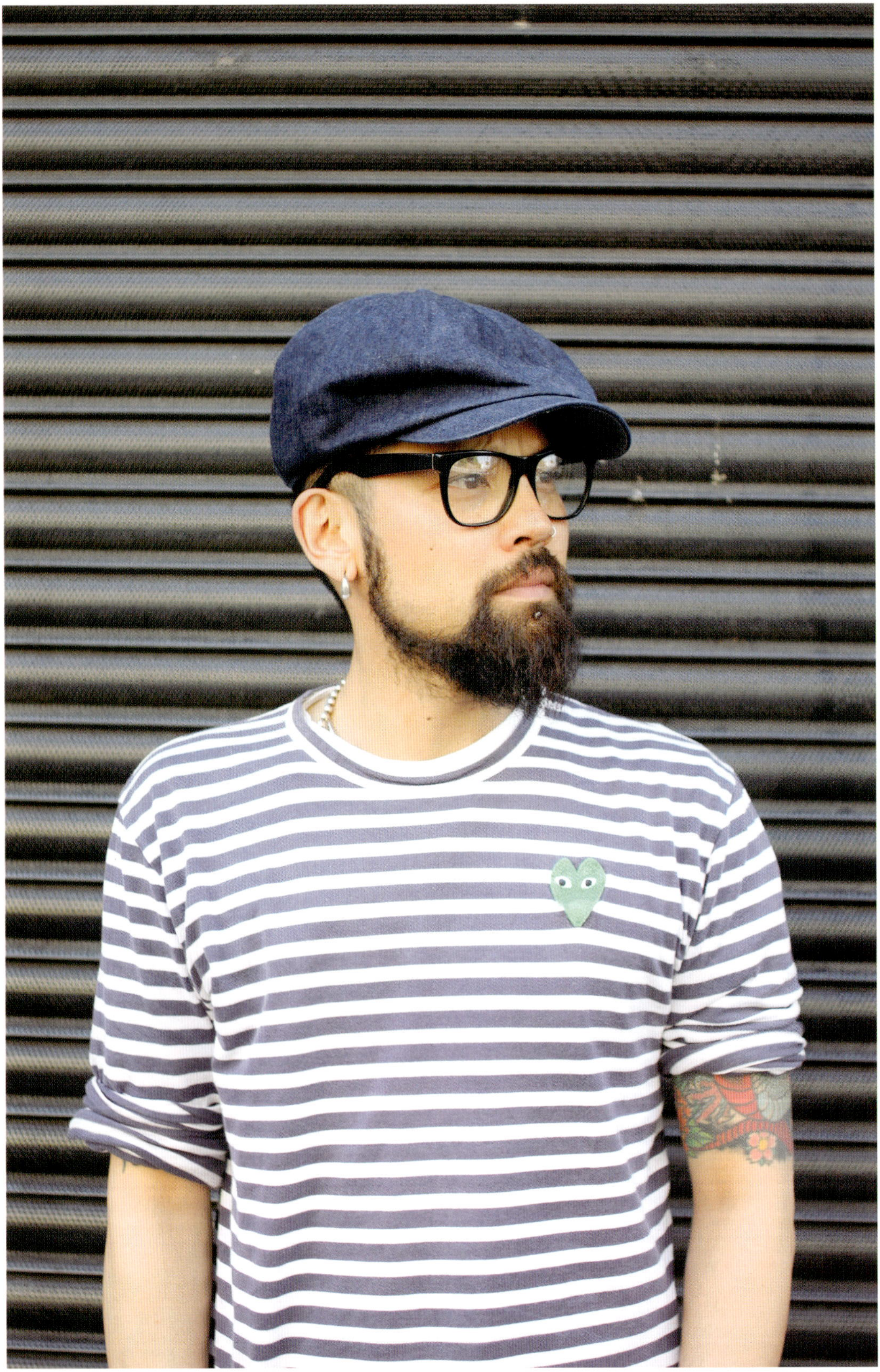

24 • Atip: Shoreditch High Street, London

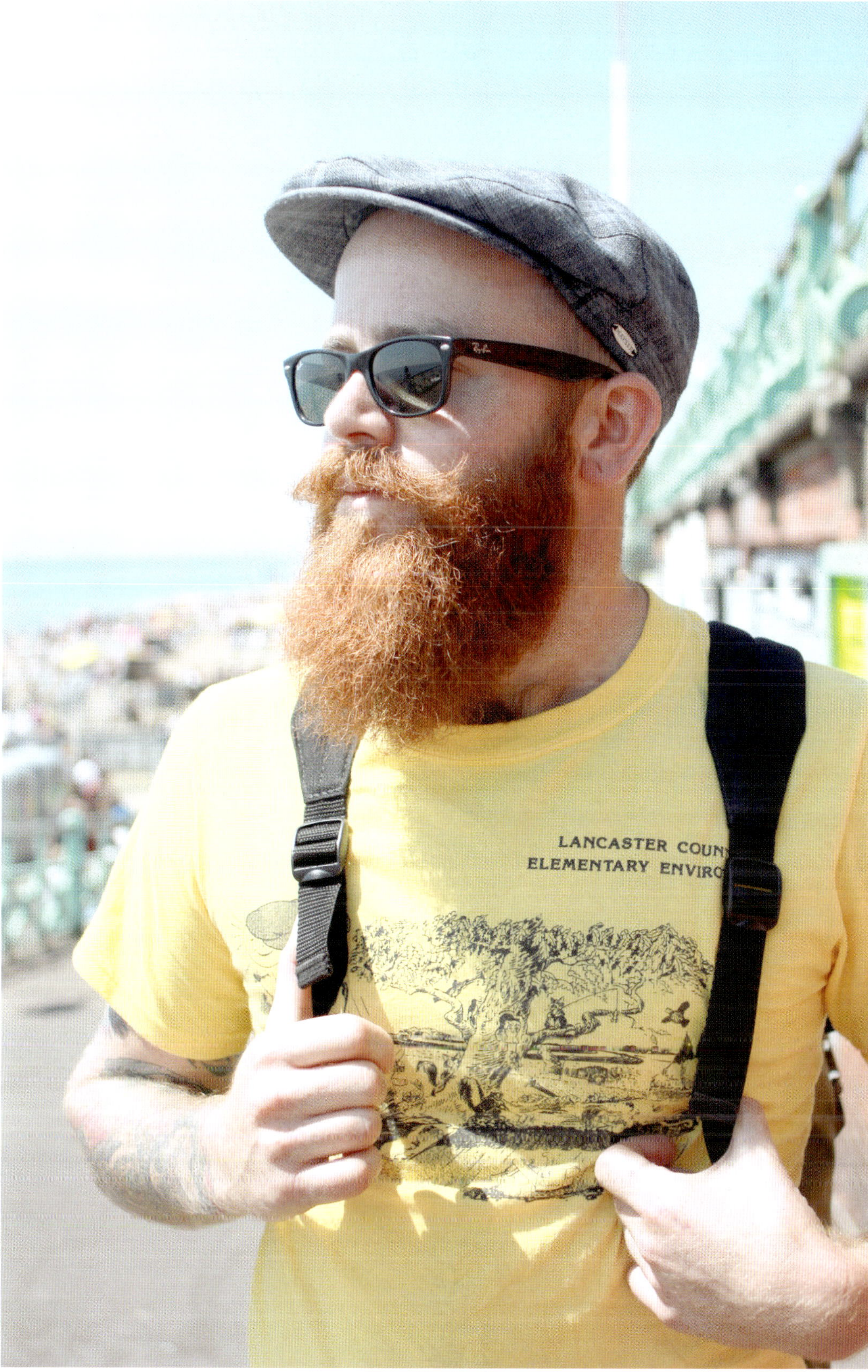

25 • Paul: Brighton Beach, Brighton

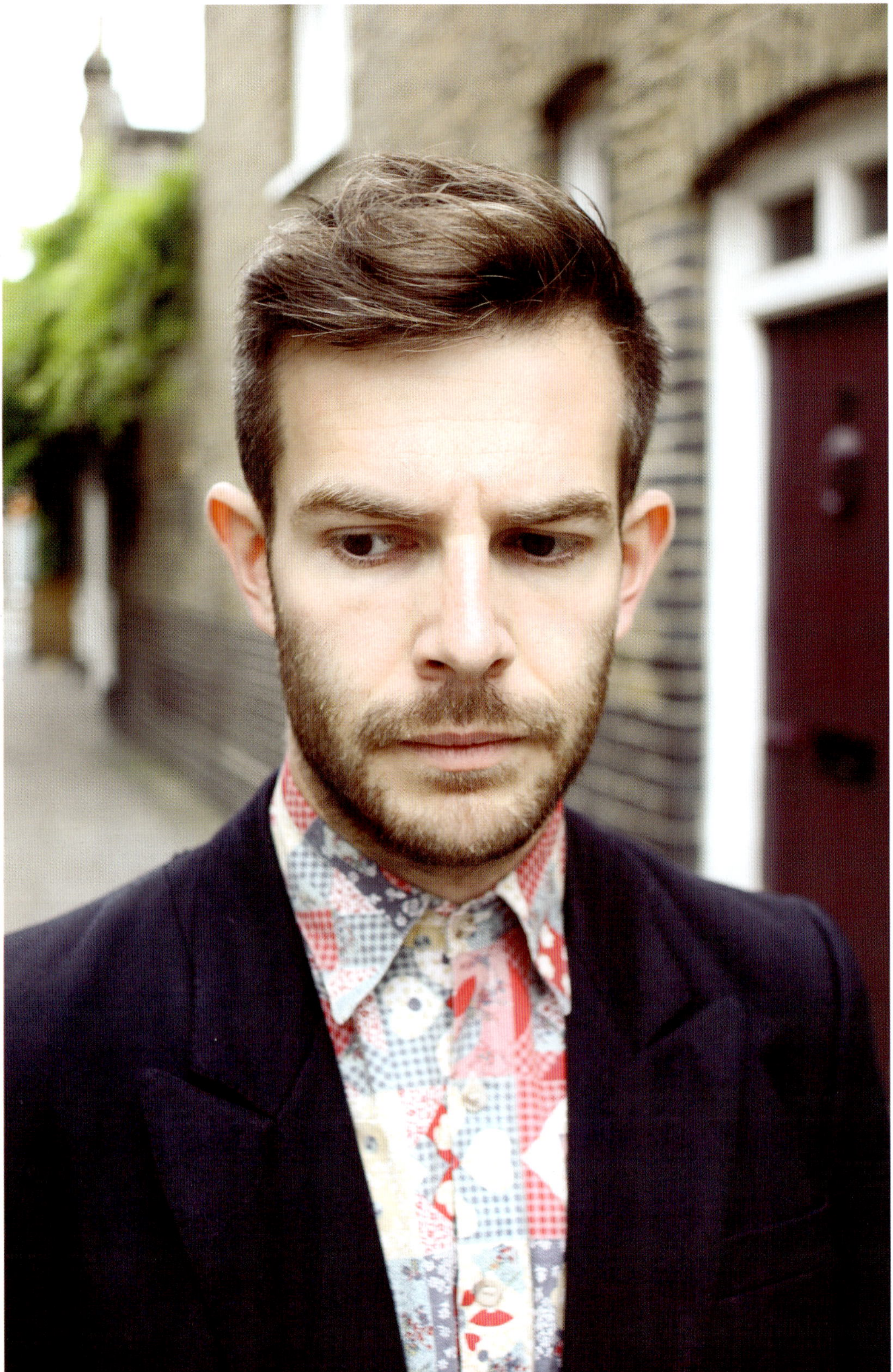

26 • Rod: Ezra St, London

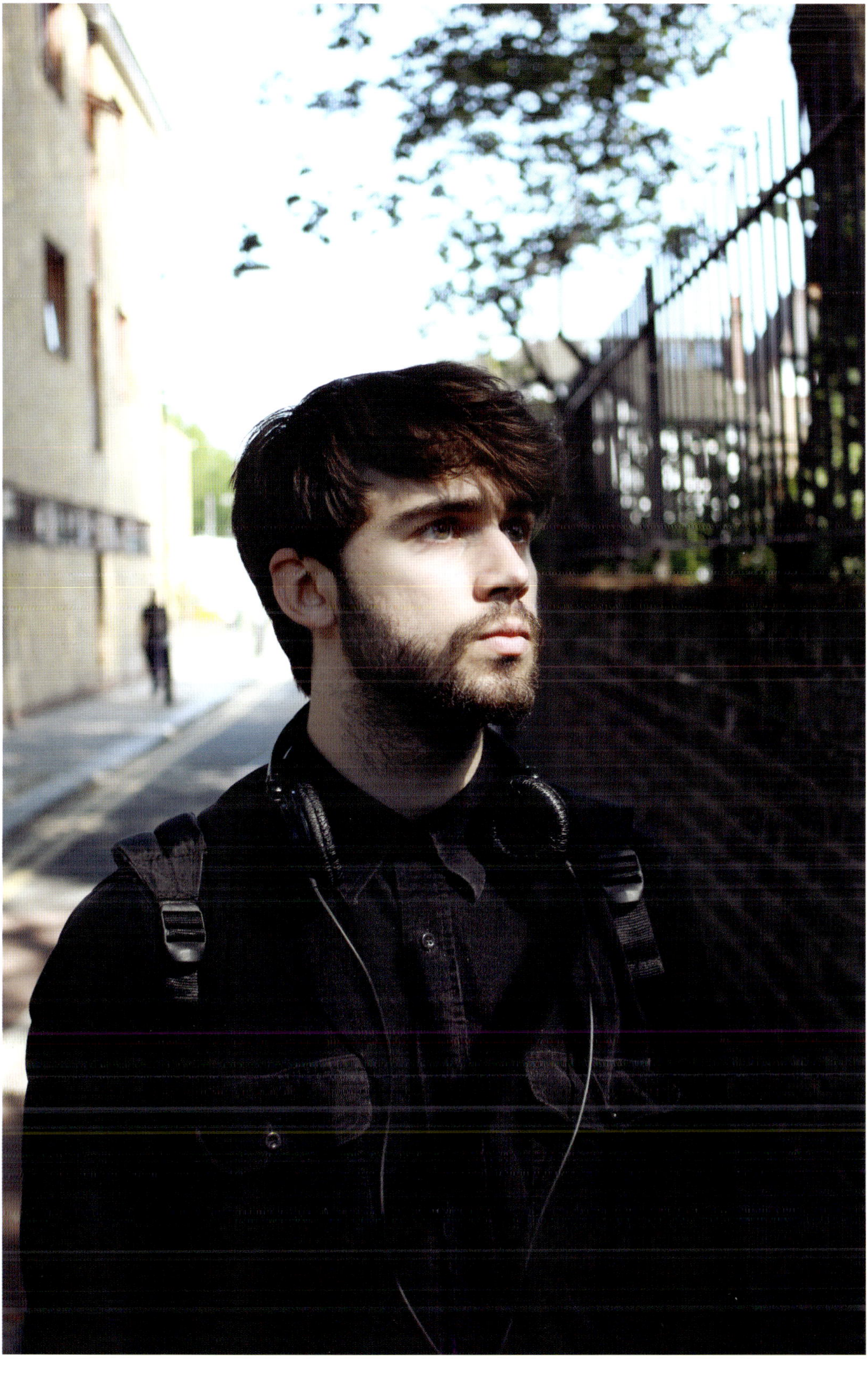

27 • Visilis: Boundary St, London

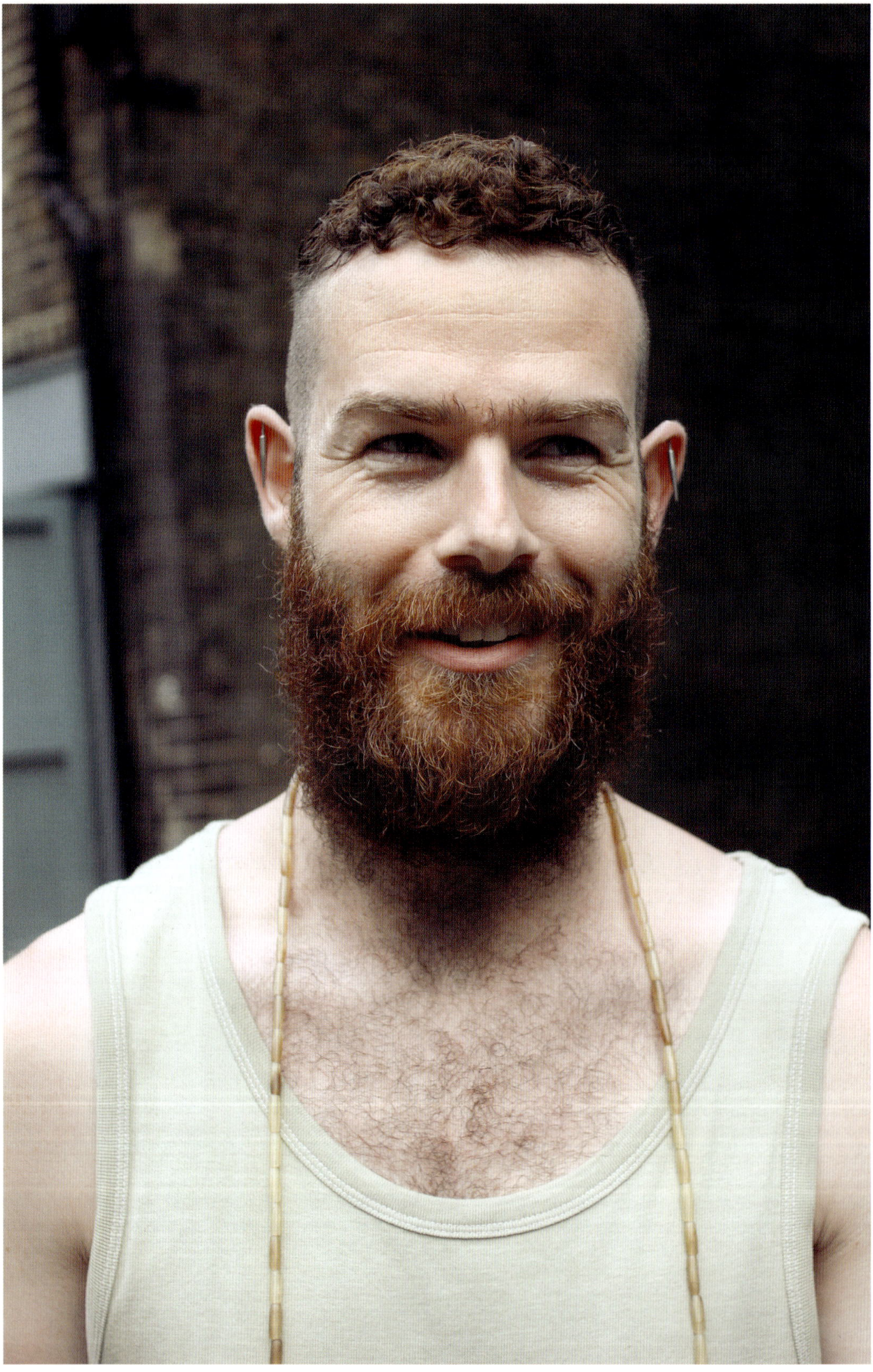

28 • Aaron: Dean St, London

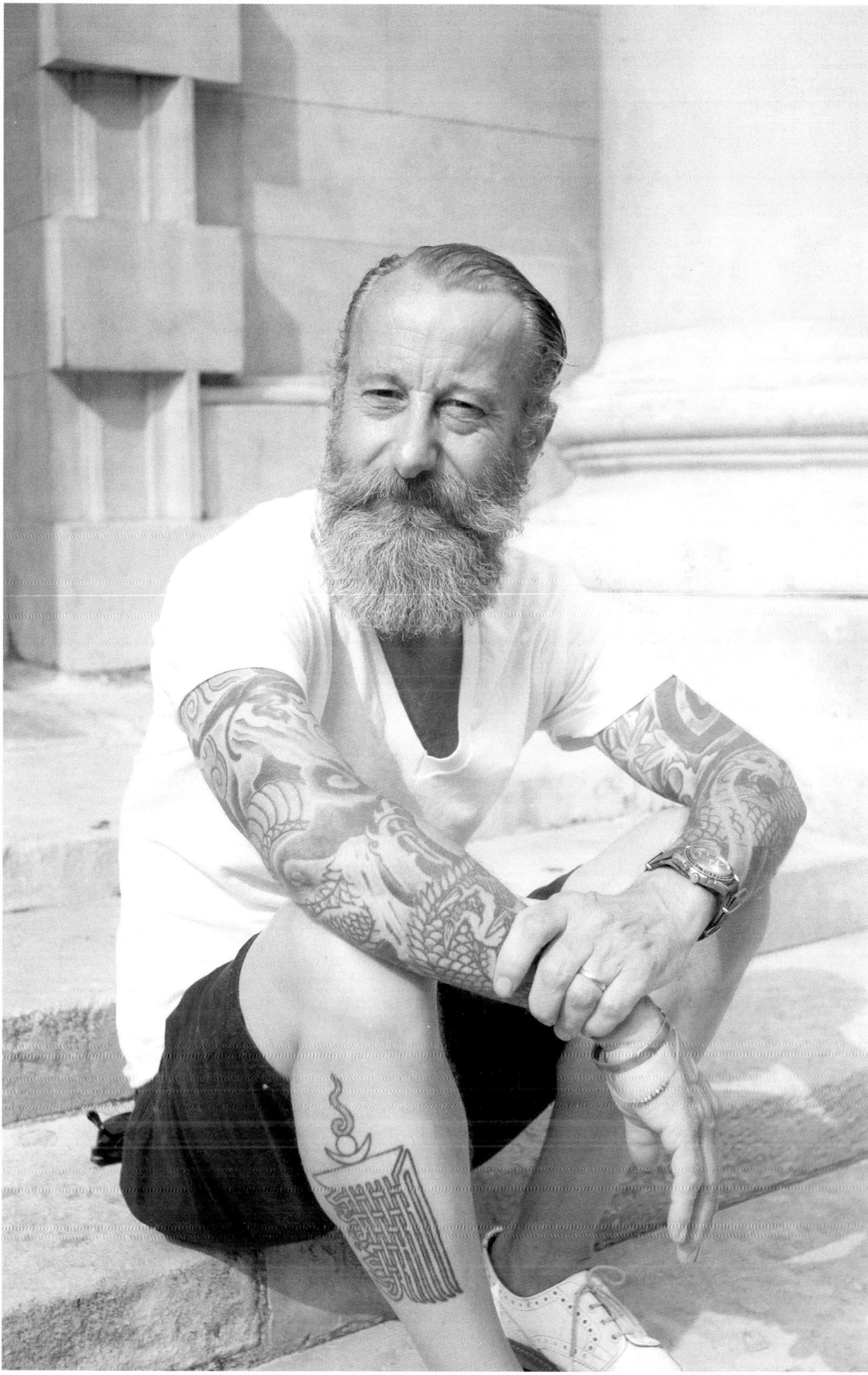

29 • Derek: St-Martin-in-the-Fields, London

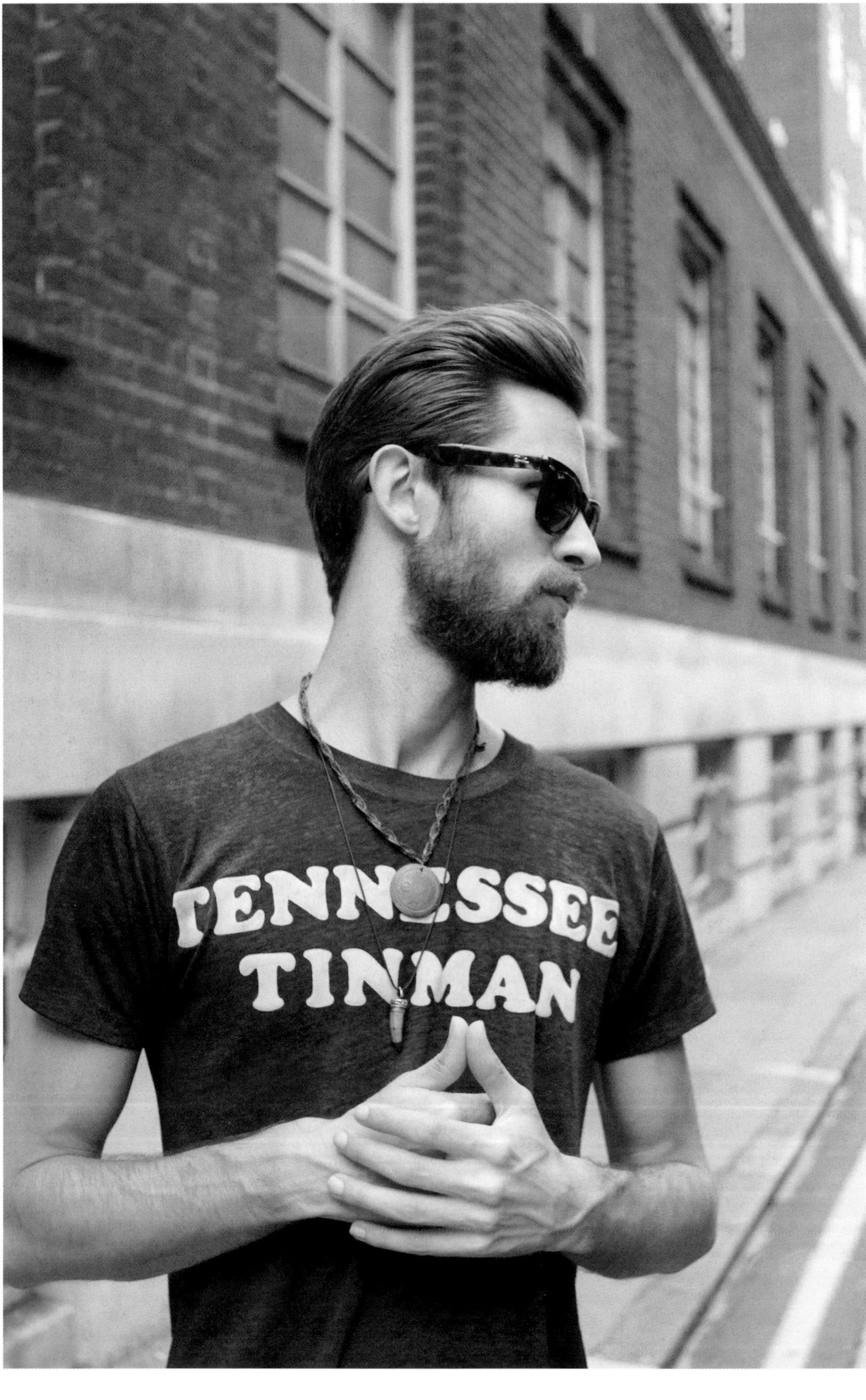
TENNESSEE
TINMAN

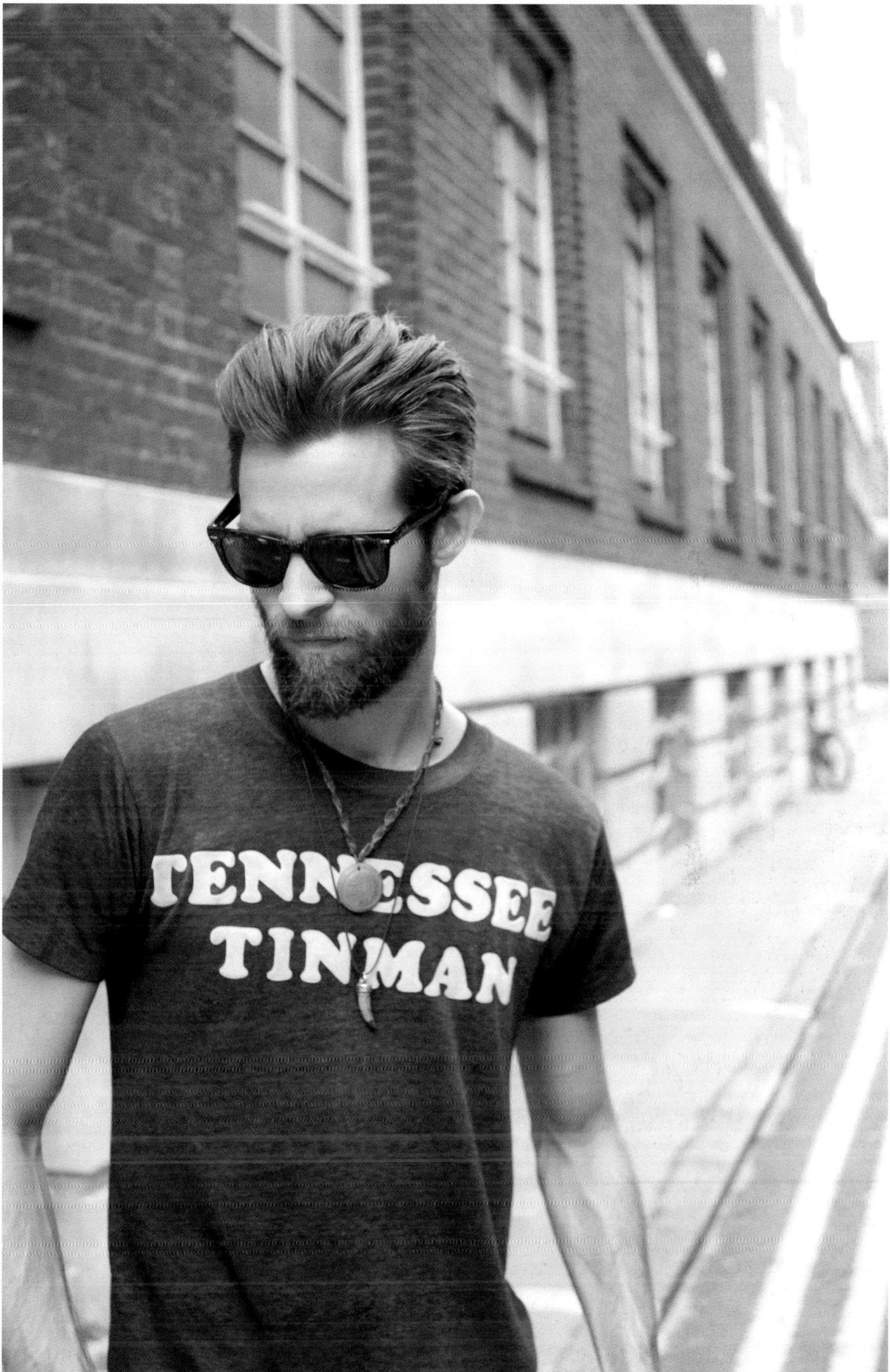

 • Justin: Great Marlborough St, London

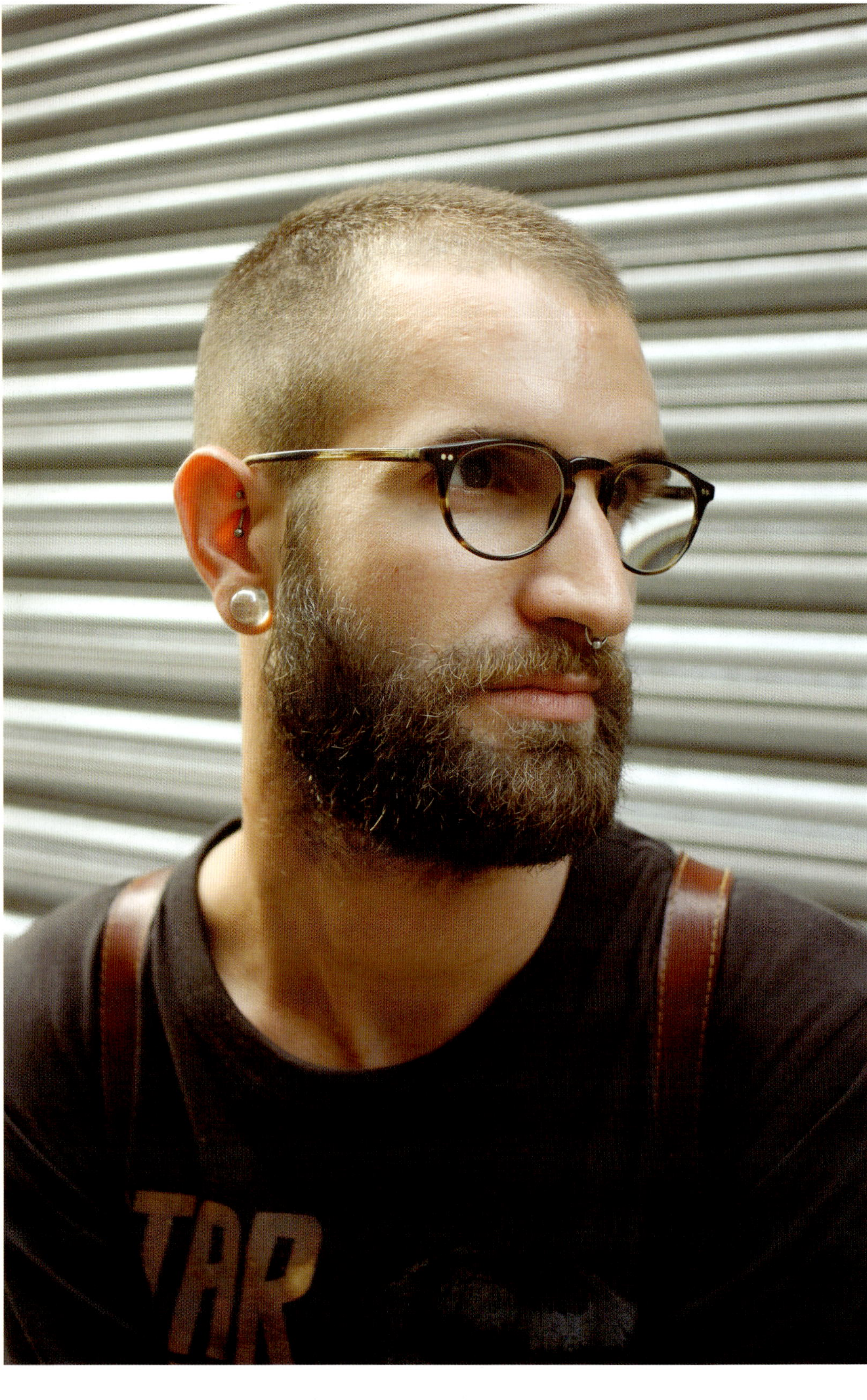
TAR

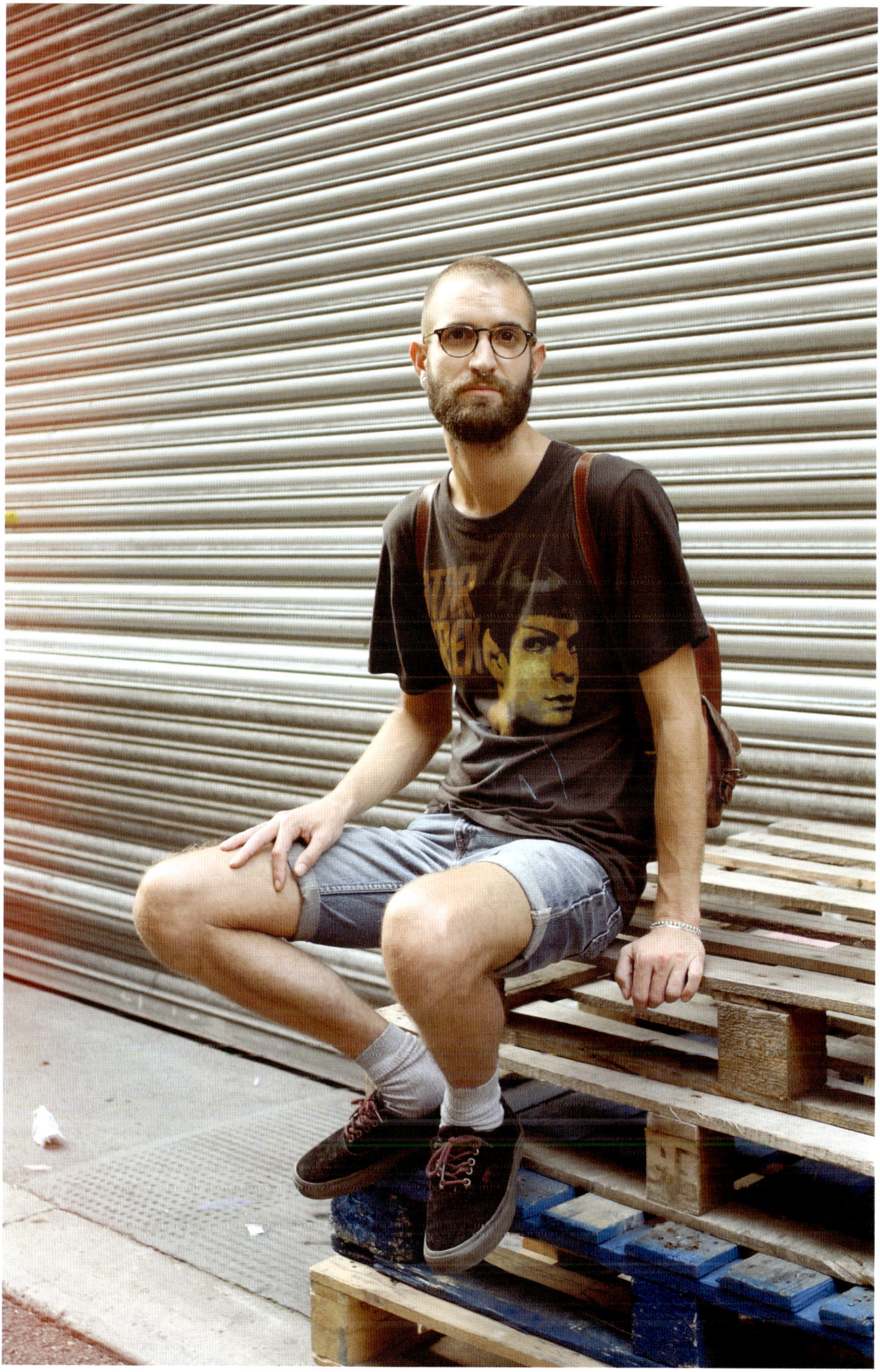

31 • Enrico: Hills Place, London

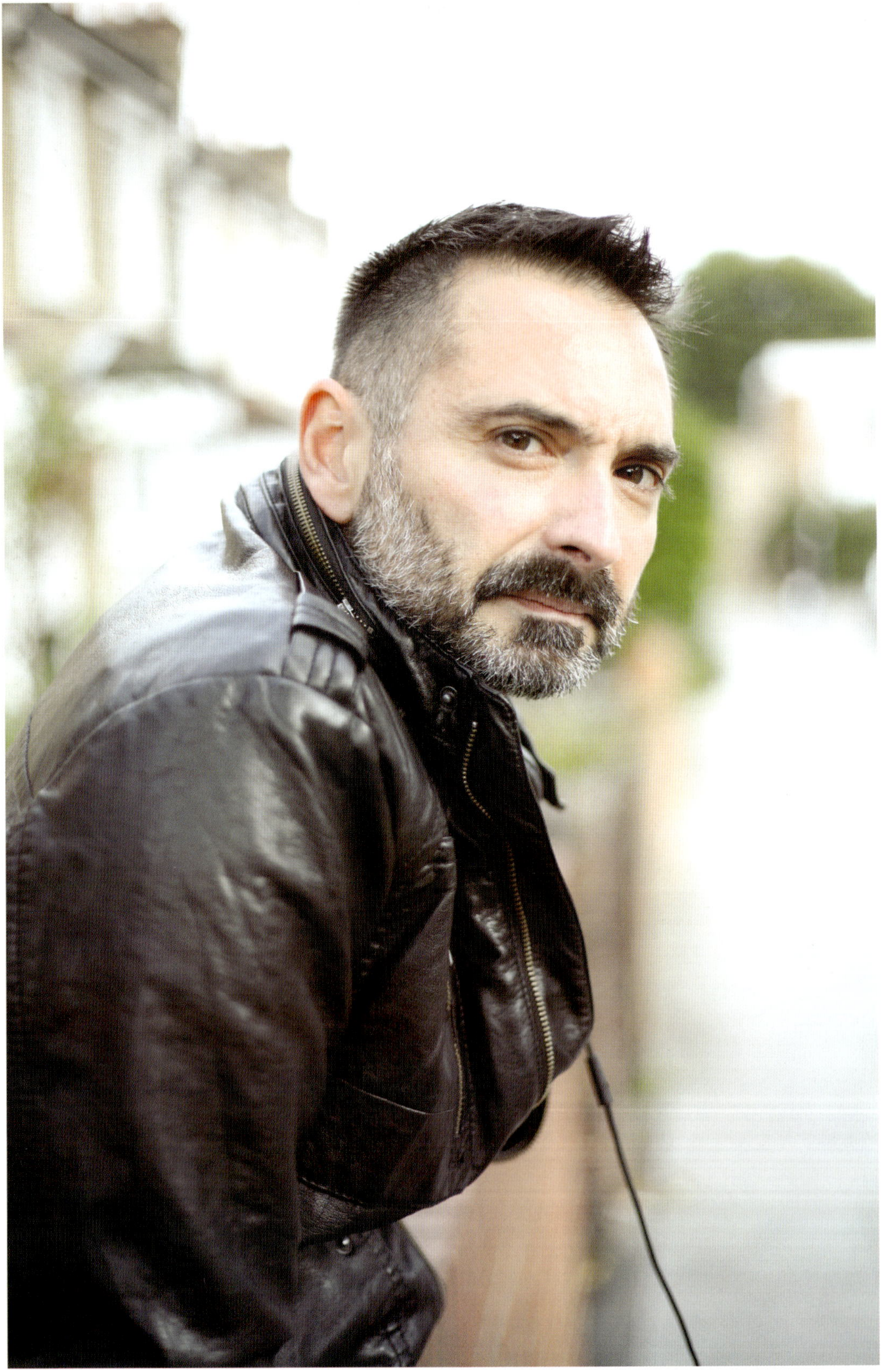

32 • Olivier: Beacon Road, London

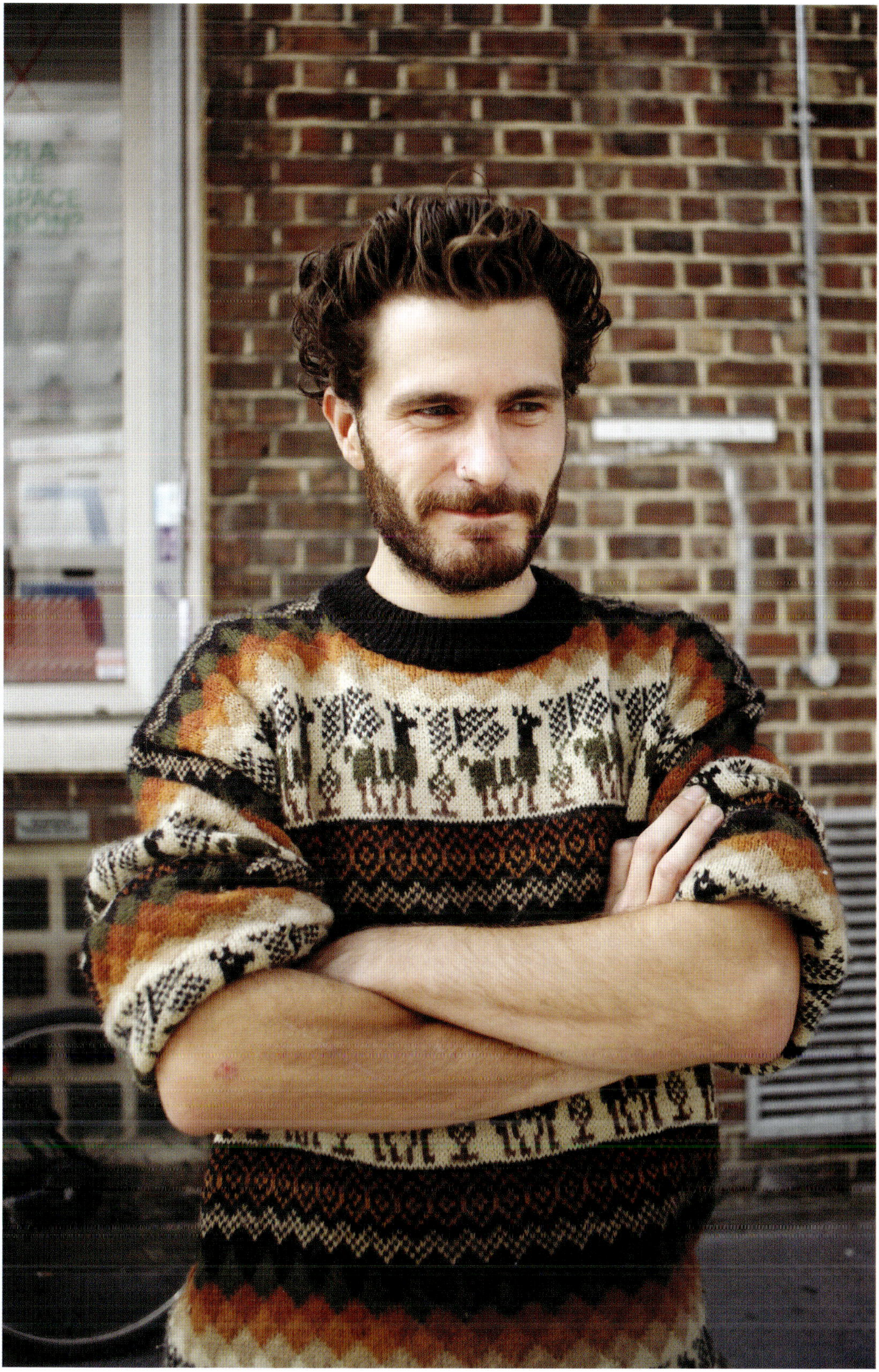

33 • Jim: Bethnal Green Road, London

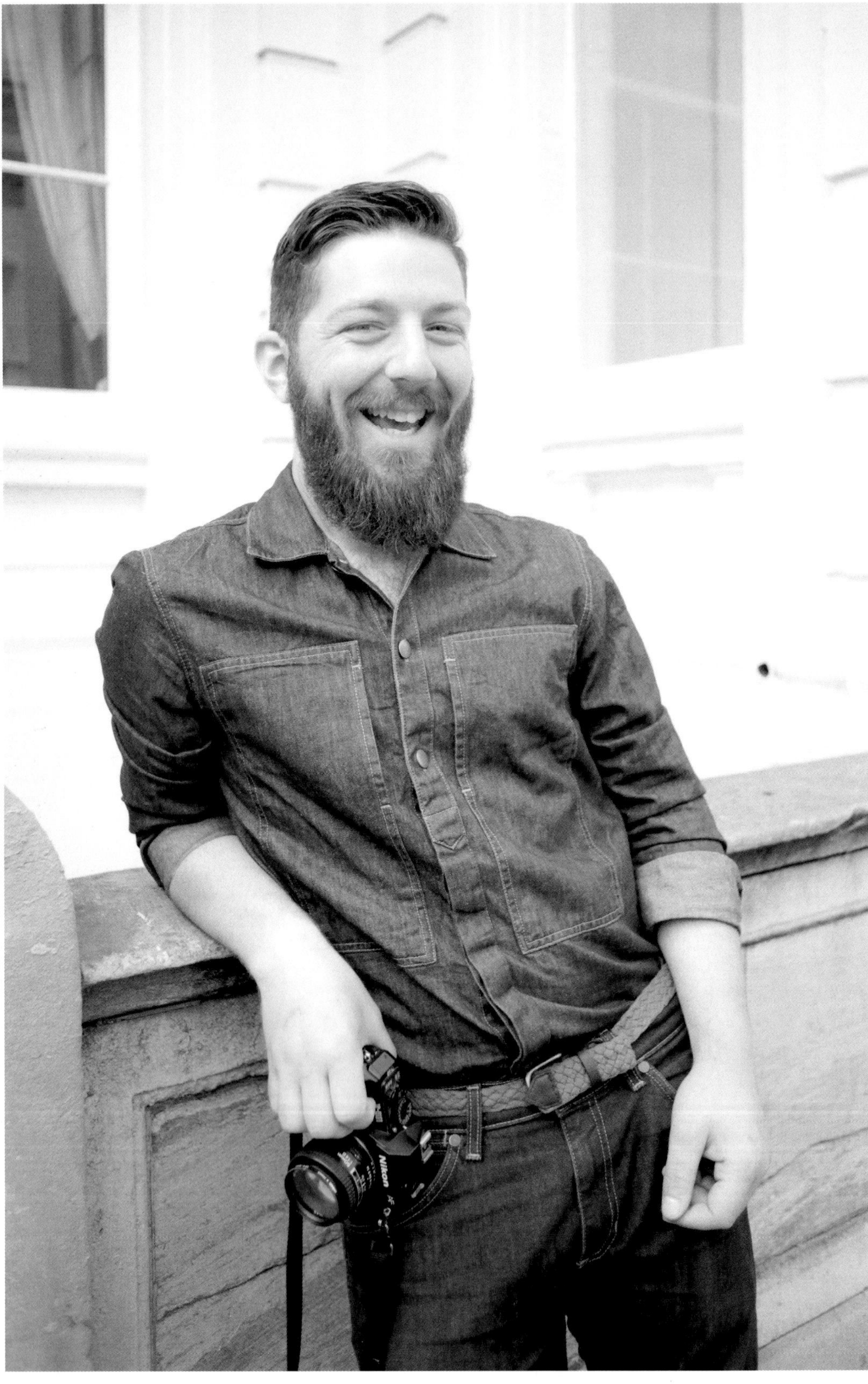

34 • Corey: Pall Mall, London

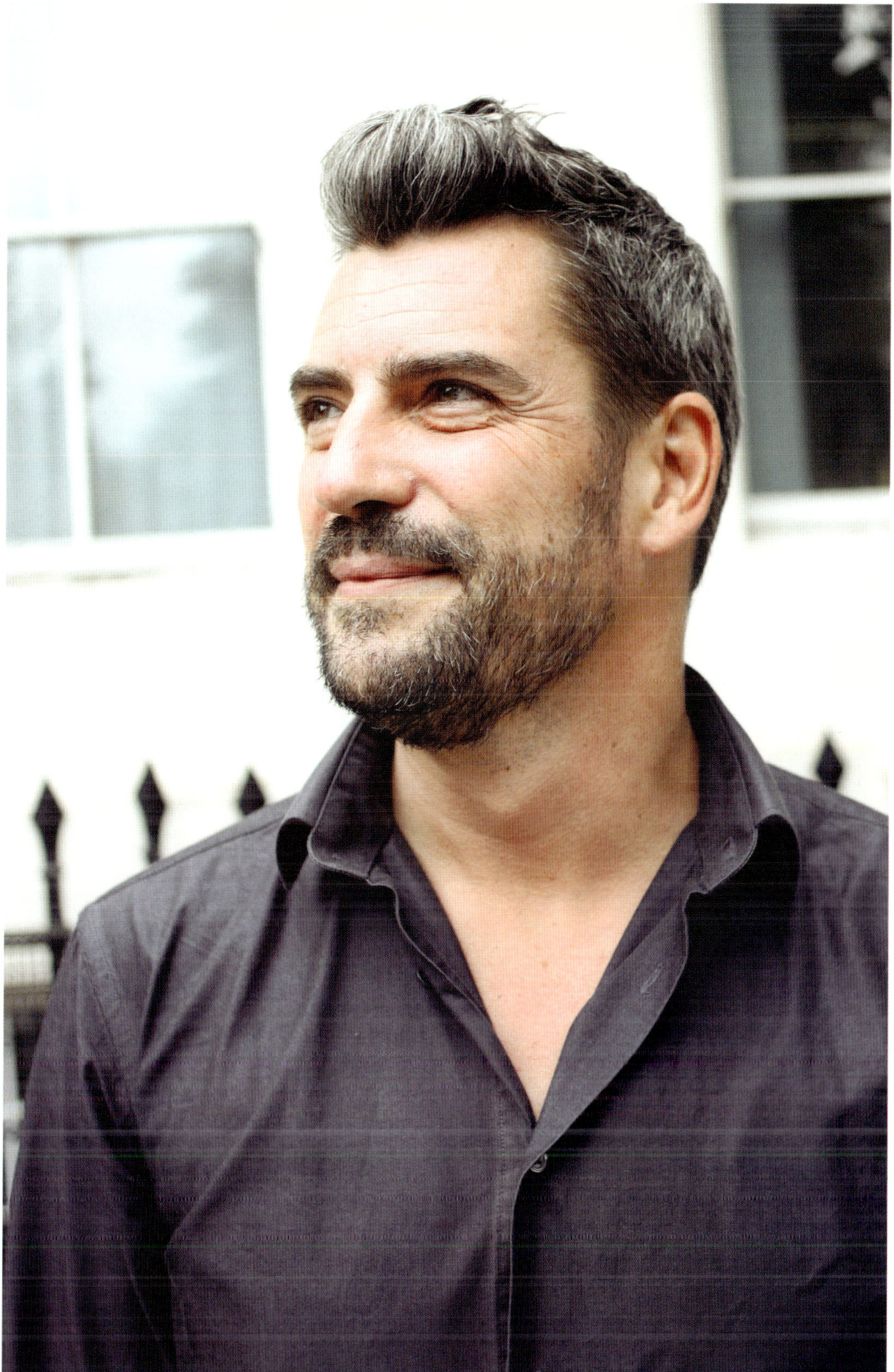

35 • Marcus: The Cut, London

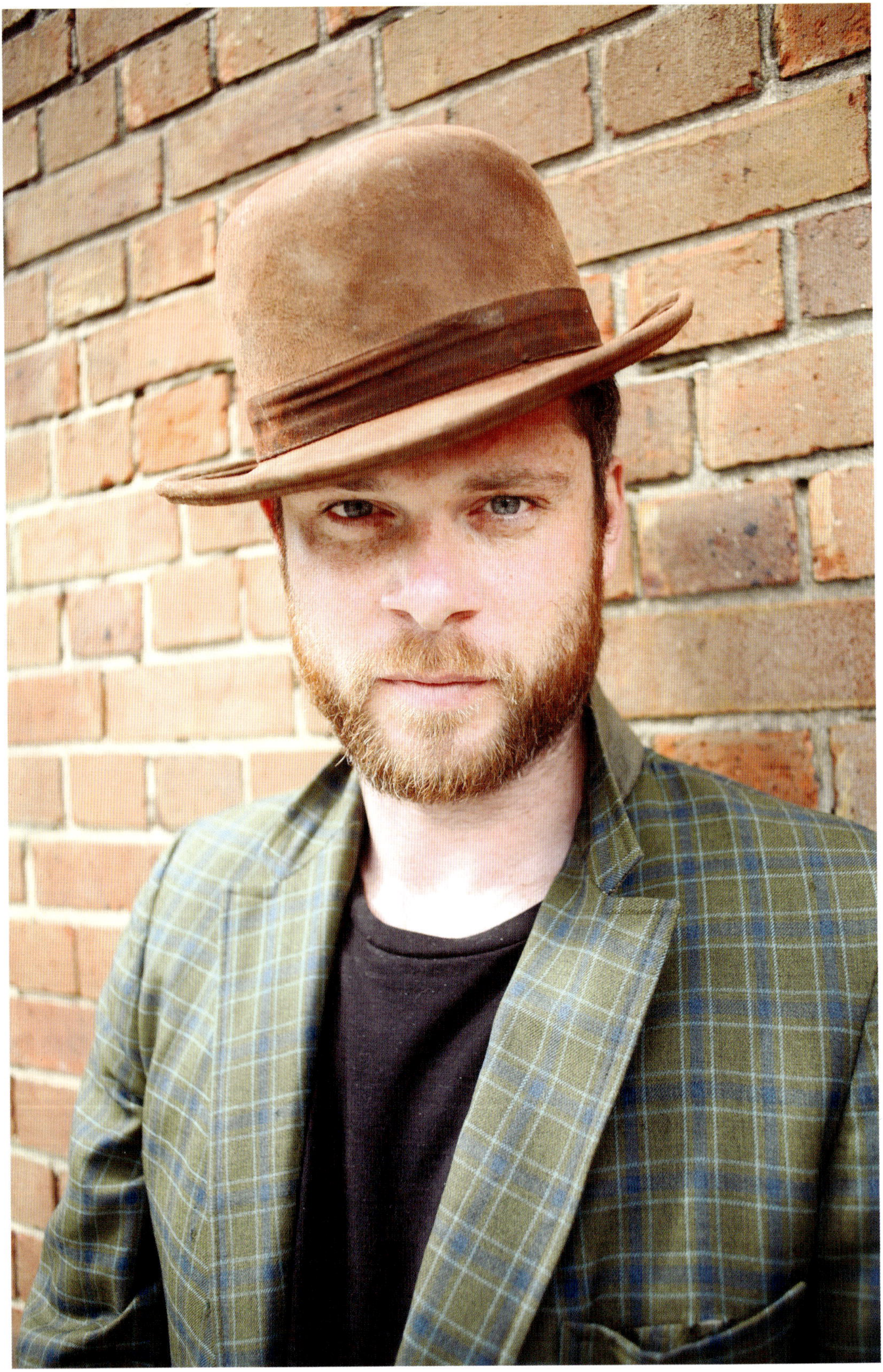

36 • Ben: Regent's Row, London

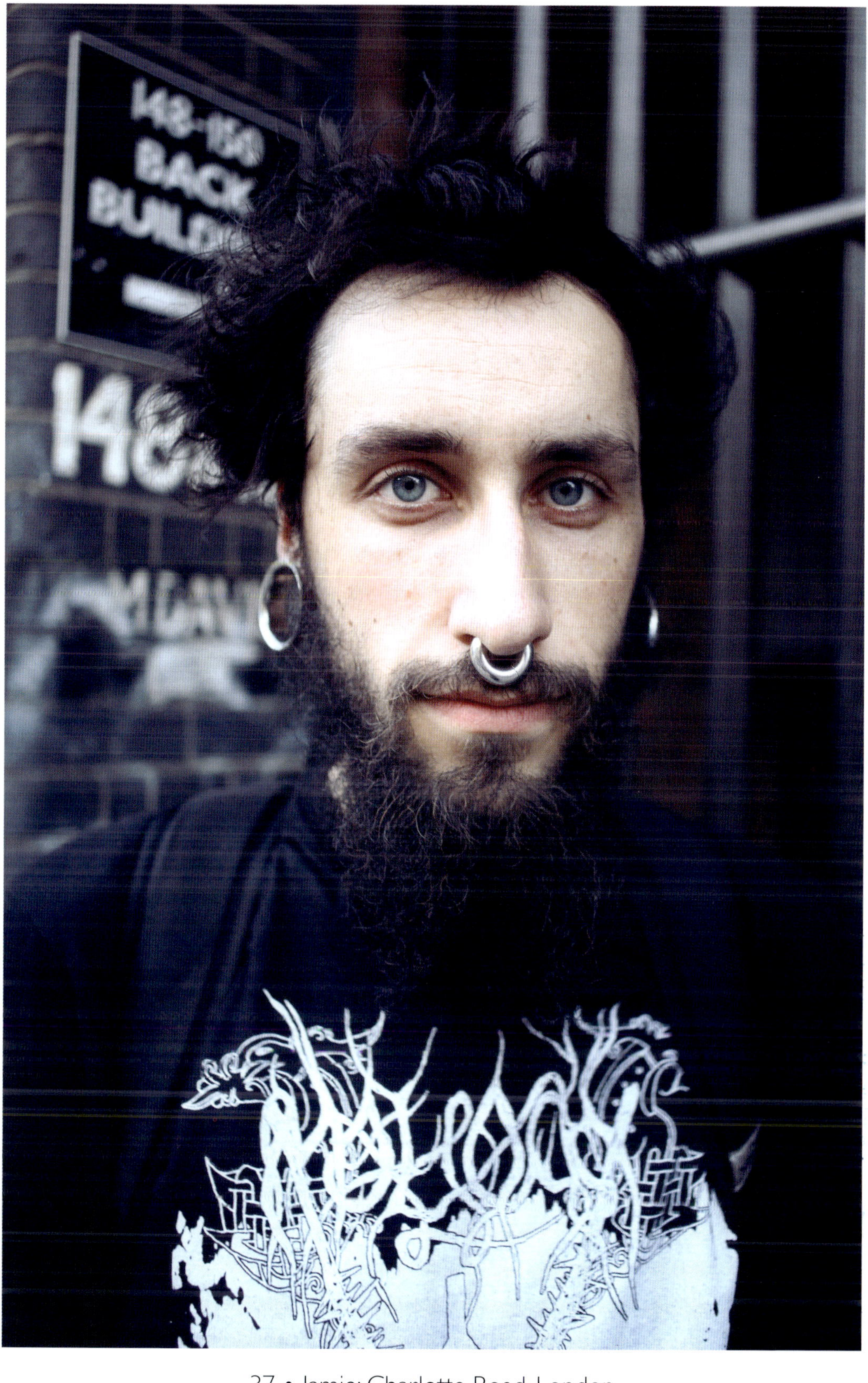

37 • Jamie: Charlotte Road, London

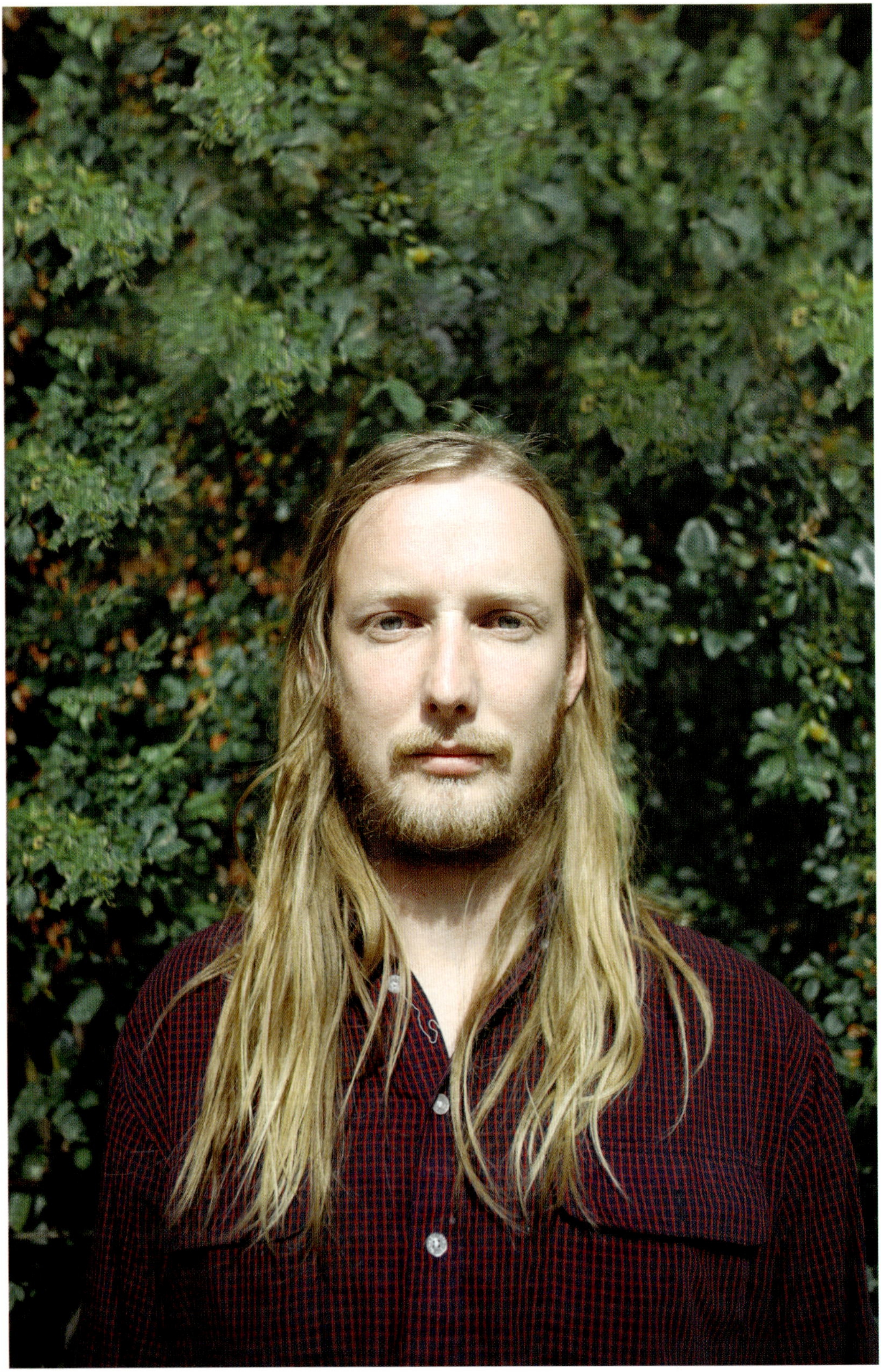

38 • Brad: Pritchard's Road, London

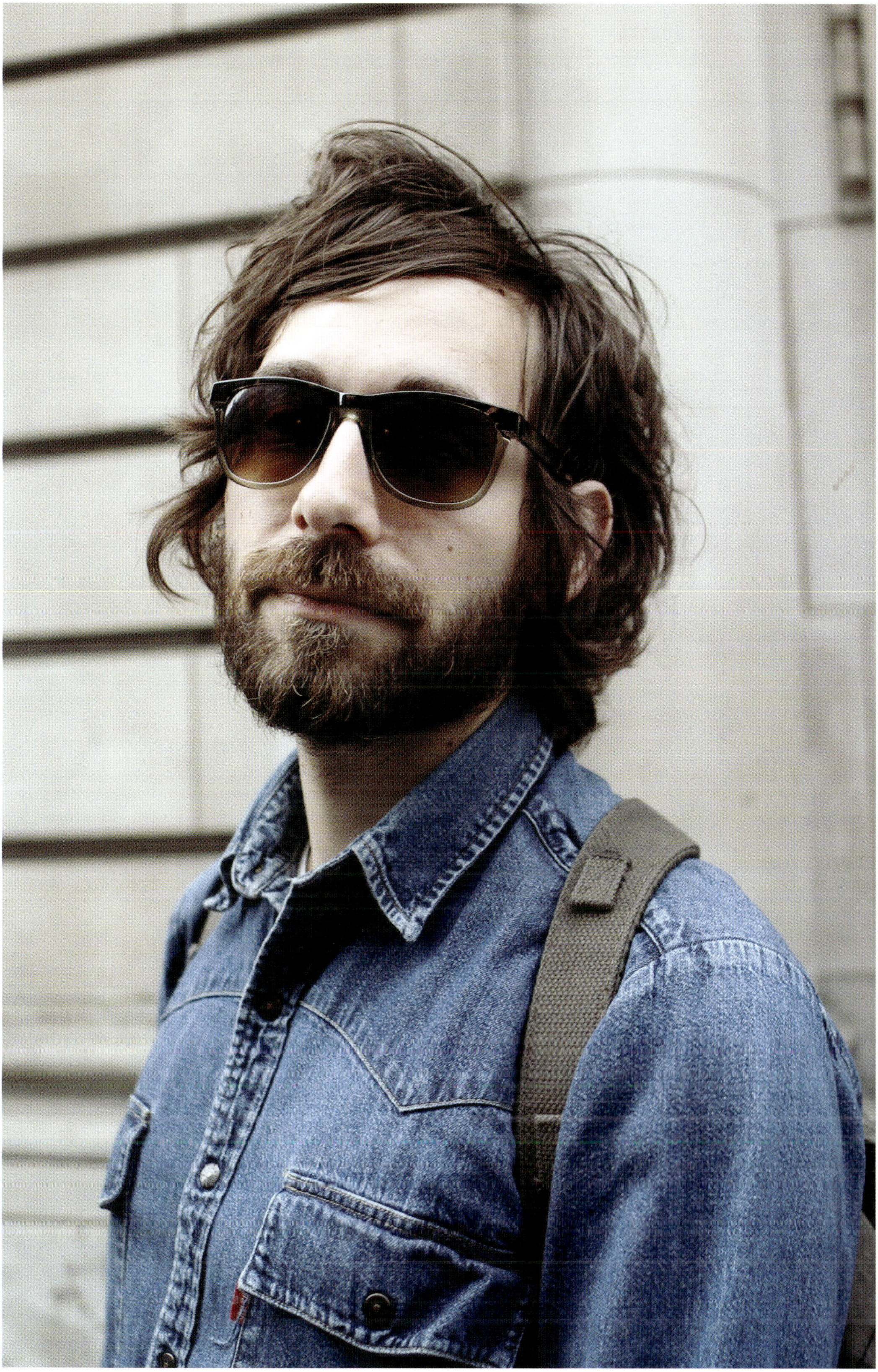

39 • Colin: Regent St, London

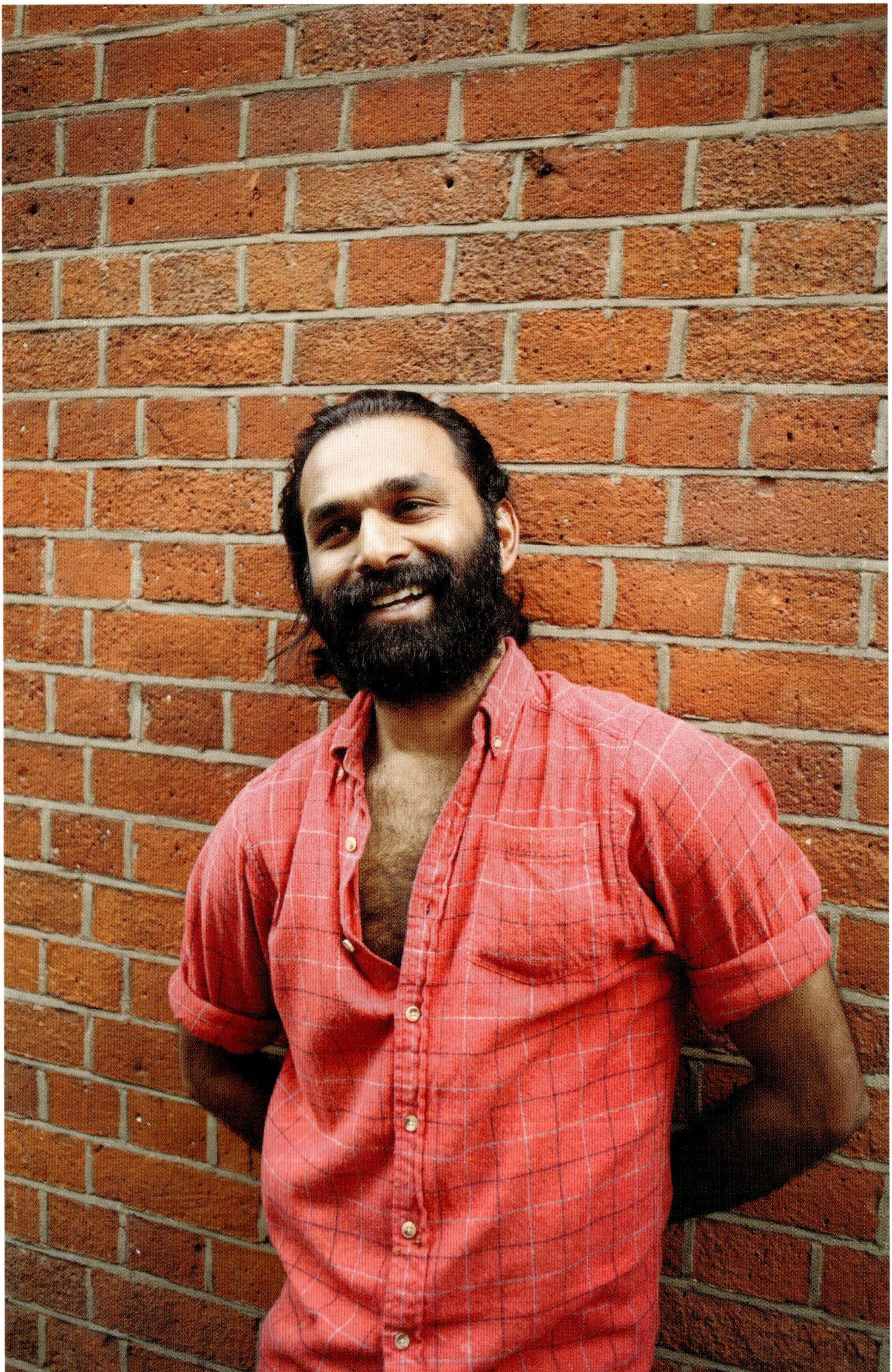

40 • Kumar: Frith St, London

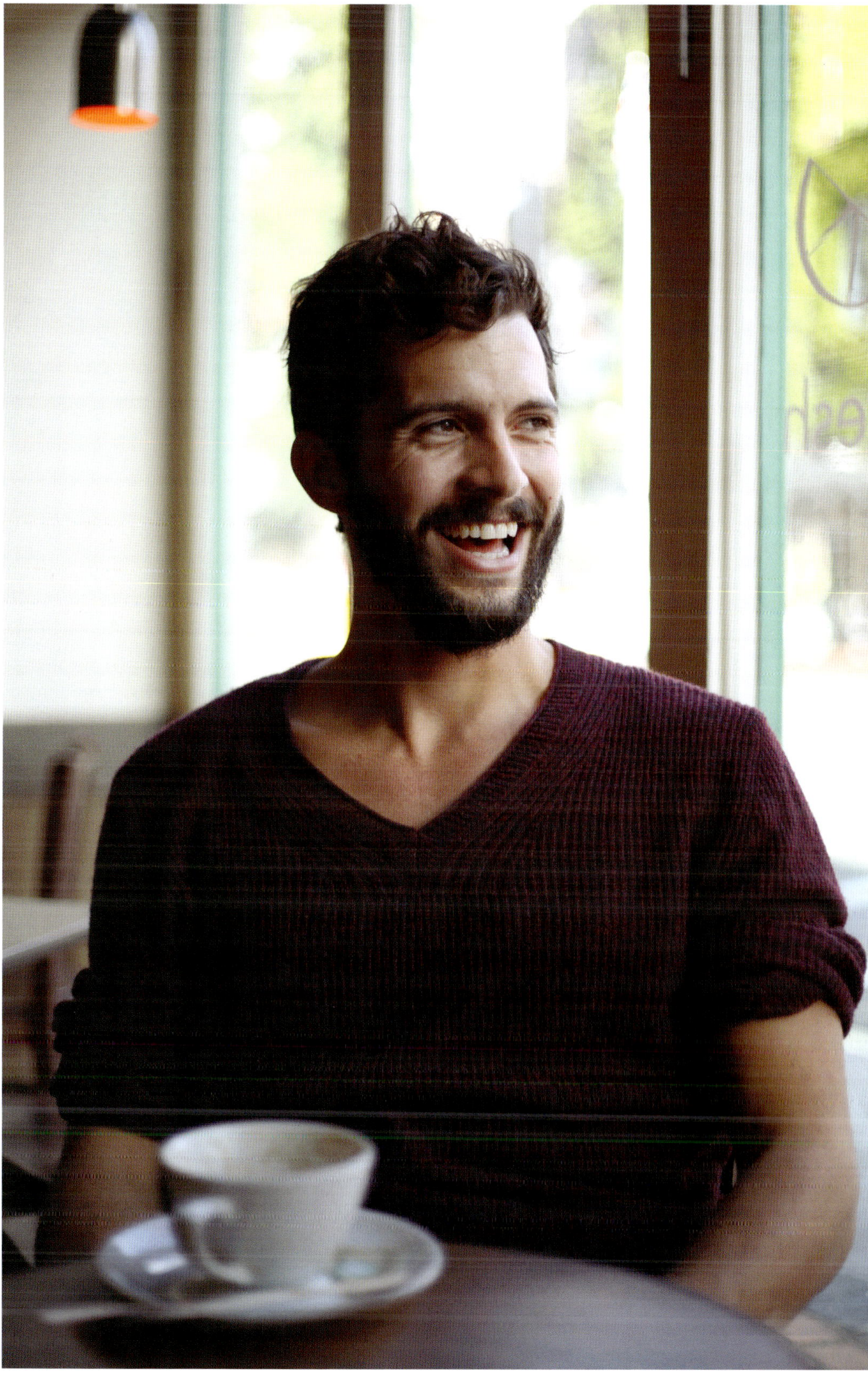

41 • Tommy: Parsons Green, London

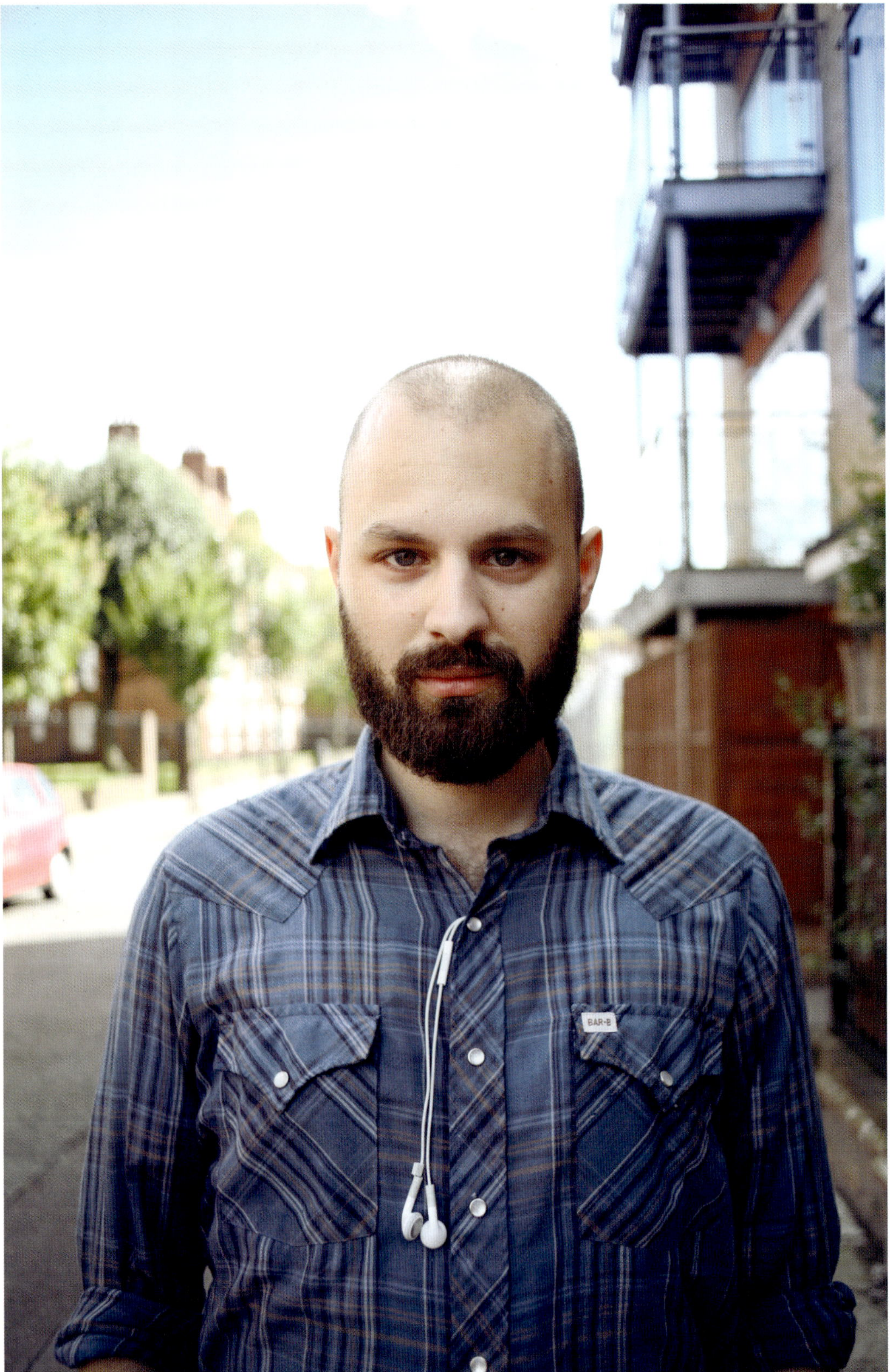

 Marko: Kay Street, London

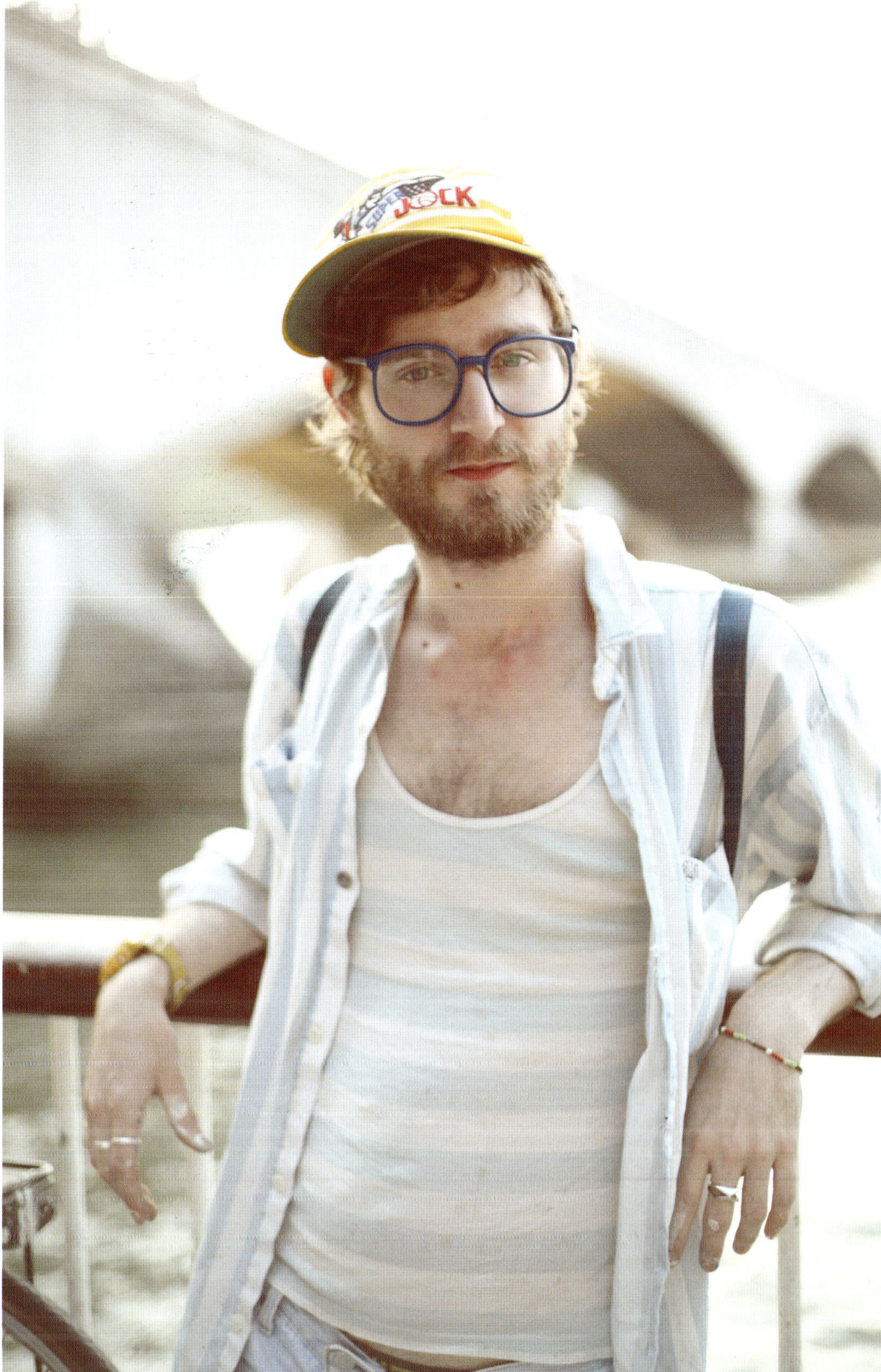

43 • Tom: Southbank, London

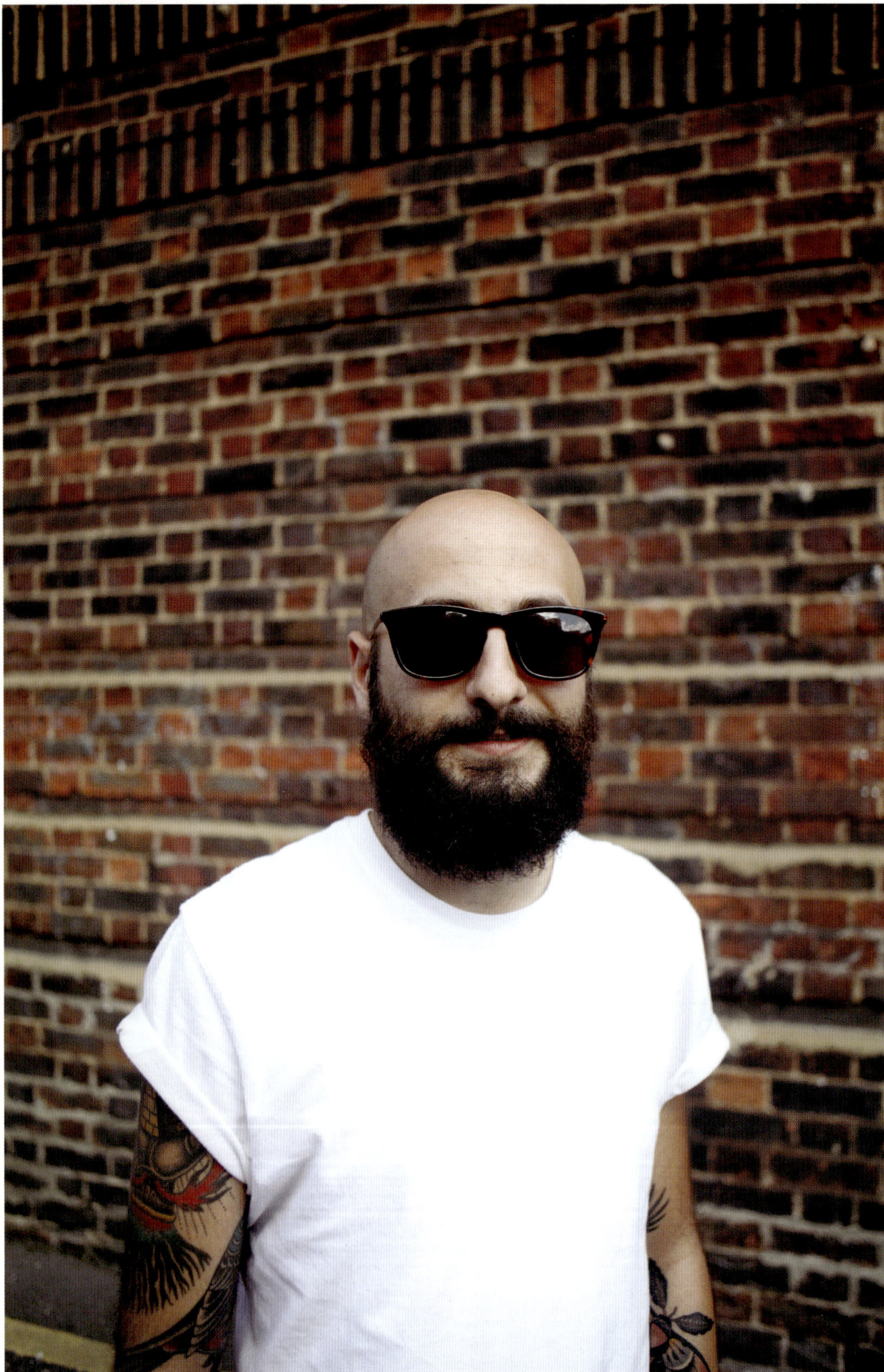

 Valerio: Sheep Lane, London

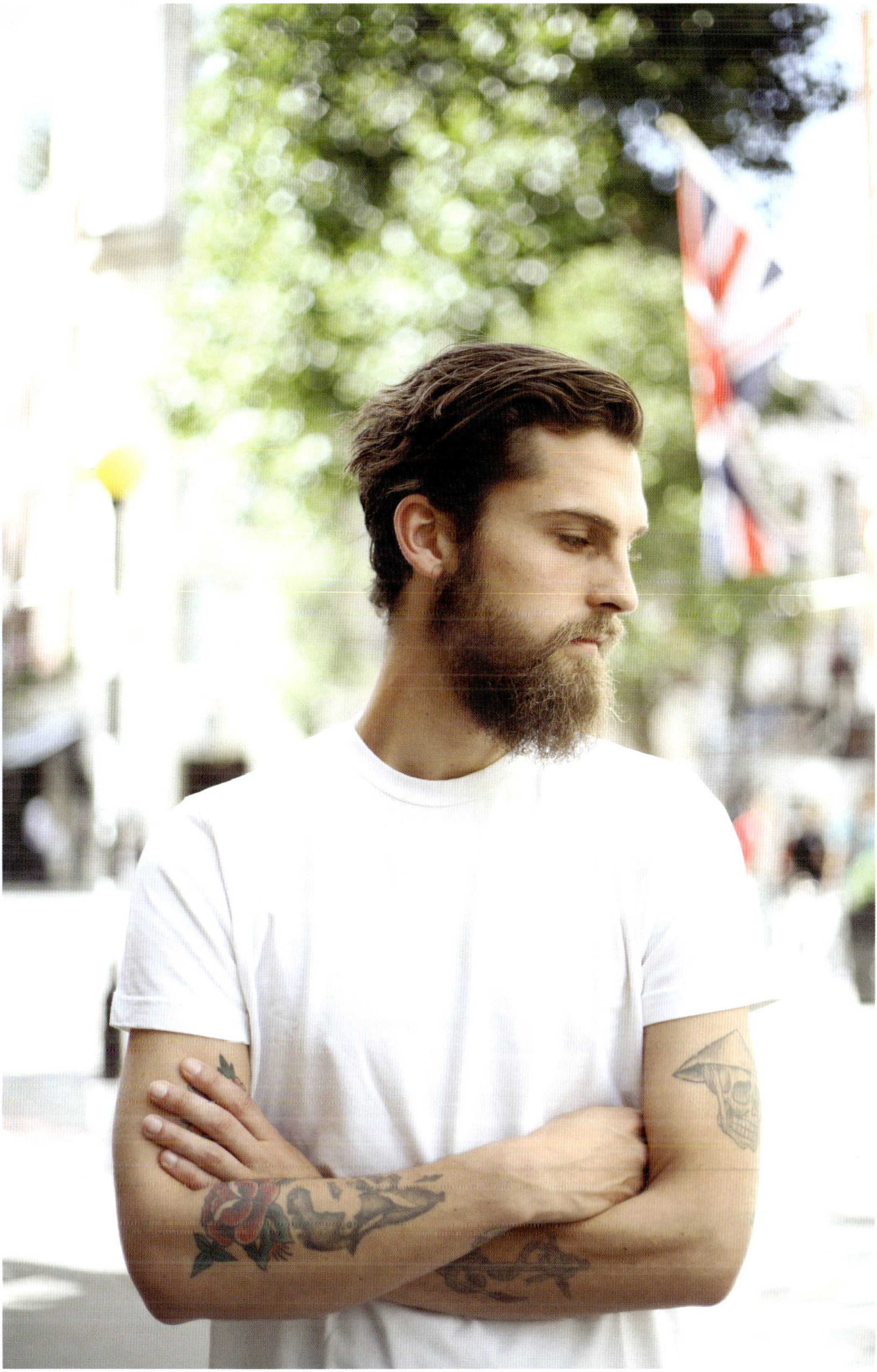

45 • Fabien: Monmouth Street, London

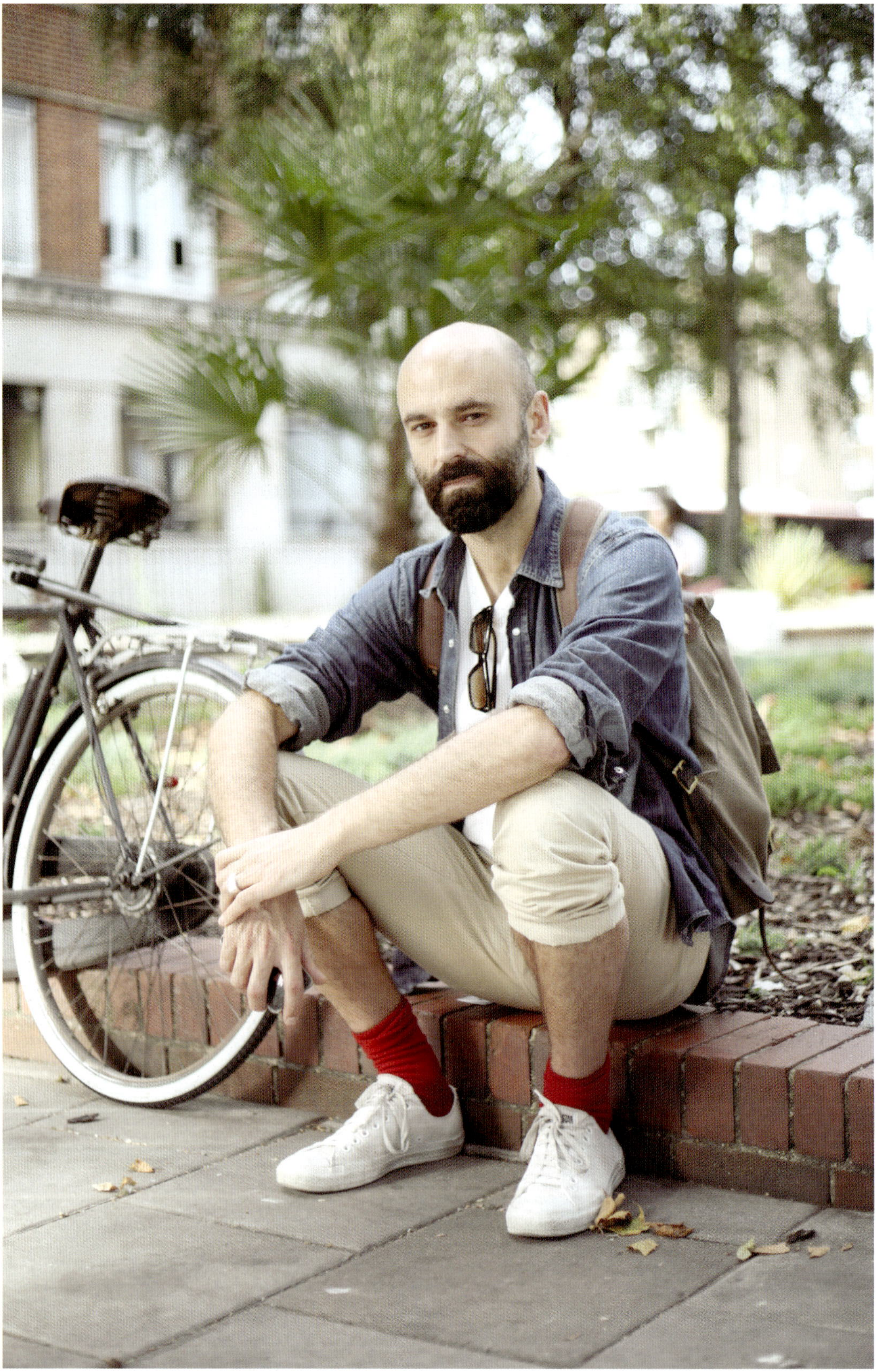

46 • Pedro: Waterloo Road, London

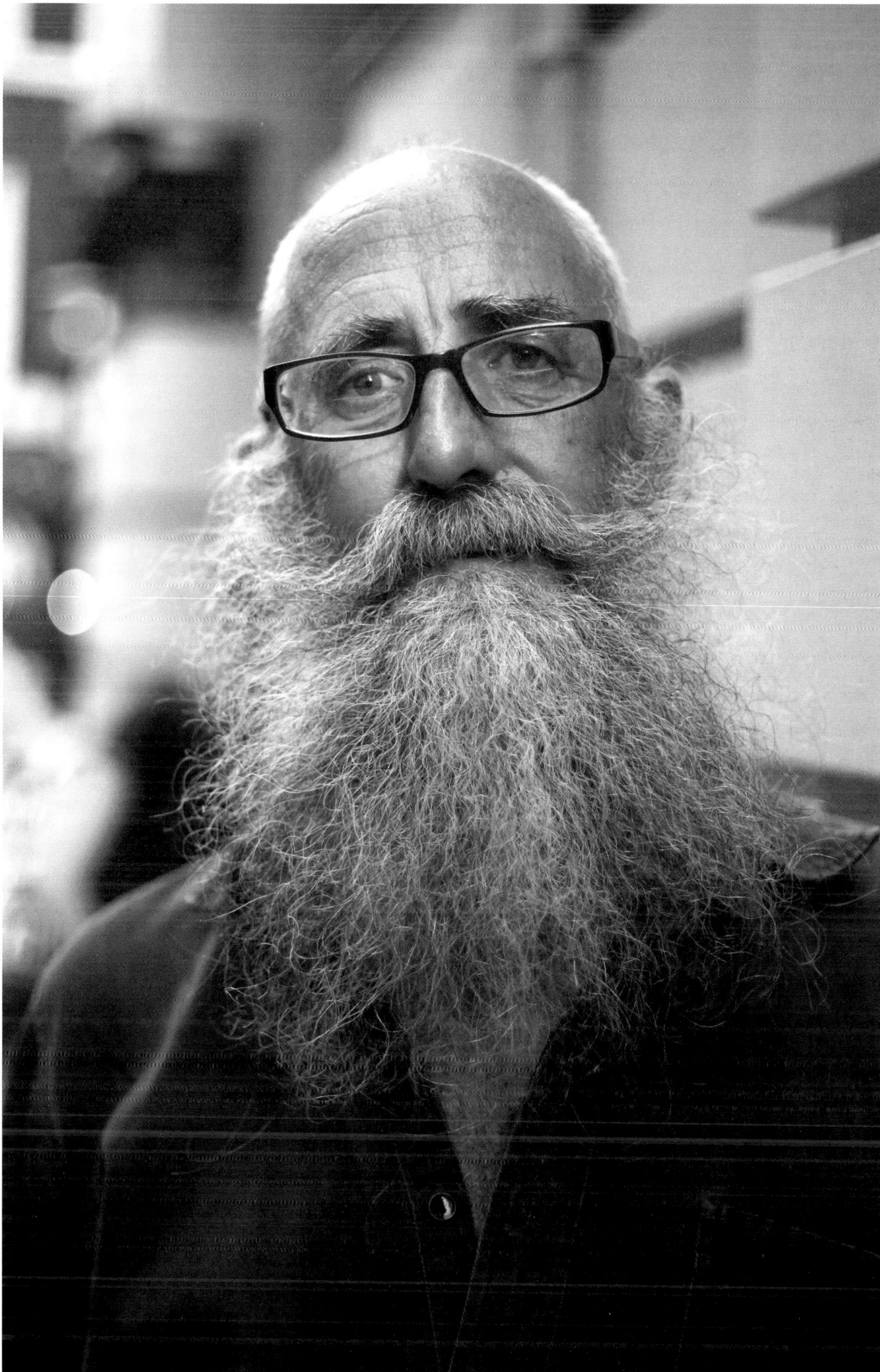

47 • Roy: Cecil Court, London

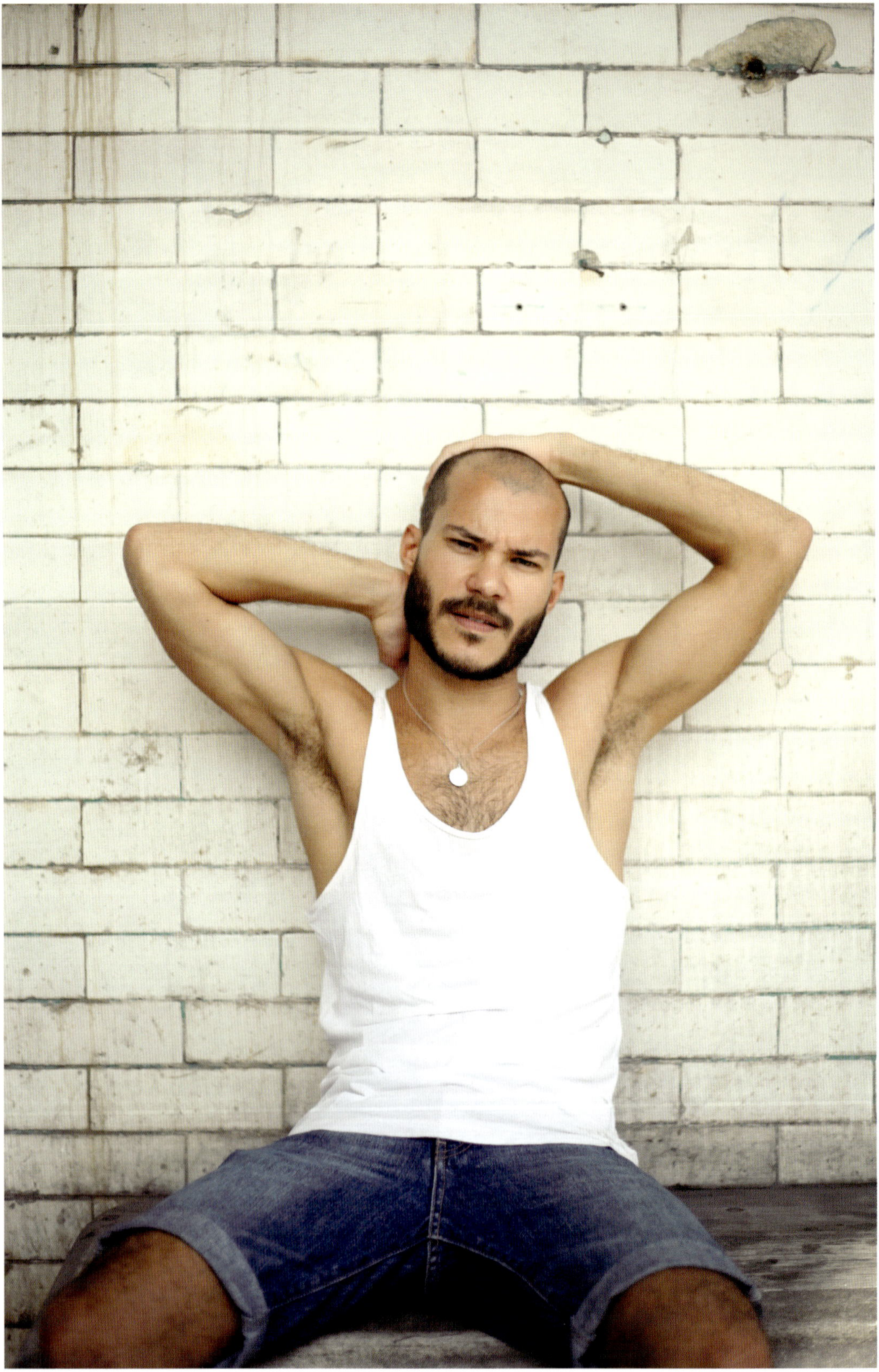

 Pedro: Southwark Street, London

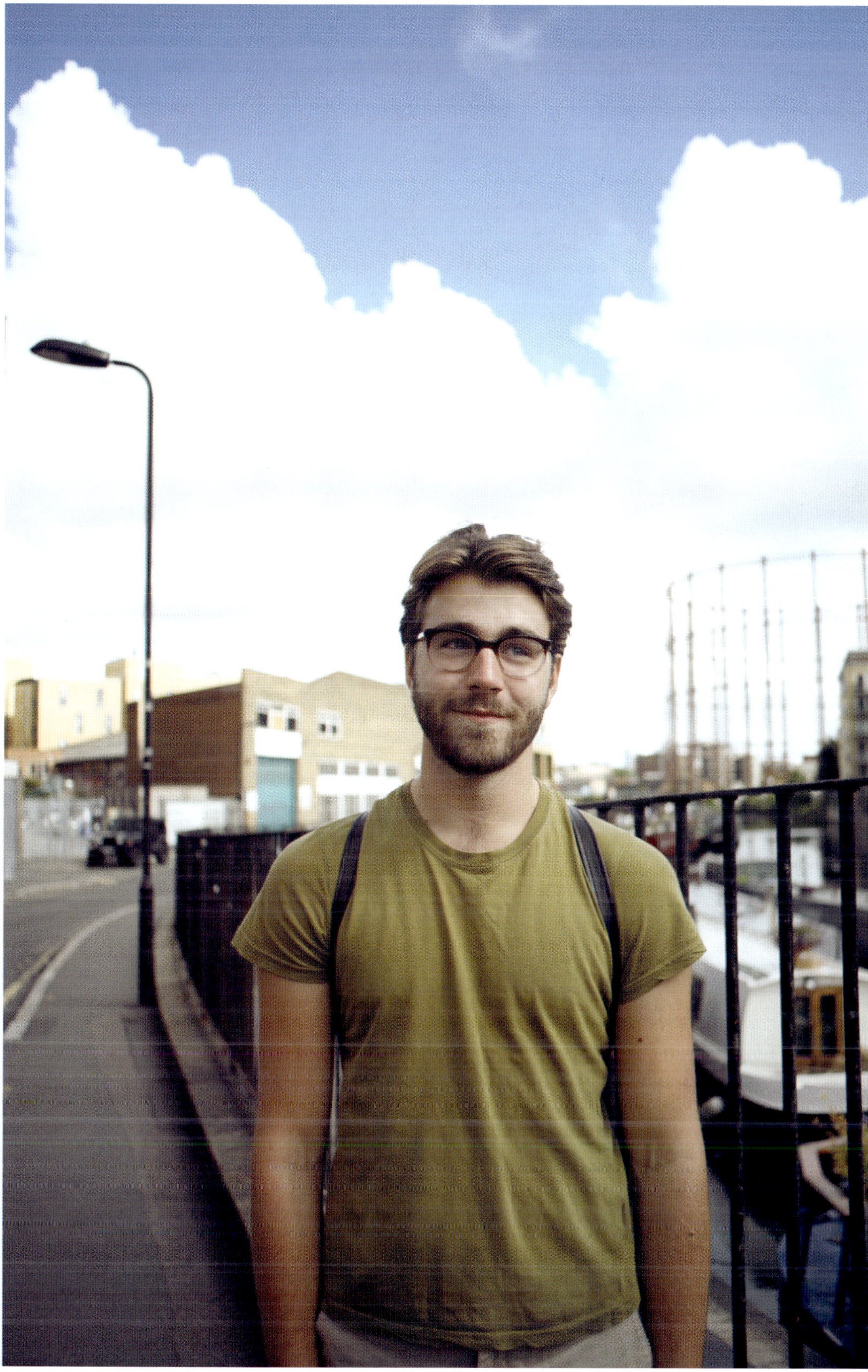

49 • Joshua: Andrews Road, London

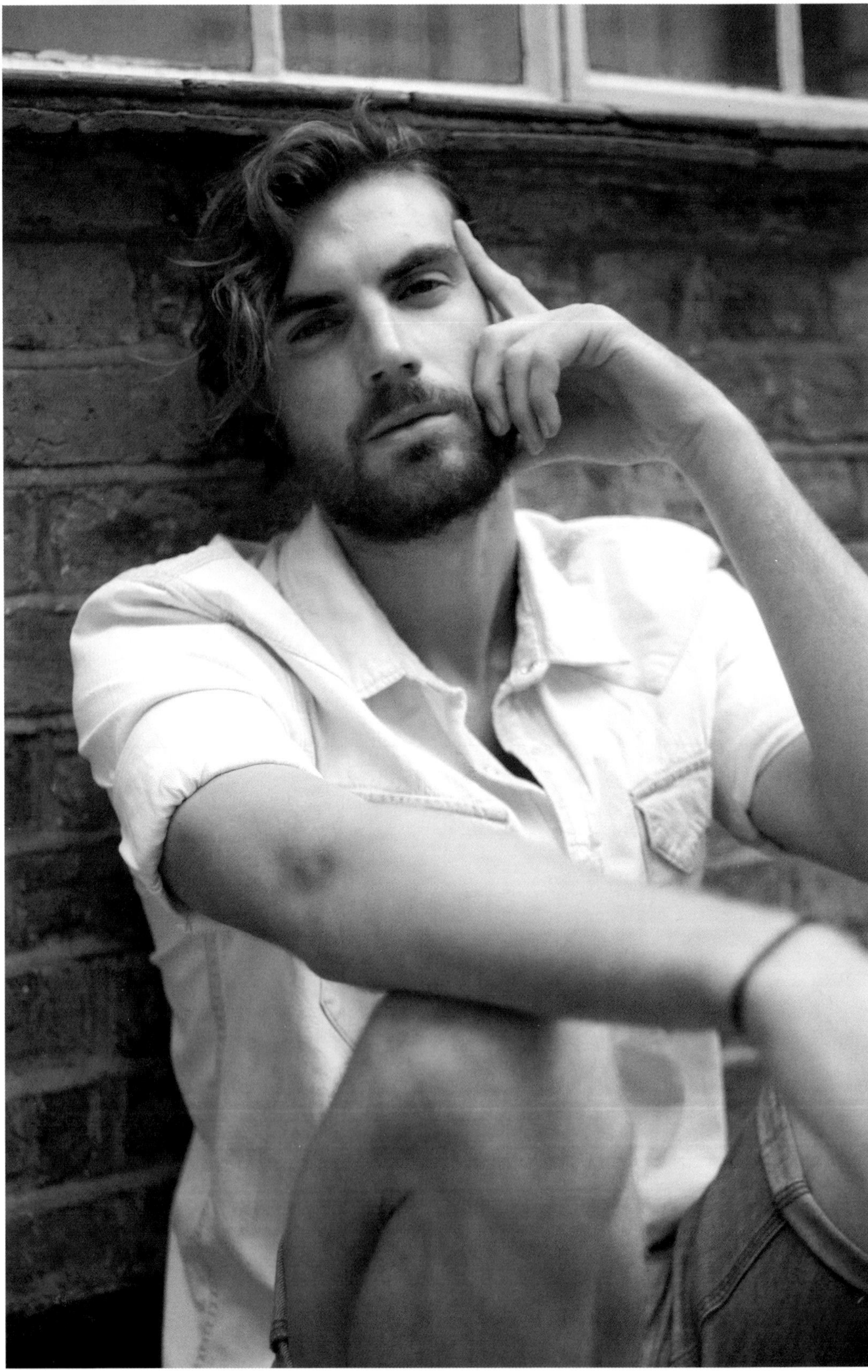

50 • Daniel: Old Church Street, London

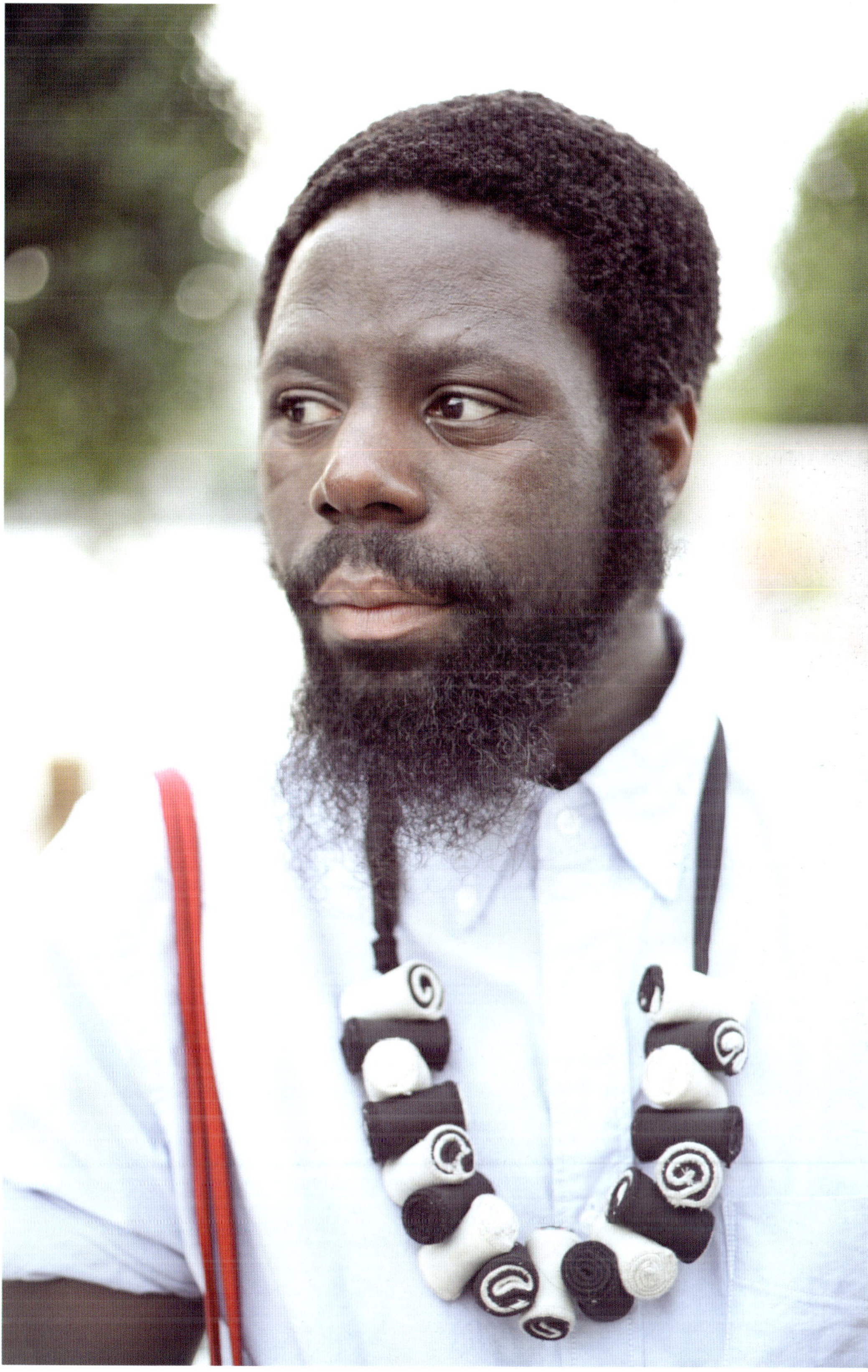

51 • Raf: Southbank, London

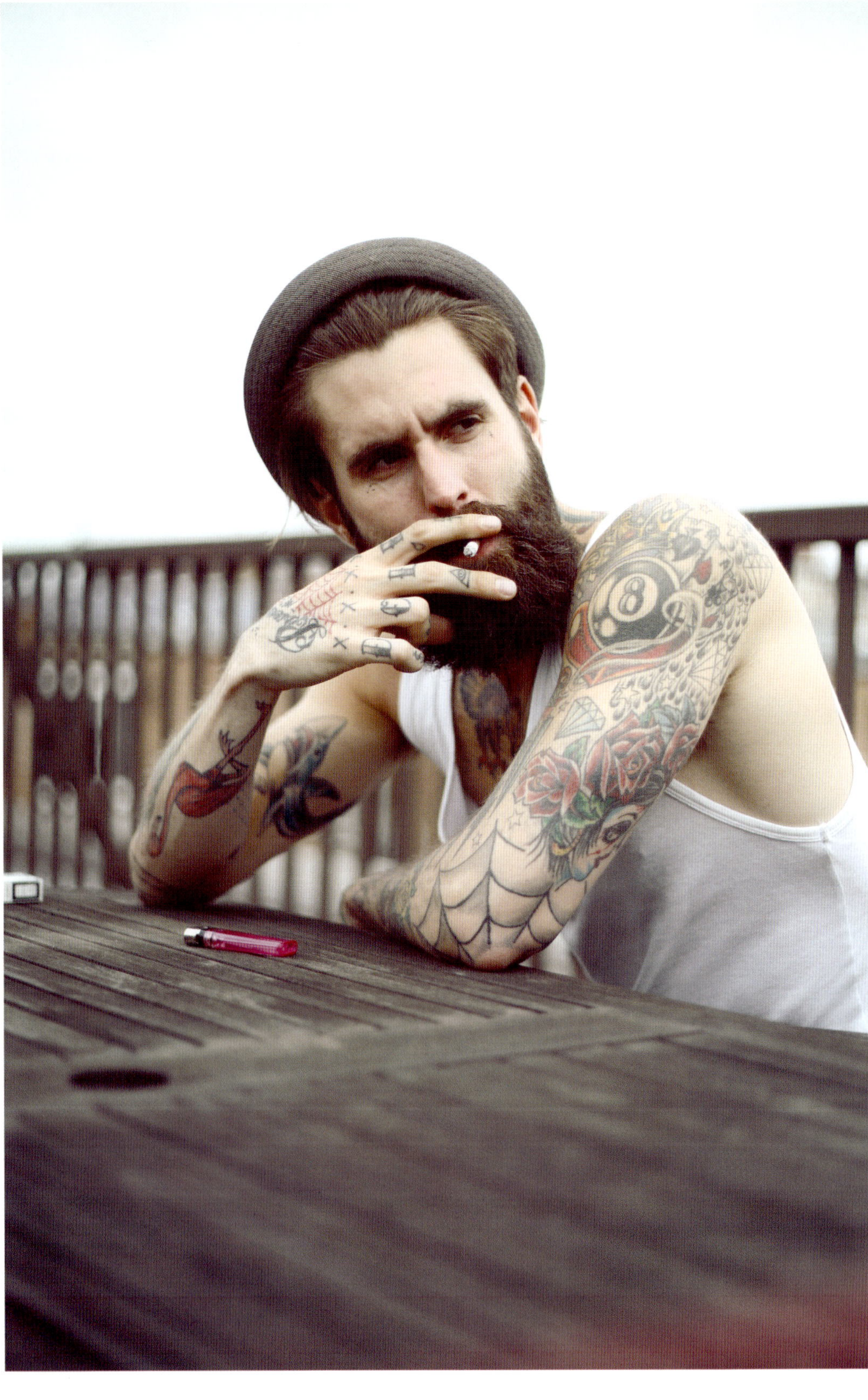

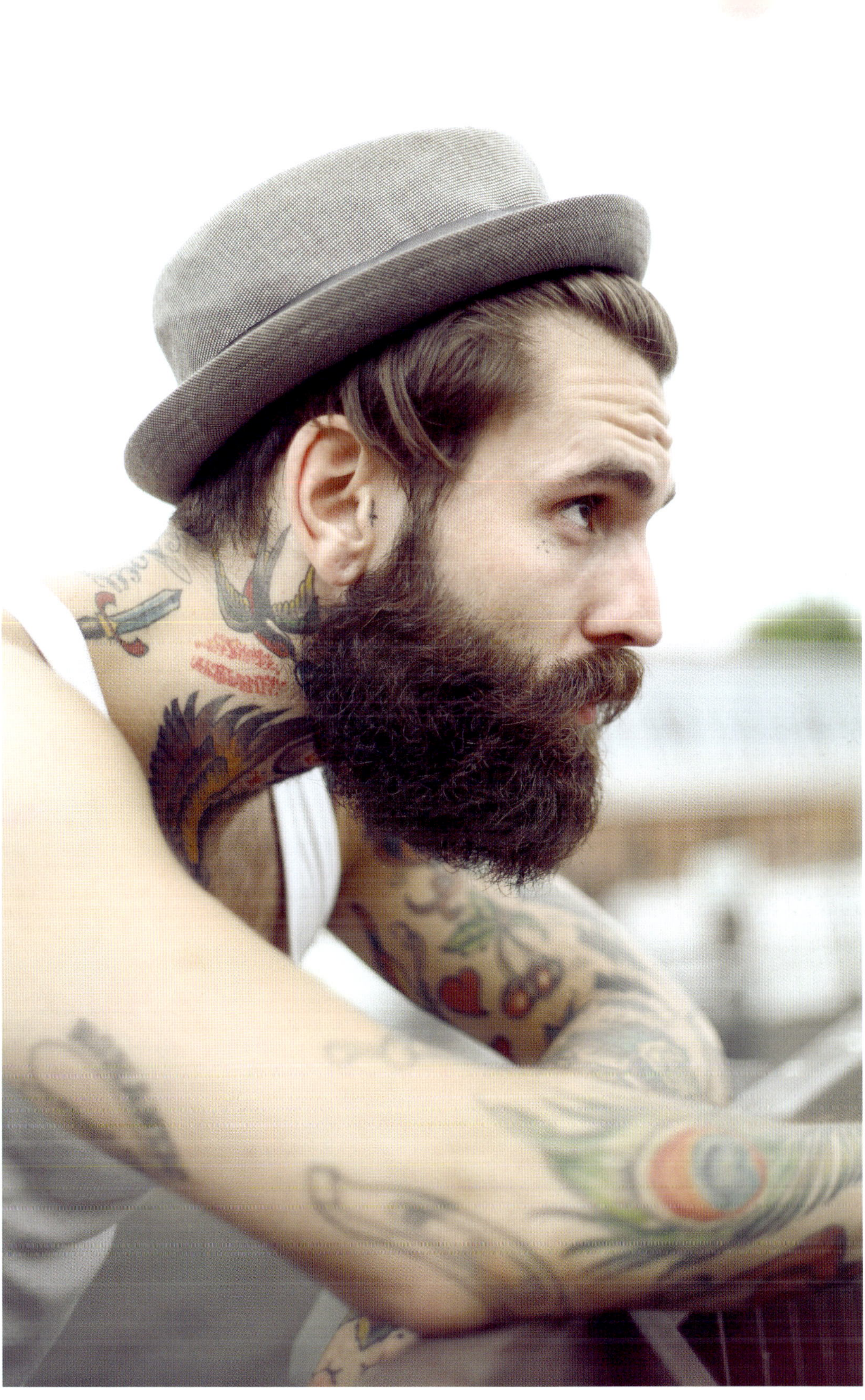

 Ricki: Kings Road, London

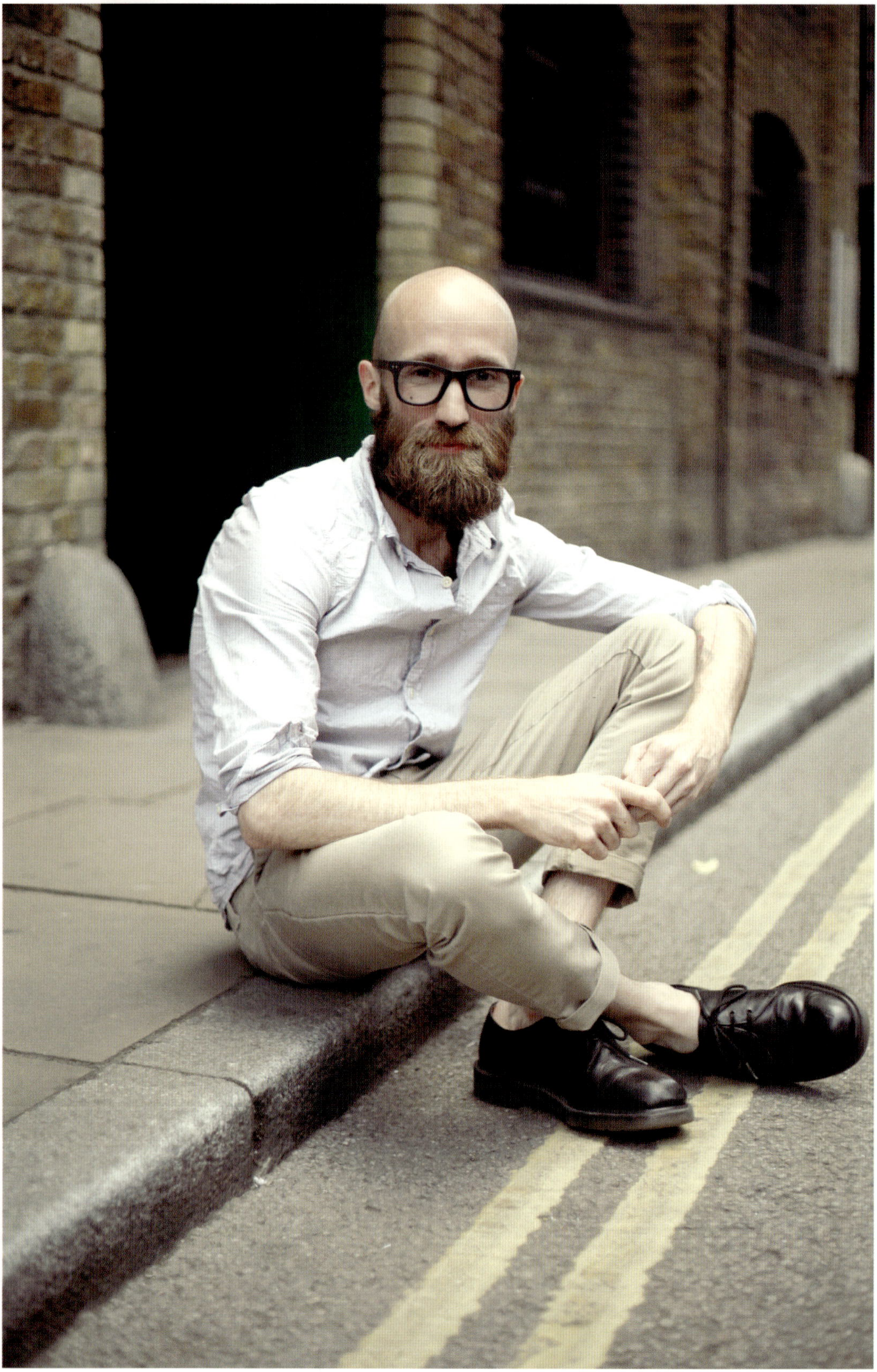

53 • Julien: Stoney Street, London

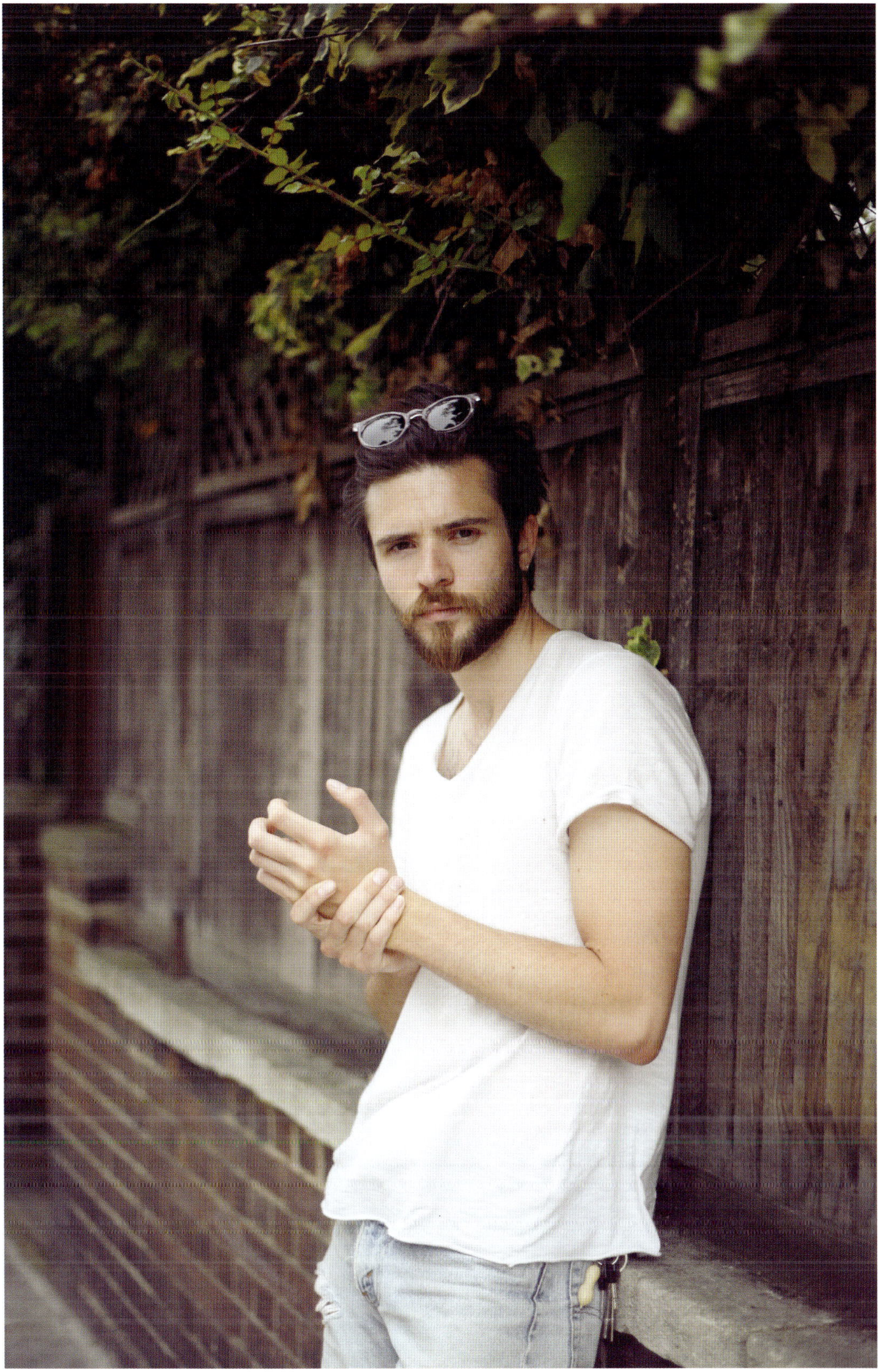

54 • Beau: Fulham Road, London

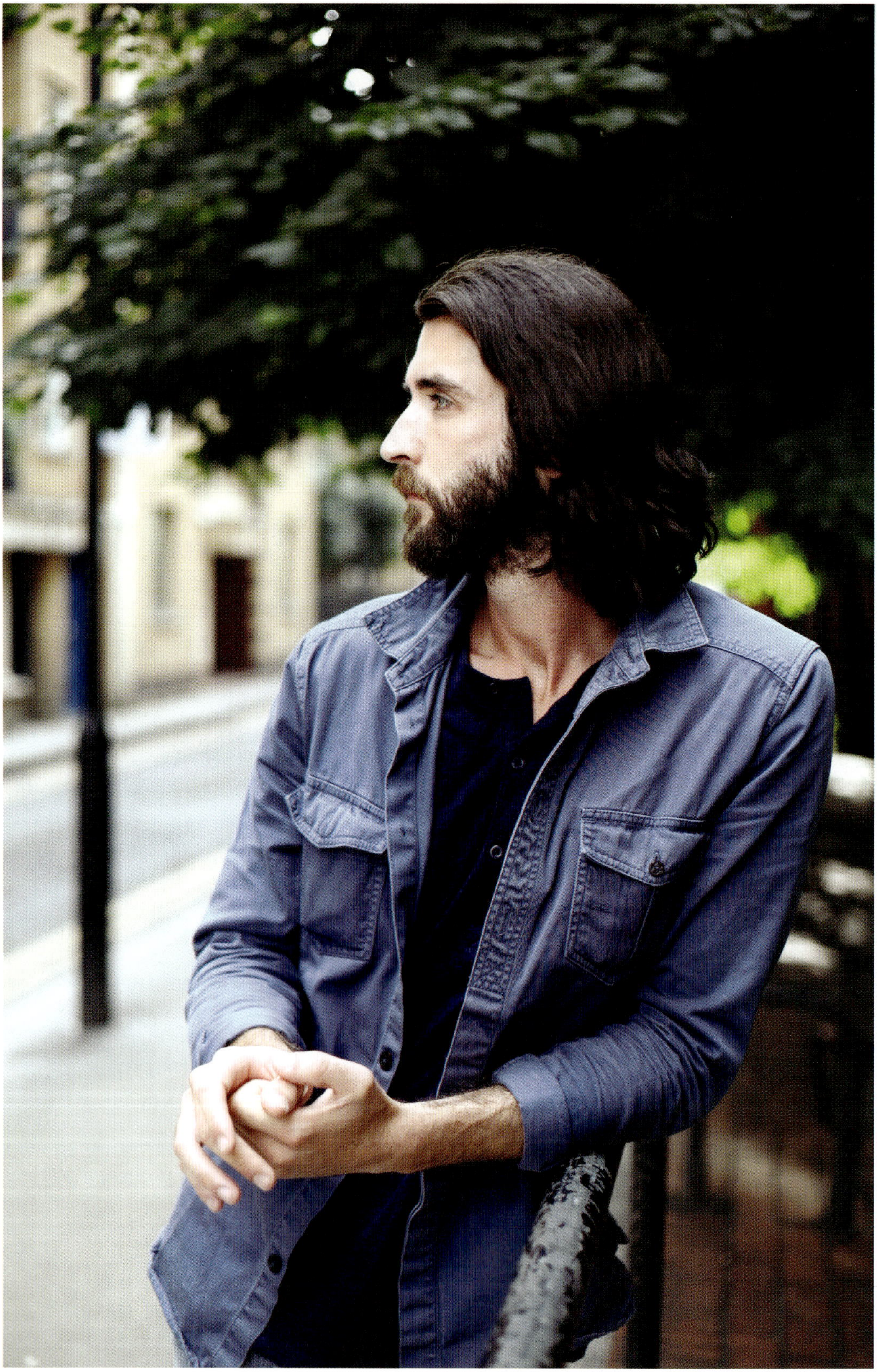

55 • Tom: Heneage Street, London

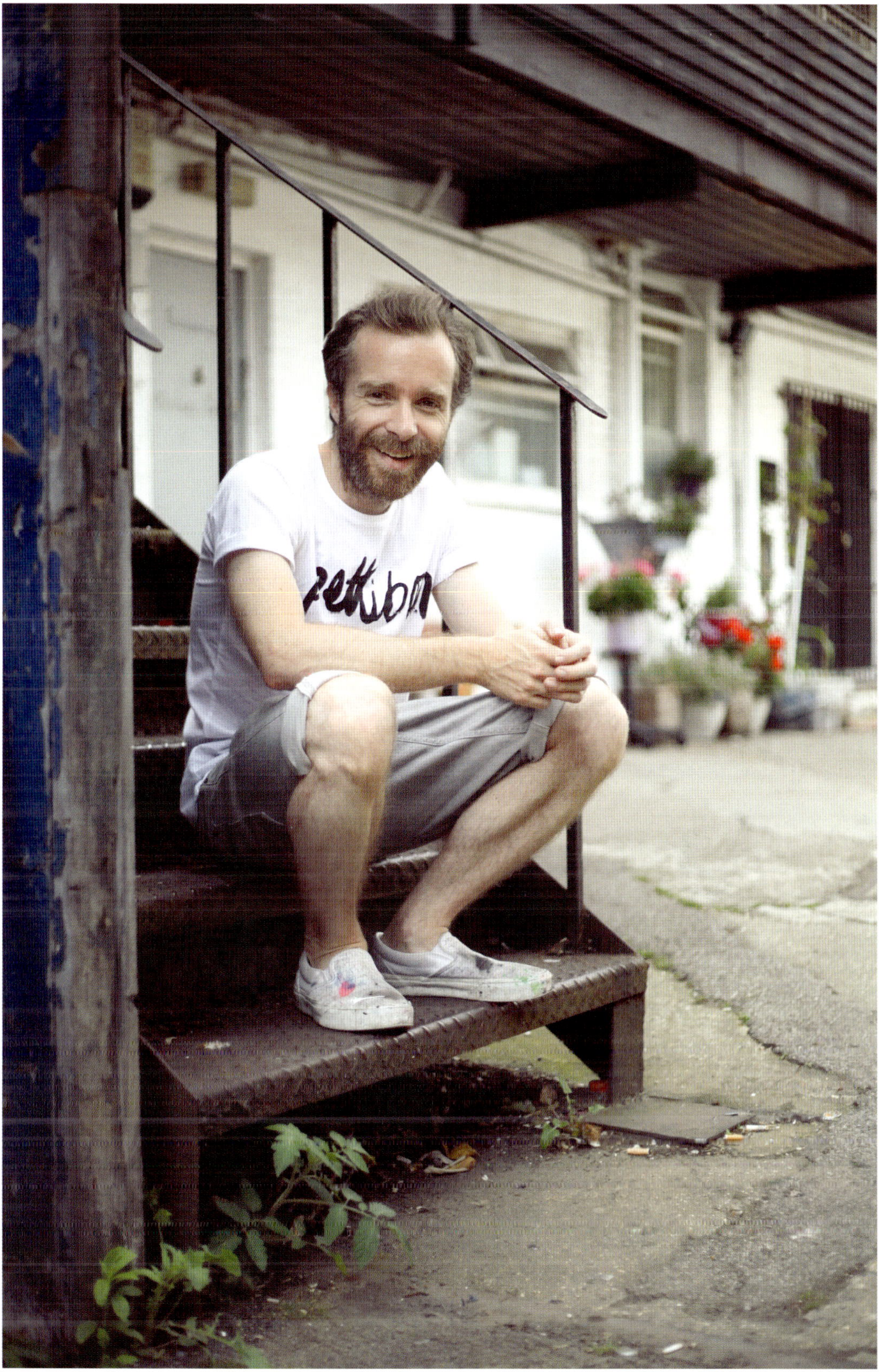

56 • Simeon: Hearn Street, London

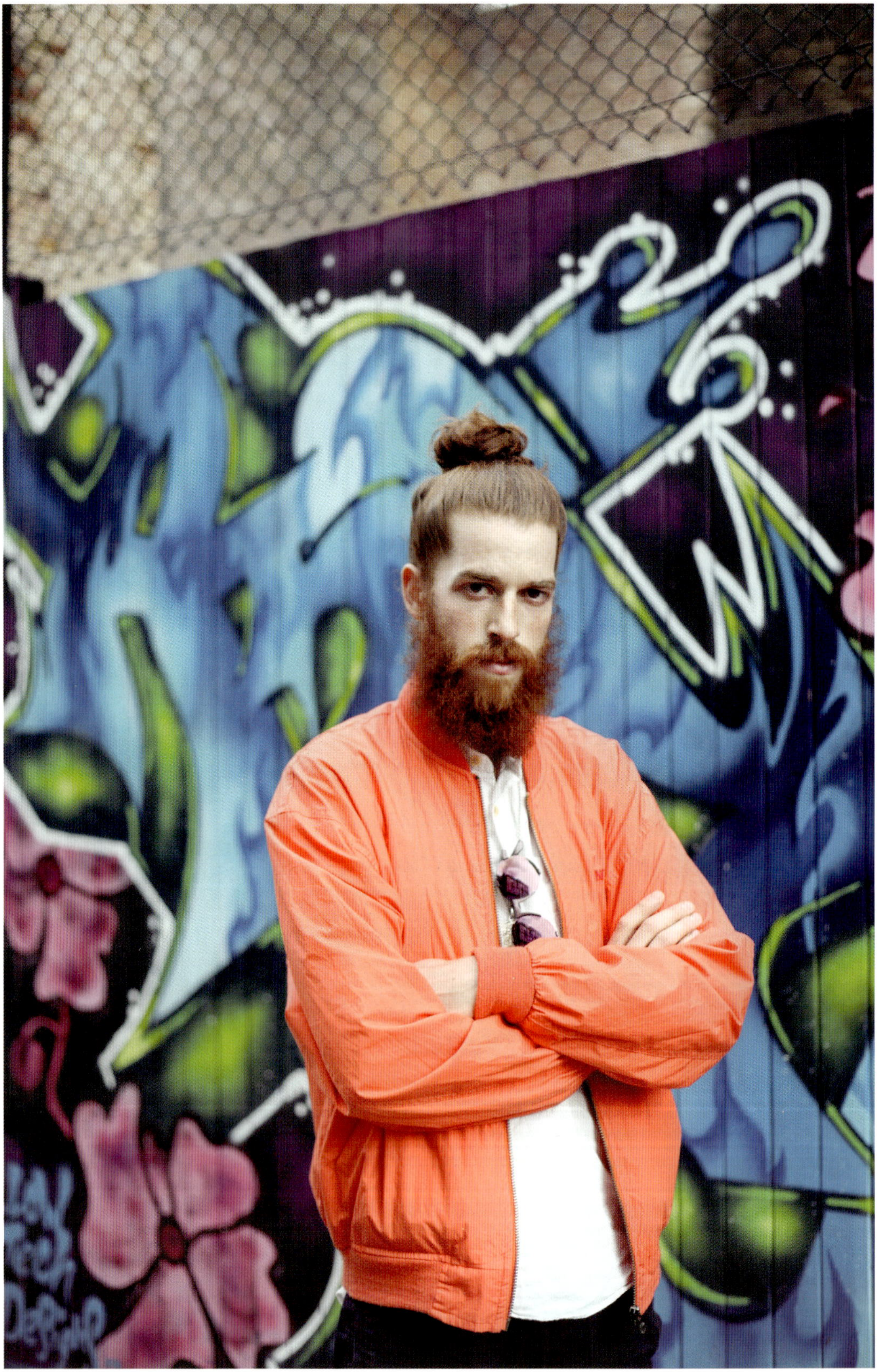

57 • Olmo: Fashion Street, London

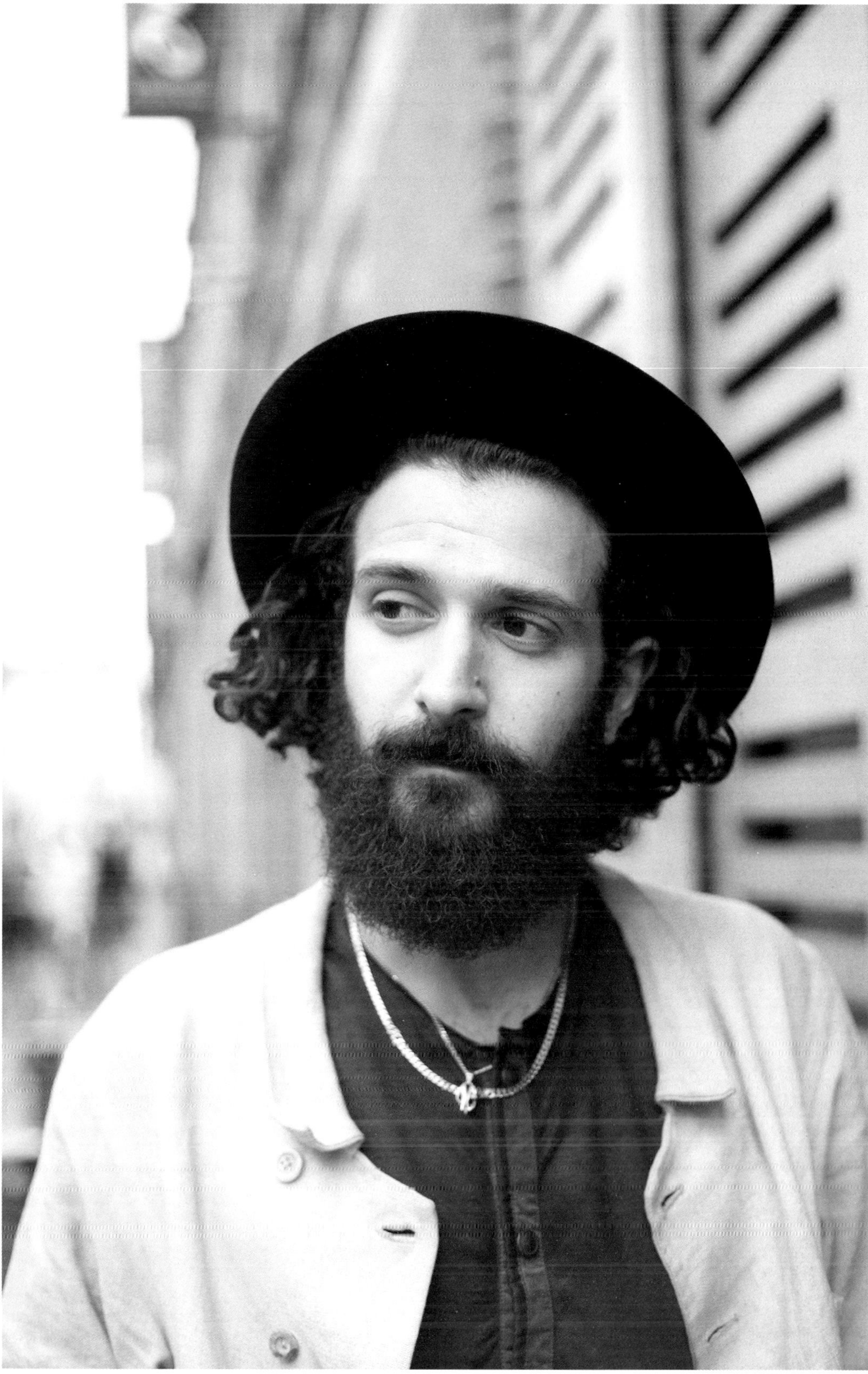

58 • Jamie: Fashion Street, London

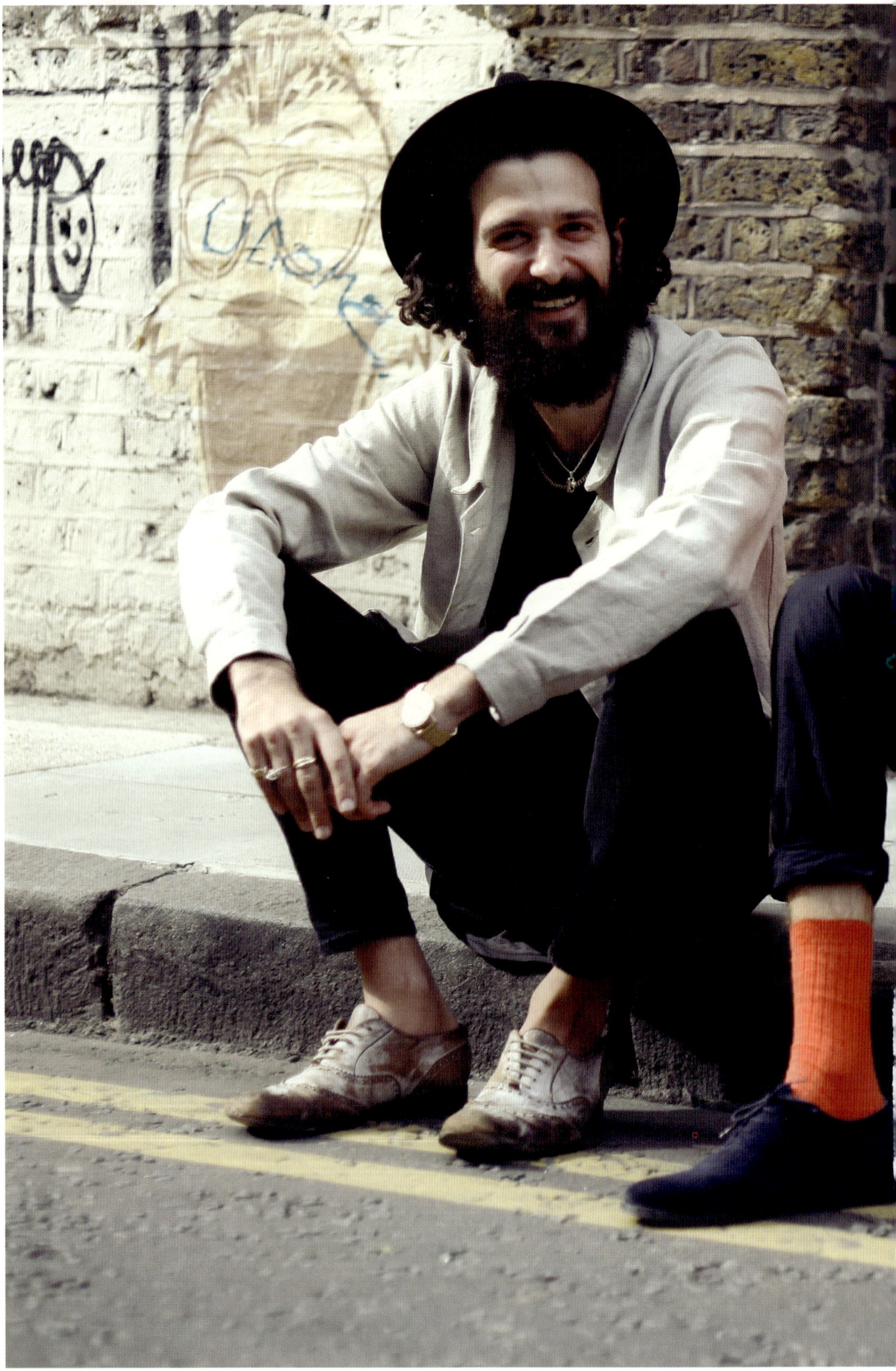

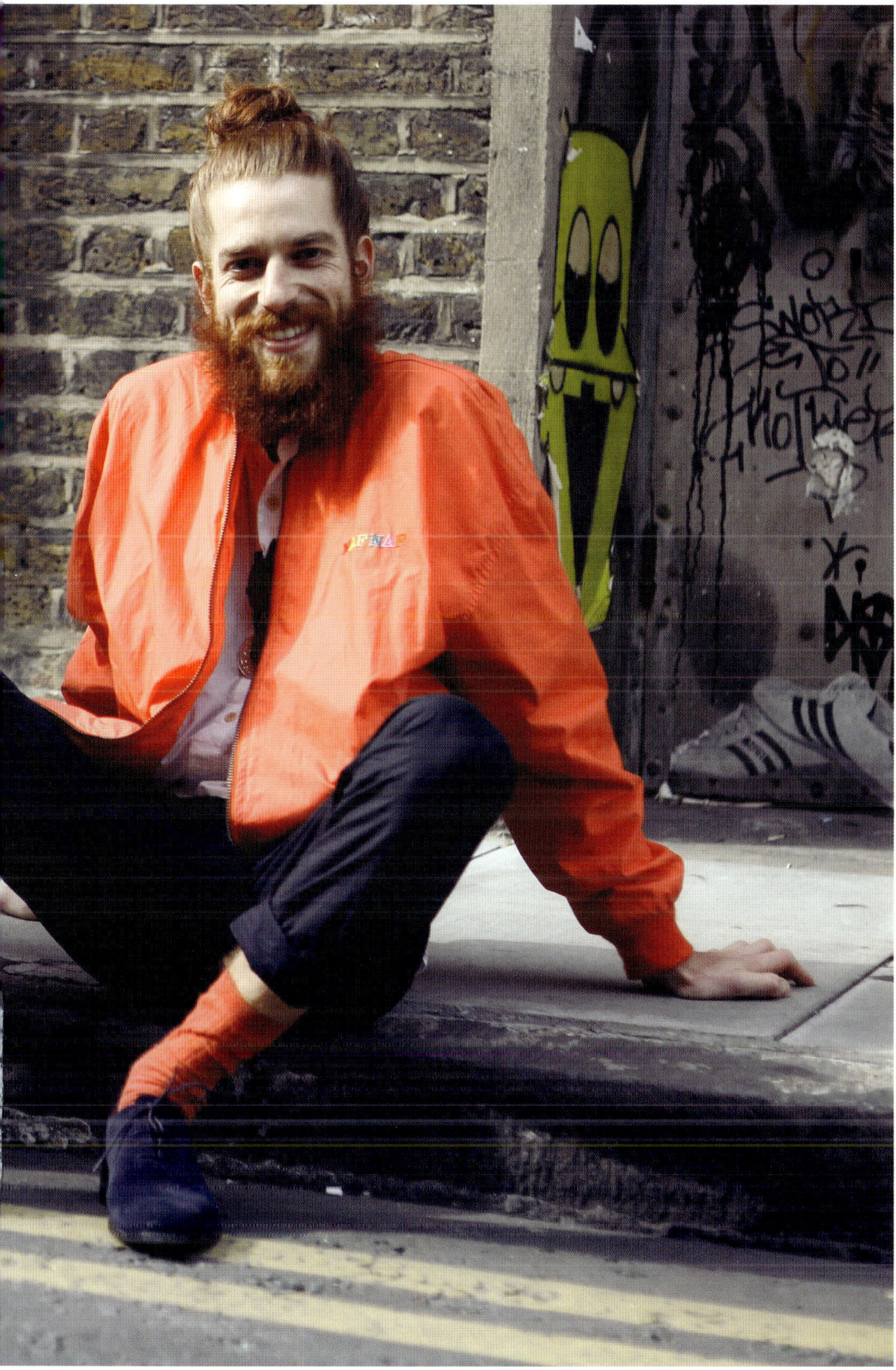

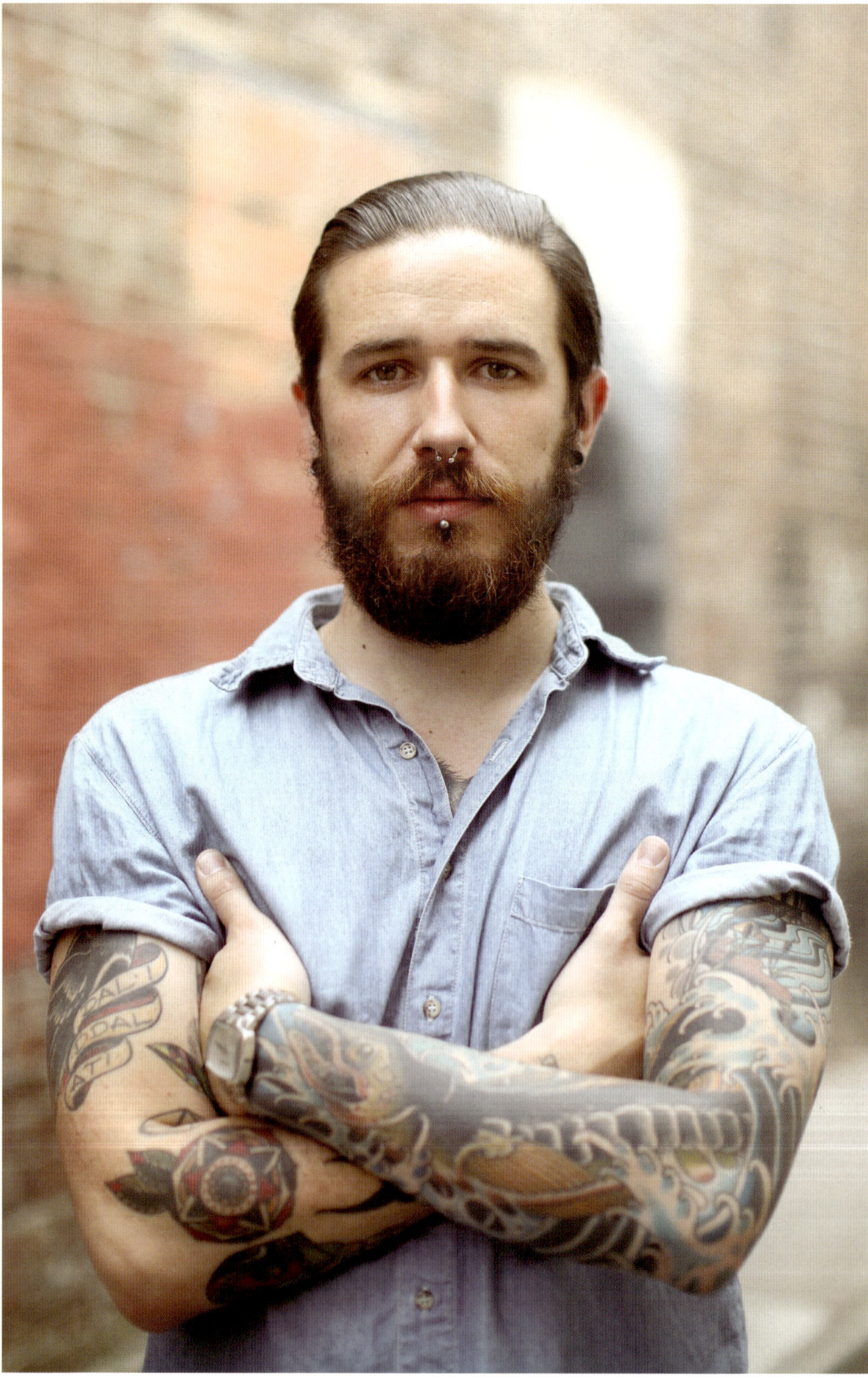

59 • Gethin: Back Turner Street, Manchester

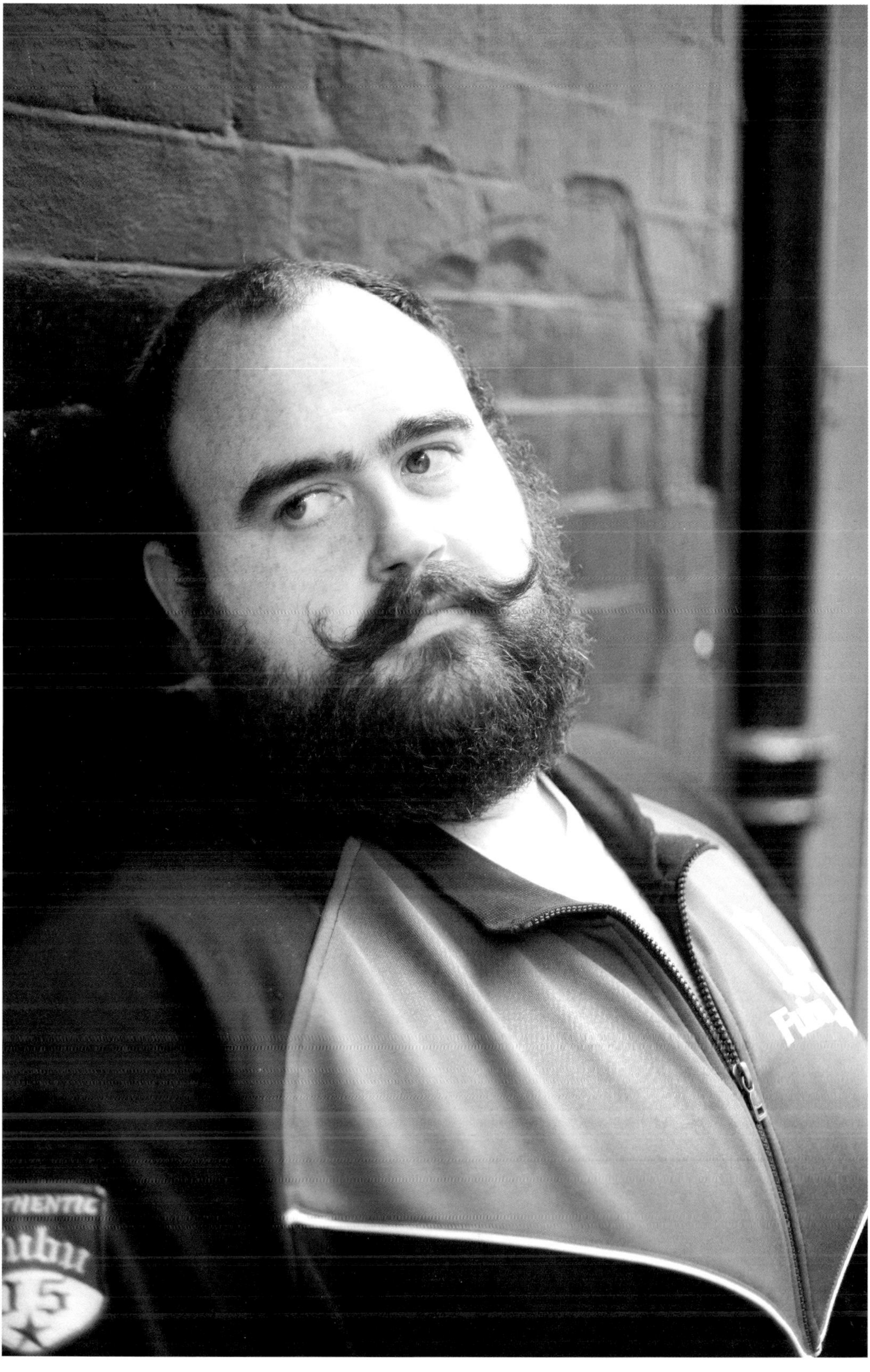

60 • Joseph: Wardour Street, London

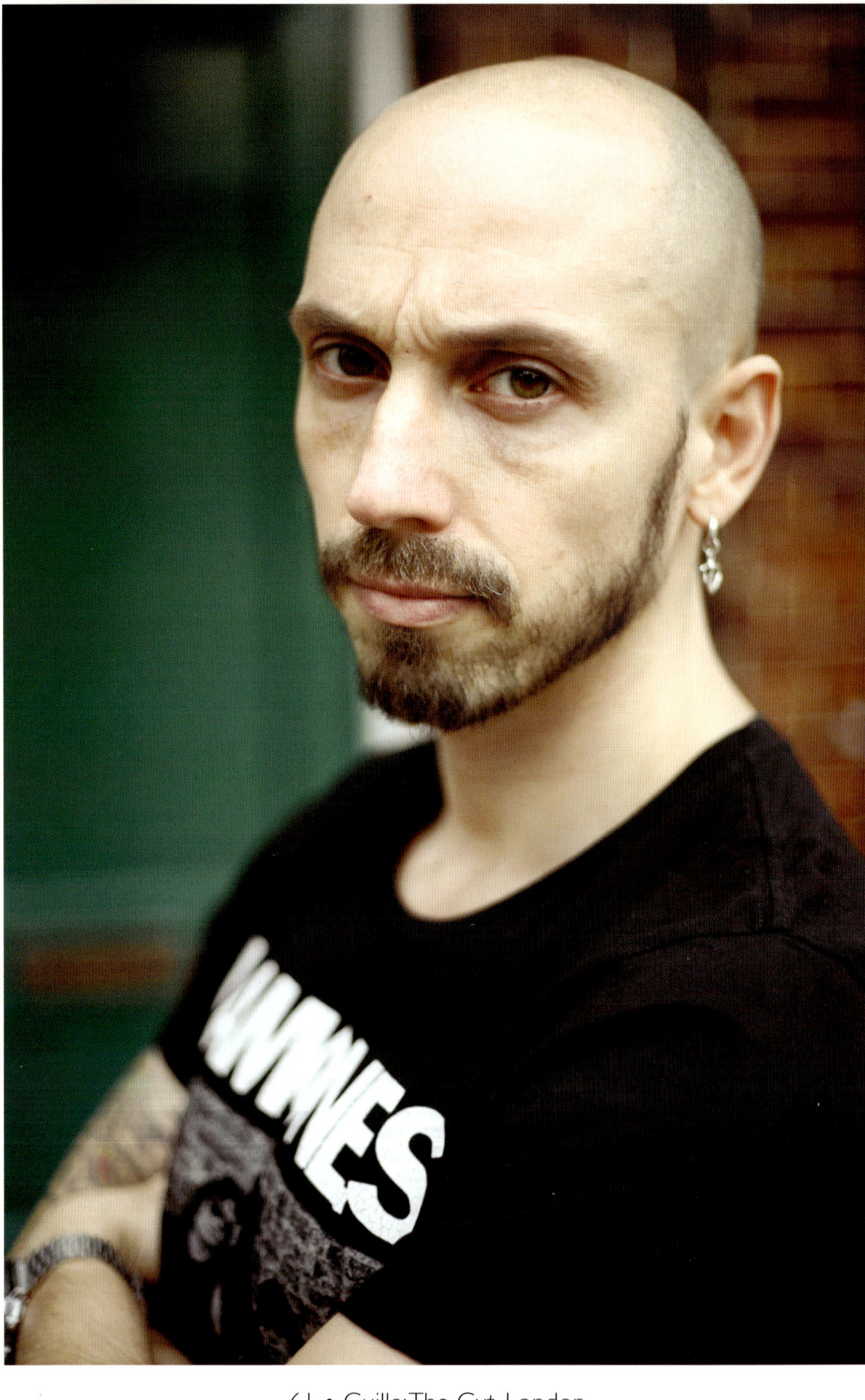

61 • Guille: The Cut, London

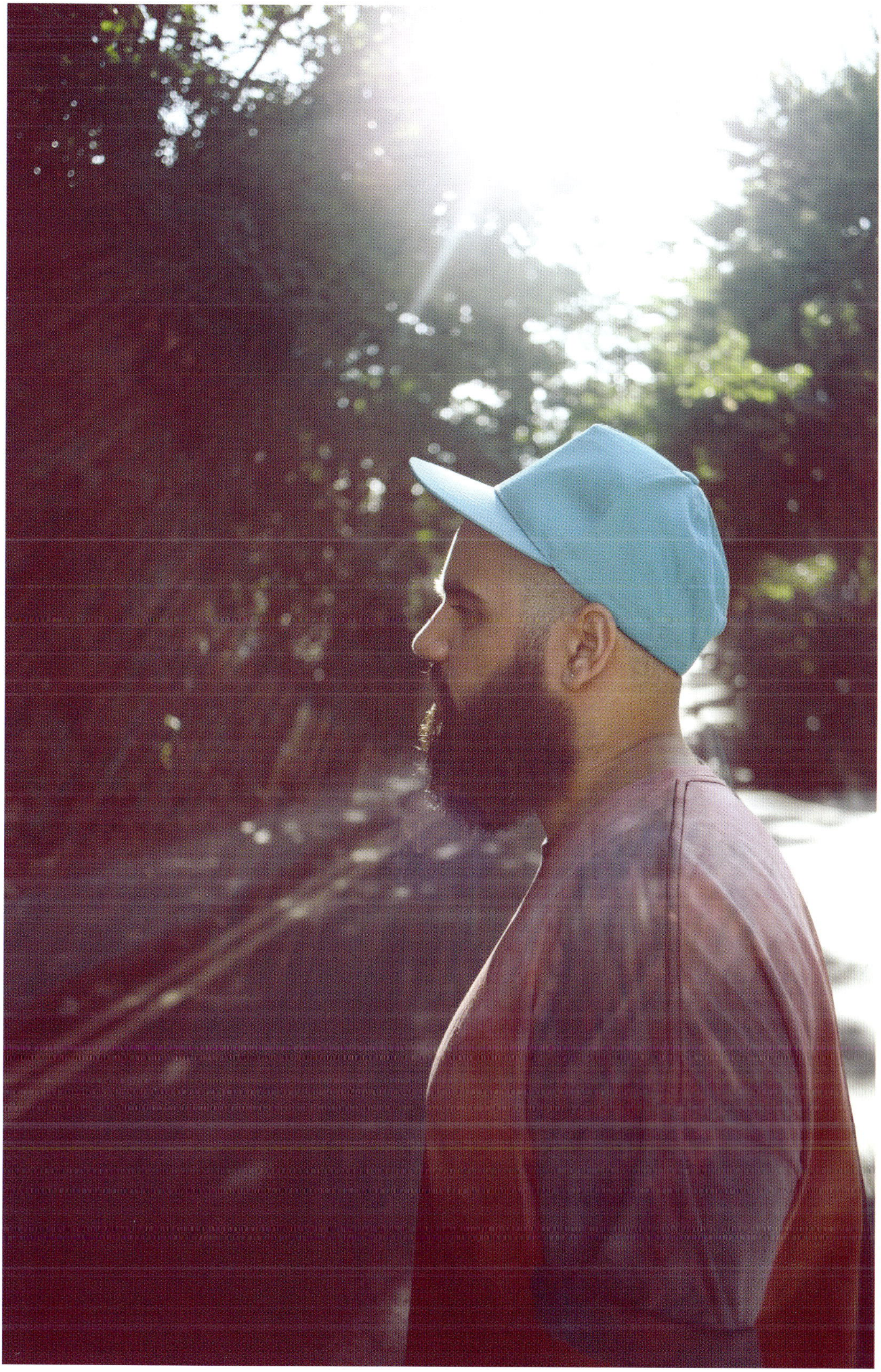

62 • Konstantino: Regent's Row, London

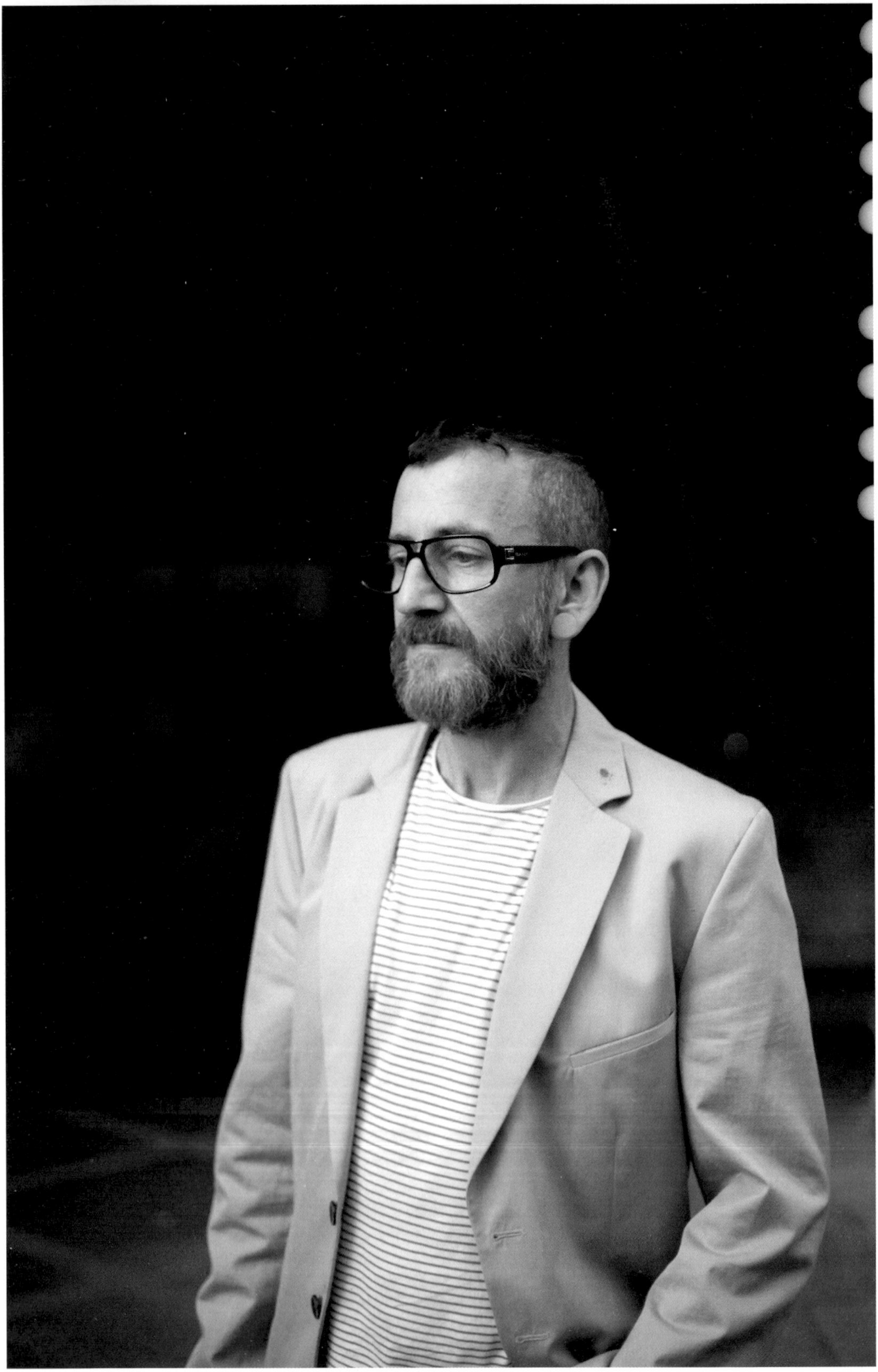

63 • Fransisco: Belvedere Road, London

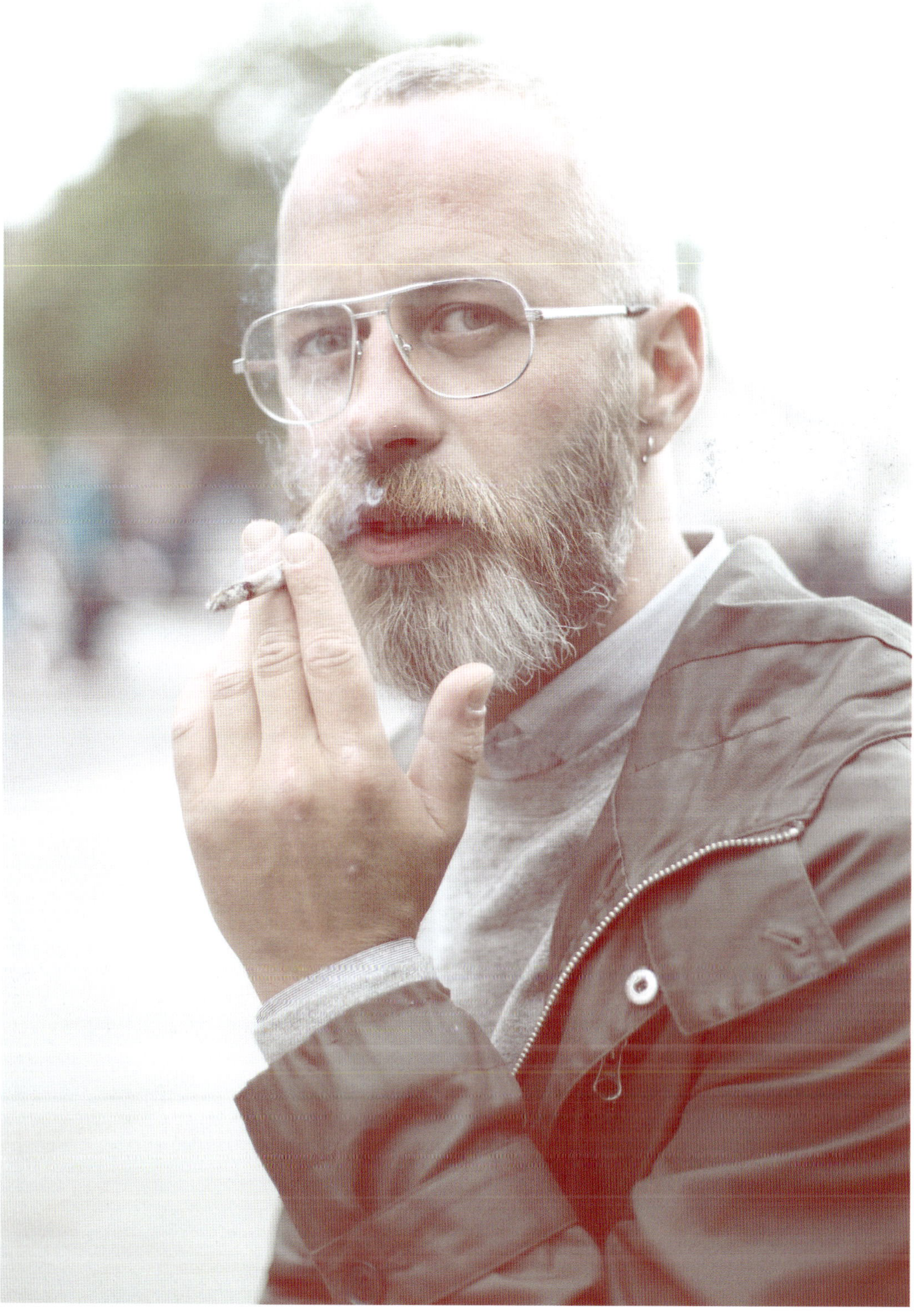

64 • Stephane: Trafalgar Square, London

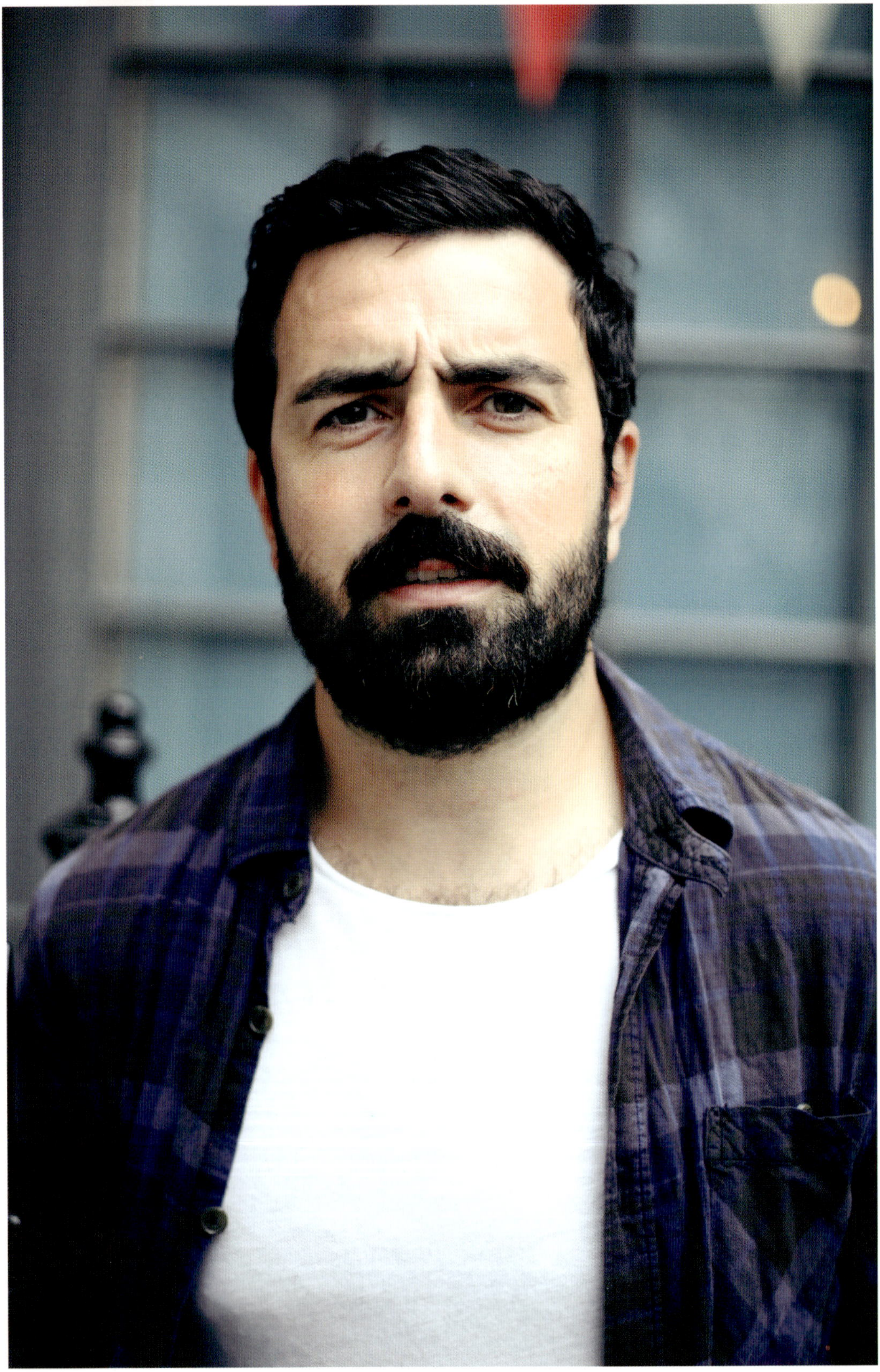

65 • Olly: St John Square, London

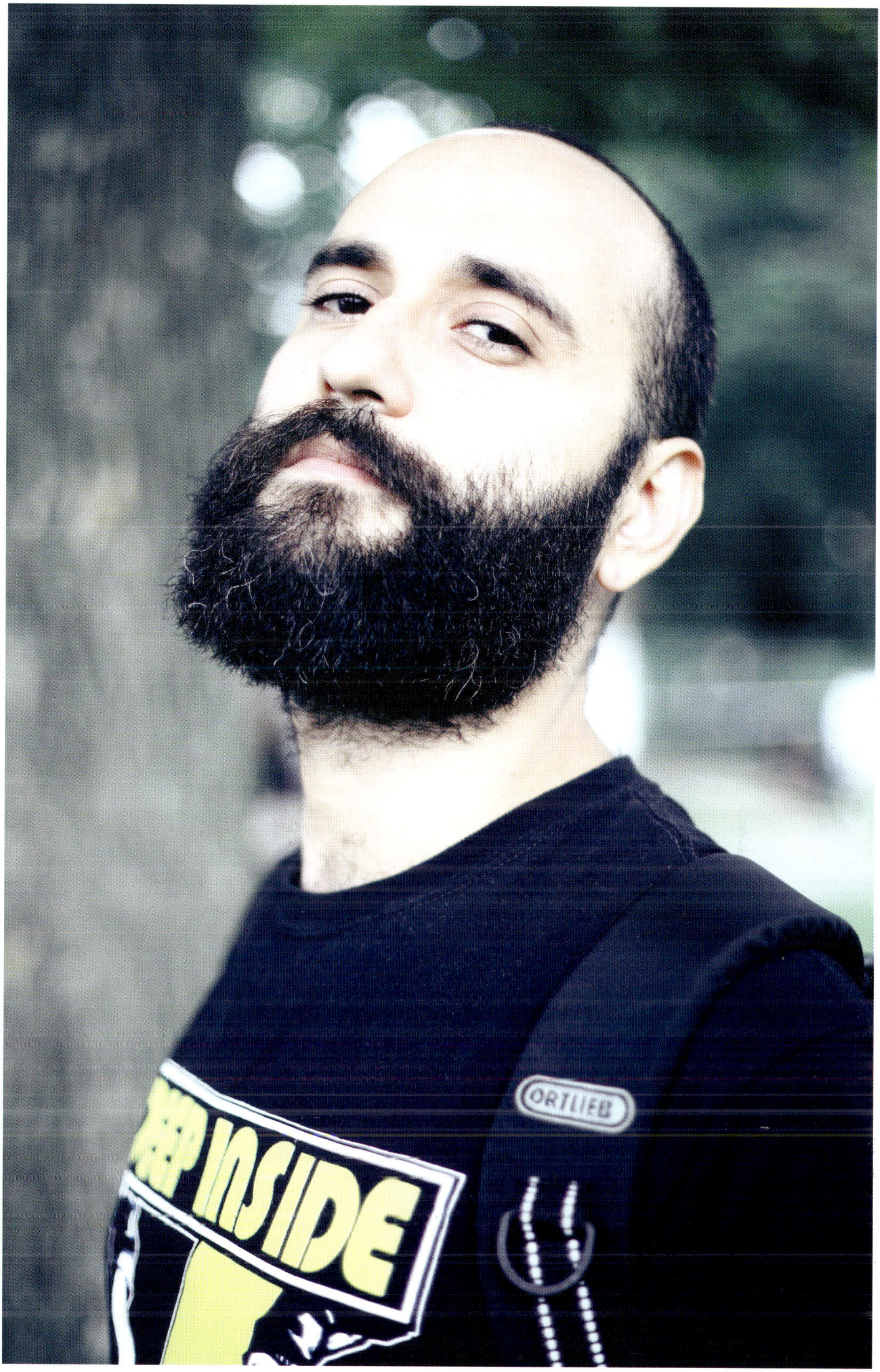

 Bruno: Preston Park, Brighton

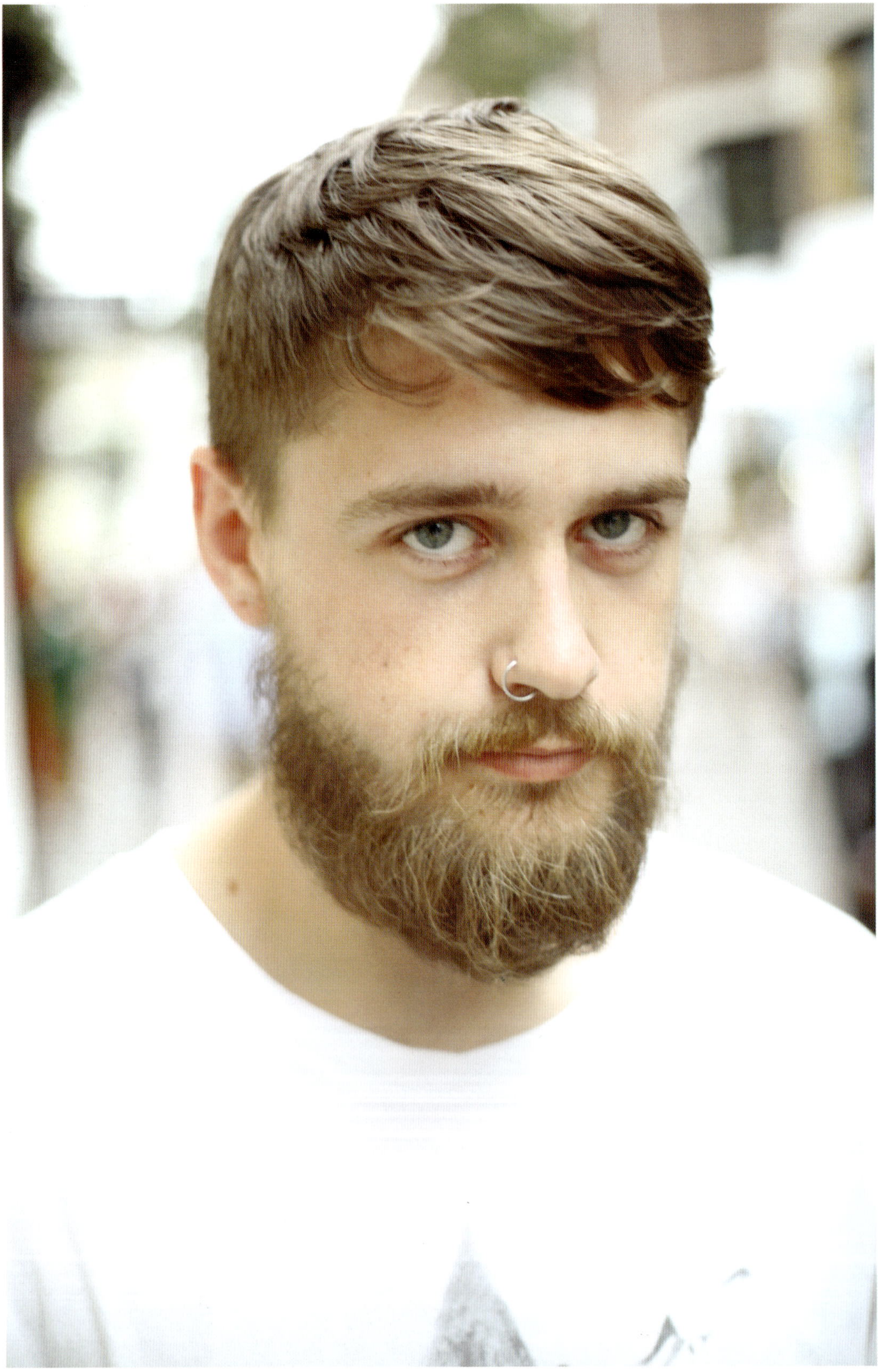

67 • Sam: Carnaby Street, London

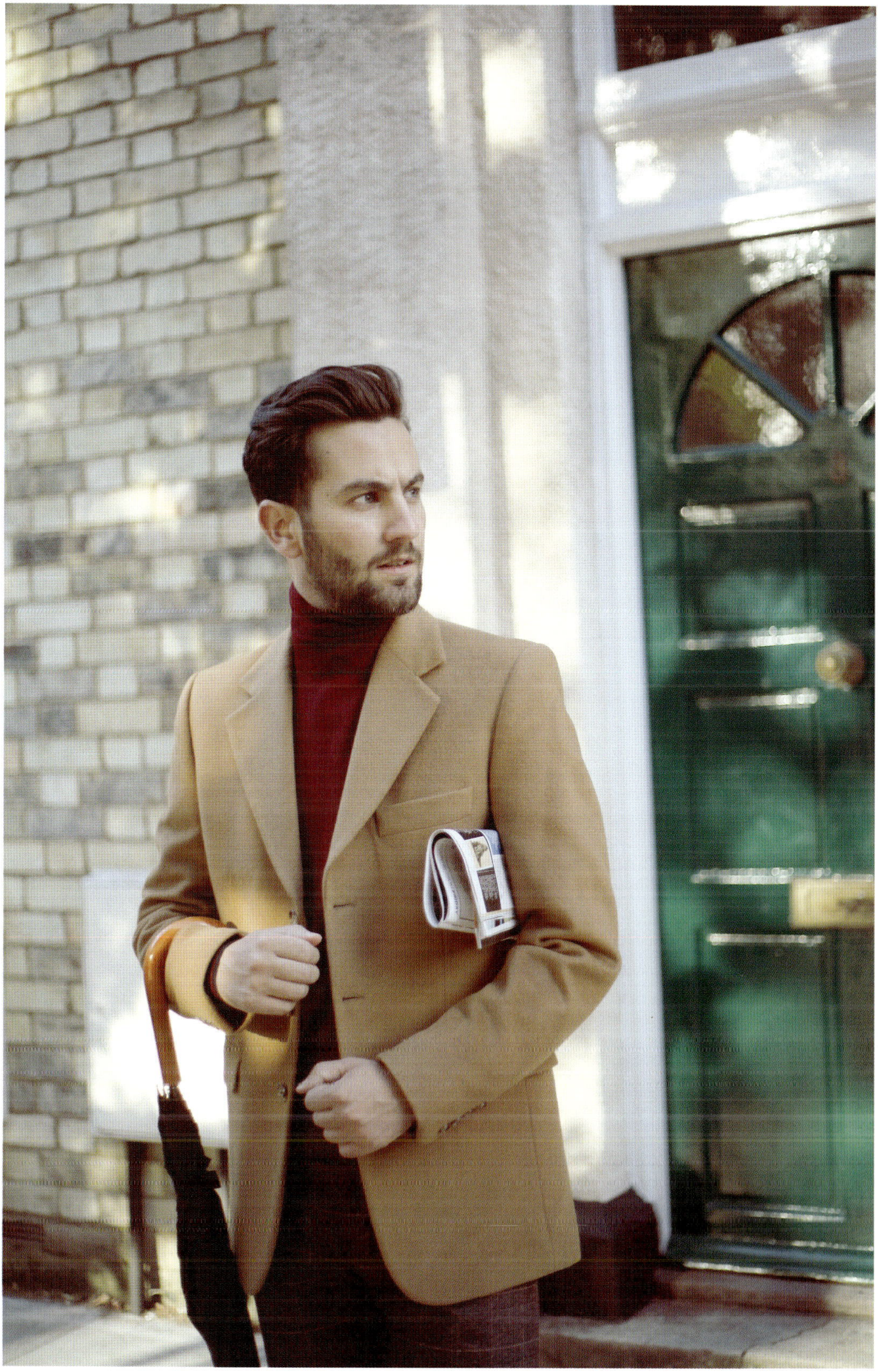

68 • Matthew: Moray Road, London

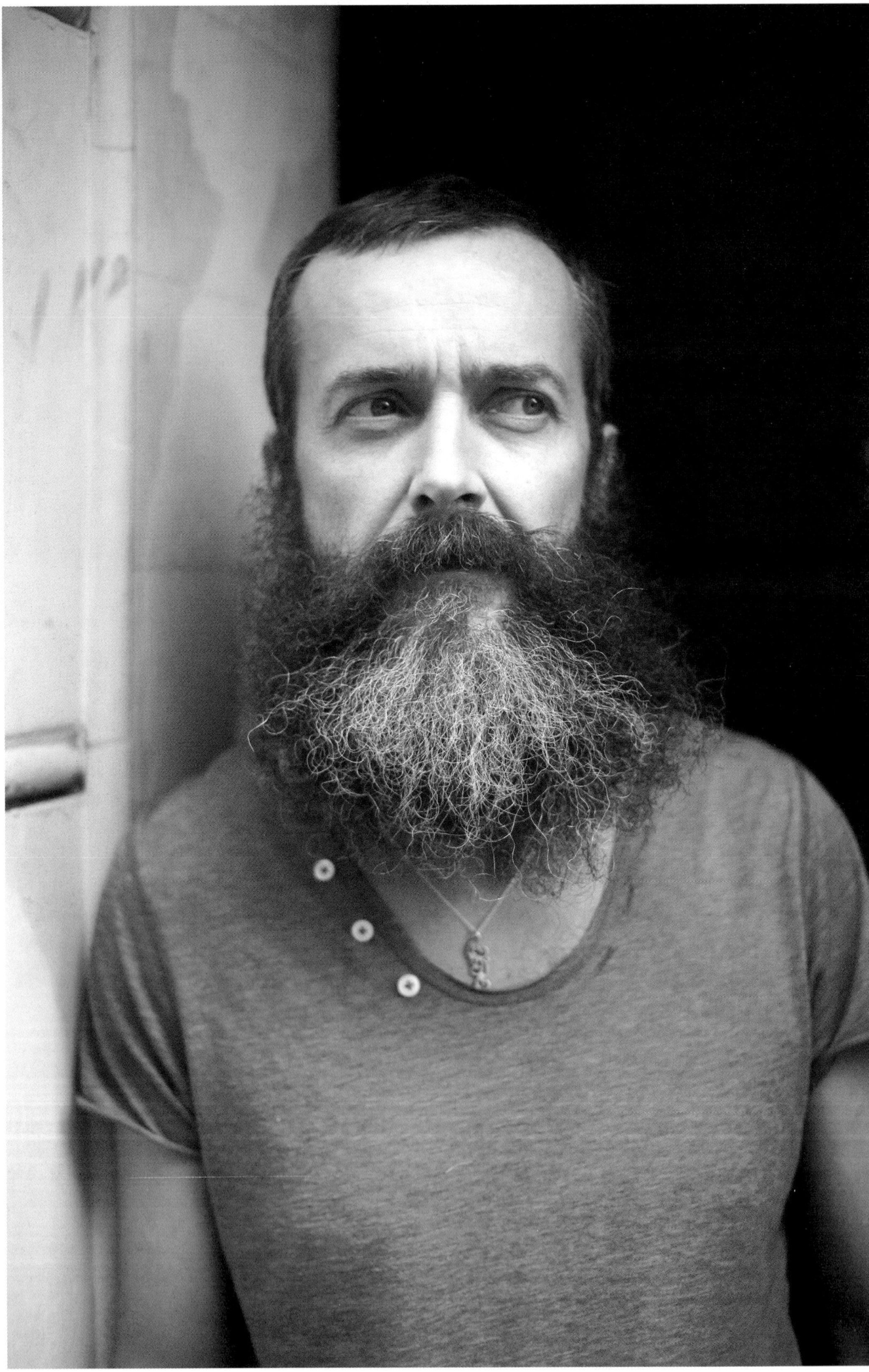

69 • Jerome: Broadwick Street, London

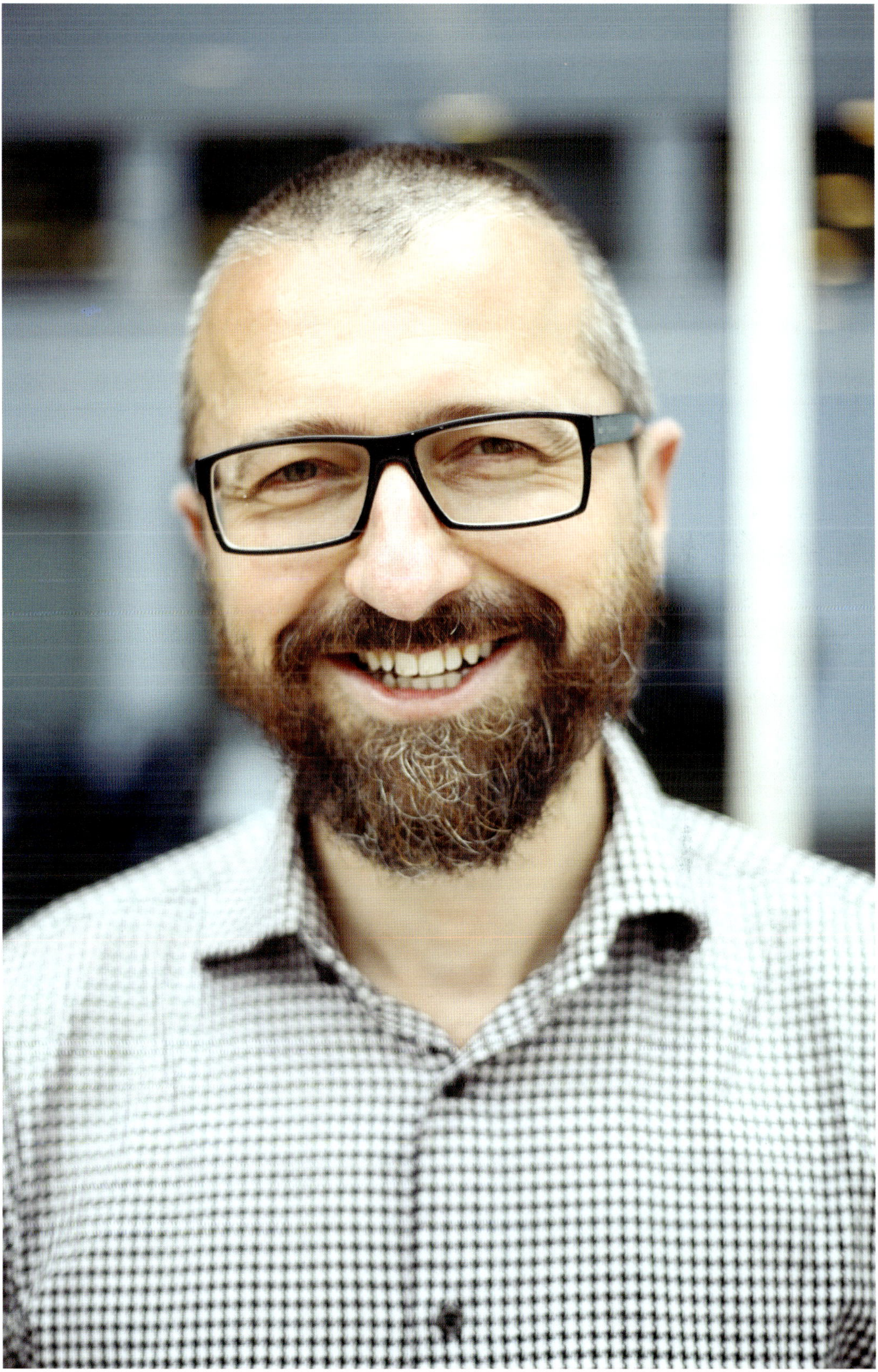

70 • Andrew: Clifford Street, London

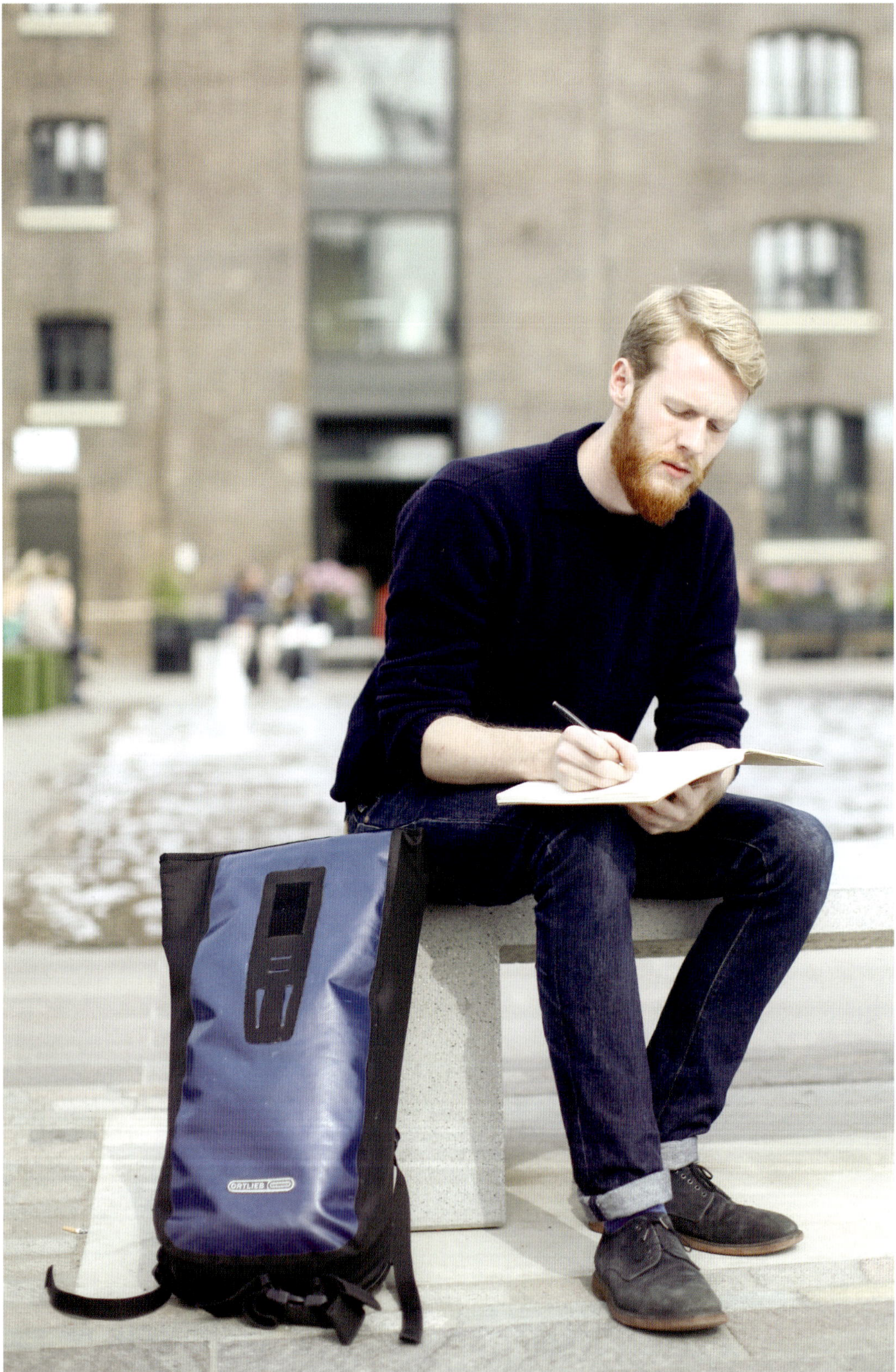

71 • Mathew: Central St Martins, London

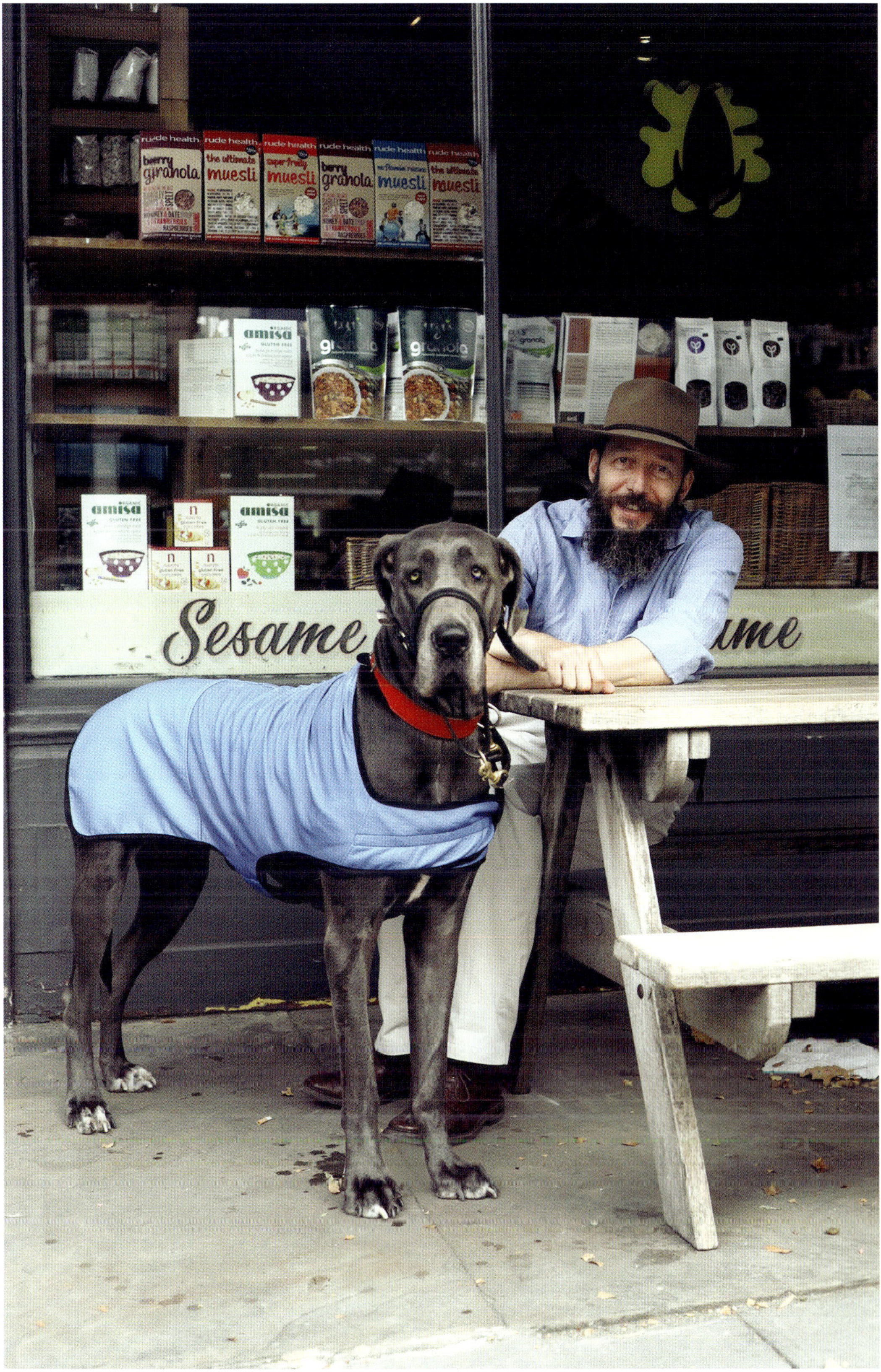

72 • Howie: Regents Park Road, London

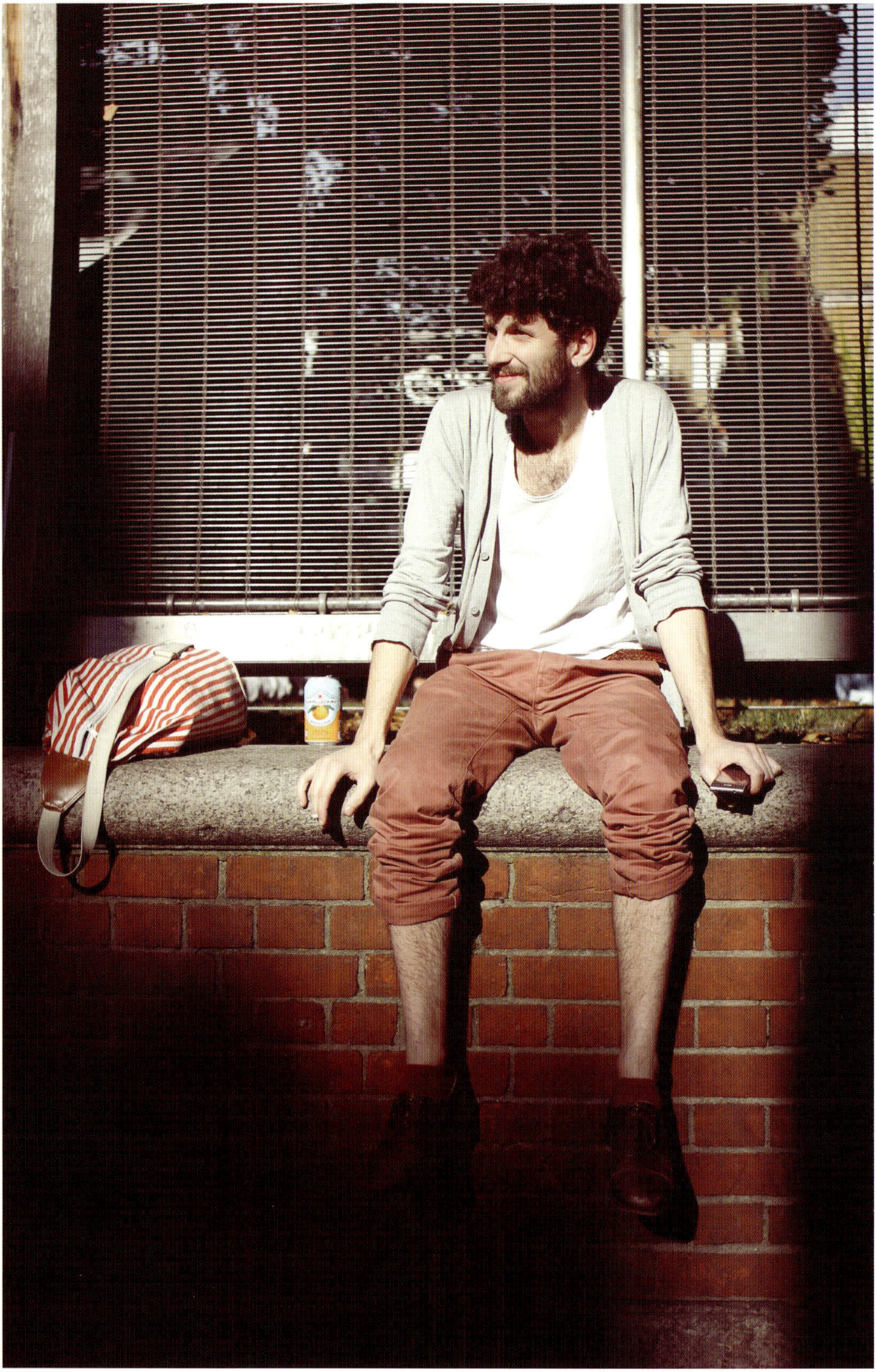

73 • Johnny: Wardour Street, London

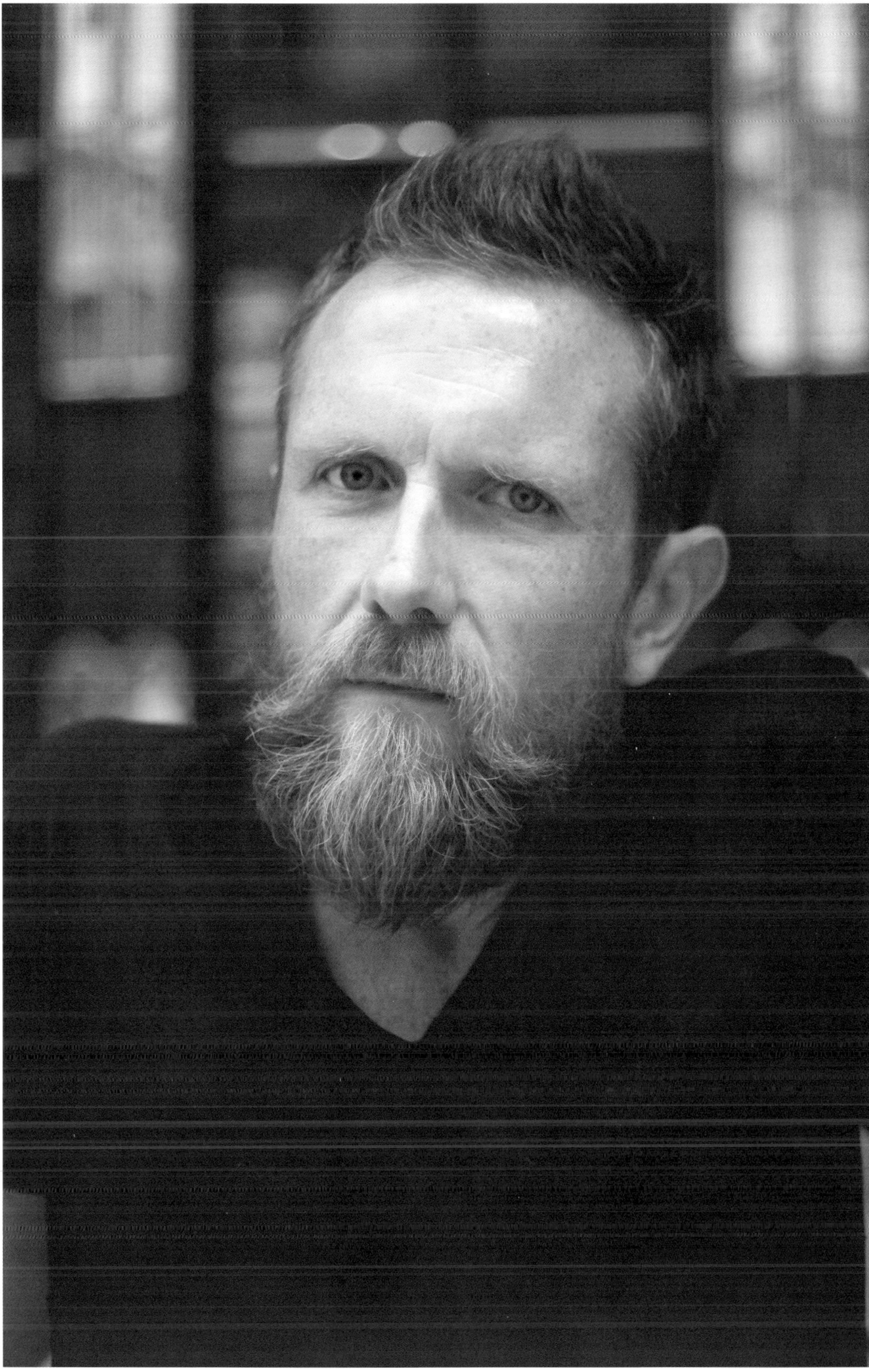

74 • John: Argyll Street, London

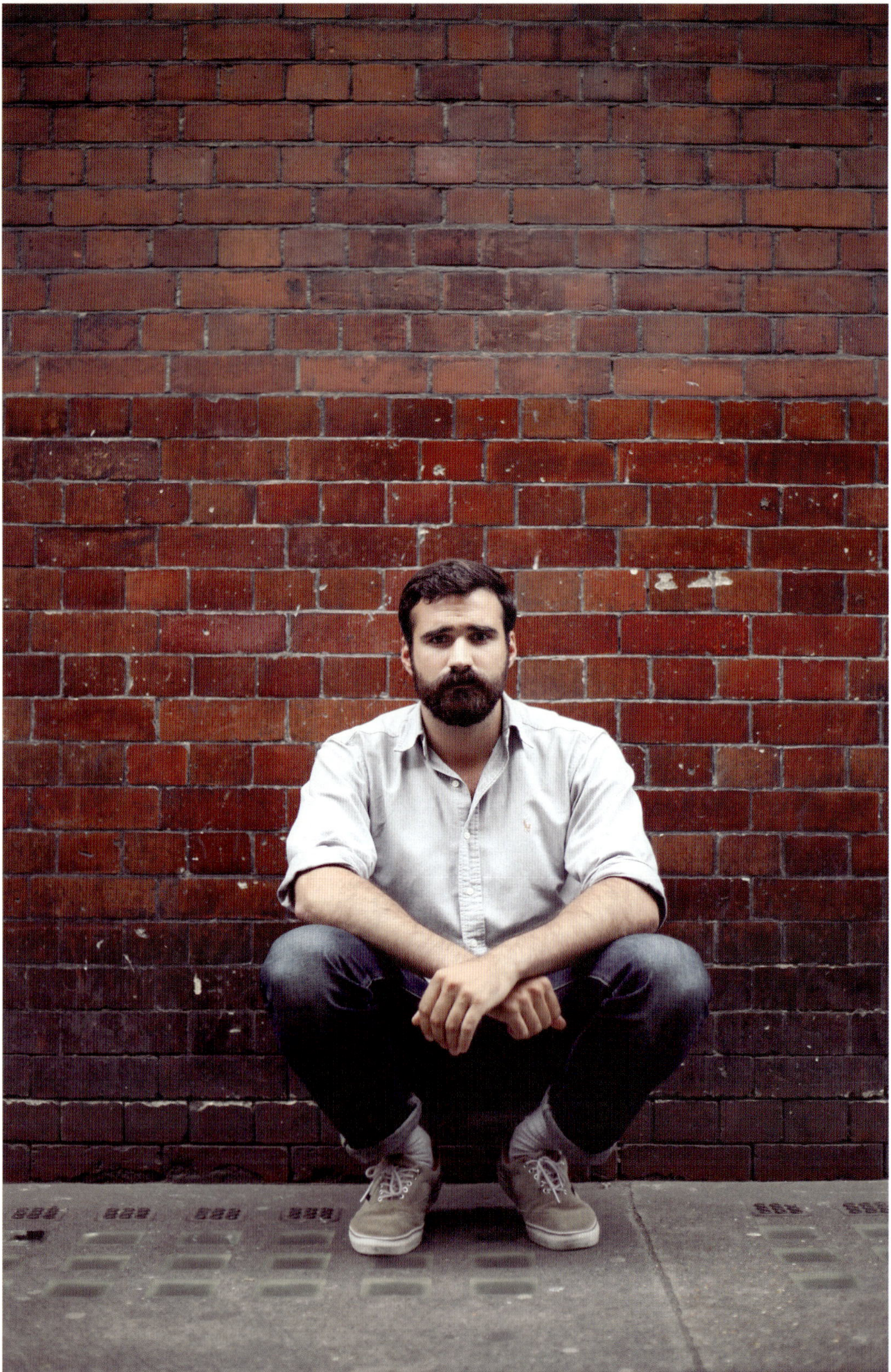

75 • Chris: Archer Street, London

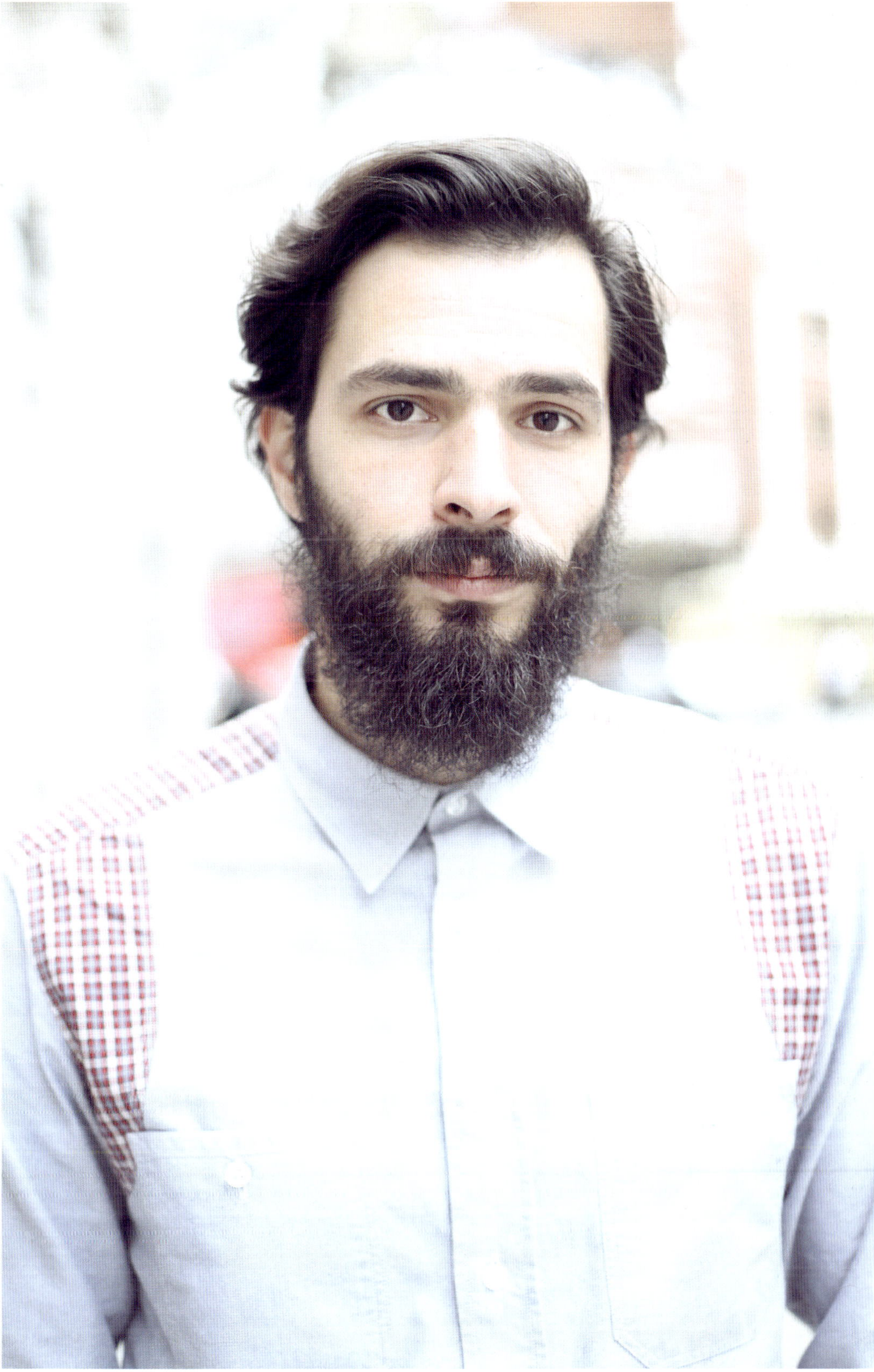

76 • Valentin: Glasshouse Street, London

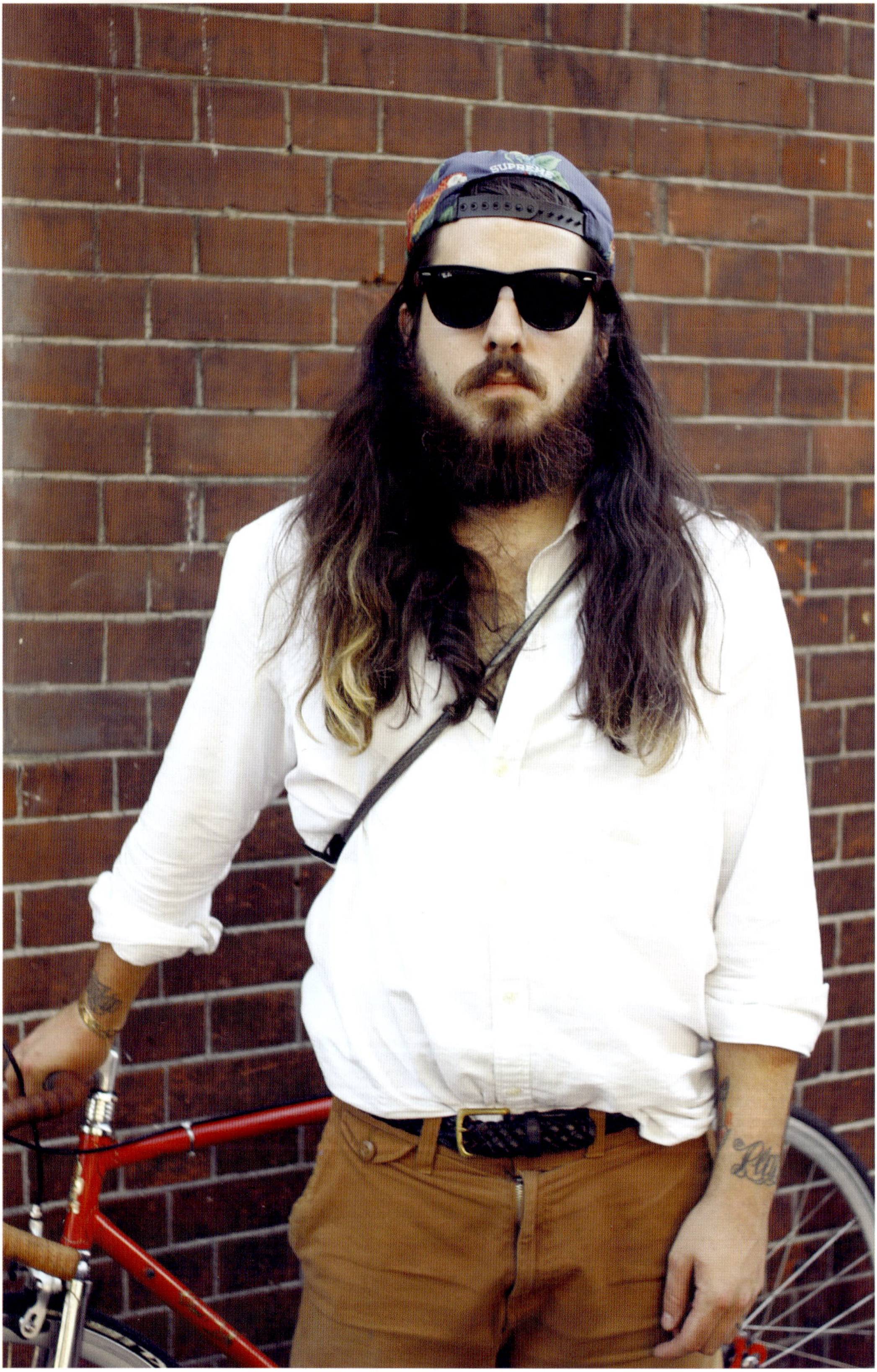

77 • Lewis: Old Compton Street, London

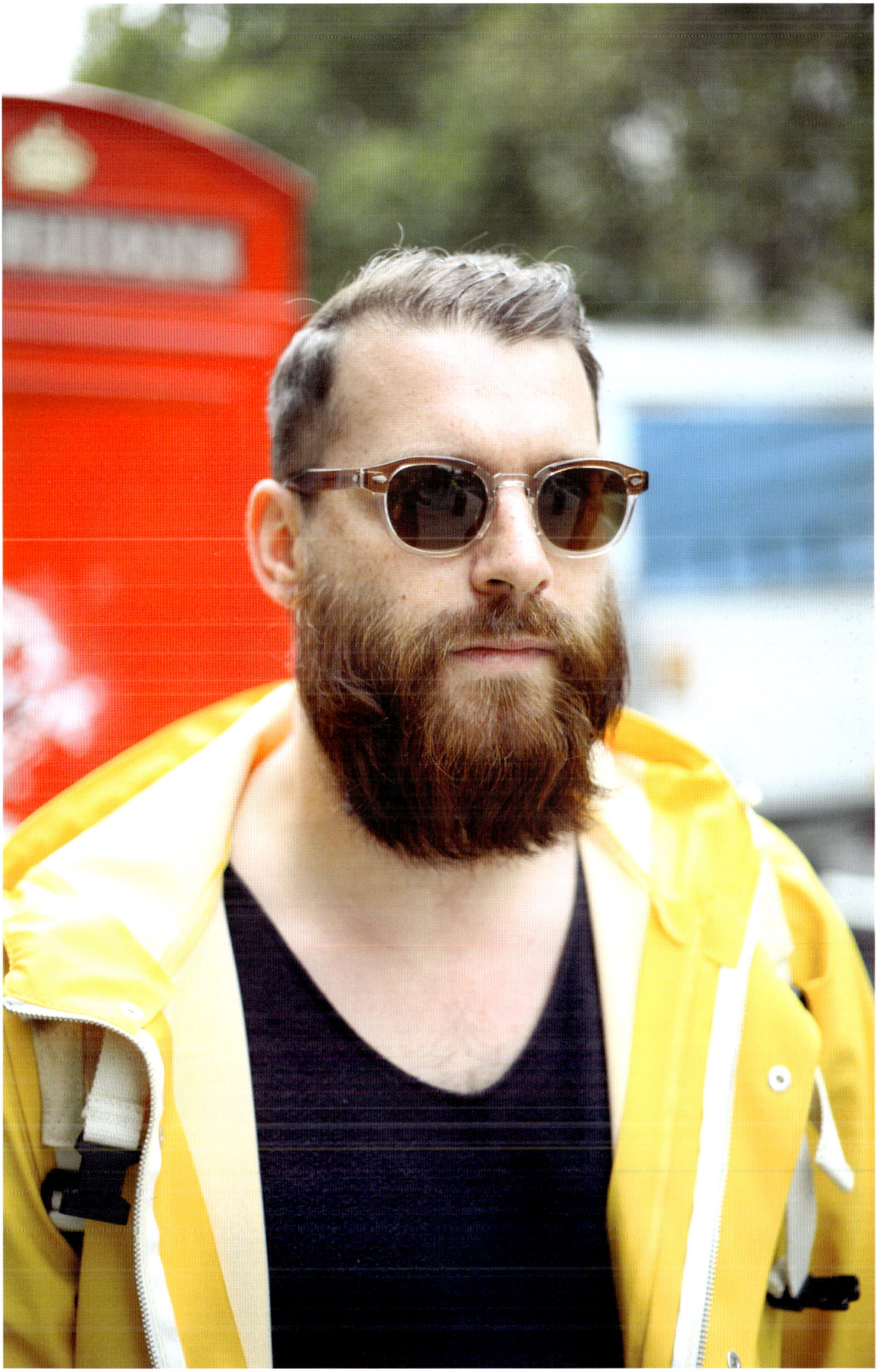

78 • Alberto: The Strand, London

"I think every man should grow a beard at least once in his life, to physically set himself apart from boyhood. The beard is, after all, the strongest and most robust mark of physical masculinity — though in no way does a beard 'make' me a man, but I think that in a certain way it made me take myself more seriously as a man.

I started growing one about 10 years ago at the age of 18. Since then I've only clean-shaved a handful of times. Once you've had the experience and enjoyment of wearing a beard, I find it impossible to go back to a clean-shaven lifestyle. I've even refused jobs for which I was asked to be clean-shaven — not for health and safety rules but arbitrary conventions and stupid ideas of conformity.

I go to a lot of music festivals, where my beard gets an enormous amount of attention, in a weird way: people feel free to just come up and touch it — which is a little uncomfortable, sometimes makes me feel a little bit like a freak-show. I'd expect a 'hello' and a 'would you mind if I touched...' otherwise it's like being beard-raped. One of my best friends decided to start charging people who came to touch my beard. I can't say we got rich, but earned a few free drinks nonetheless...

I absolutely despise shaving — it wastes an unnecessary amount of time, it's not a nice feeling, it gives me rashes — just to end up looking like a 12 year old. Plus, at the end of the day, there's nothing more elegant than a bearded man in a sharp suit!

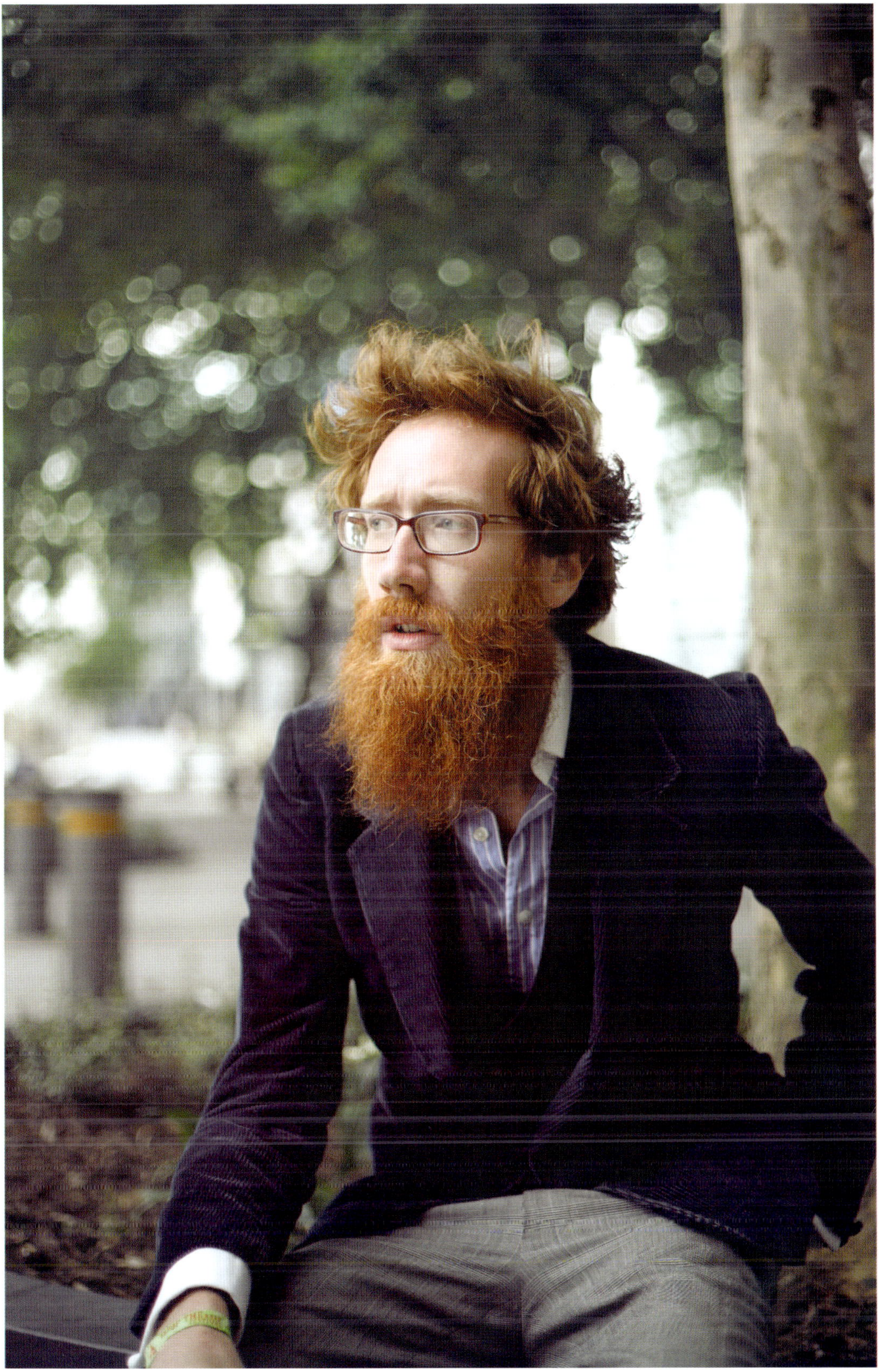

79 • Gregory: Old Street, London

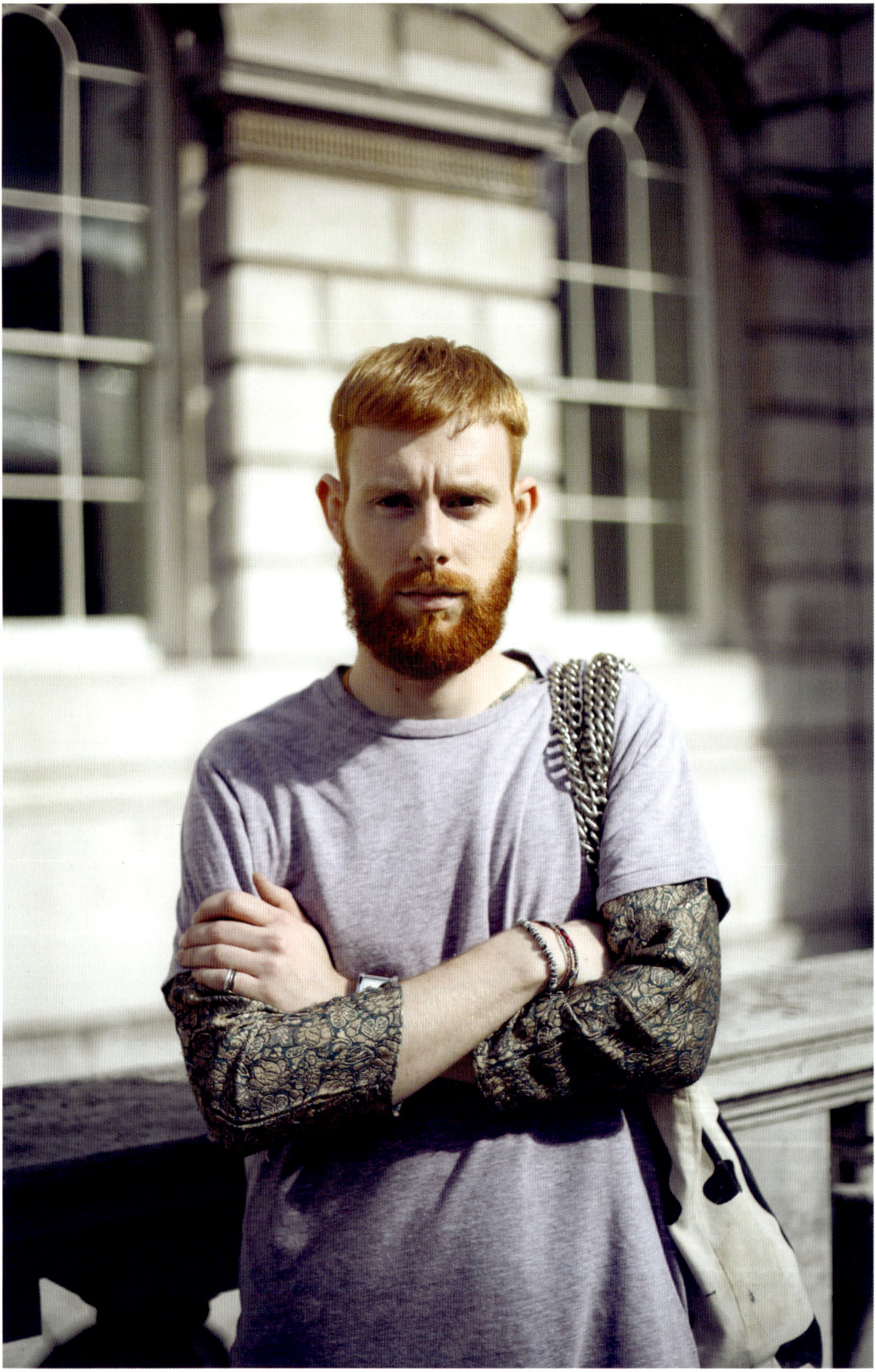

80 • Rowan: Somerset House, London

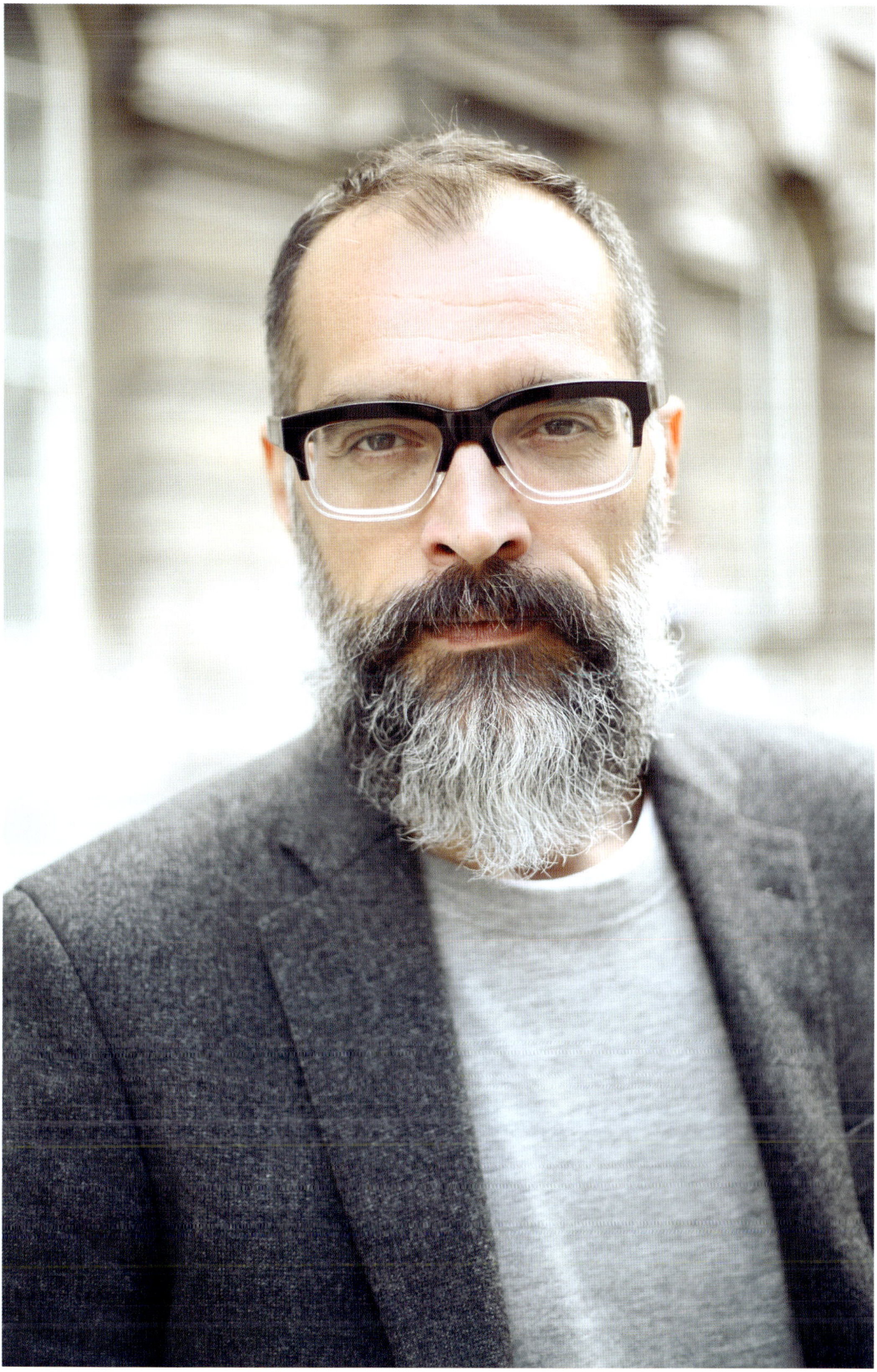

81 • Alex: Somerset House, London

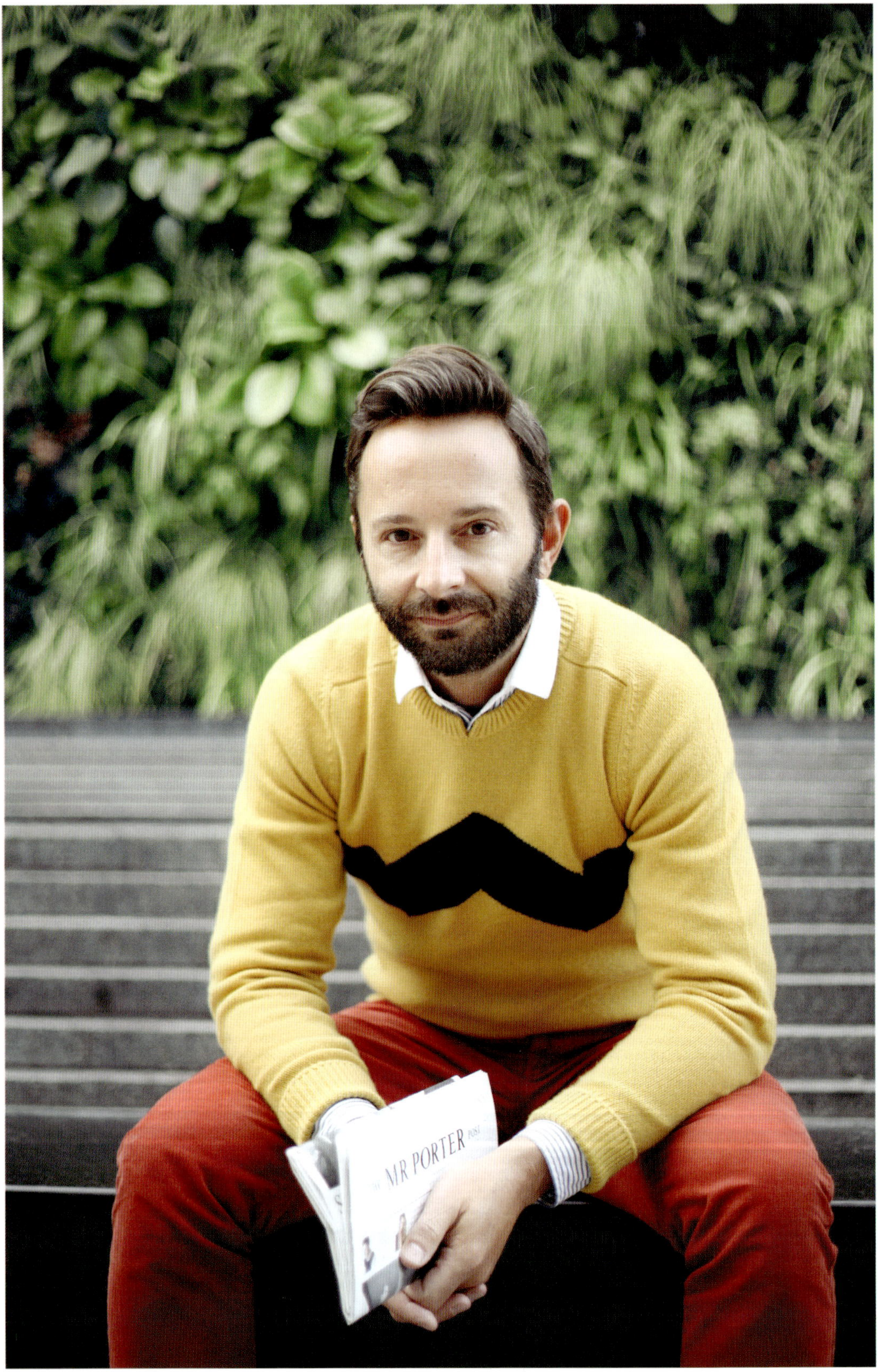

82 • Jeremy: Shepherds Bush, London

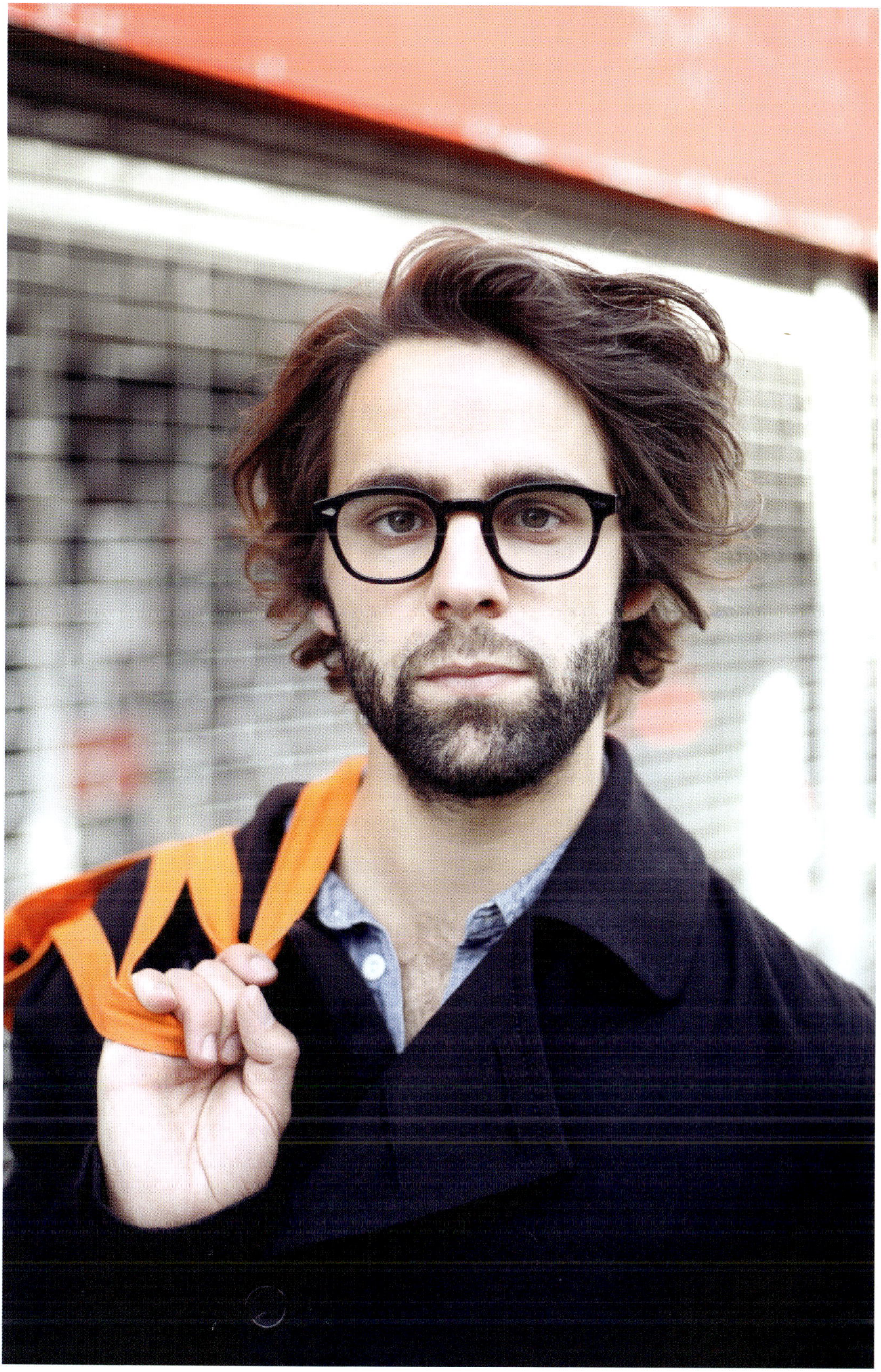

83 • Richard: The Strand, London

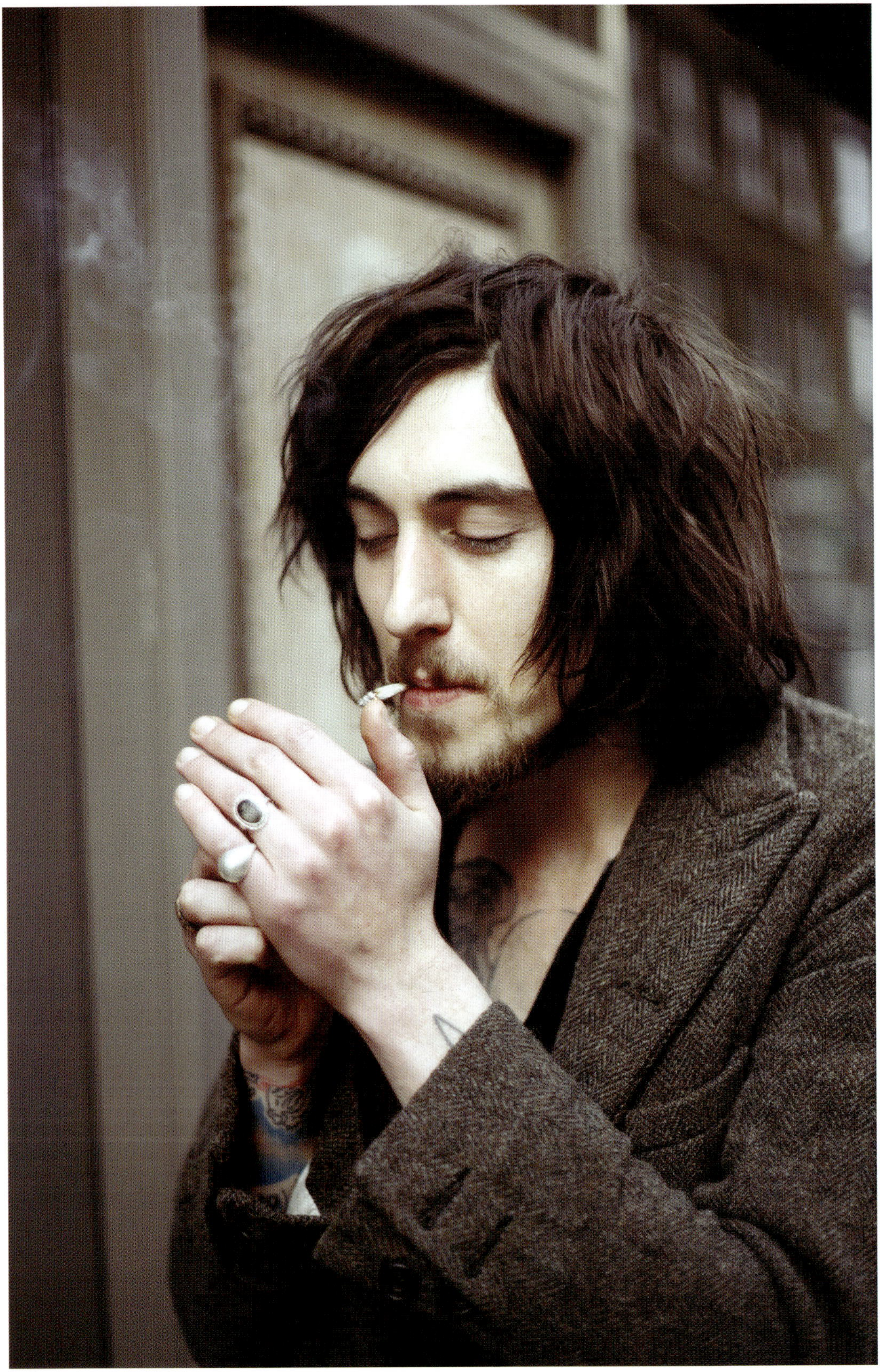

 Richard: Rivington Street, London

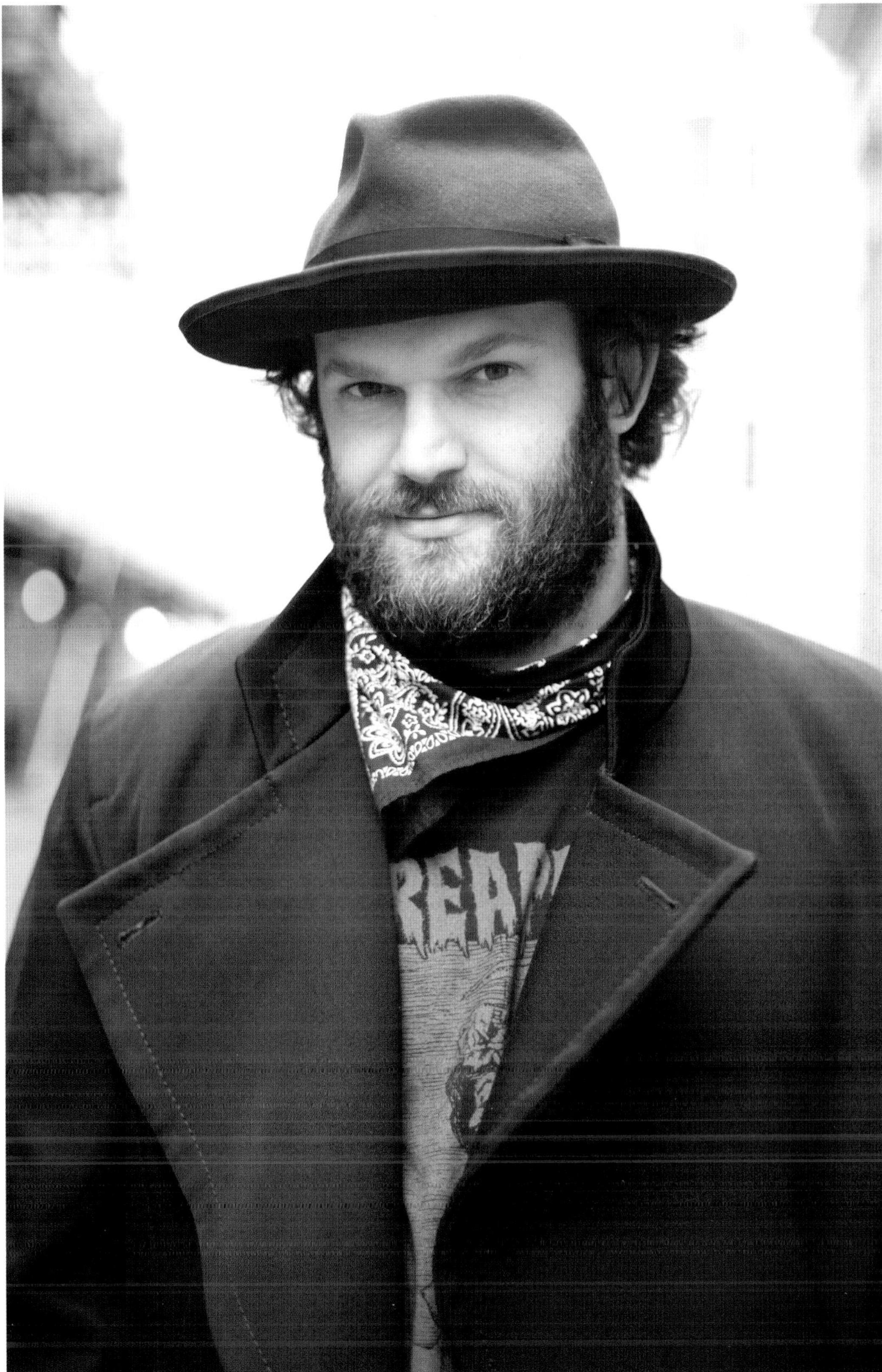

85 • Dylan: Burleigh Street, London

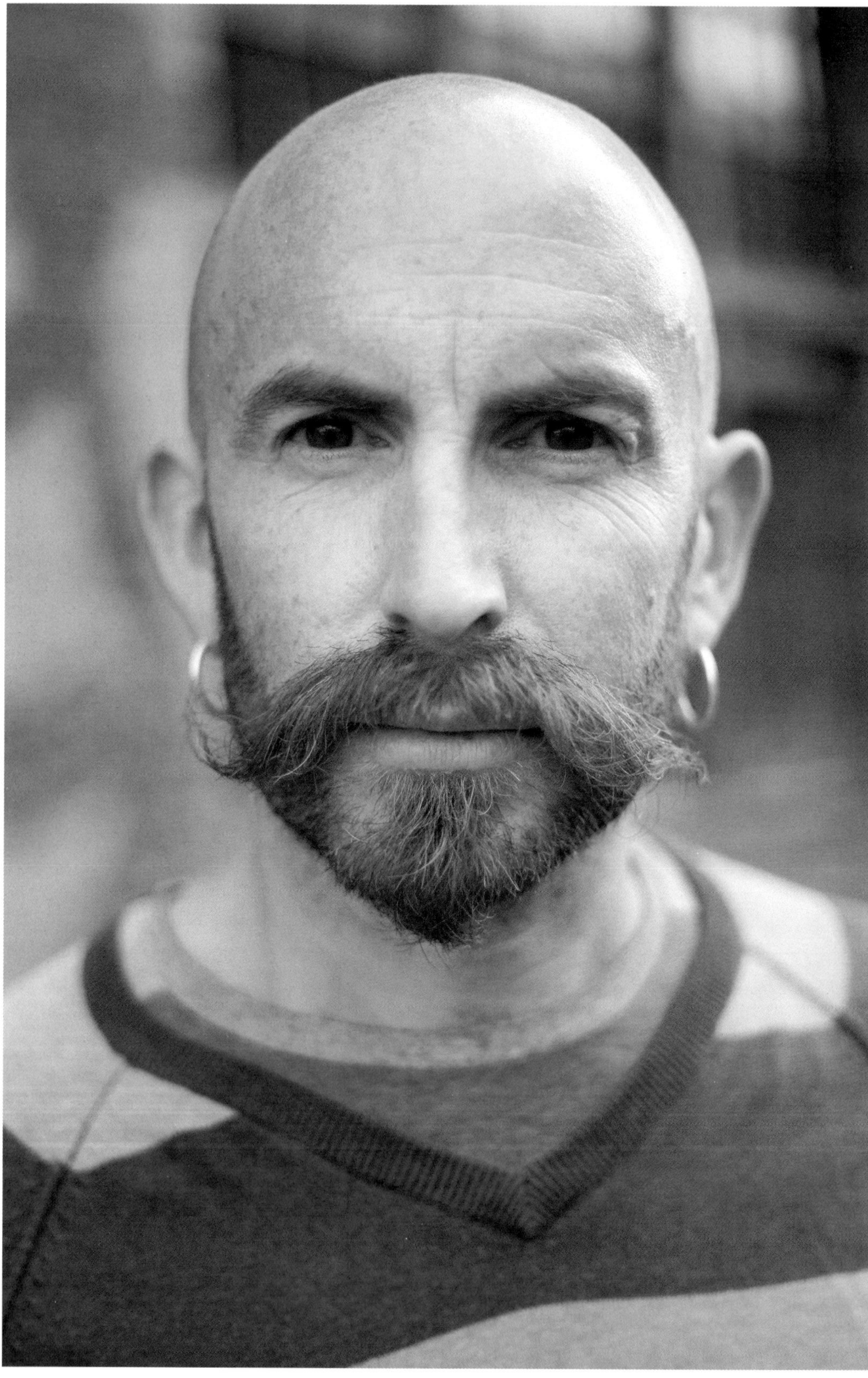

86 • Dennis: Delancey Street, London

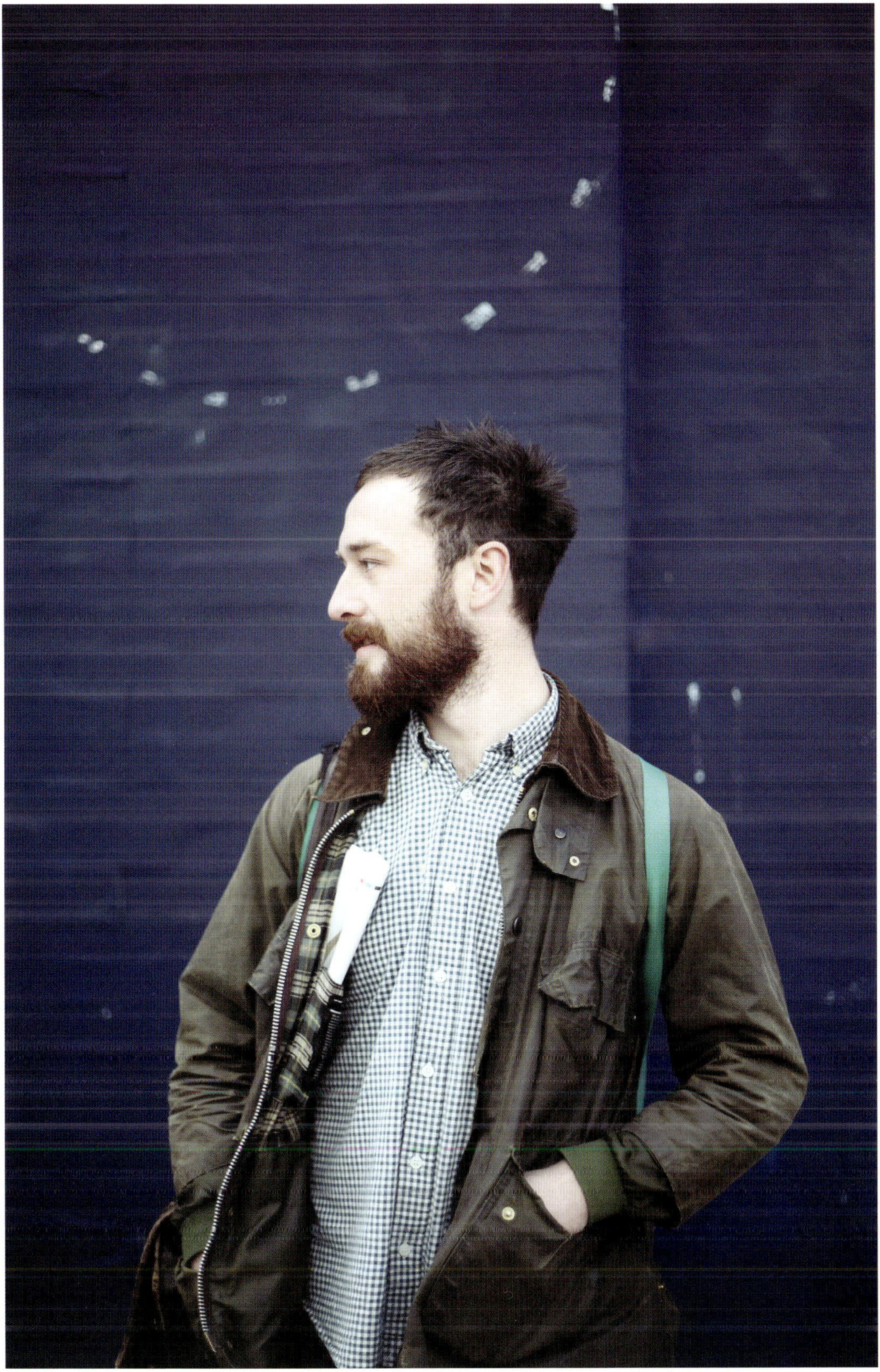

87 • Callum: Rivington Street, London

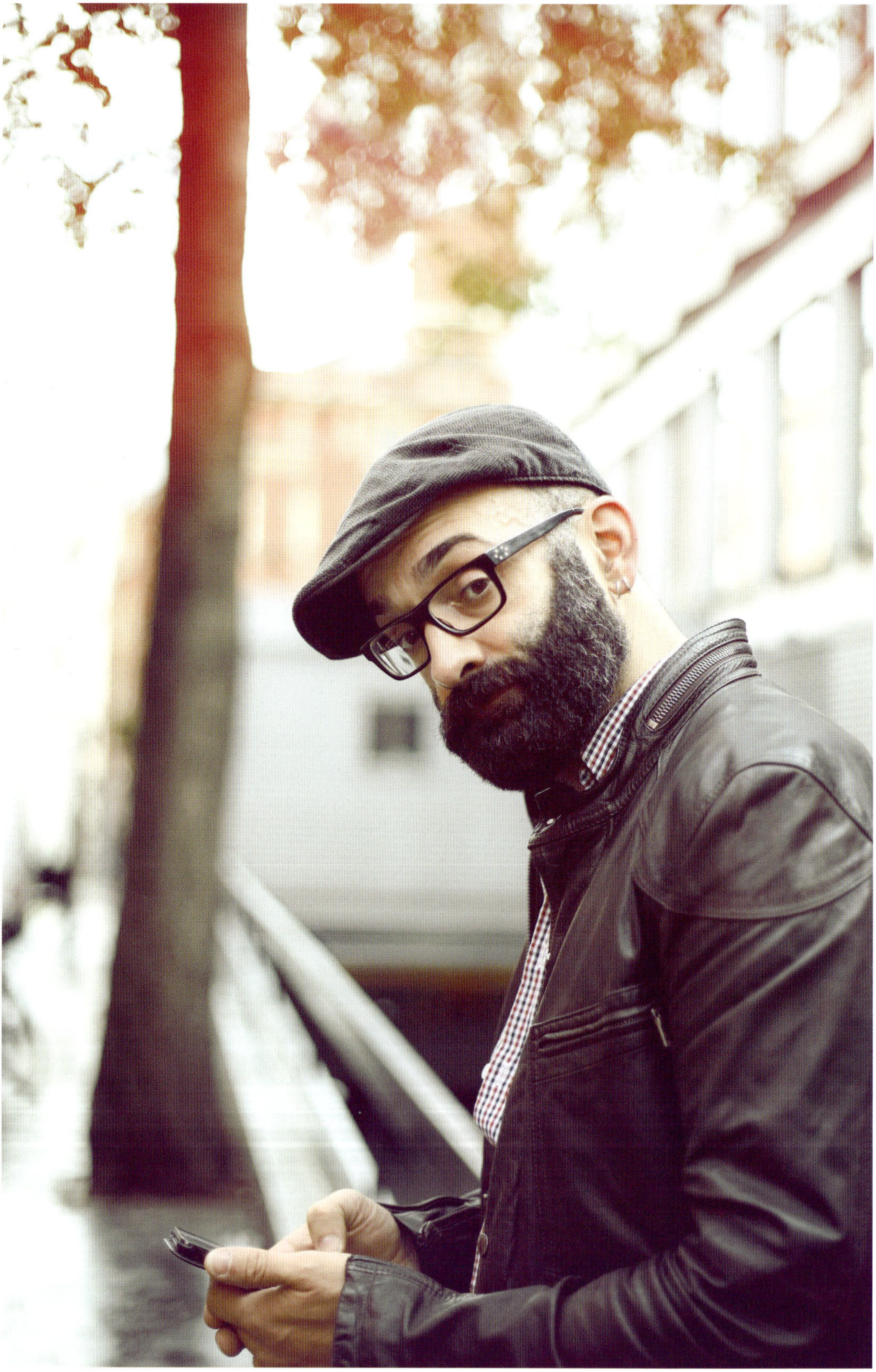

88 • Nic: Garrick Street, London

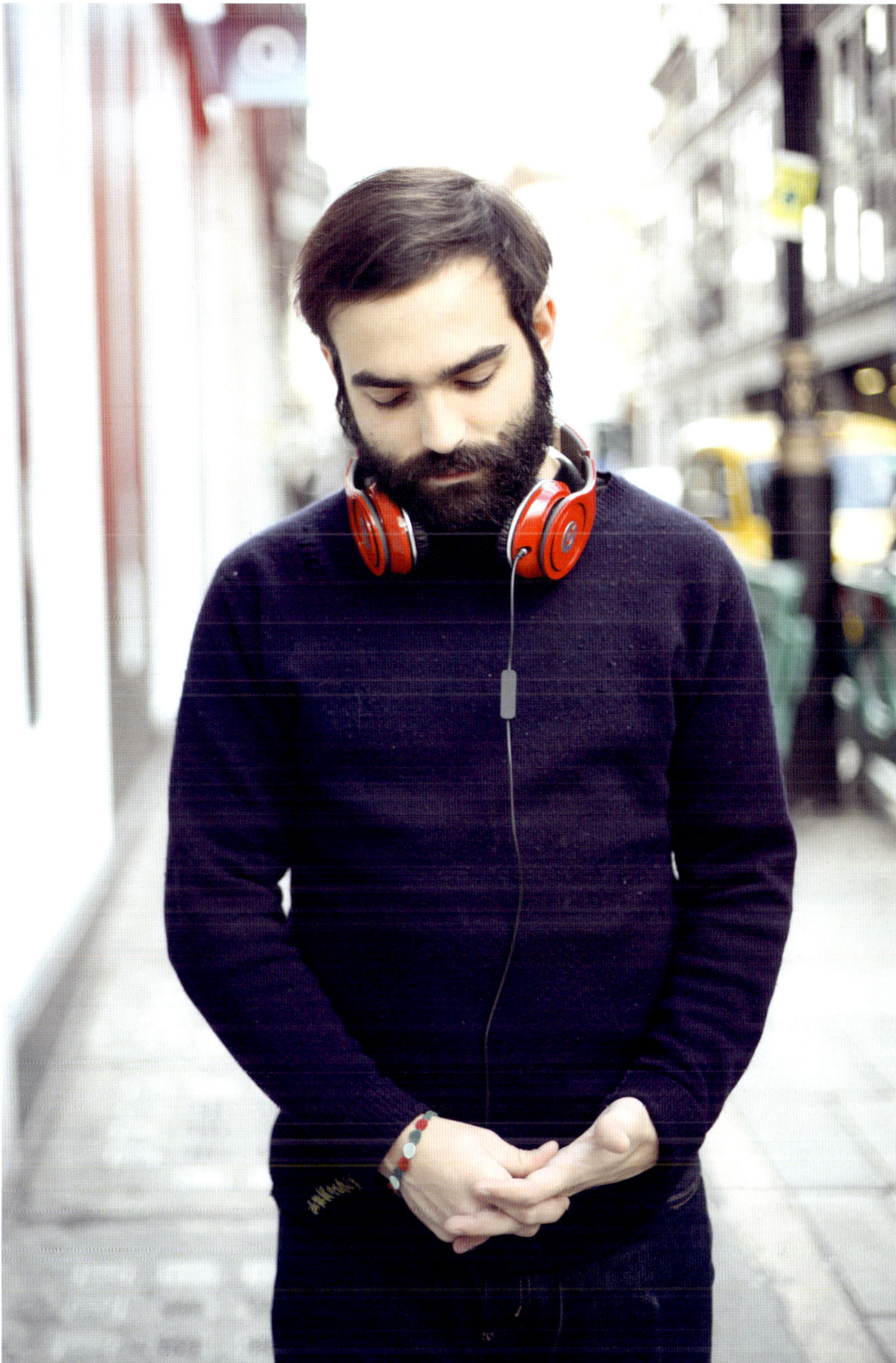

89 • Edoardo: Wells Street, London

Facial hair is something that represents man and spirituality. I believe it is a gift from nature. It is divine. We are intended to be this way by nature. If you cut your hair, it always grows back. That has a message itself, it is like a friend to me that has been there since my birth. I have never cut my hair and I will never. It is a part of a tradition given to the Sikhs of Guru Gobind Singh ji. Hair has a frequency of its own and in most cultures reflects splendour. It is a journey and I can't wait to see what it looks like when I am old.

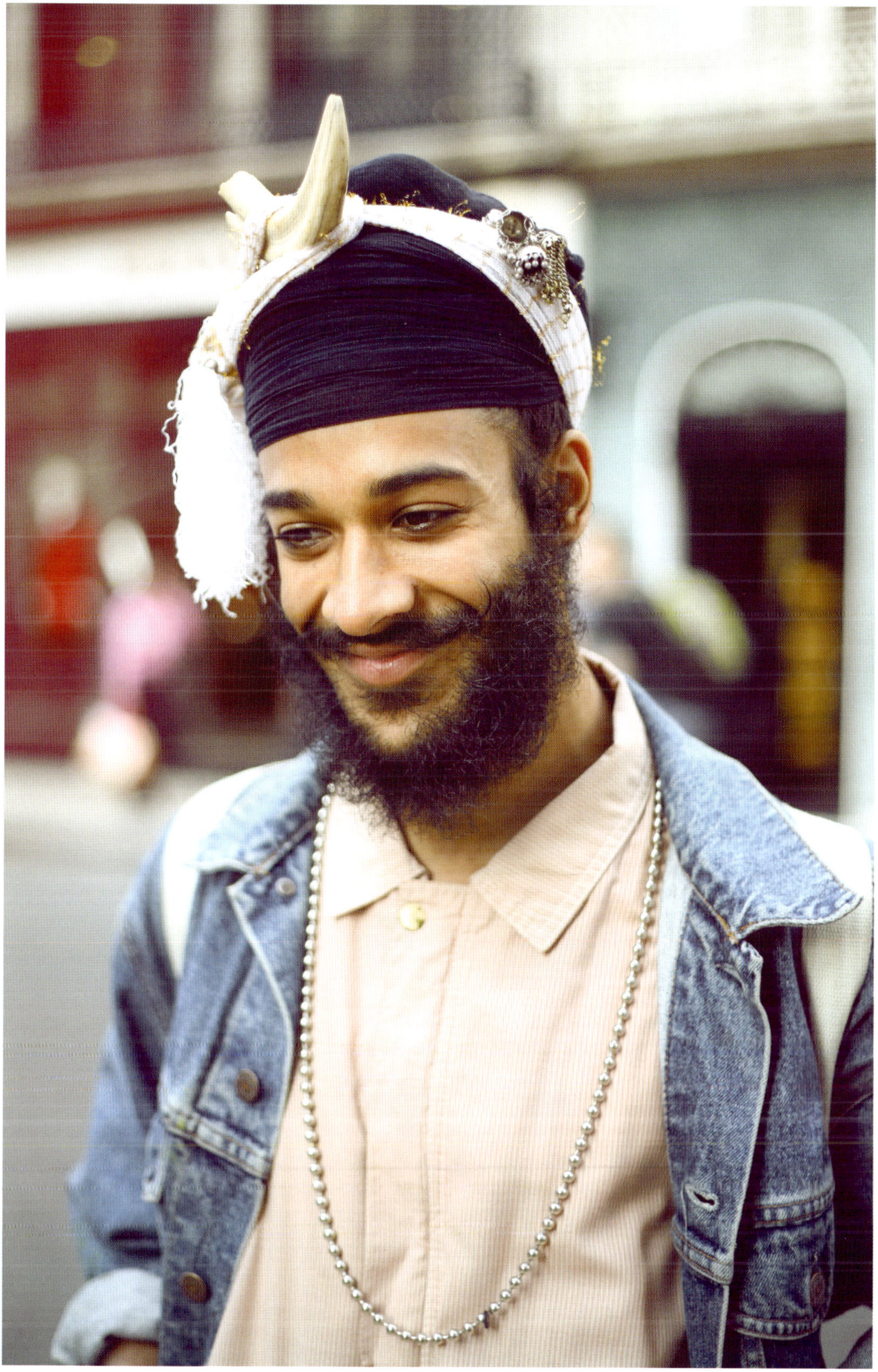

90 • Jatinder: Old Bond Street, London

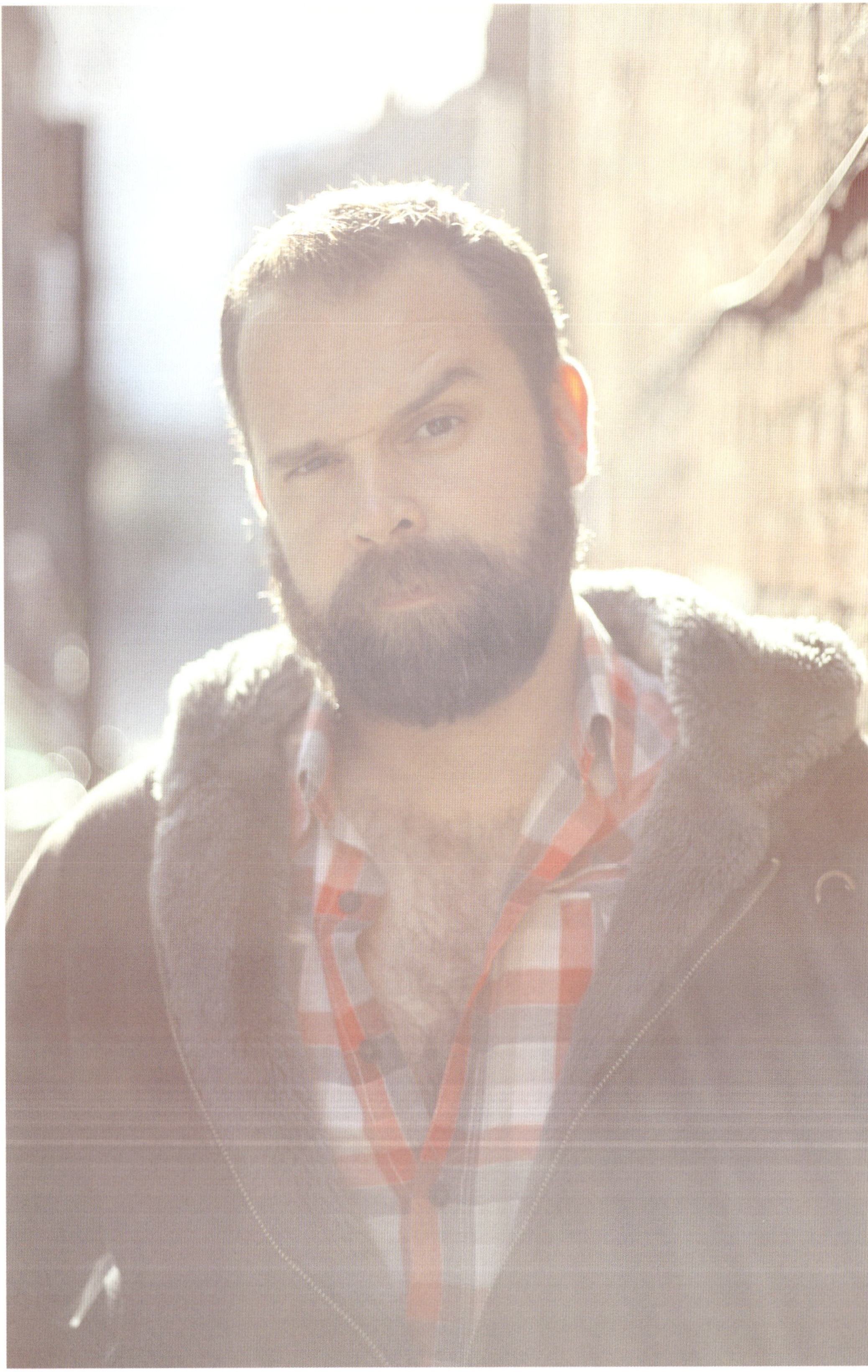

91 • Rob: Mercer Street, London

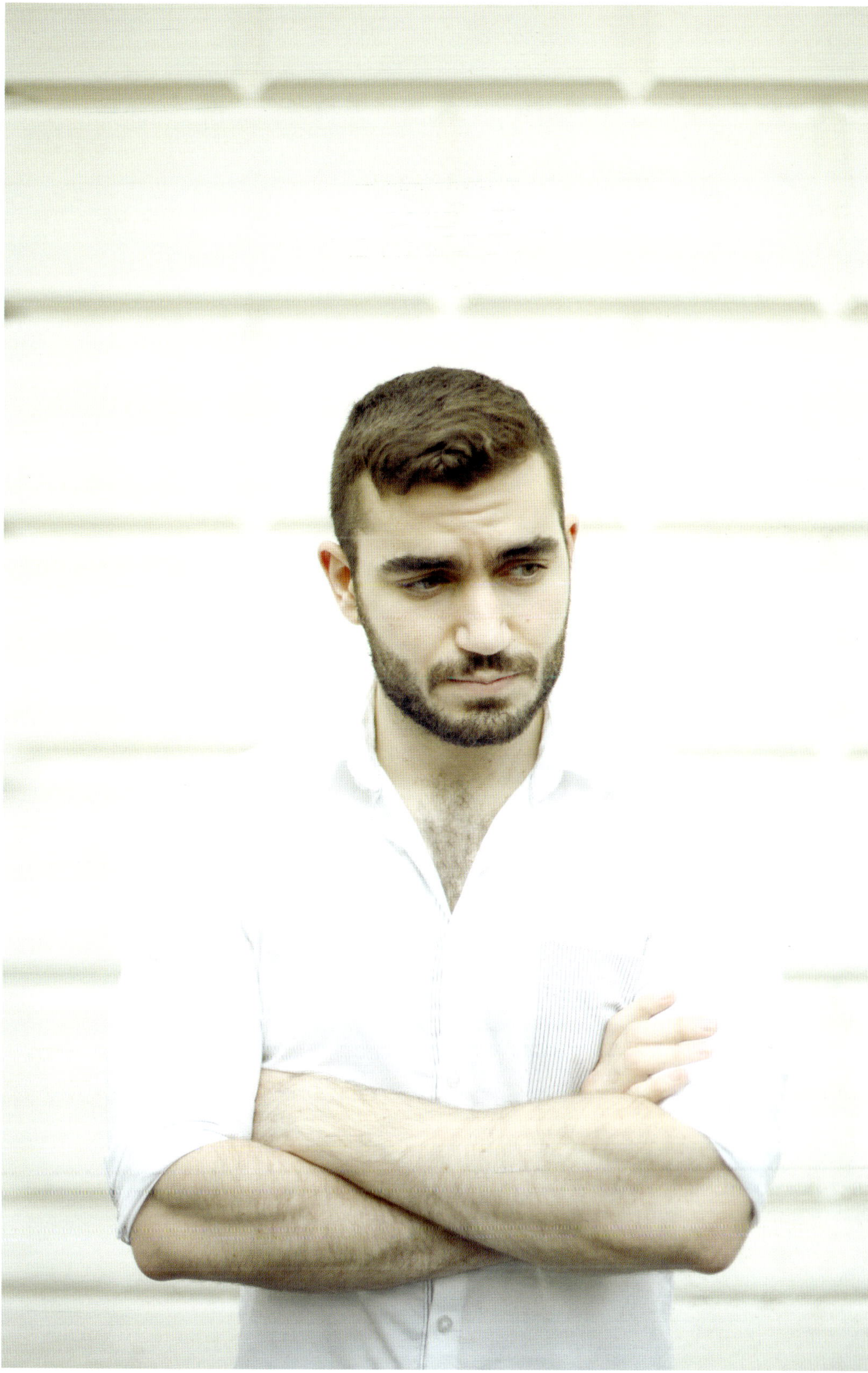

92 • Andreas: The Mall, London

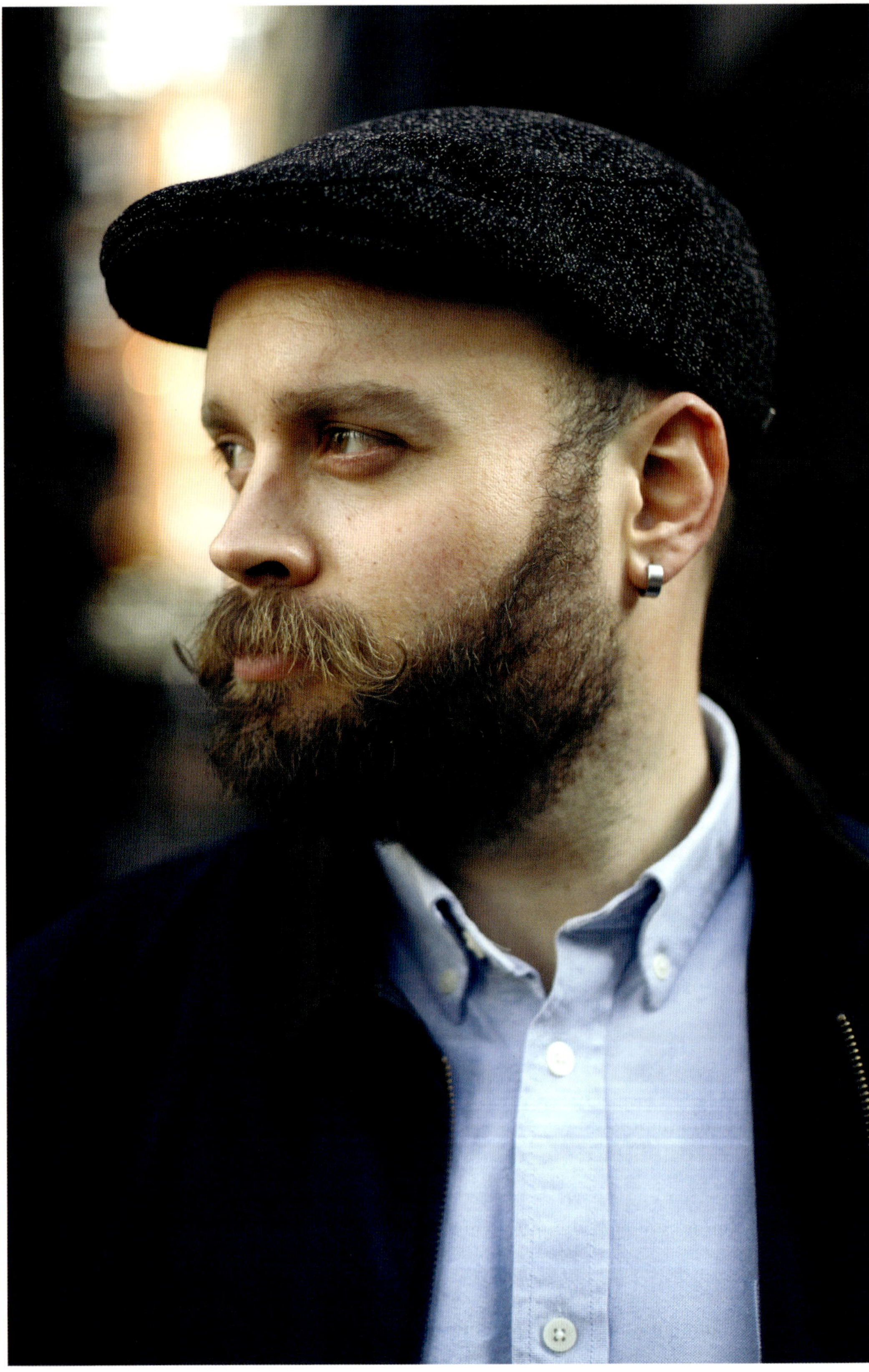

93 • Tom: Meard Street, London

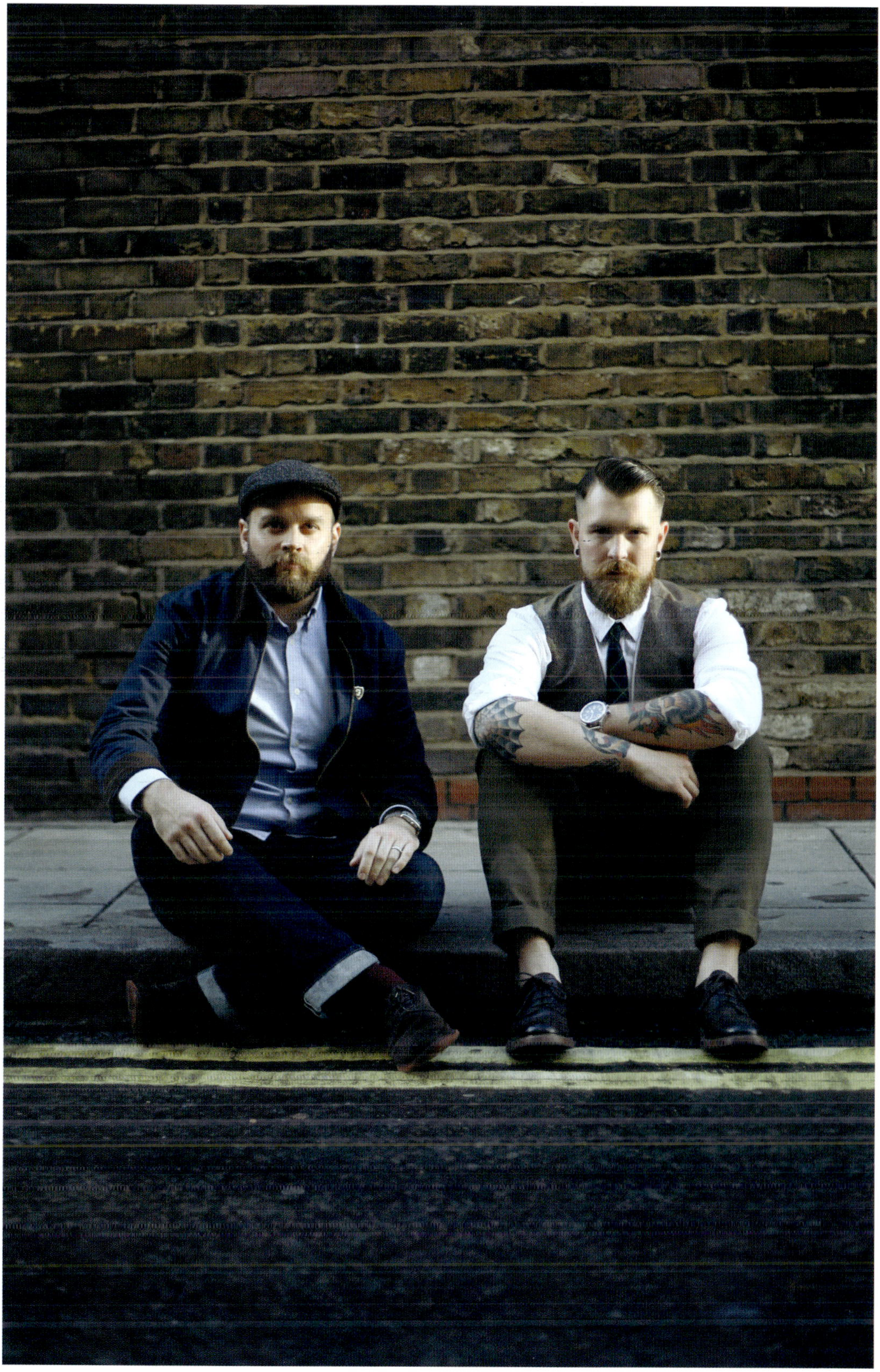

Tom & Kial: Meard Street, London

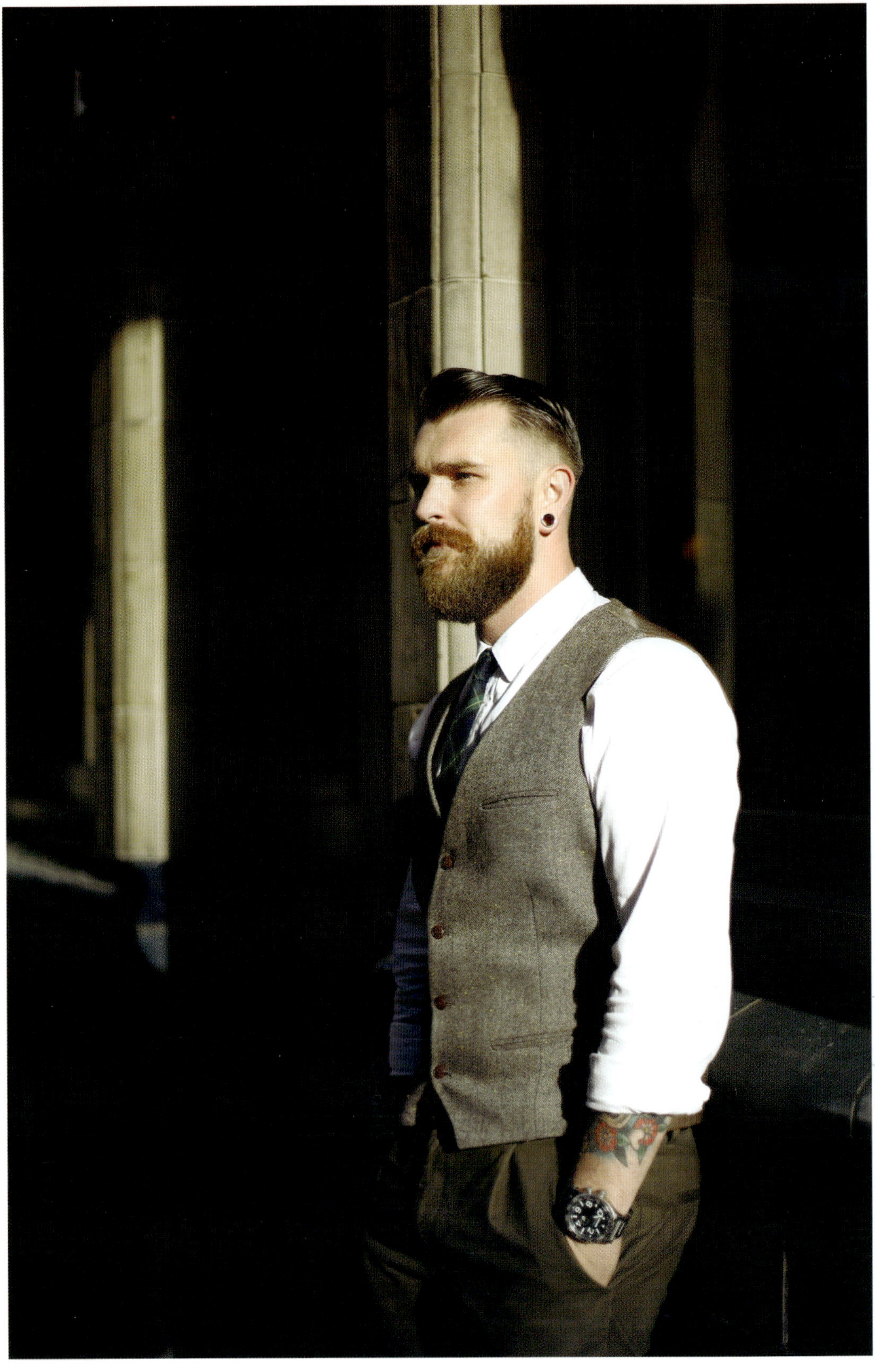

 • Kial: Dean Street, London

There's no denying the popularity of beards worldwide. I manage a barber shop in London where I consult dozens of guys a week about their beards. Just when I start to think this might be some kind of trend that is soon to be on the way out, it becomes stronger and even more popular as it filters down to the masses. It's not just hipster cool guys from Shoreditch now, it's becoming a socially acceptable look in the corporate world — with editorial and advertising depicting the beard done up in expensive tailoring, changing the perception of who should be allowed to have a beard and how good a beard can look when dressed up. Some beards are certainly stronger than others, but I think we are all united in how they make us feel. It's always personally given me confidence and helped me attract more attention than if I was clean shaven. There's a romanticism for me in the lumberjack-woods-cabin ruggedness of it all, especially when you live in a concrete jungle. All I need now is my own cabin in the woods.

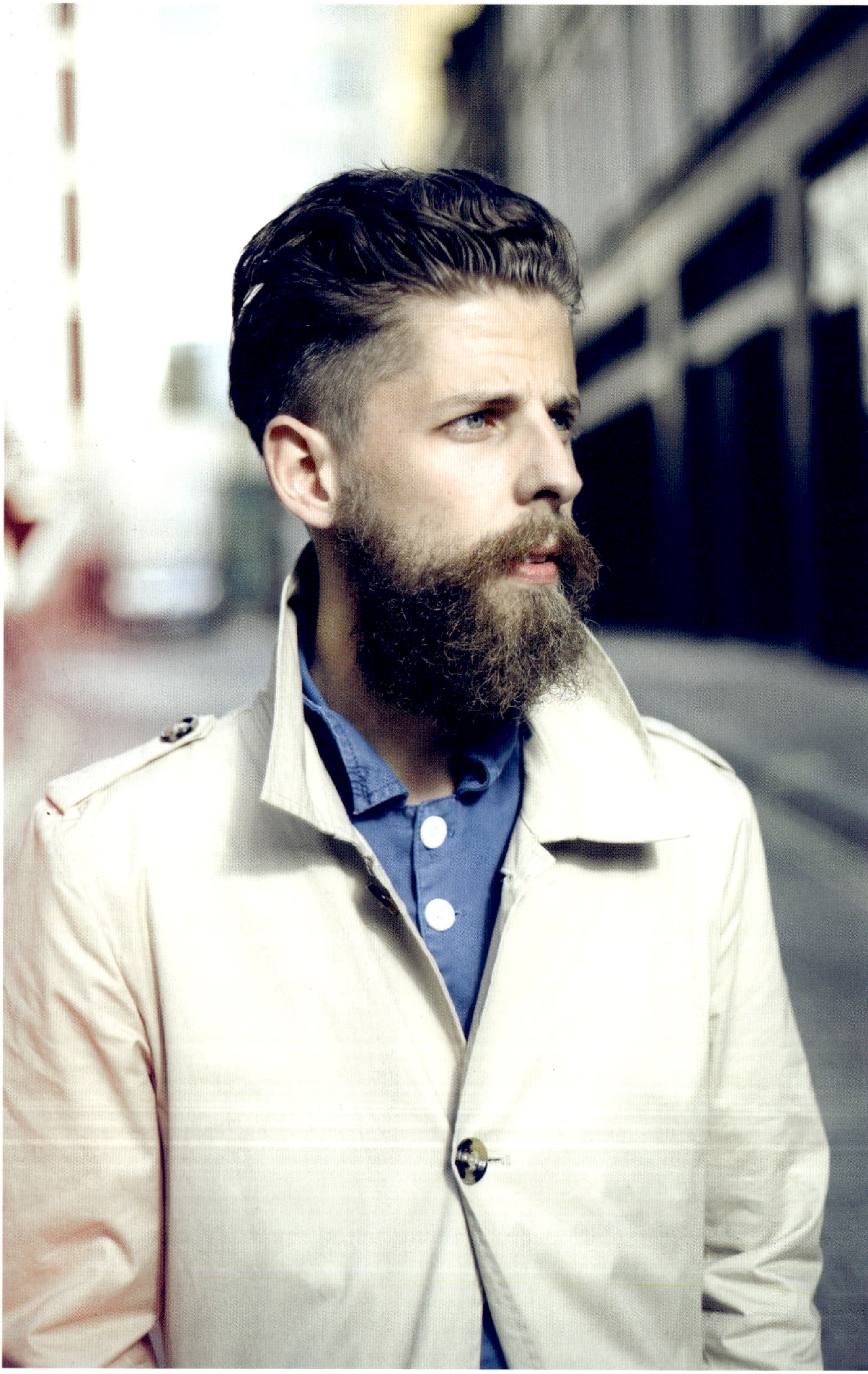

95 • Paul: New Burlington Place, London

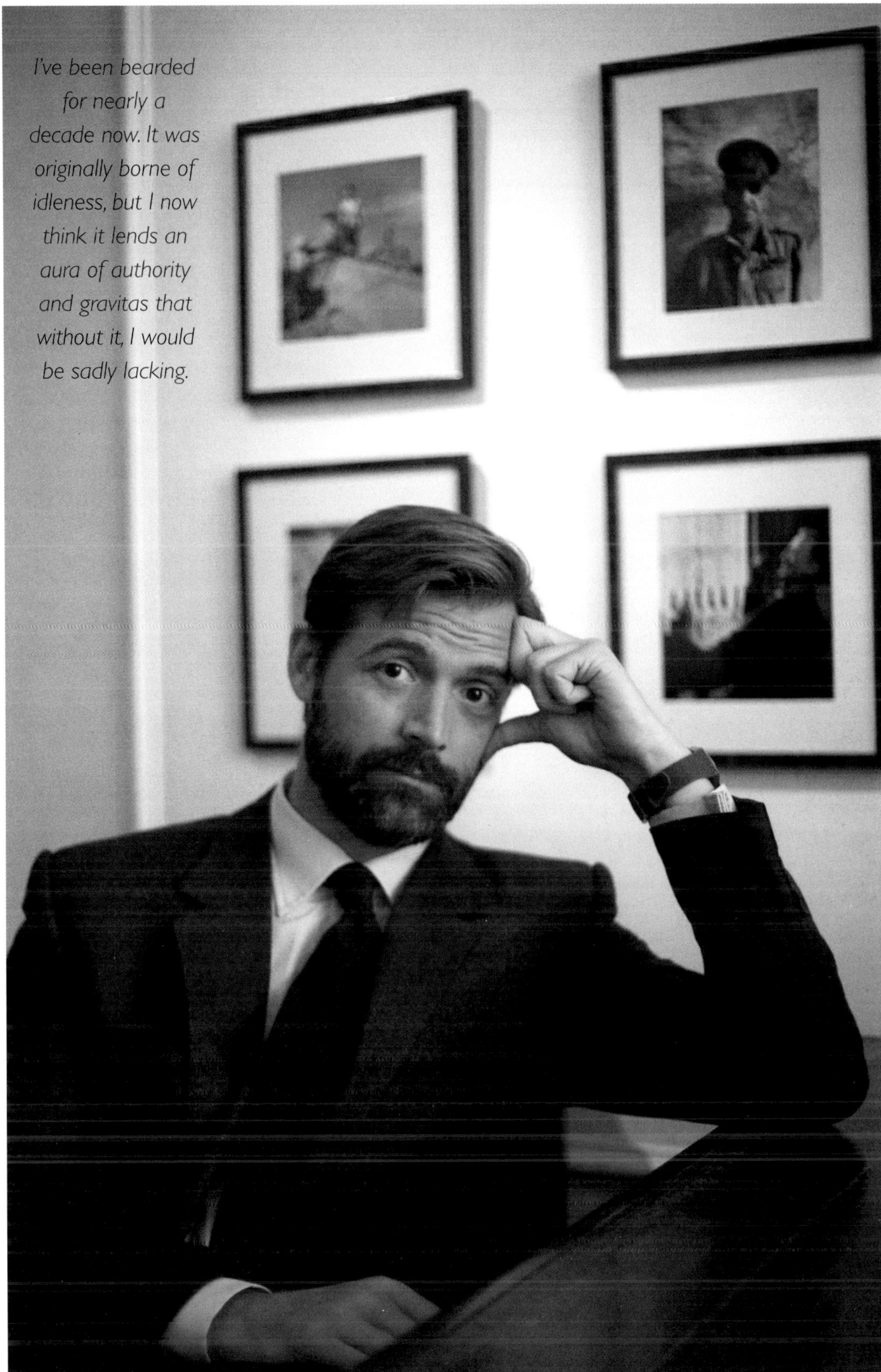
I've been bearded for nearly a decade now. It was originally borne of idleness, but I now think it lends an aura of authority and gravitas that without it, I would be sadly lacking.

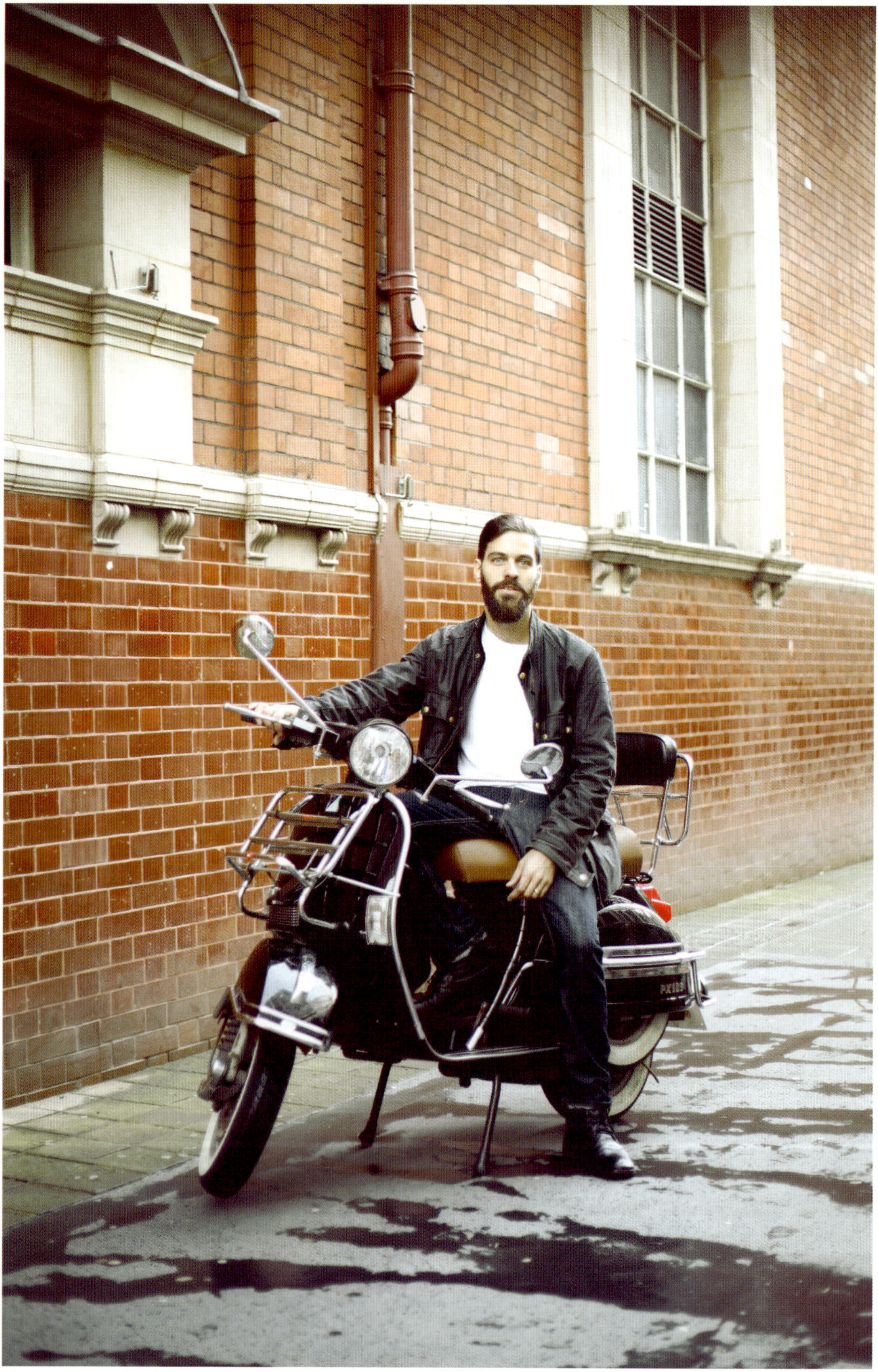

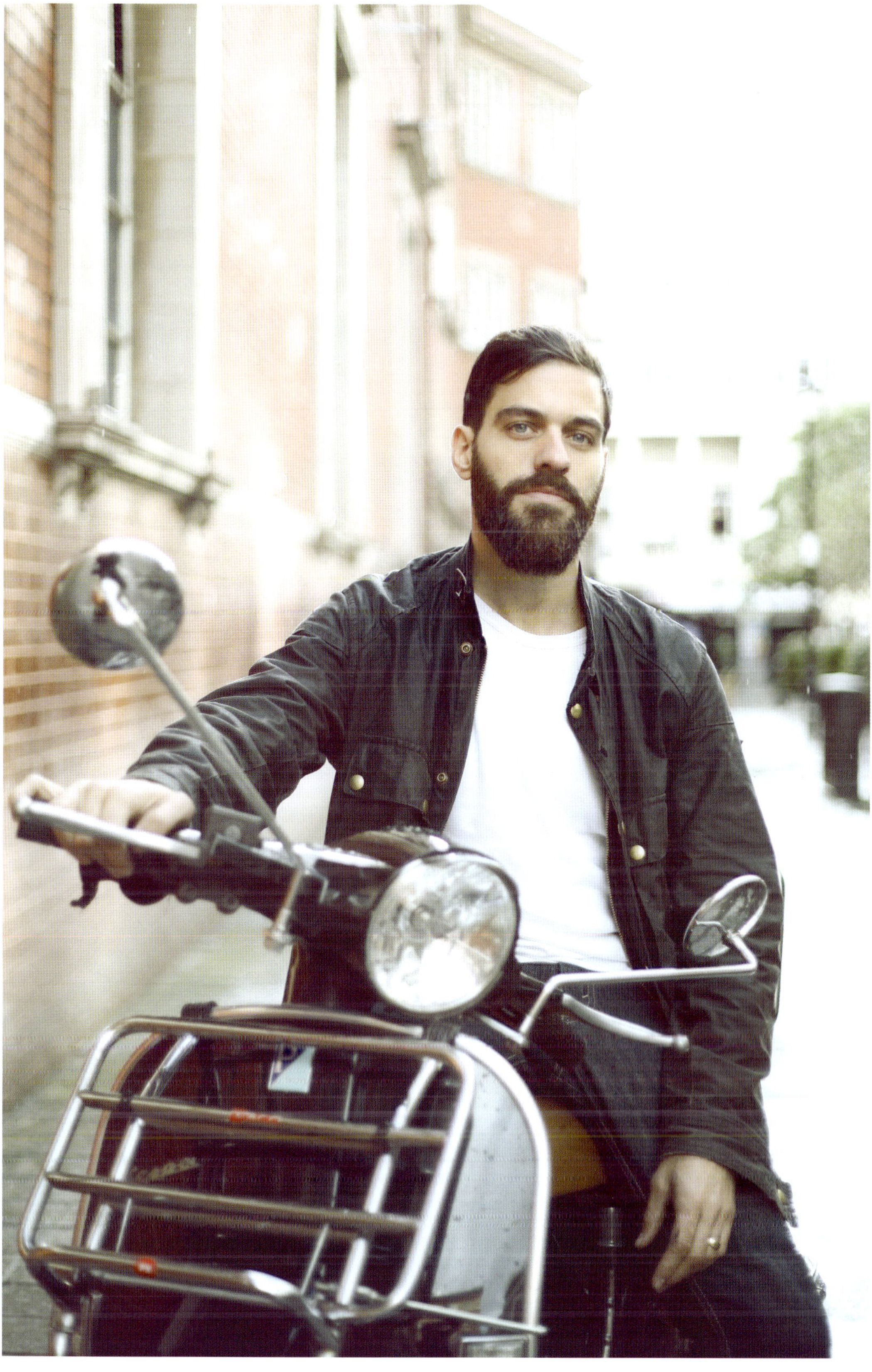

97 • Michael: Mays Court, London

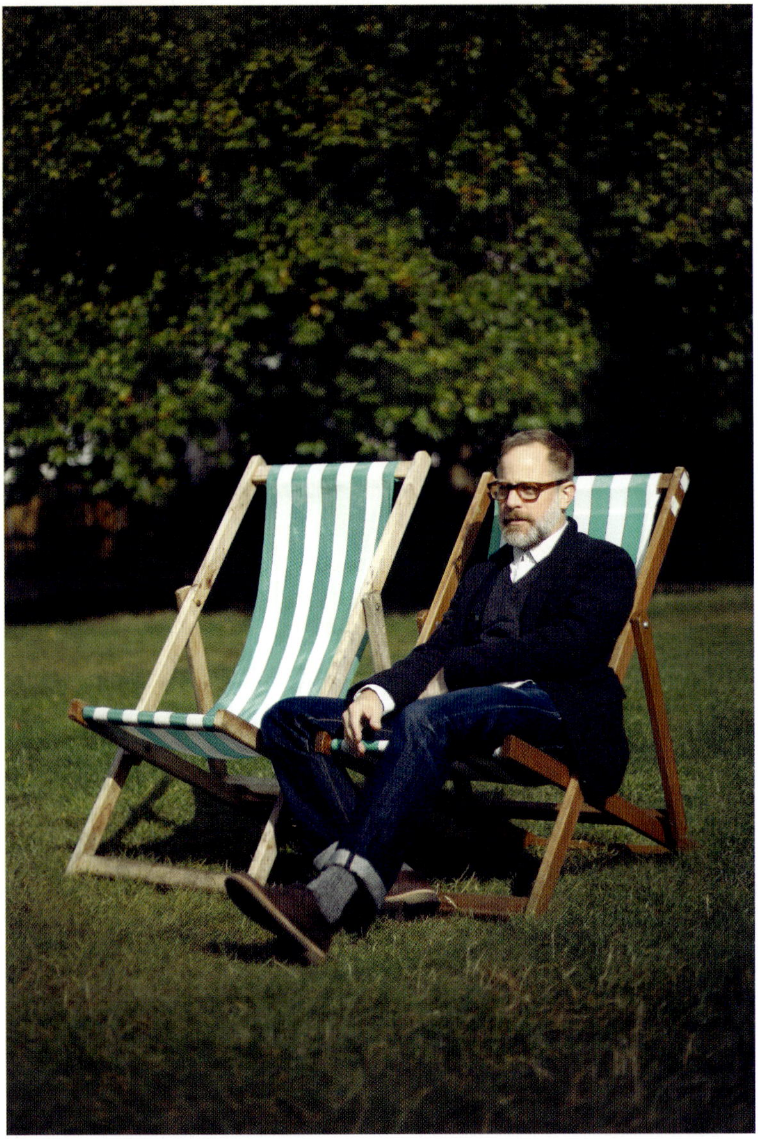

My beard sporting started unexpectedly: I was travelling in Maine with a dear friend in October, during the off–season. It was stark and cold and no visitors were around — just a lot of locals that didn't seem to take too kindly to outsiders. We'd been on the road for a few days and I had gotten lazy with shaving. I recognized that the locals were all pretty grizzly, so decided to keep mine going as a way to be less of an uninvited guest. It was itchy as all hell, but gradually I got used to it and really liked not having to shave every day. When I got back to New York City my boss was a bit surprised but I persisted in keeping it.

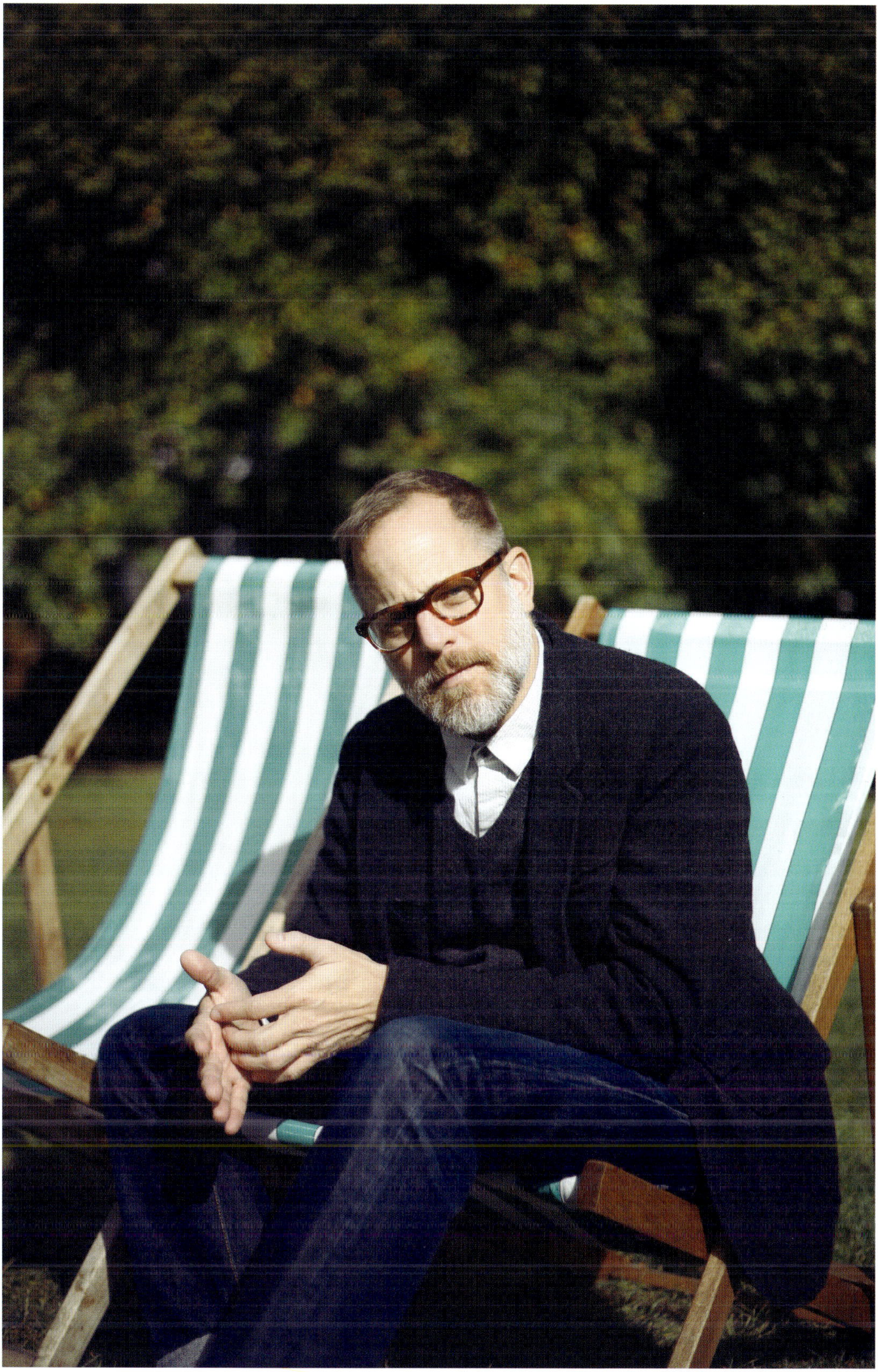

98 • Bruce: Green Park, London

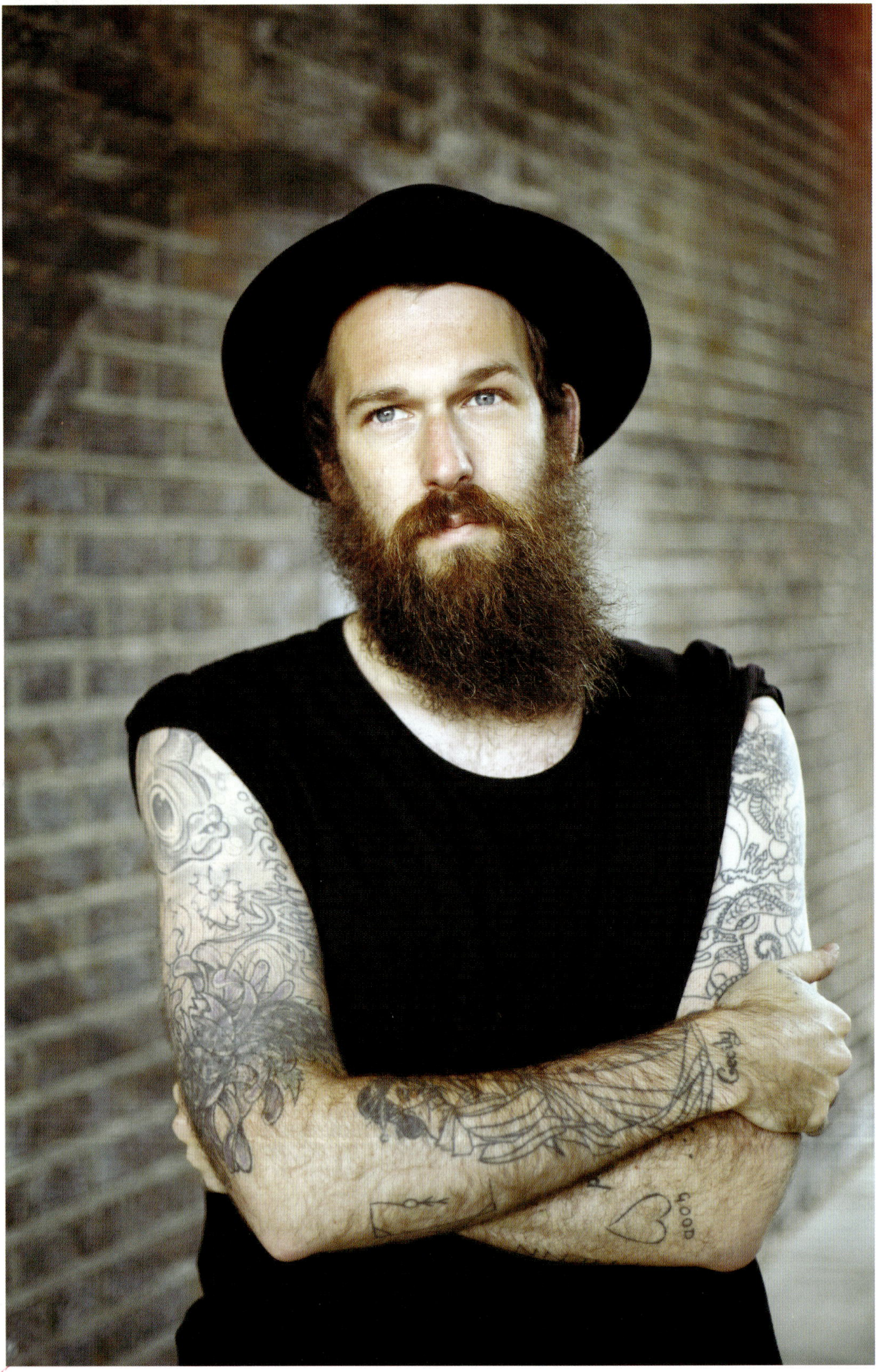

99 • Rich: Arbutus Street, London

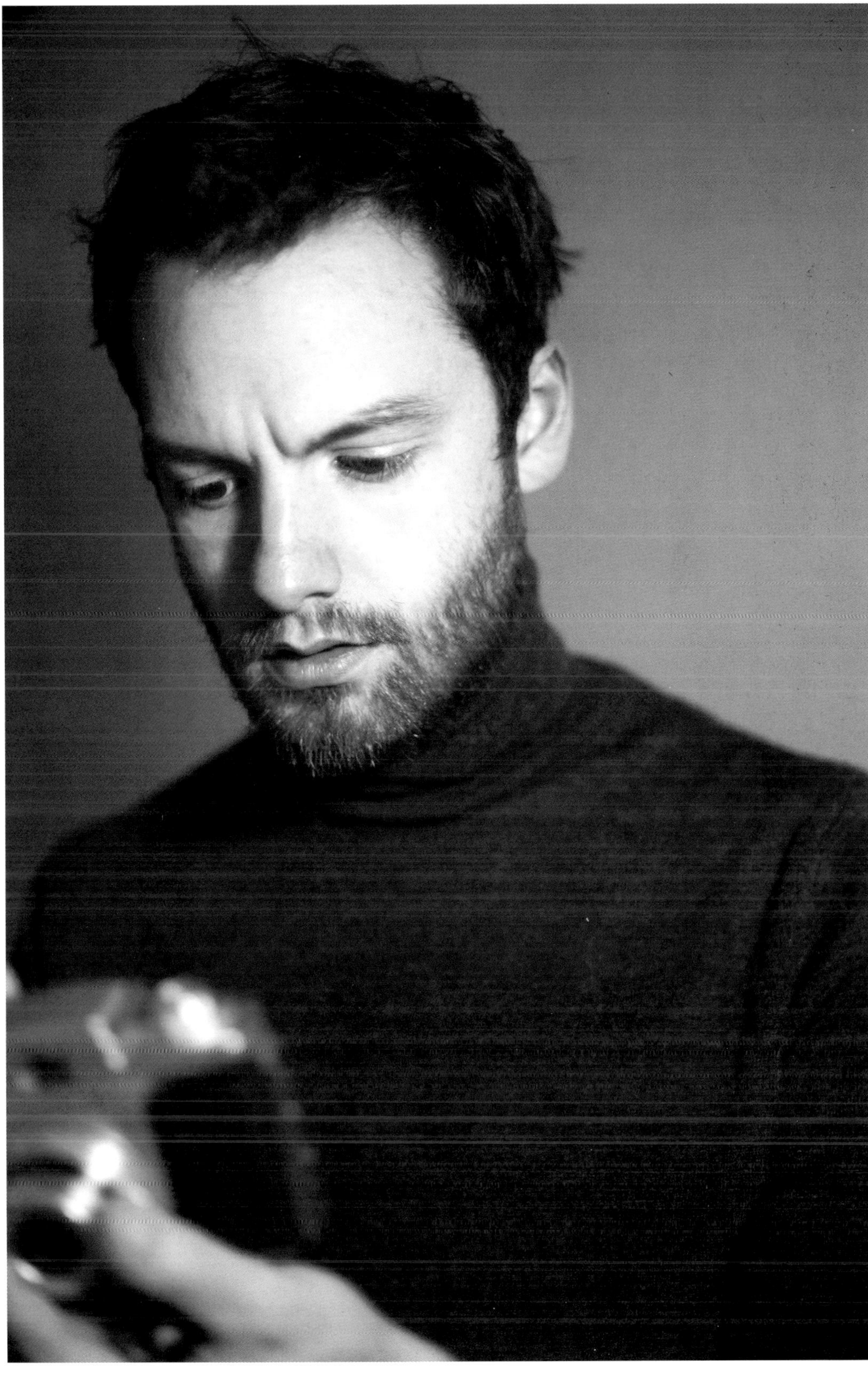

100 • Jonathan: Studio, London

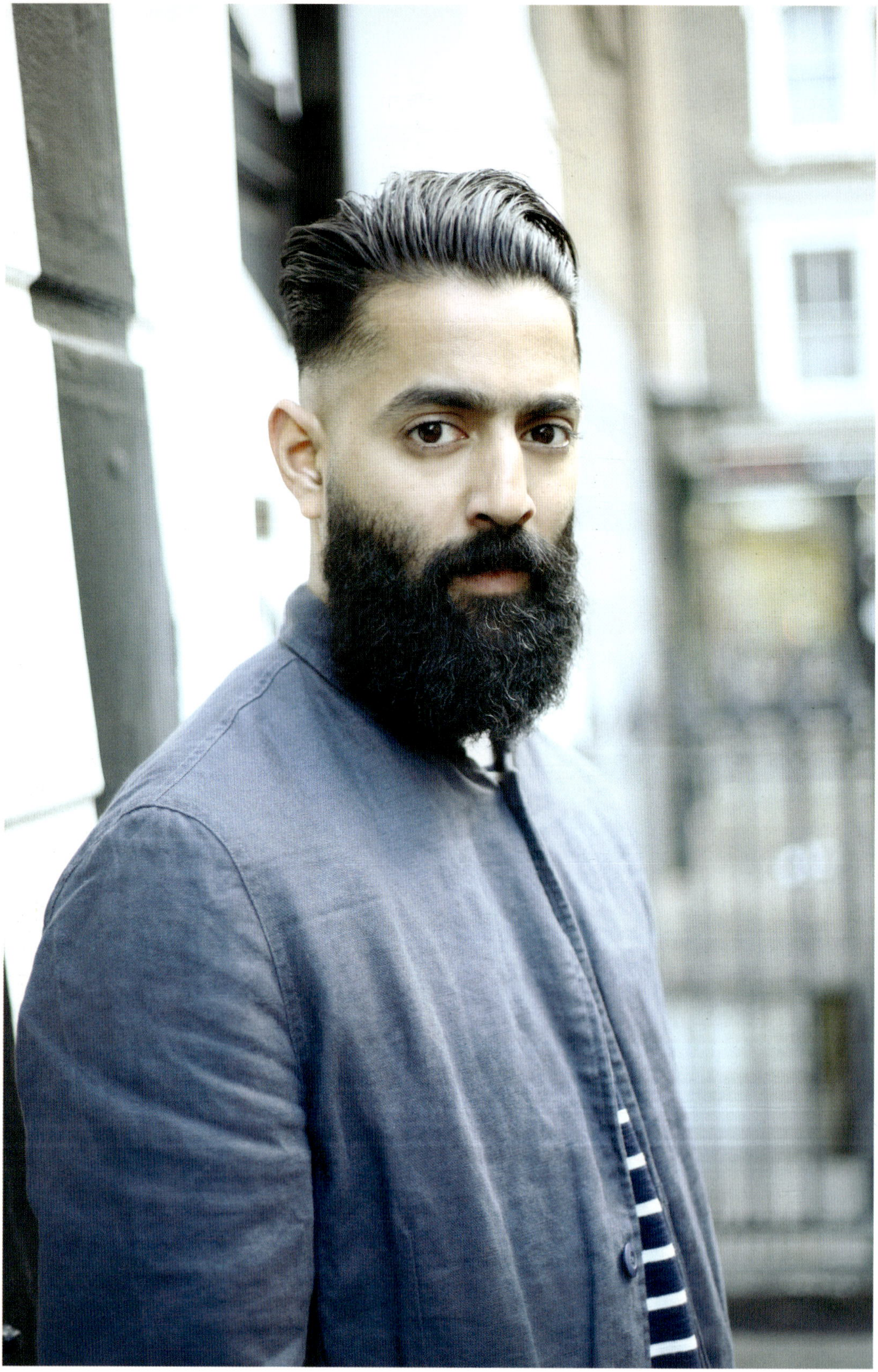

101 • Nehjat: Lexington Street, London

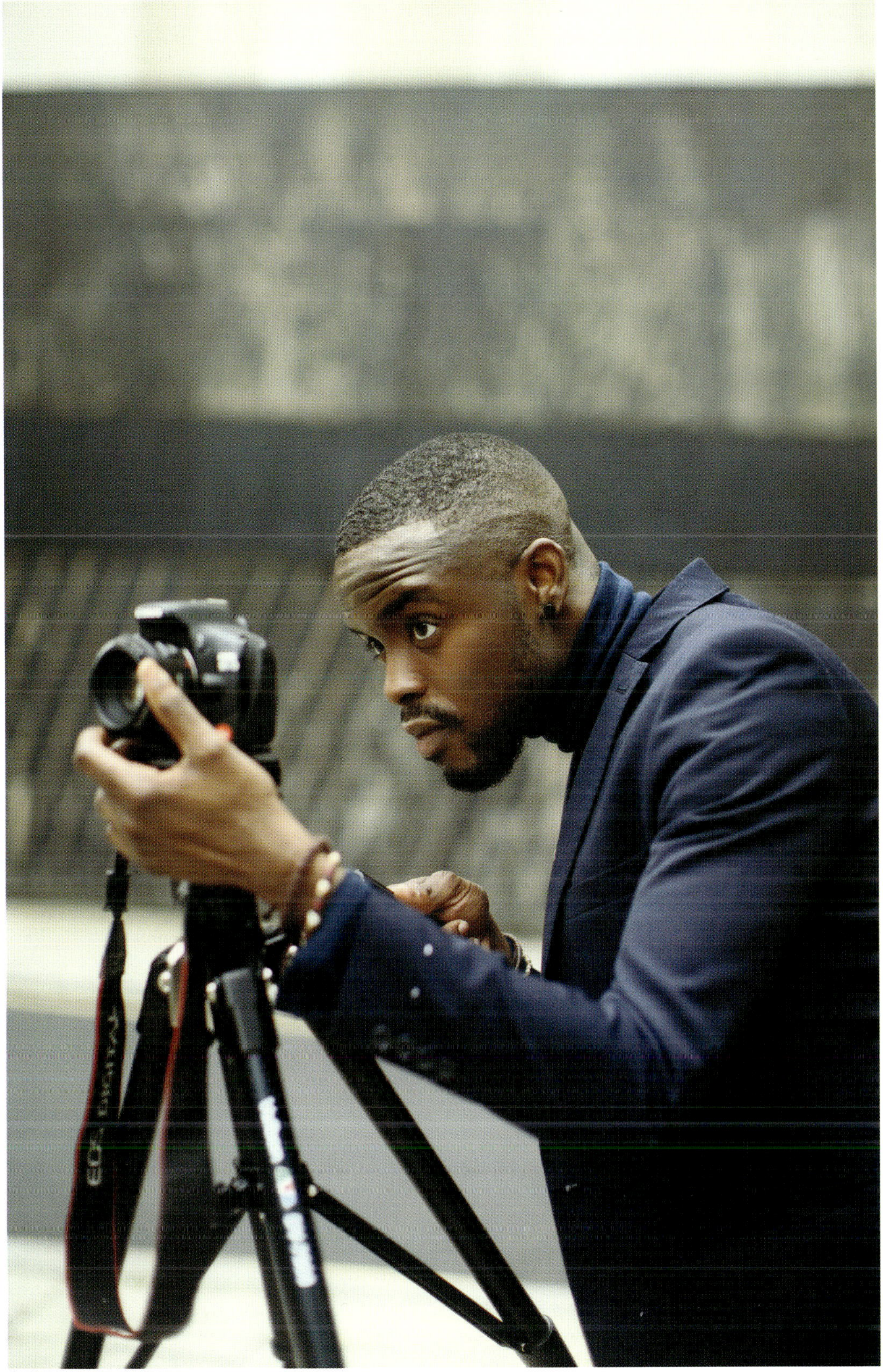

 Seye: Museum Street, London

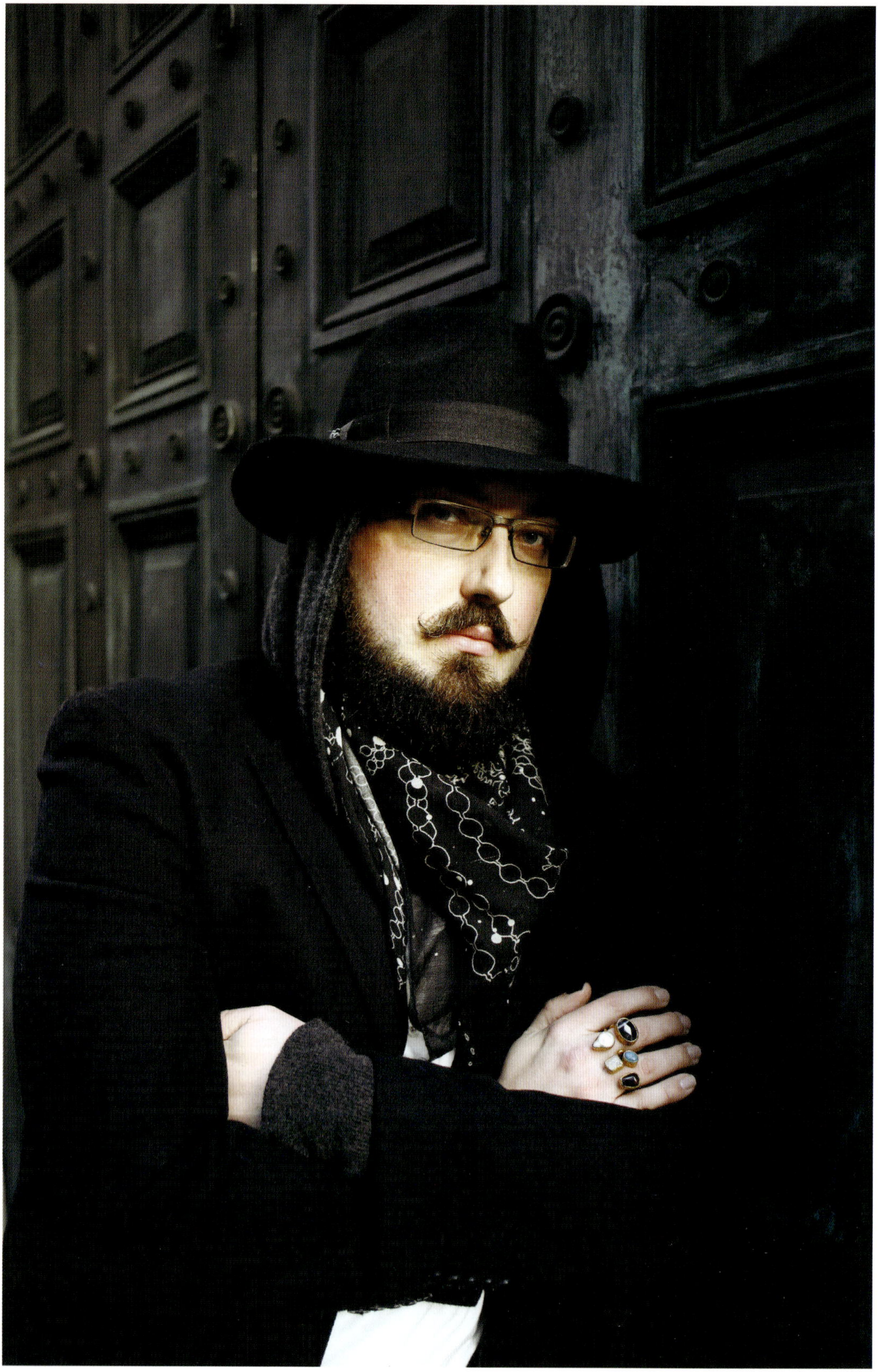

My facial hair has been transformative for me — not just in appearance, but on a very personal level. It seems to have broken down a lot of social barriers, as people don't think twice about approaching me in the street to talk about my beard, get advice or reminisce about a childhood memory of an uncle with facial hair. I've also discovered my partners automatically place me in a dominant masculine role in our relationship which has been quite a liberating experience.

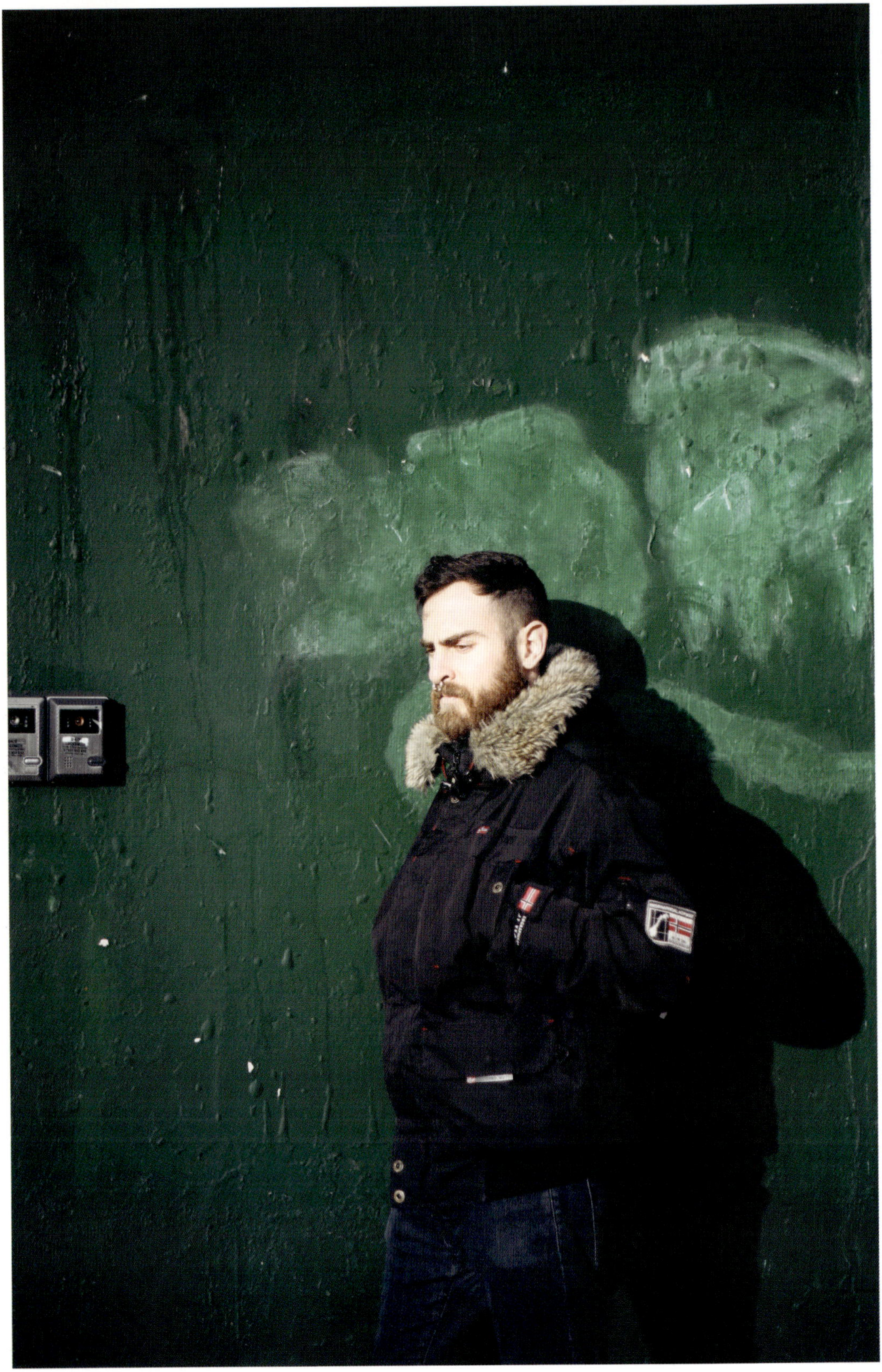

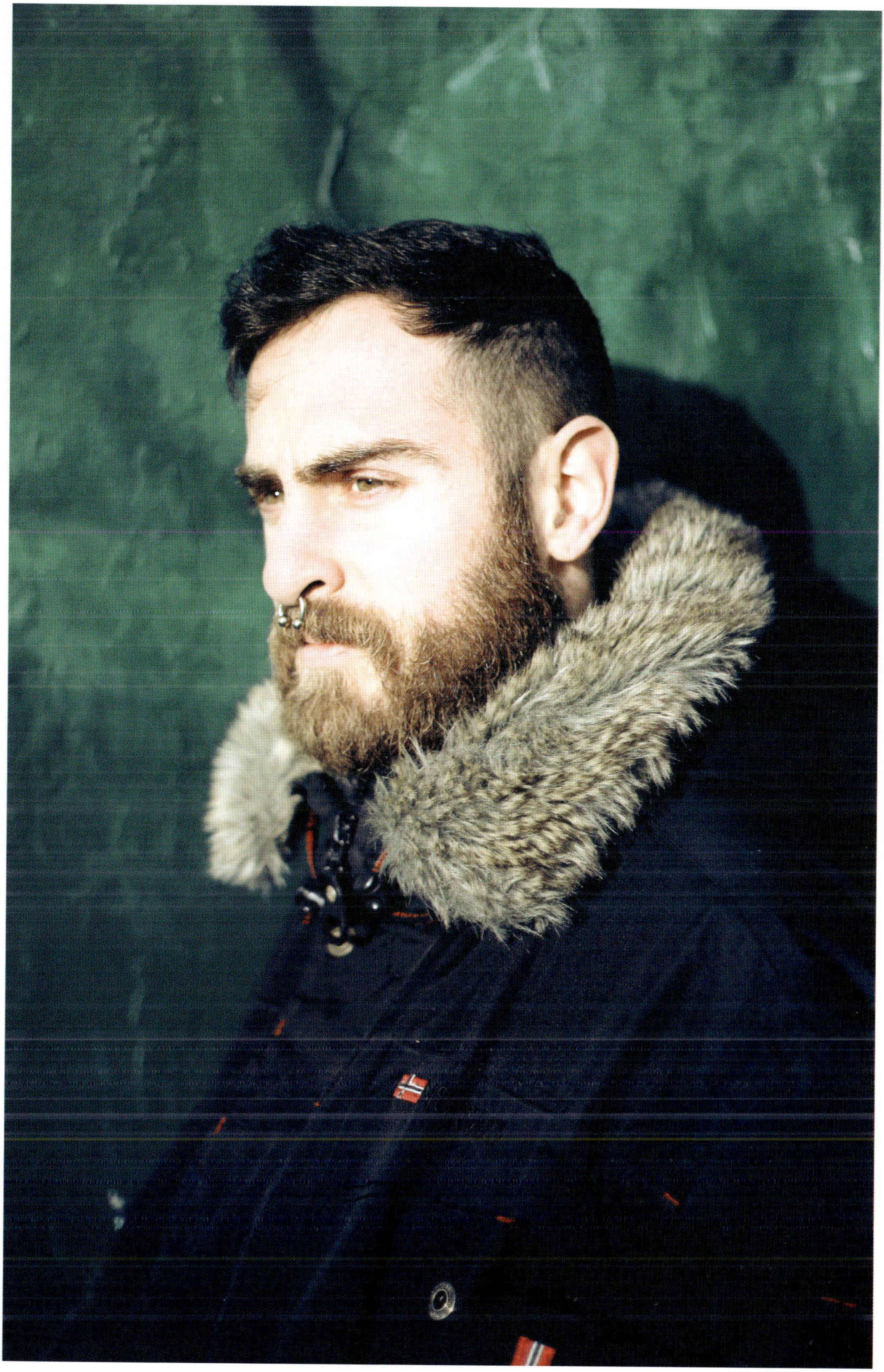

 Abraham: Old Street, London

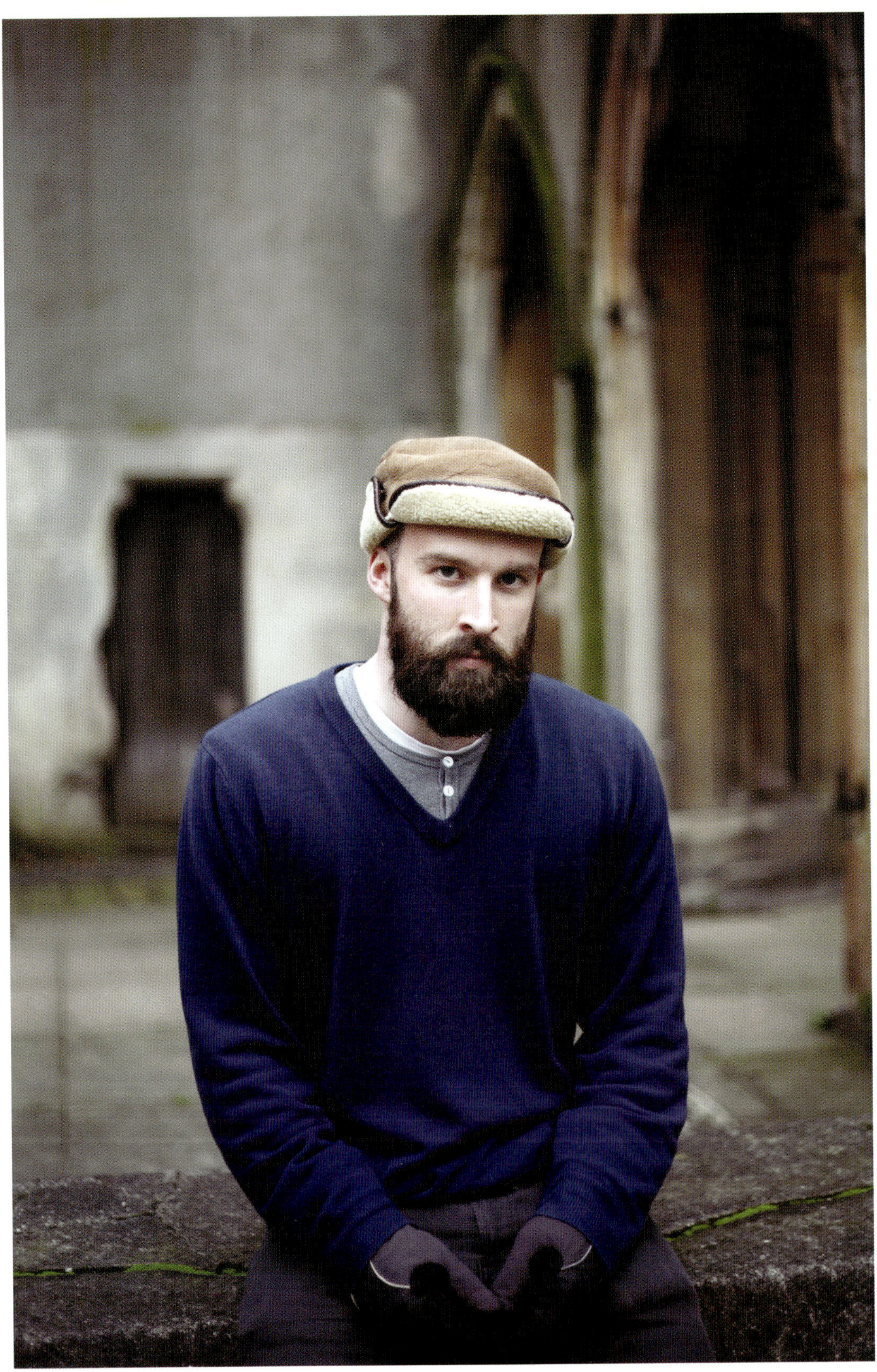

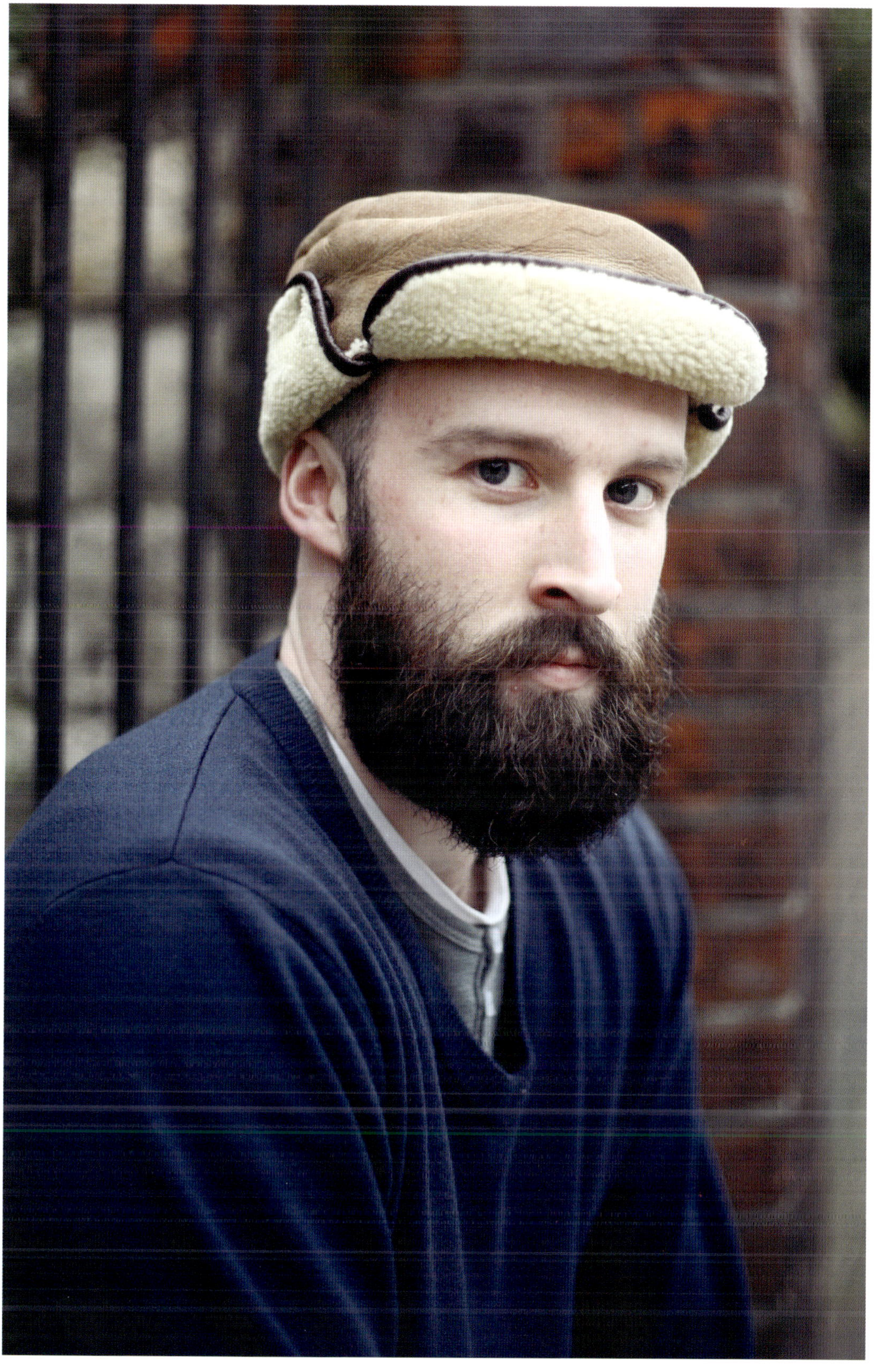

105 • Max: Kennington Park Road, London

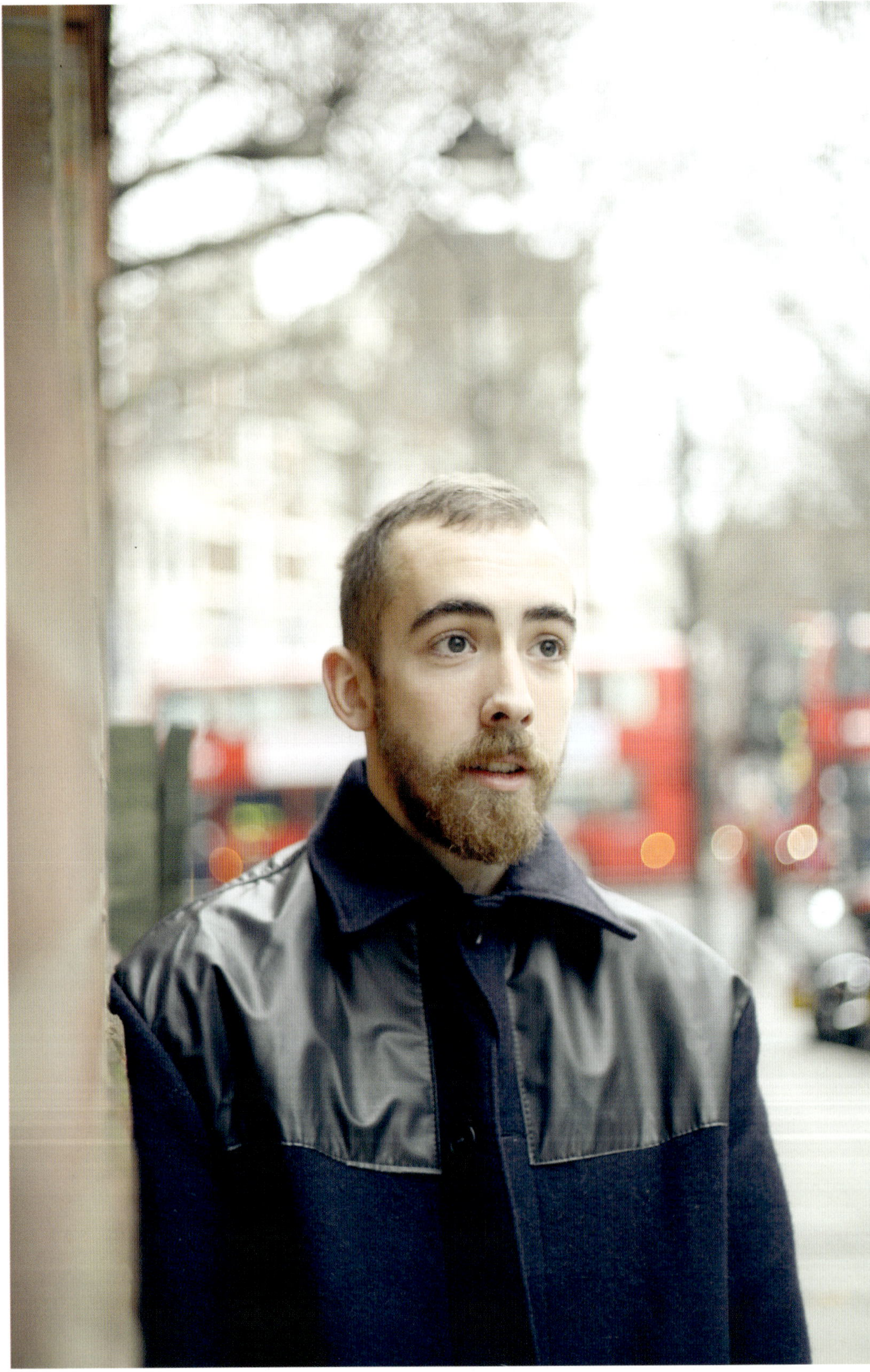

 Matthew: Endell Street, London

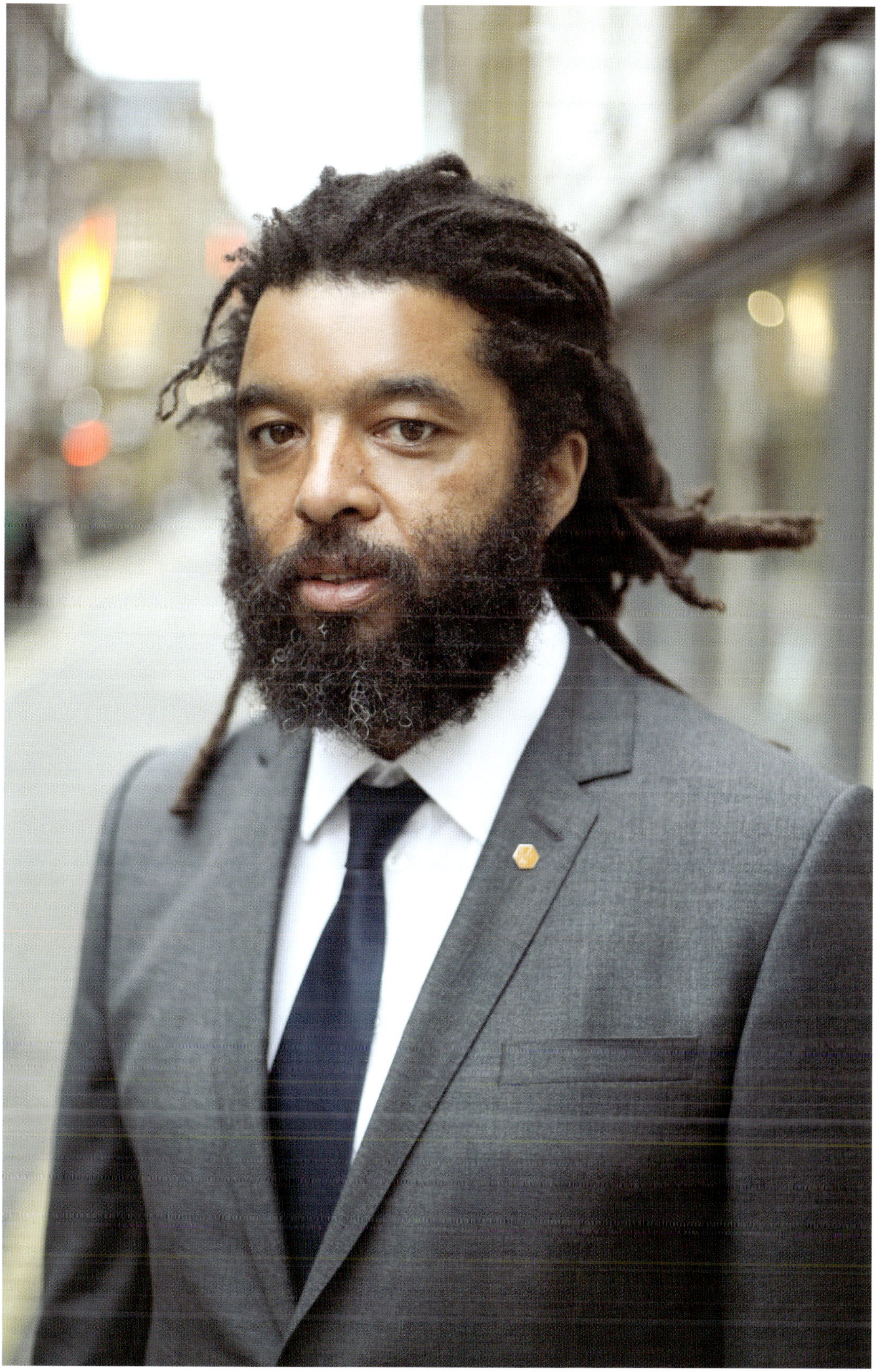

107 • Marc: Shorts Gardens, London

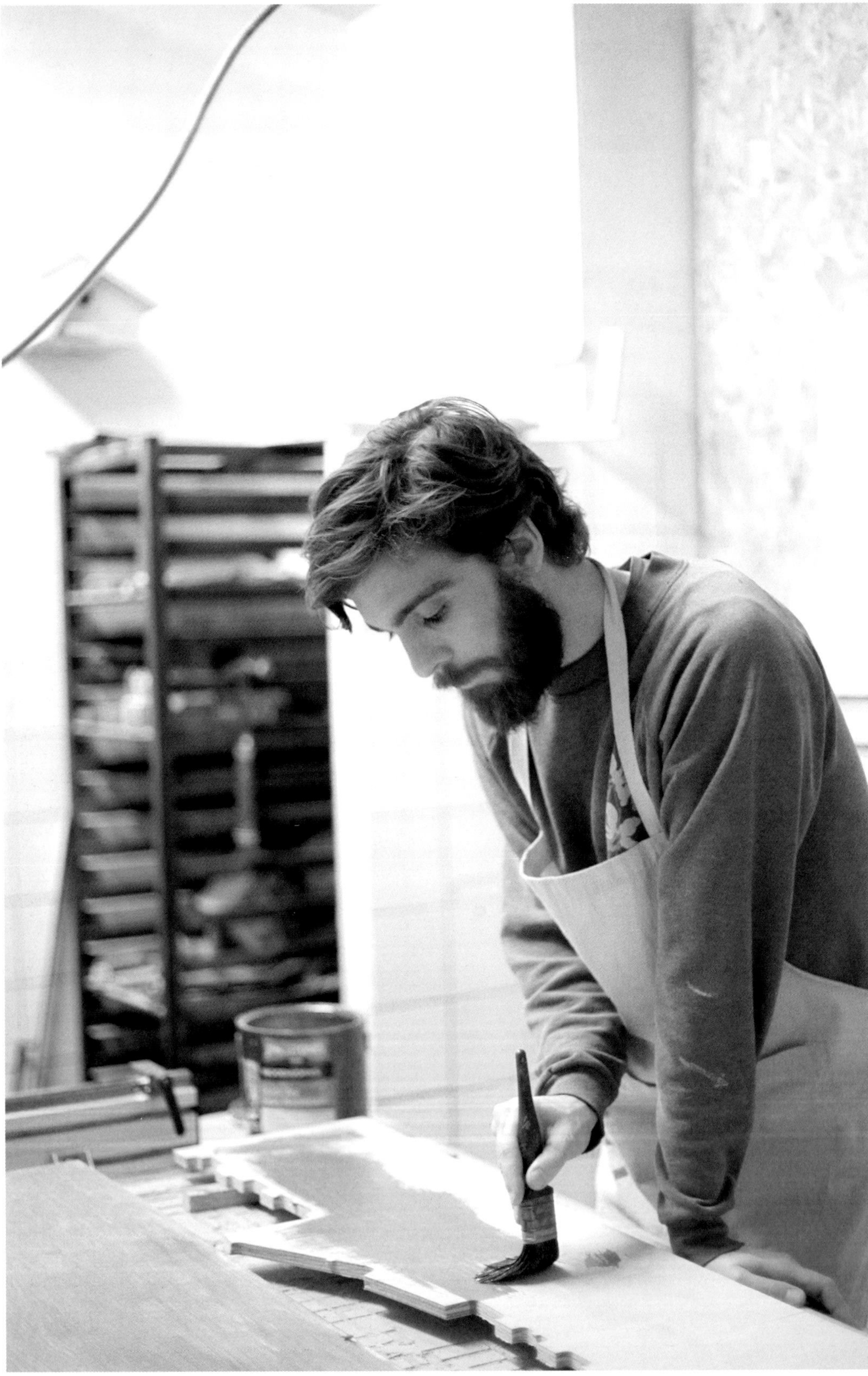

108 • Christopher: Lower Marsh, London

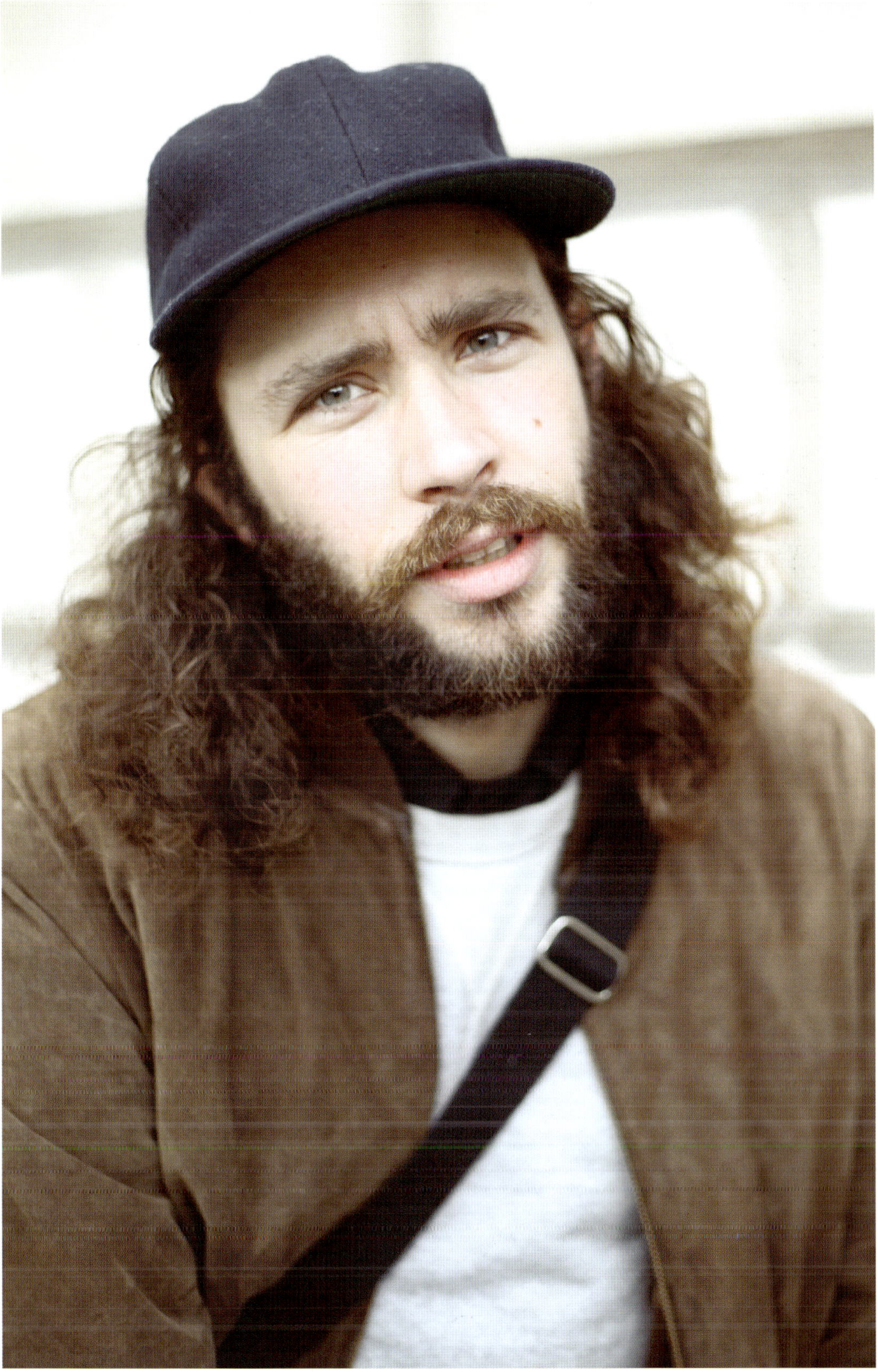

109 • James: Somerset House, London

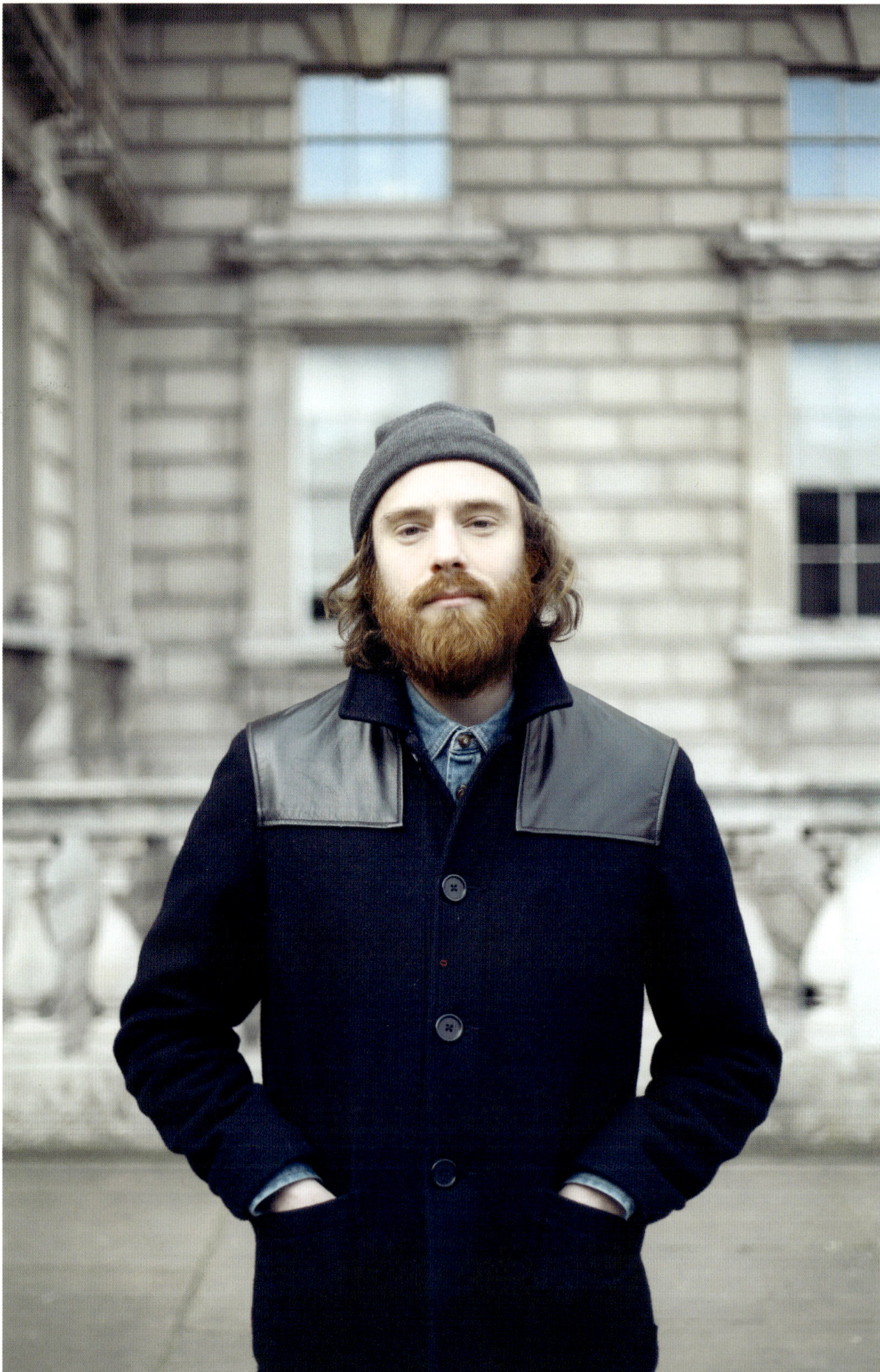

110 • Christopher: Somerset House, London

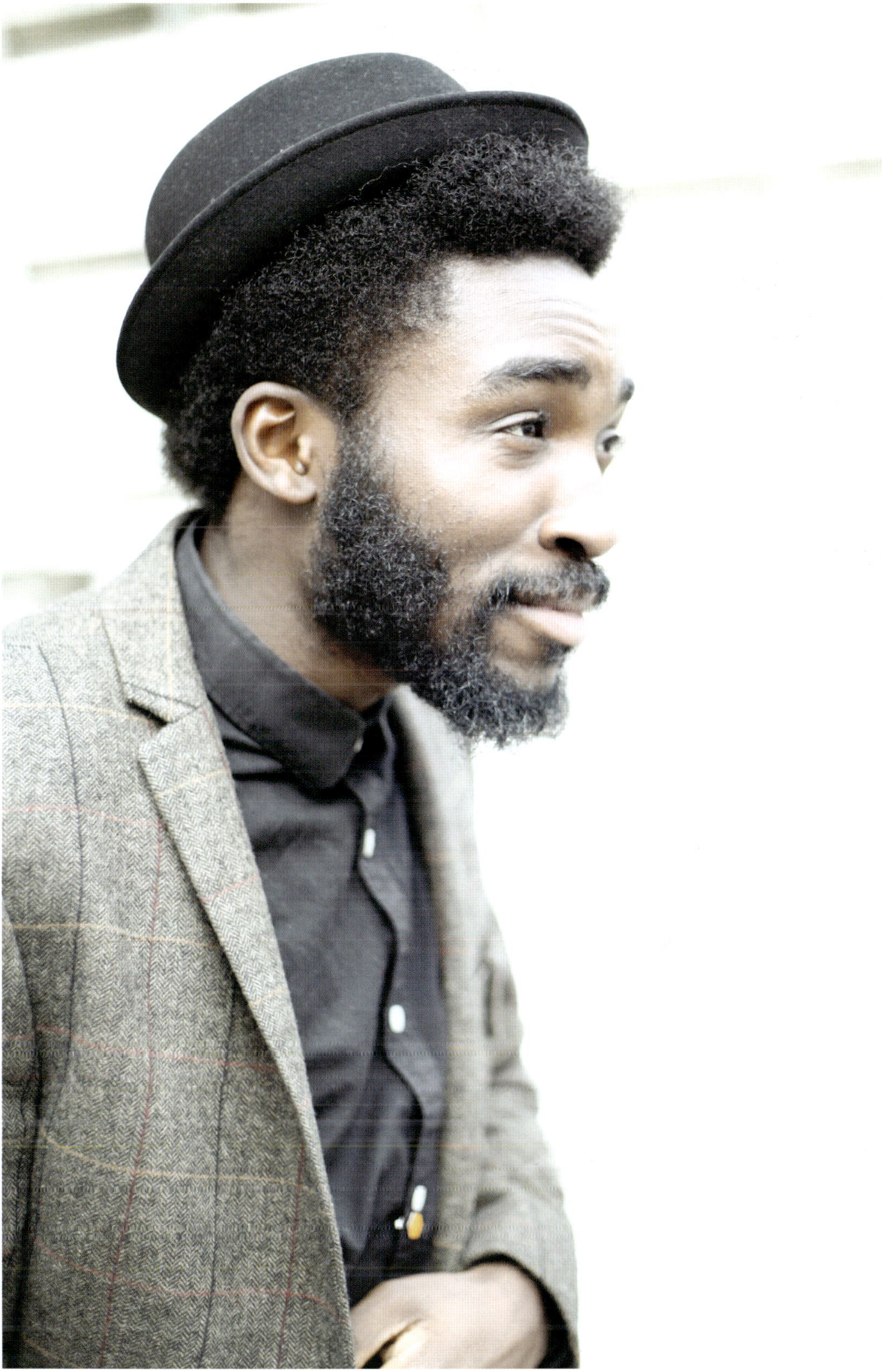

111 • James: Somerset House, London

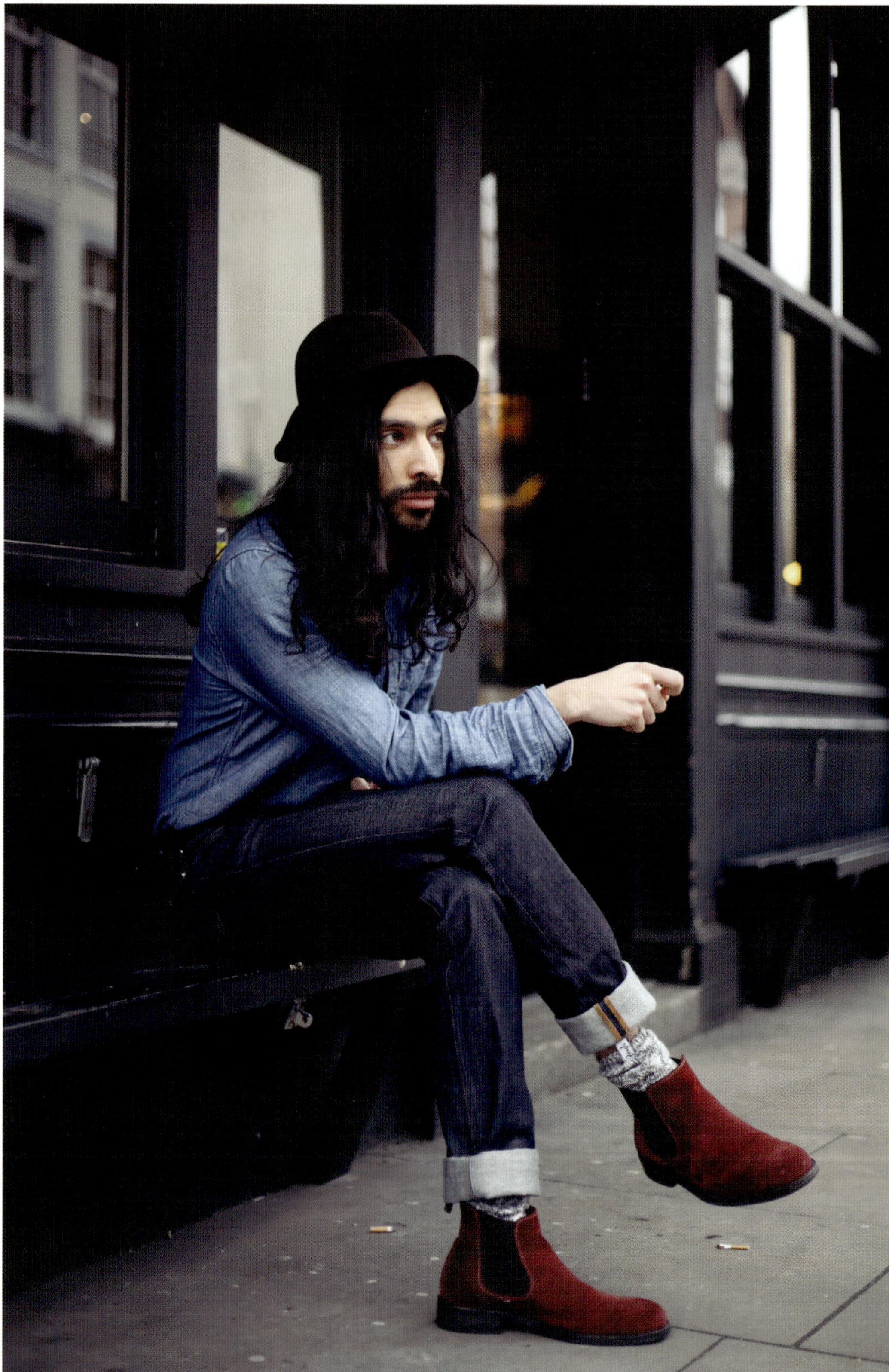

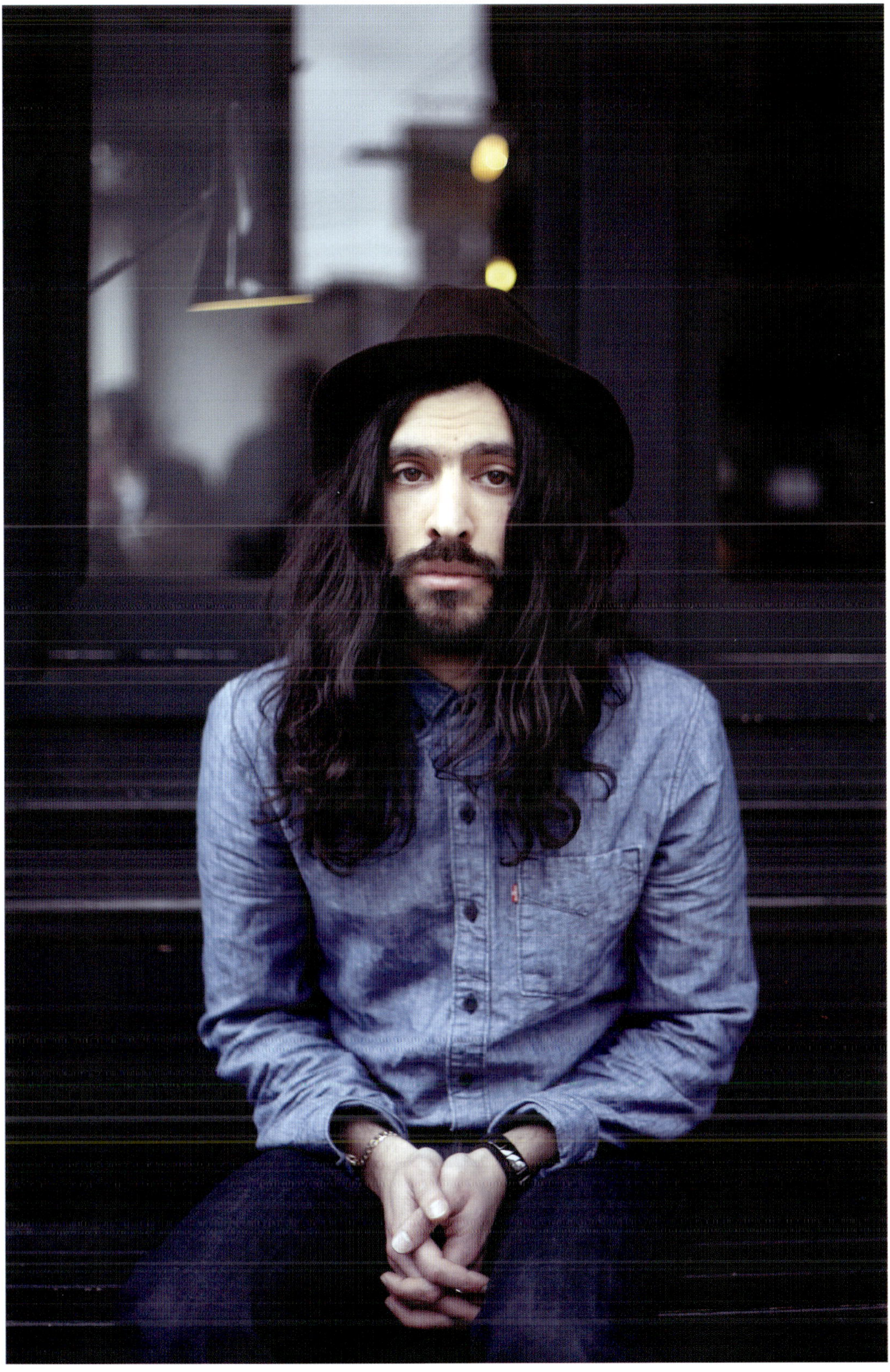

112 • Macks: Curtain Road, London

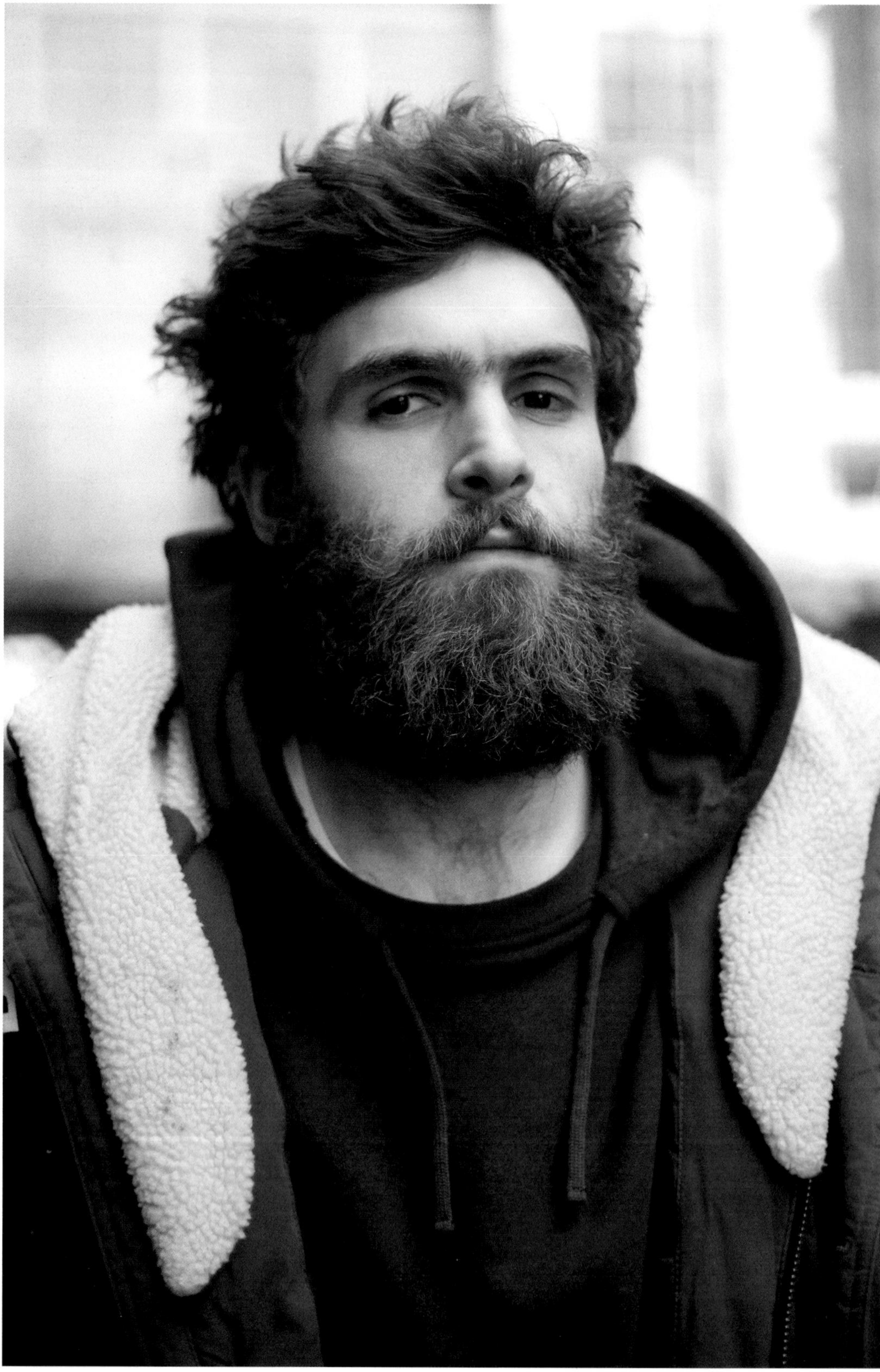

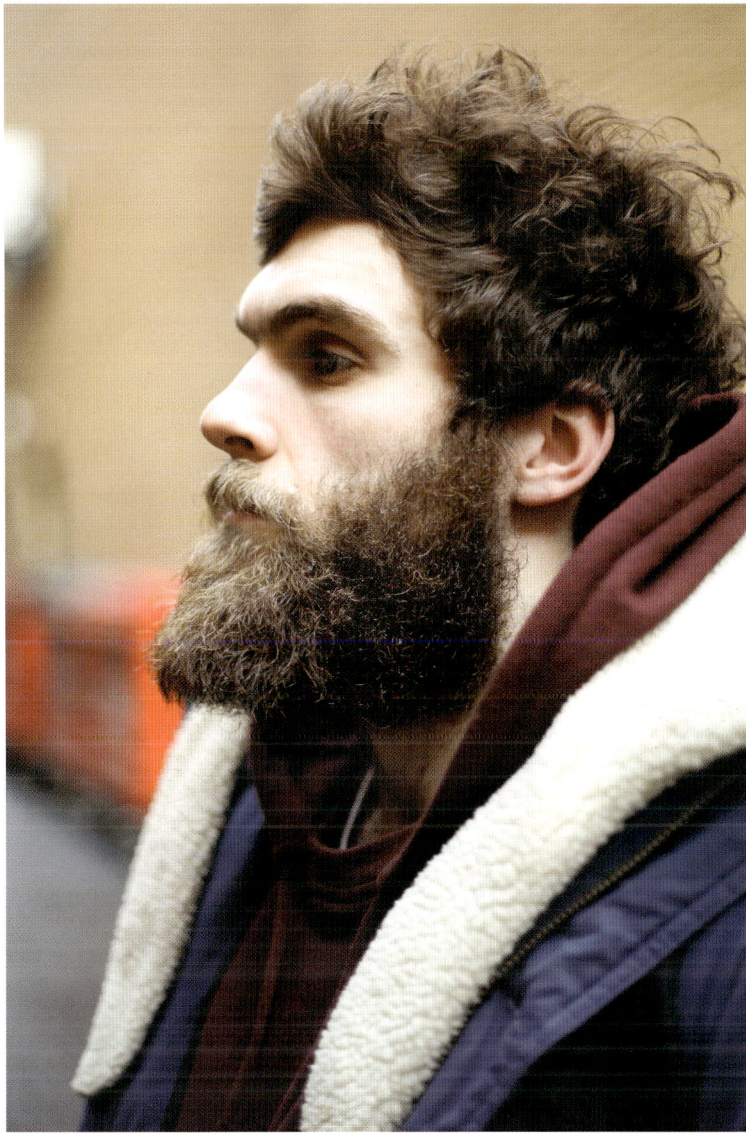

For me, the beard is a sign of heritage. I take a lot of pride in my beard because of it's colouring. Not many people get the pleasure of sporting a full-coloured Norse beard. It reminds me of where I come from. Recently, beards have become fashionable and people comment on it all the time. I normally get 'the heads-up' from people I'm walking with that every other passing person is taking a good hard look. I think people are forever trying to find a way to be unique and a beard can present you with that opportunity: in fashion and statement. What's more unique than something you grow yourself? One thing is for sure, if beards become unpopular at sometime in the future, I'll still have one. It's part of me now. For better or for worse.

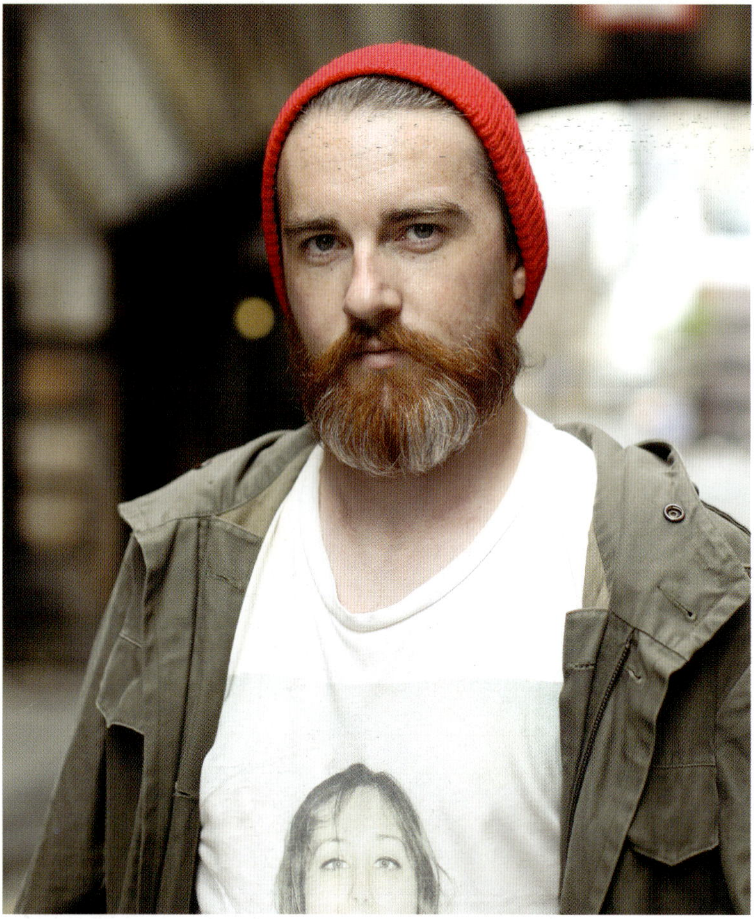

My beard has taken many forms over the years, and is currently a long and wild, but not unkempt, ginger and white expanse. I originally grew a beard because I didn't really like my face. My beard became a mask. The longer it got indicating the more I wanted to hide. Now it has become a symbol of pride and latterly has brought me the most joy, yet at times has also left me dumbstruck at the unwanted attention it draws. To have a thick beard you must also have a thick skin! I have received so many positive comments from strangers and spoken to those that I may never have before my facial fuzz. One day I was walking through a local park in Glasgow when I came past some kids who had kicked their football into the duck pond. As I approached I was spotted by one of the boys who pointed at me and whispered to another, audibly enough for me to hear, "Check out Jesus." The other boy turned and instantly pointed at the strewn ball bobbing on the pond and shouted to me... "Here big man! Can you walk out there and get our ball back?" With a great beard comes great sensibility it would seem.

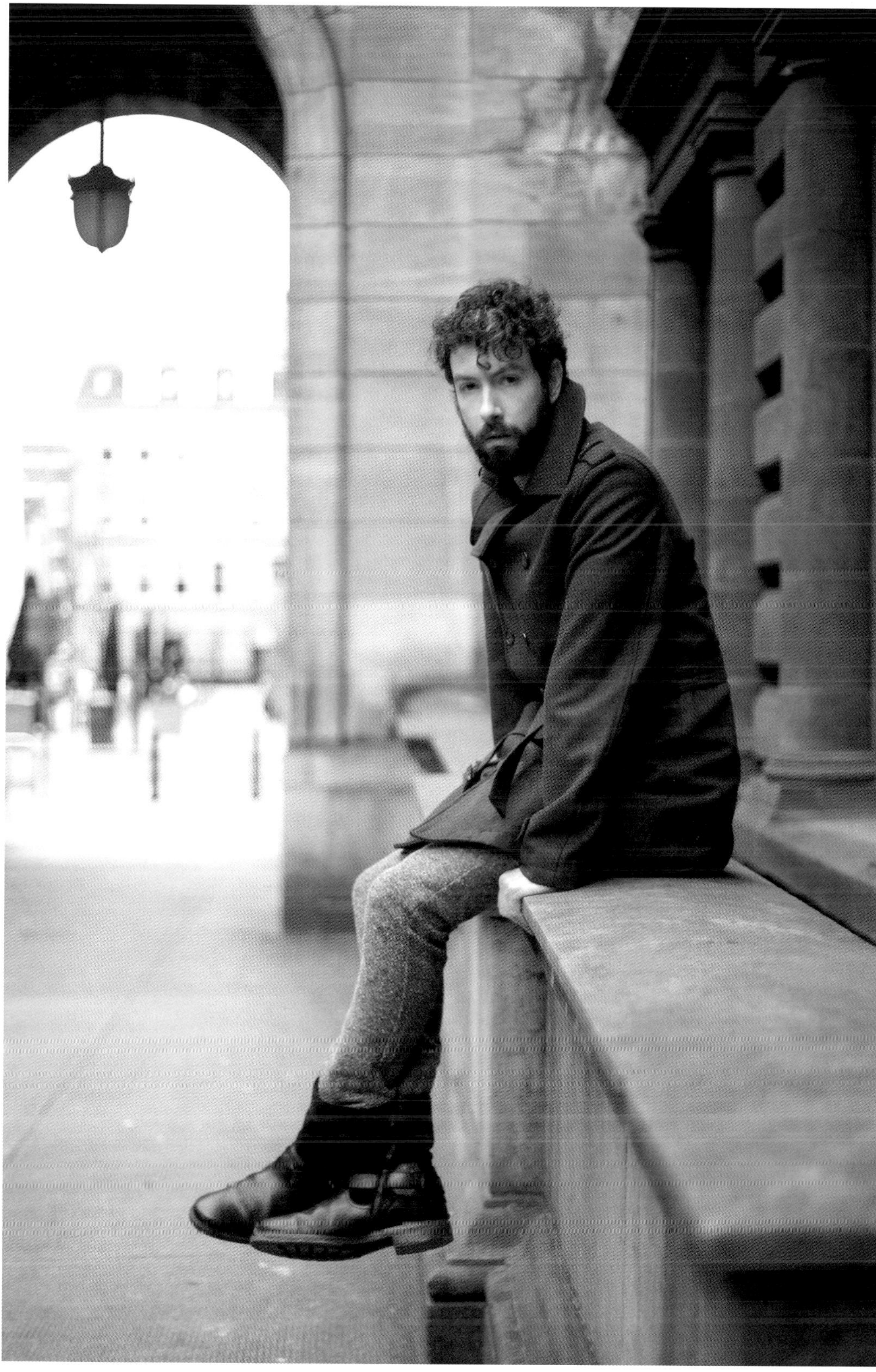

115 • Portis: John Street, Glasgow

Initially I was worried that if I grew a beard I would lose my boyish looks. I did lose them, but exchanged them for man-ish ones instead. The beard connects me to something that's very wild and deeply masculine. I celebrate it on a daily basis. The more I celebrate it for myself, the more other people compliment me on it. Having a beard is like having a teddy bear constantly cuddling your face. There are a million and one reasons that it's great to have a beard. Pick a few which work for you and grow your own or, ladies, get your man to grow one and let him tickle your fancy in all the right ways.

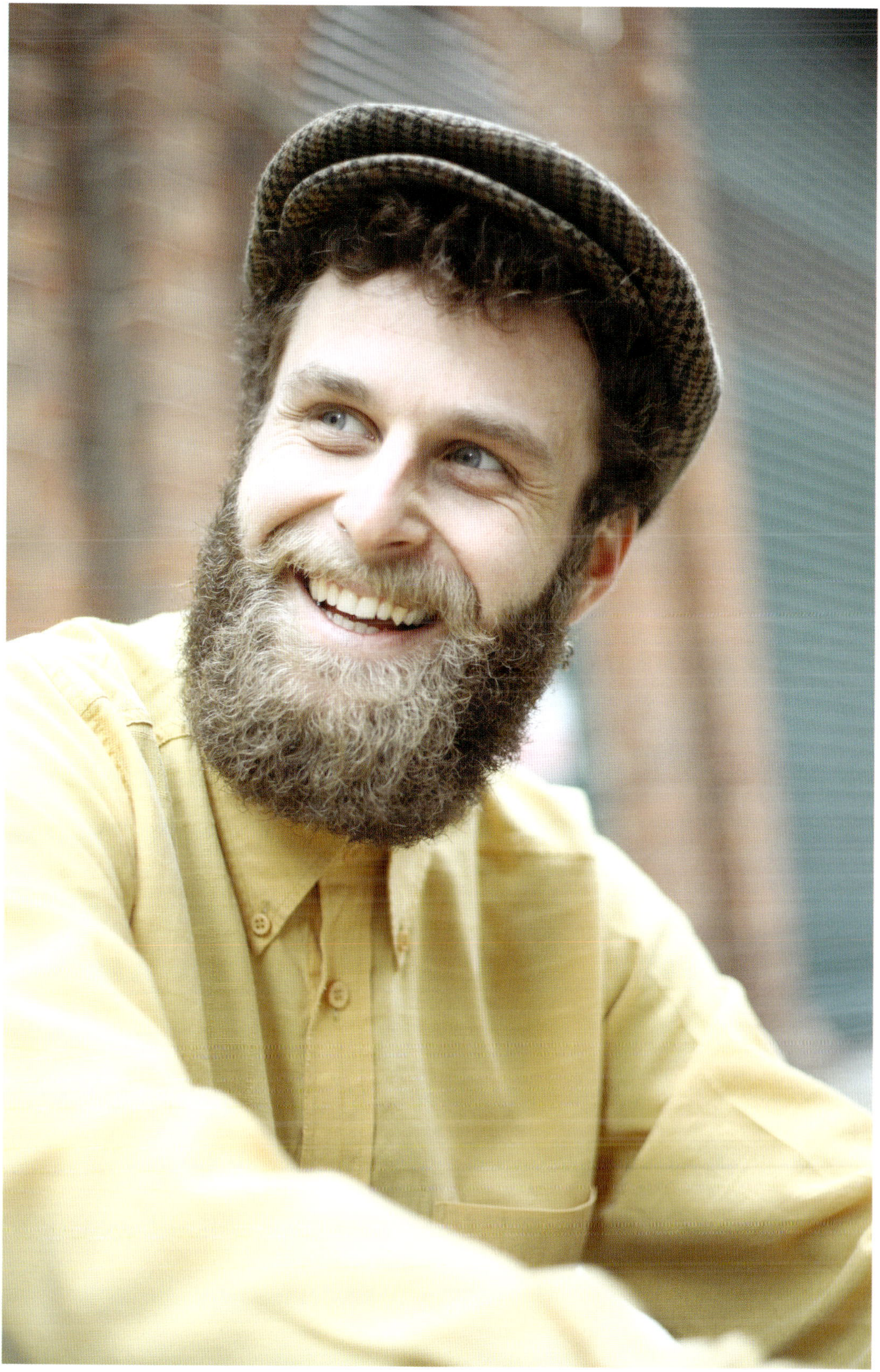

116 • Nate: Bedford Street, London

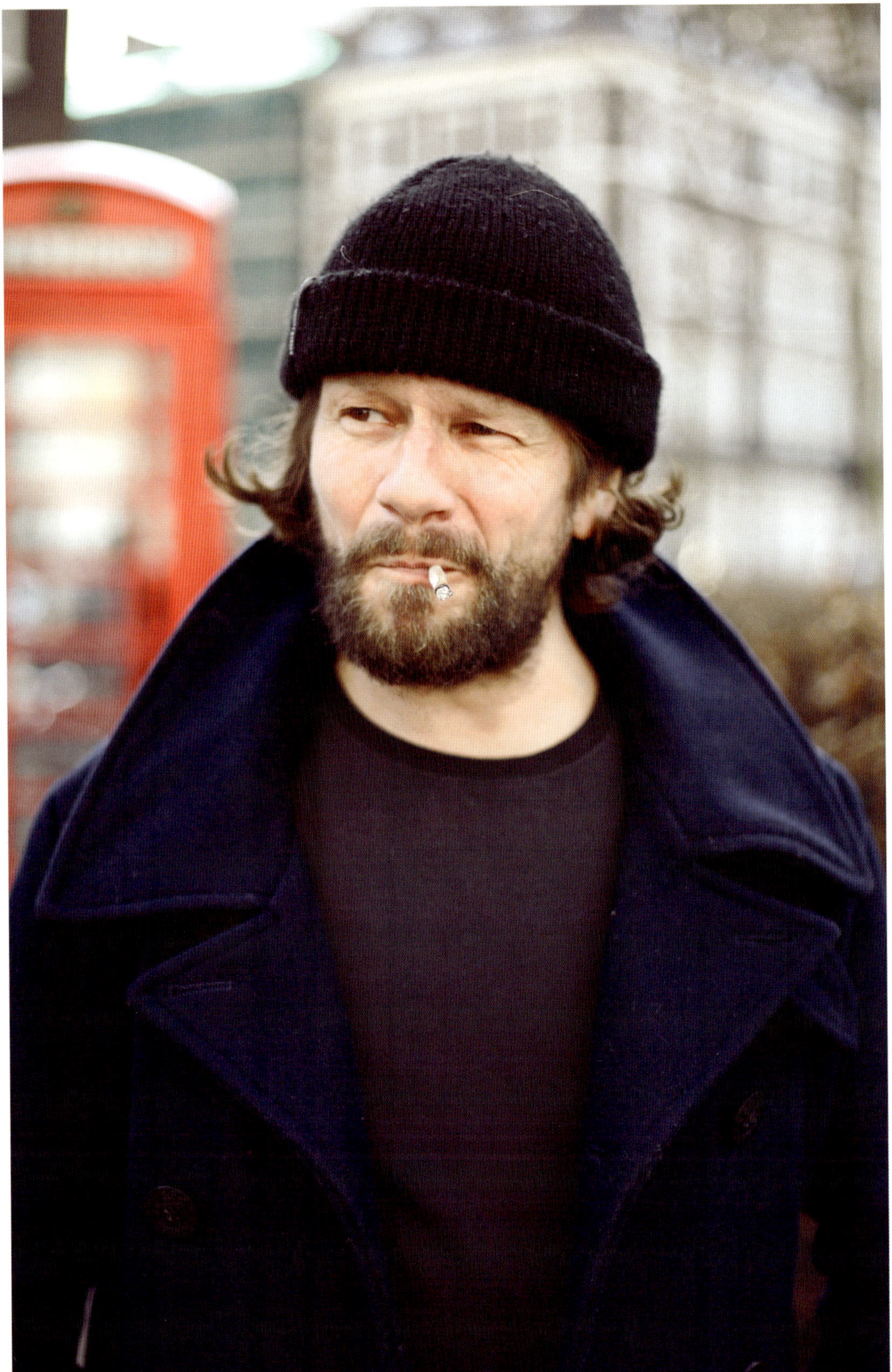

117 • David: Victoria House, London

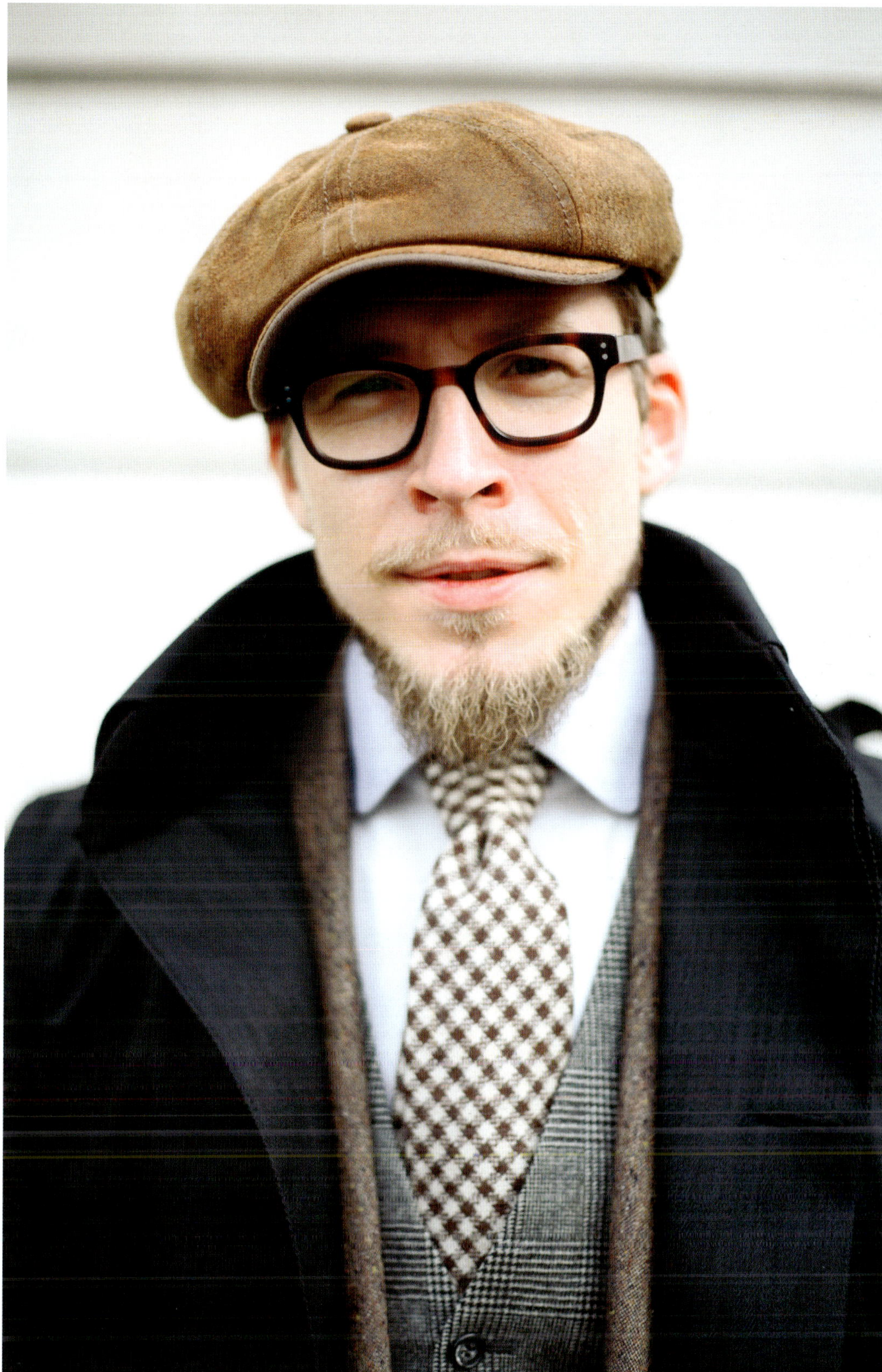

 Alexander: Victoria House, London

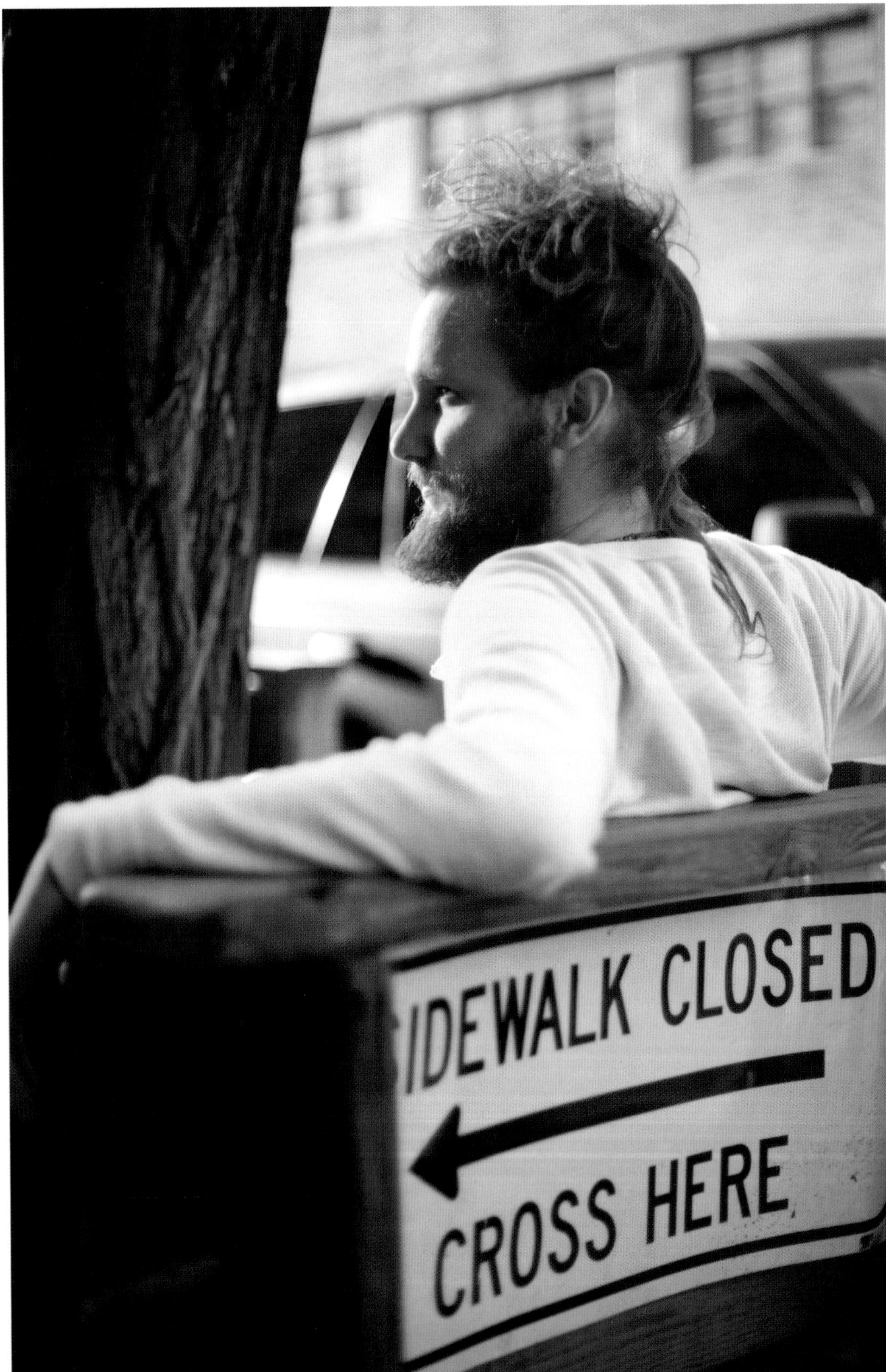

119 • Ryan: Greenwich Street, New York

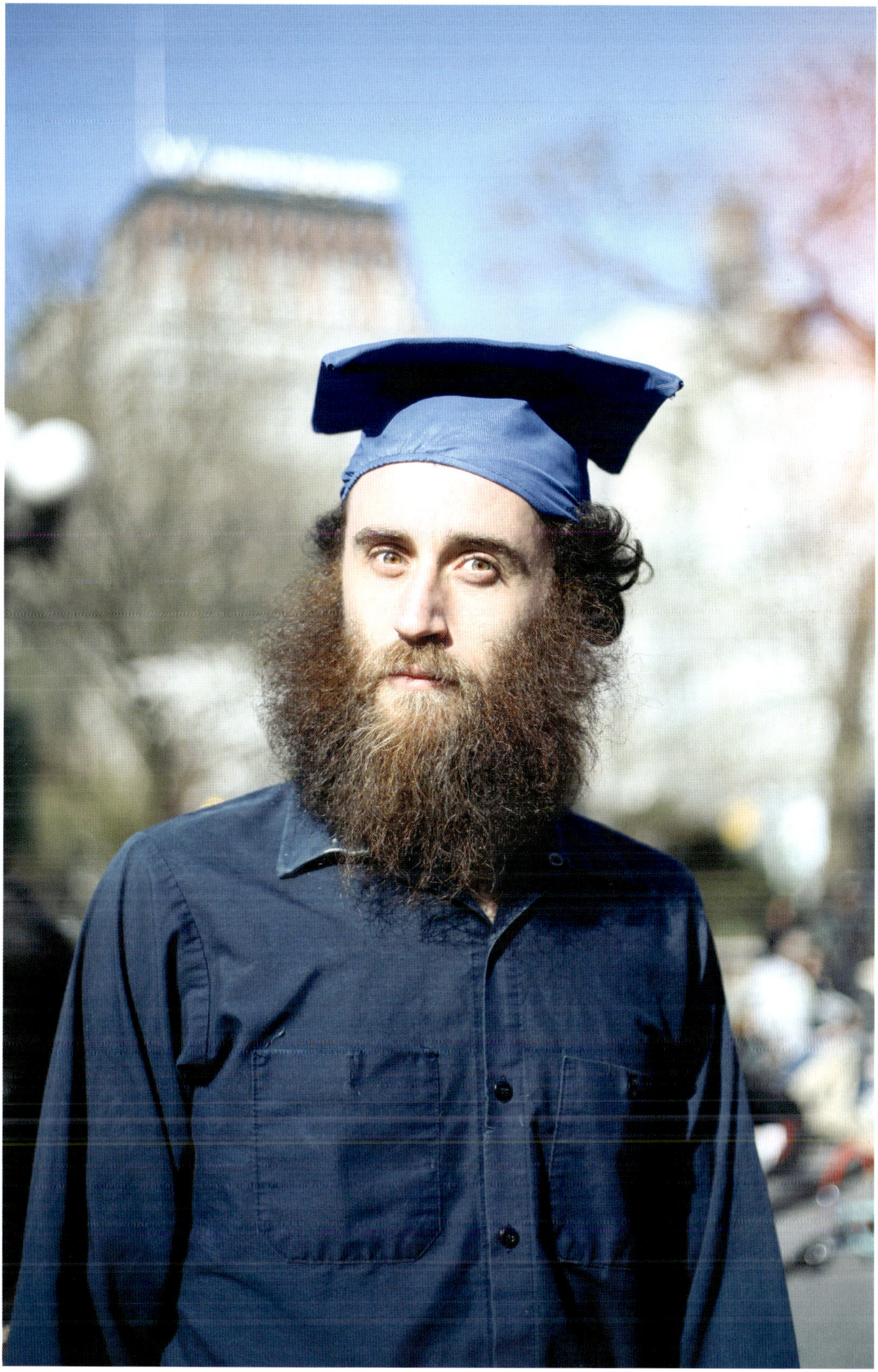

120 • Matthew: Union Square, New York

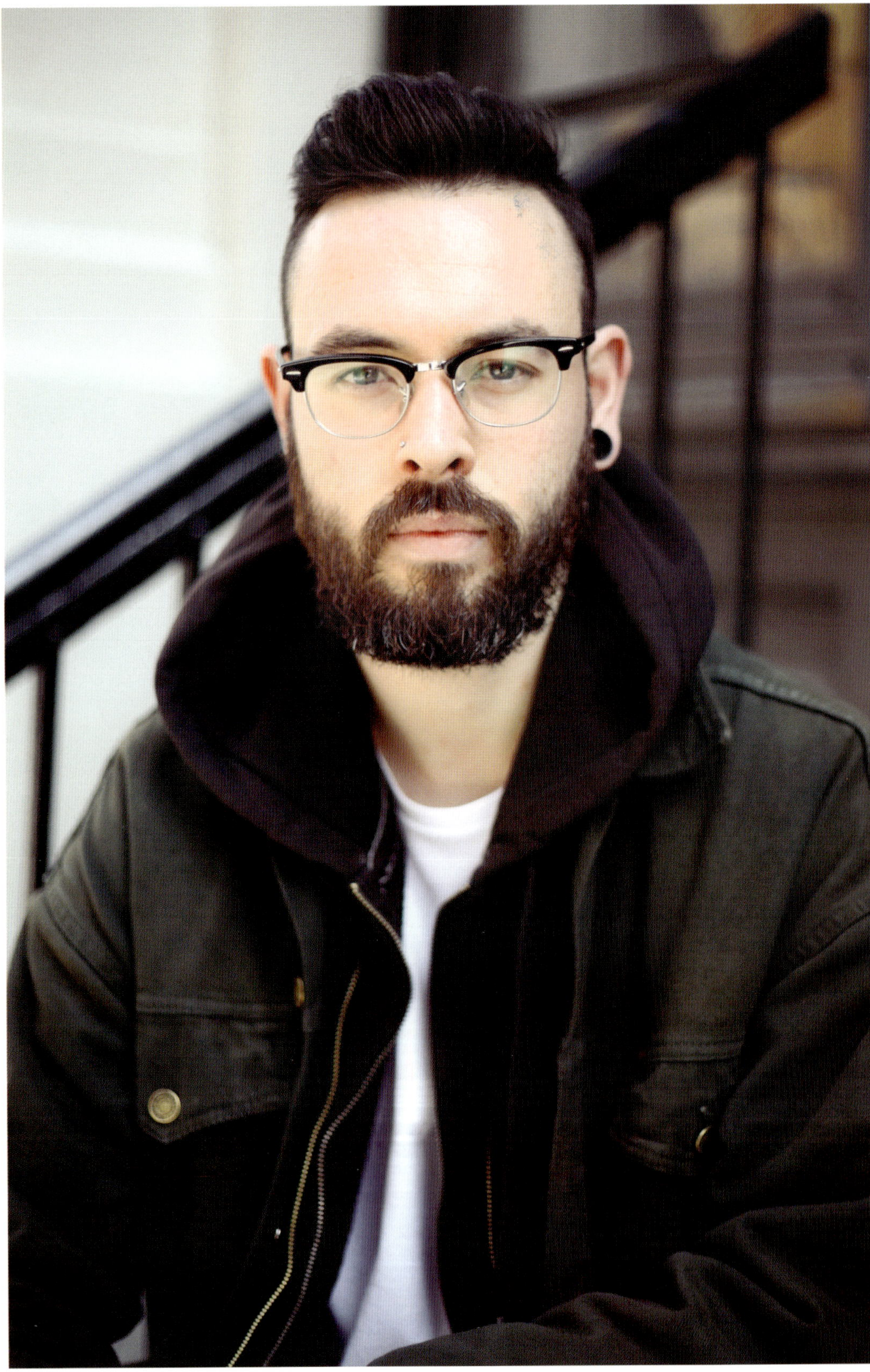

121 • Liam: Mercer Street, New York

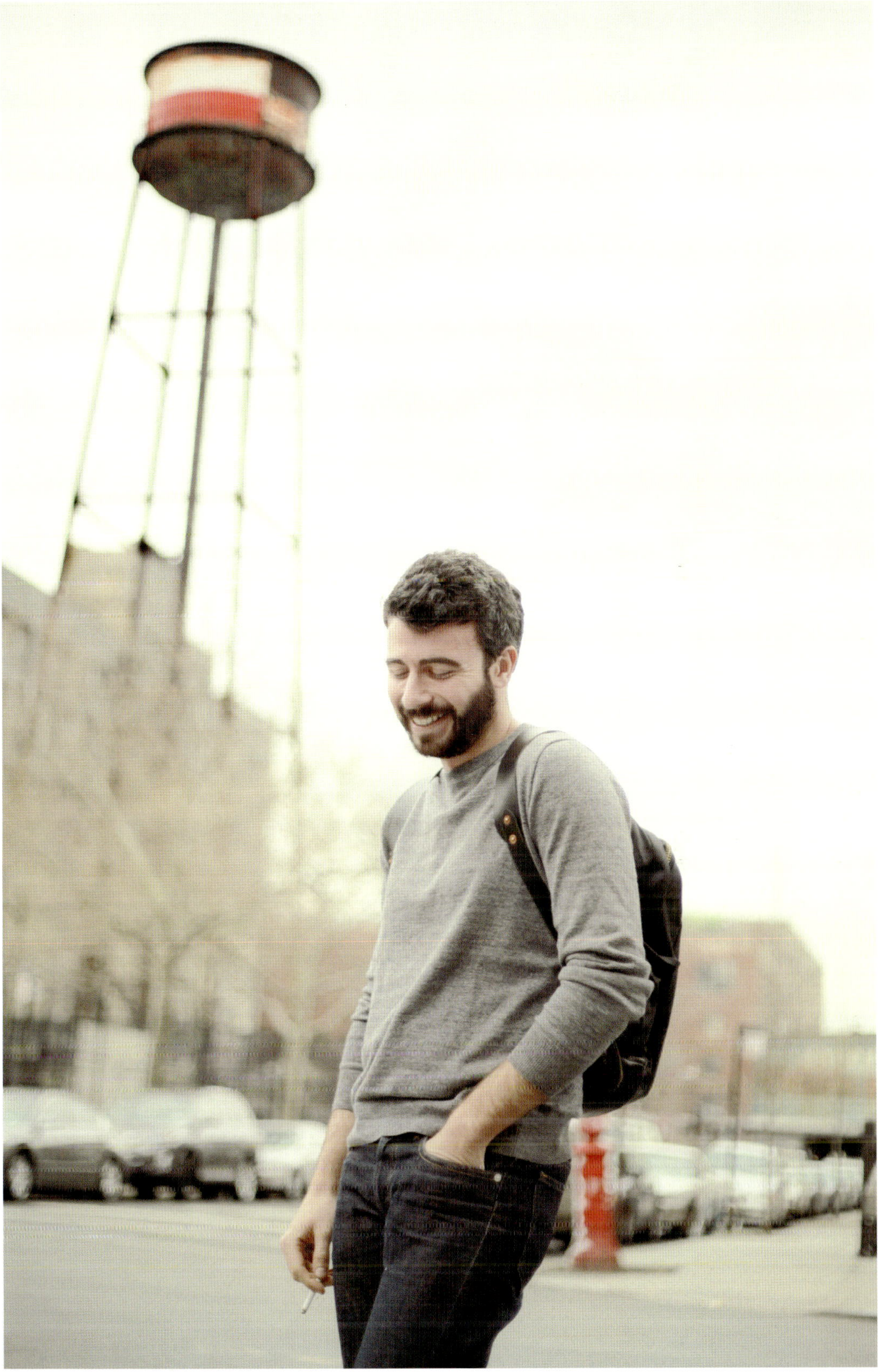

122 • Ernest: Manhattan Avenue, New York

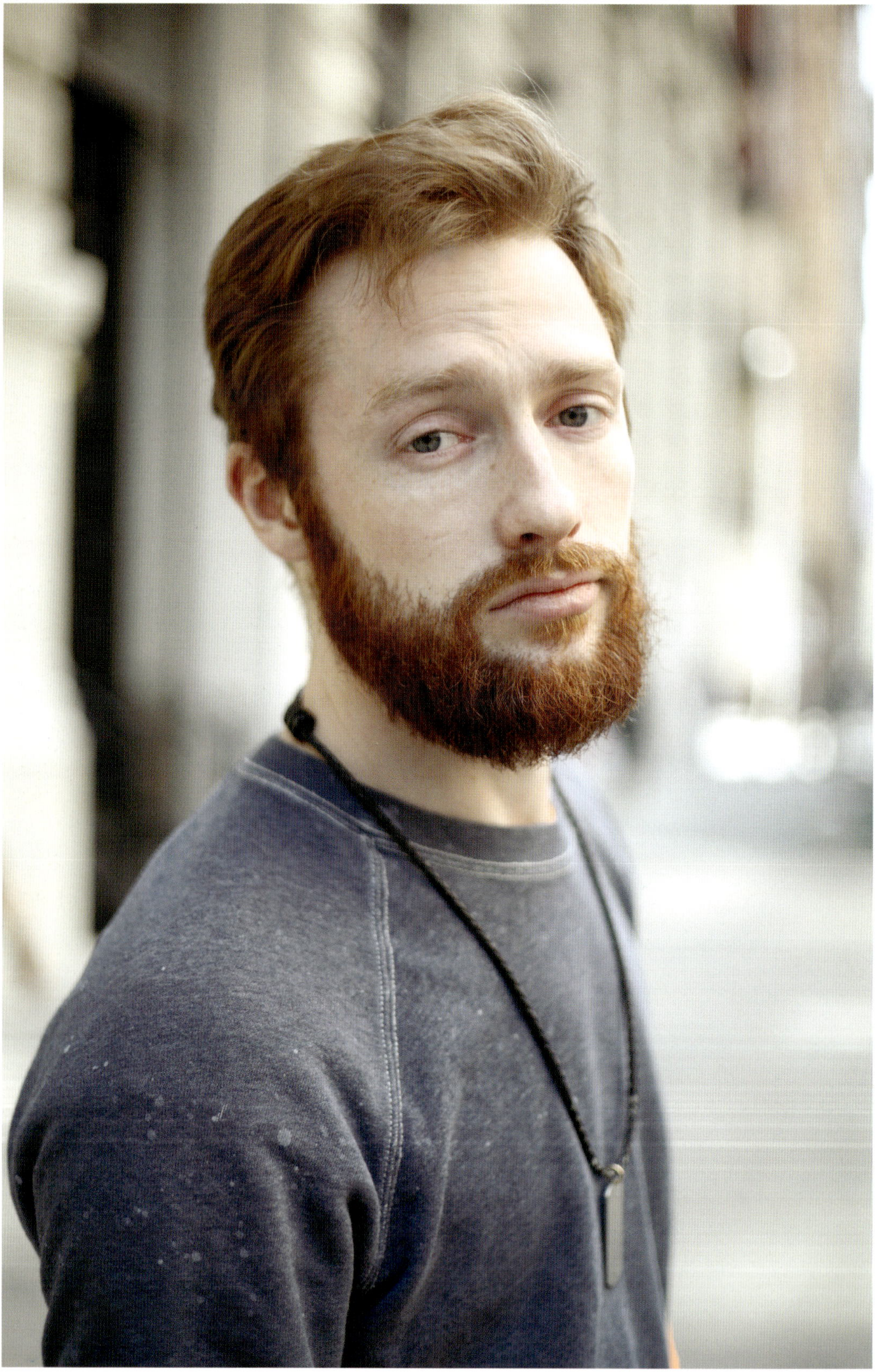

123 • Nick: East 10th Street, New York

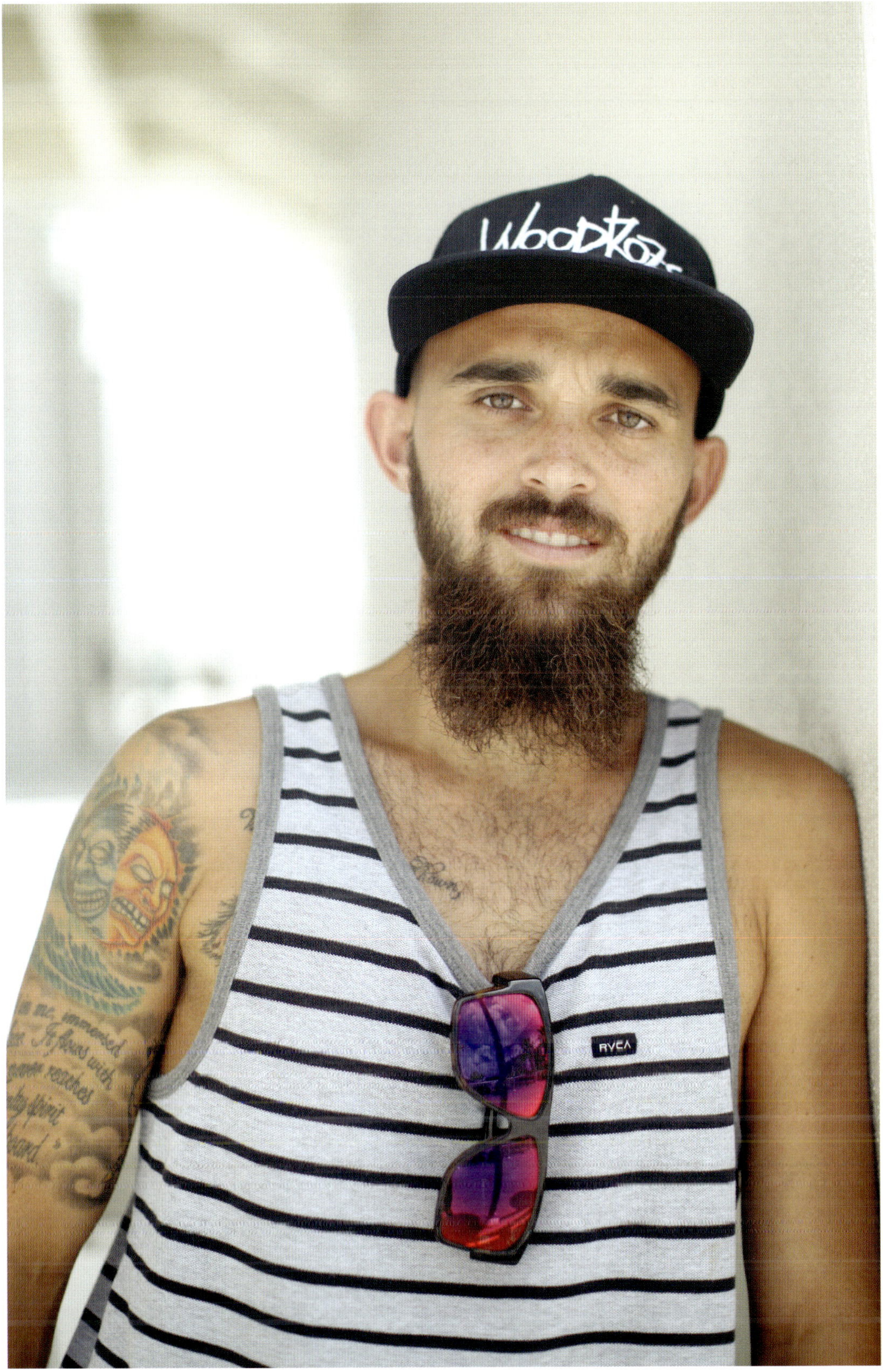

124 • JP: International Boulevard, Orlando

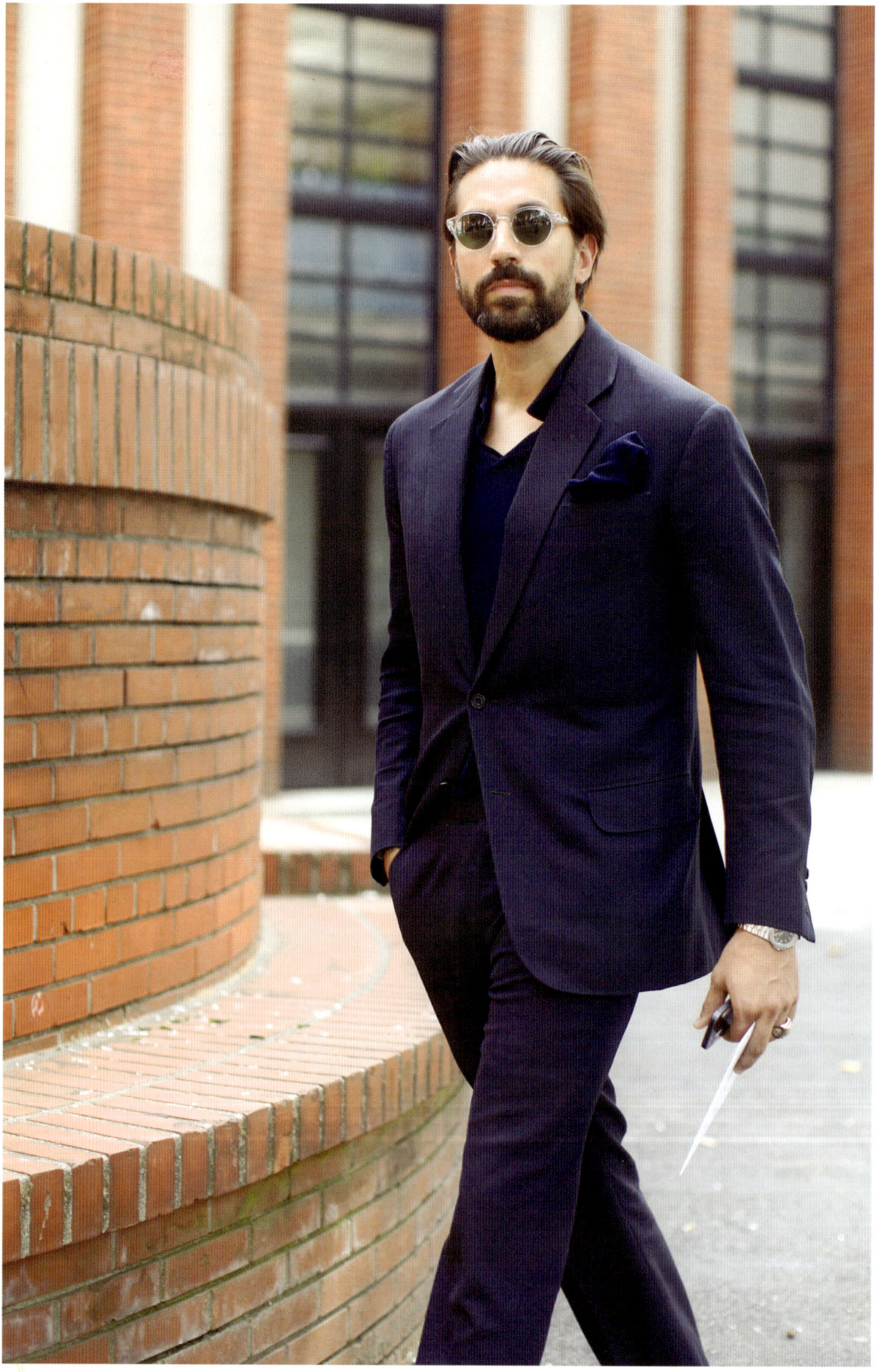

125 • Ben: Porte de Saint Cloud, Paris

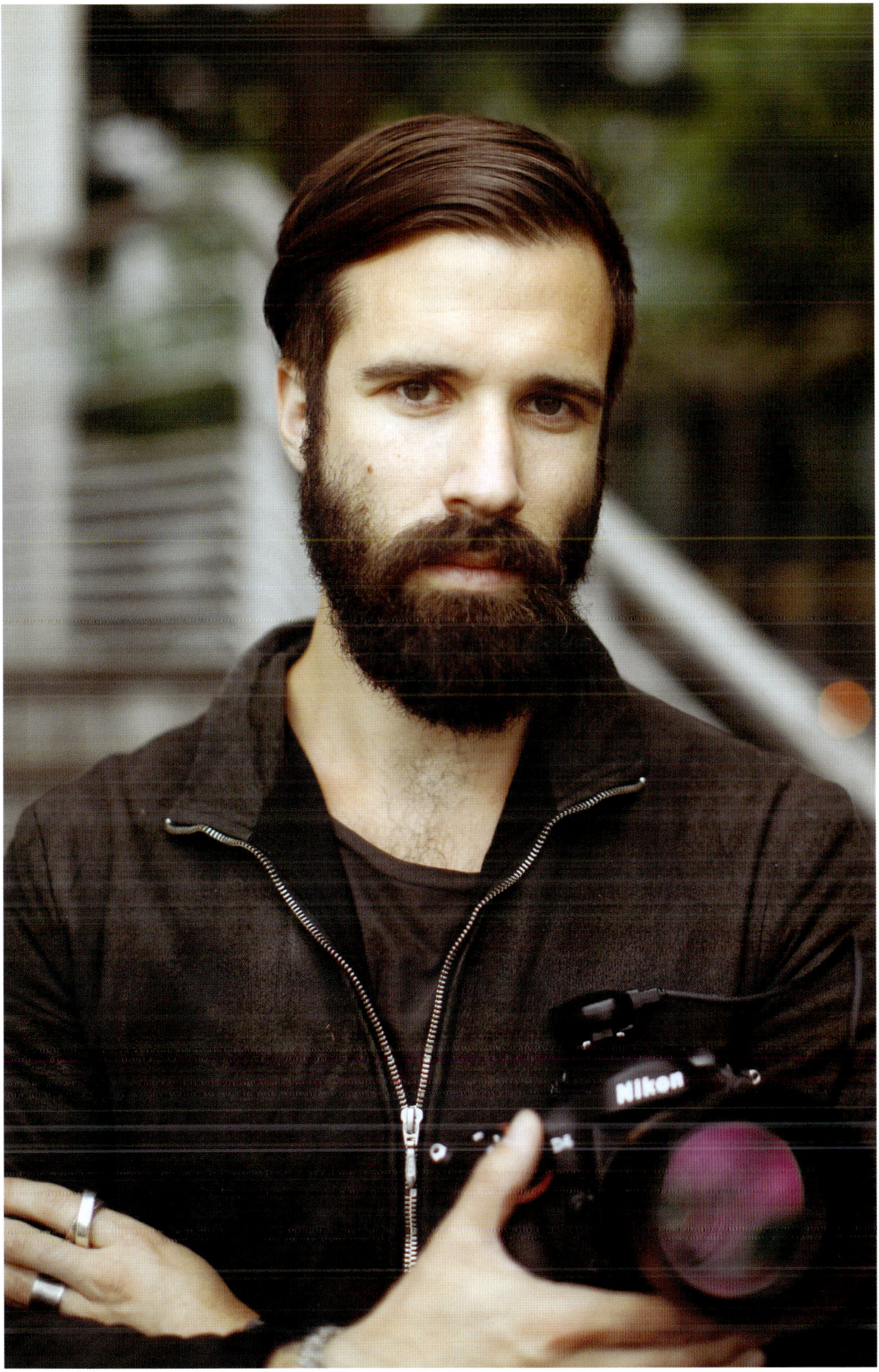

126 • Adam: Quai d'Austerlitz, Paris

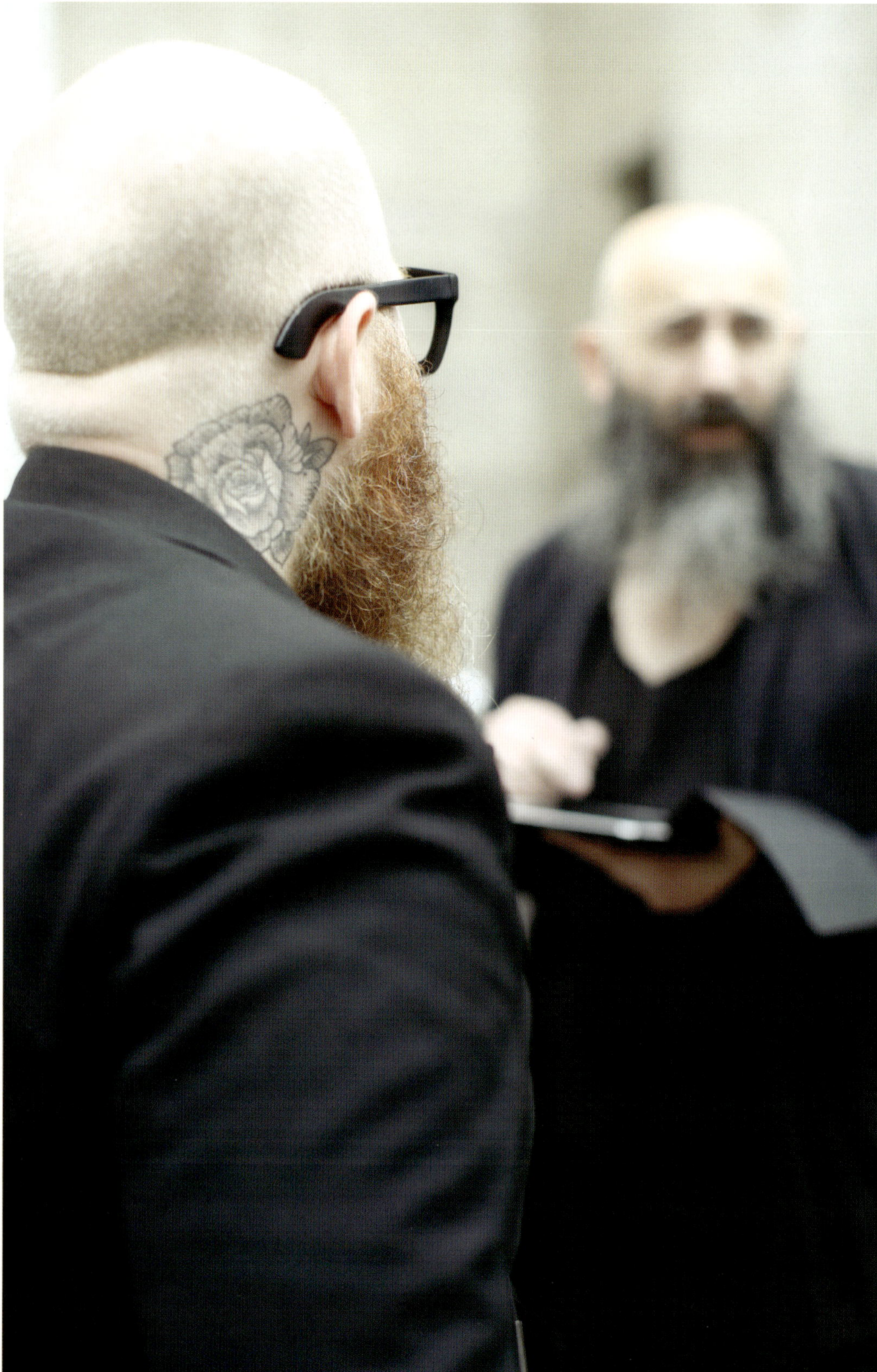

127 • Bruno: Palais de Tokyo, Paris

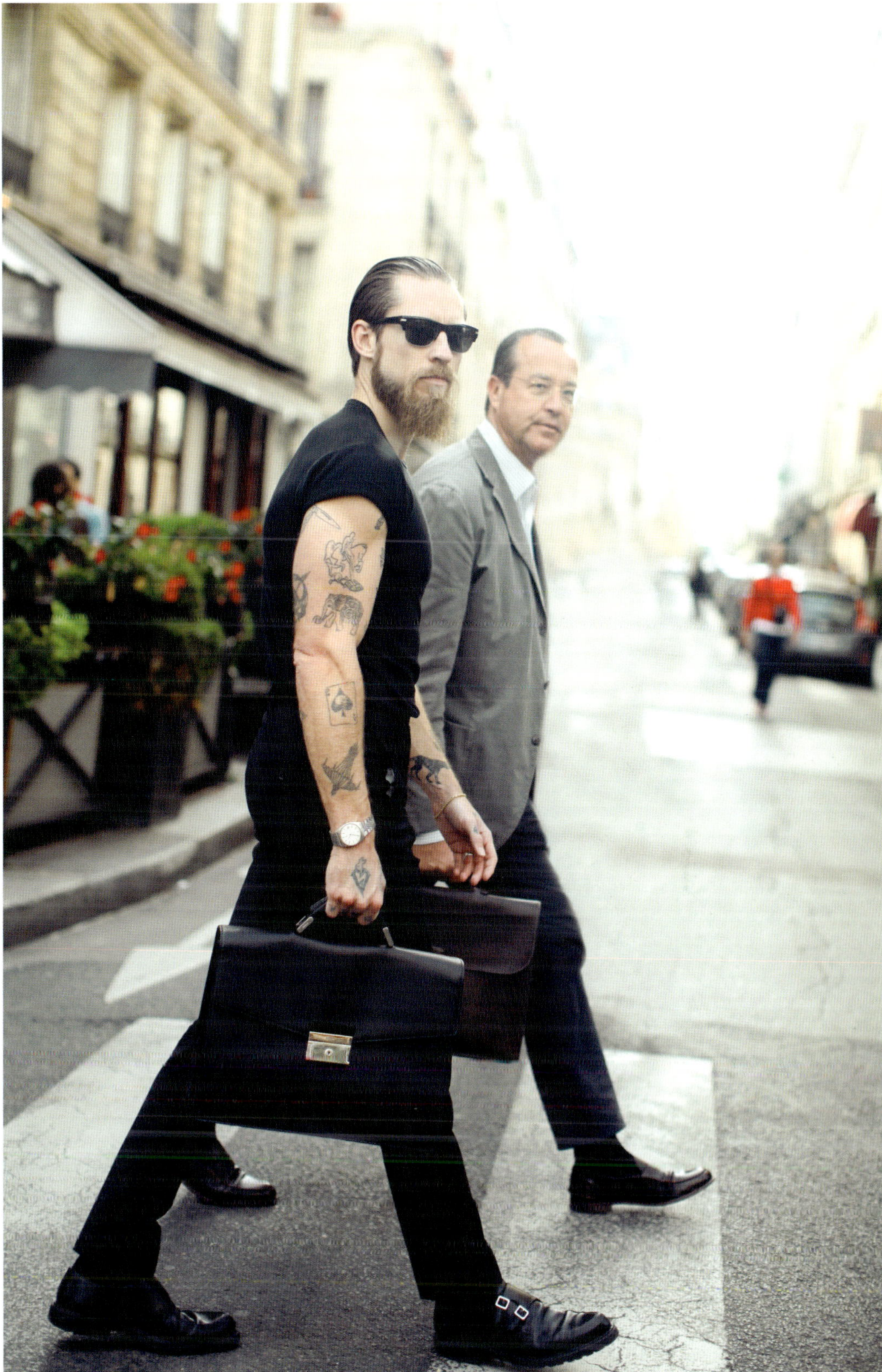

 Justin: Rue Jacob, Paris

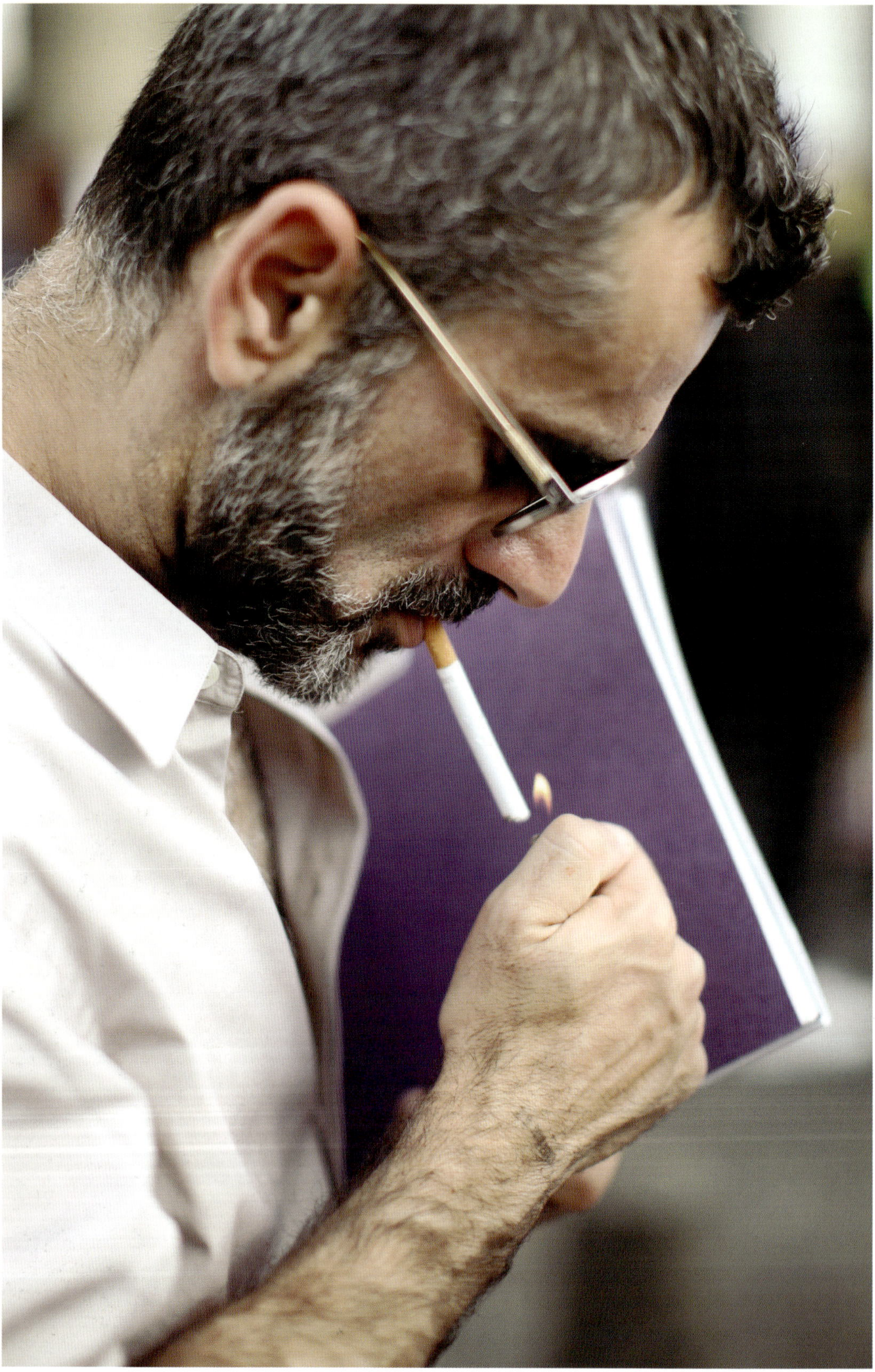

129 • Michael: Palais-Royale, Paris

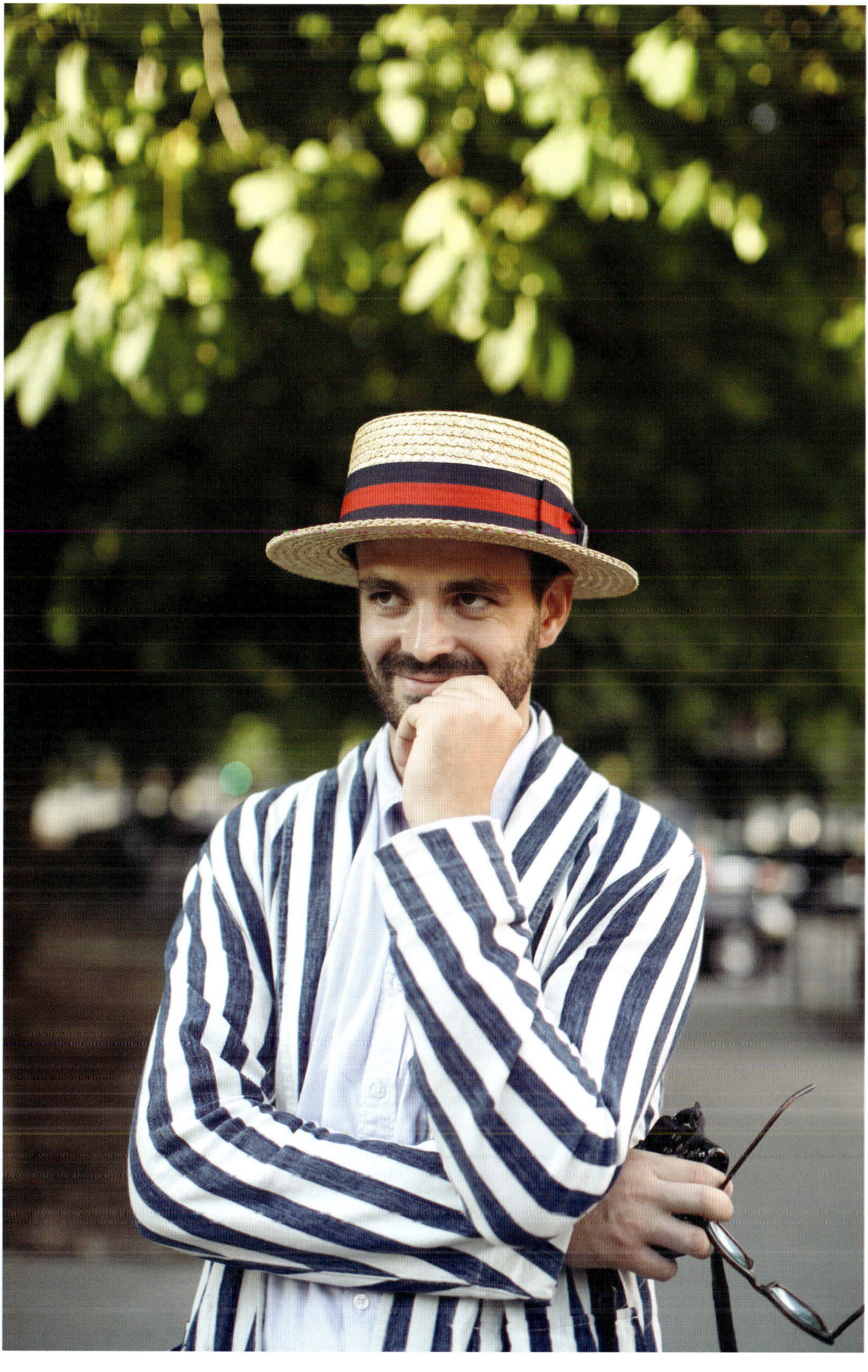

130 • Maxime: Avenue du Général Eisenhower, Paris

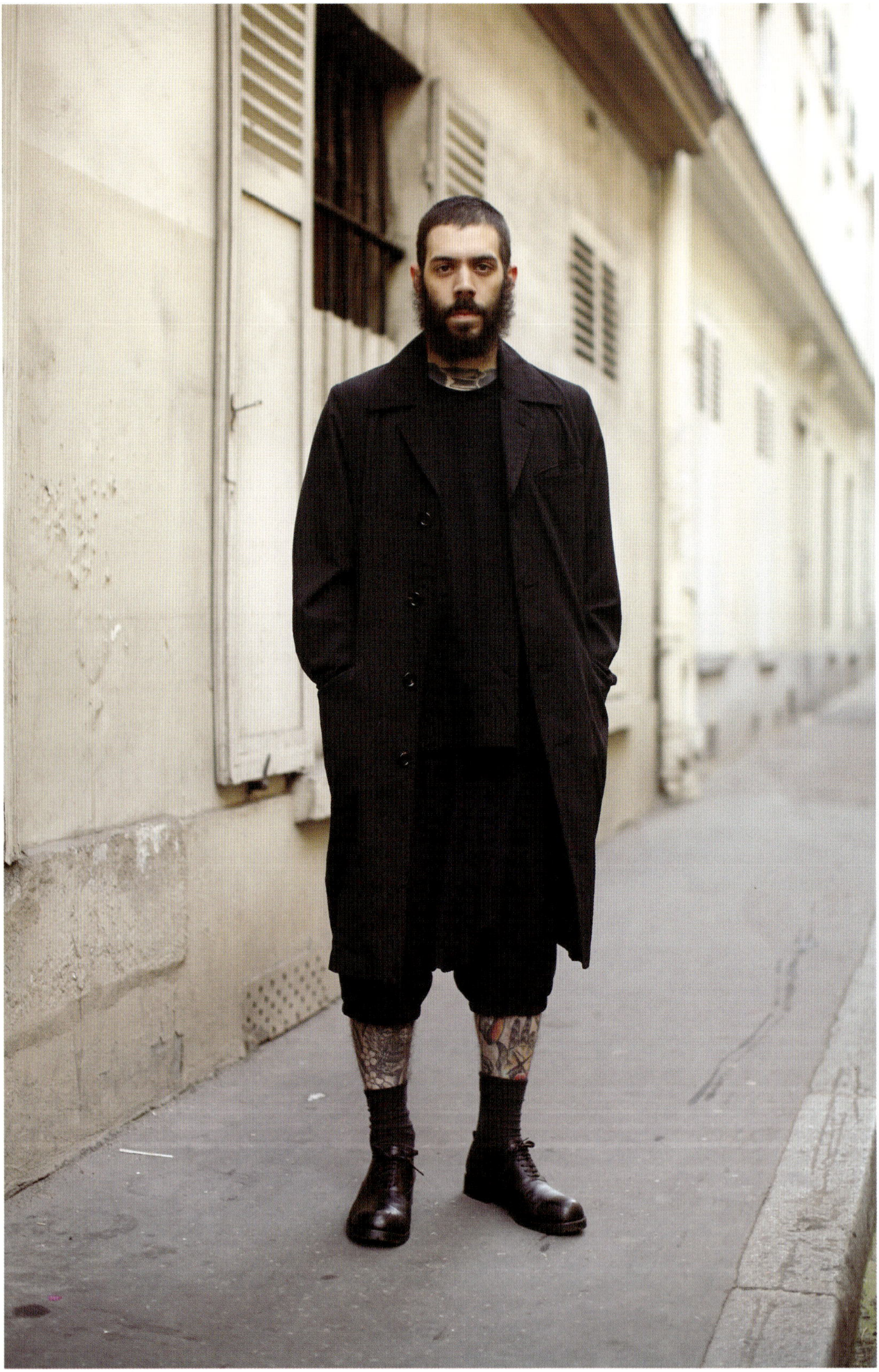

131 • Paride: Rue de Martyrs, Paris

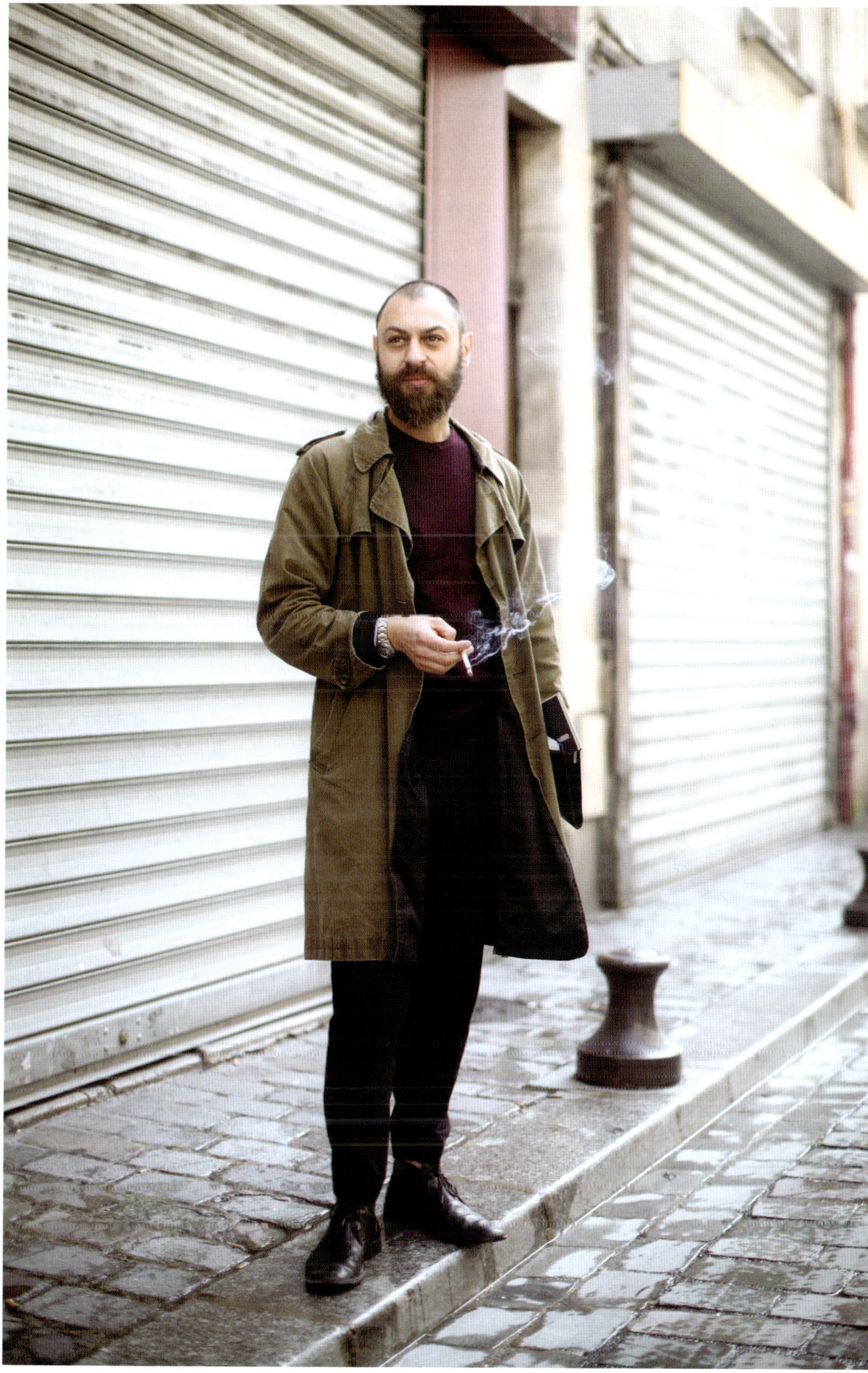

132 • Phillipe: Rue de la Roquette, Paris

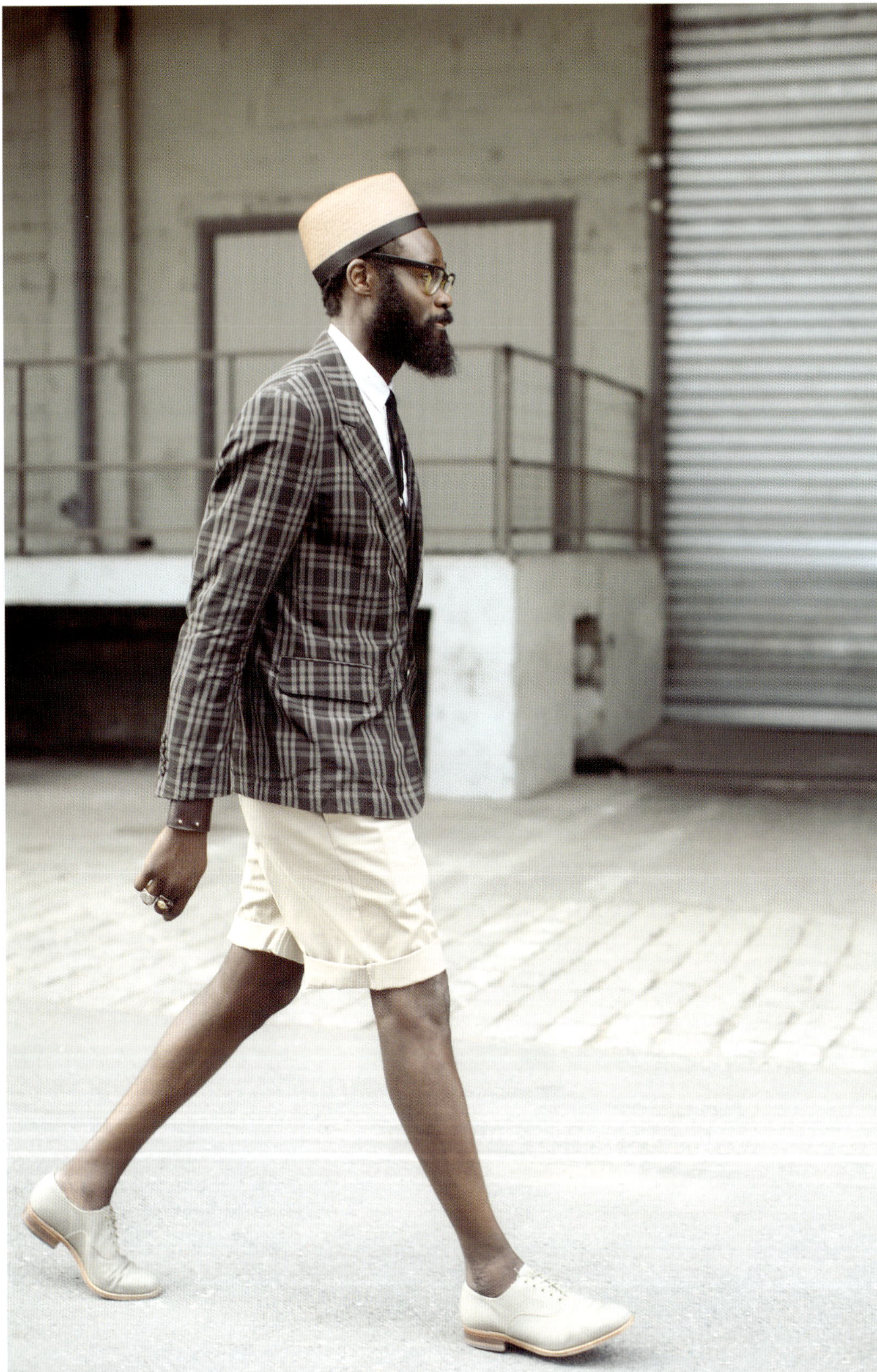

133 • Shaka: Quai d'Austerlitz, Paris

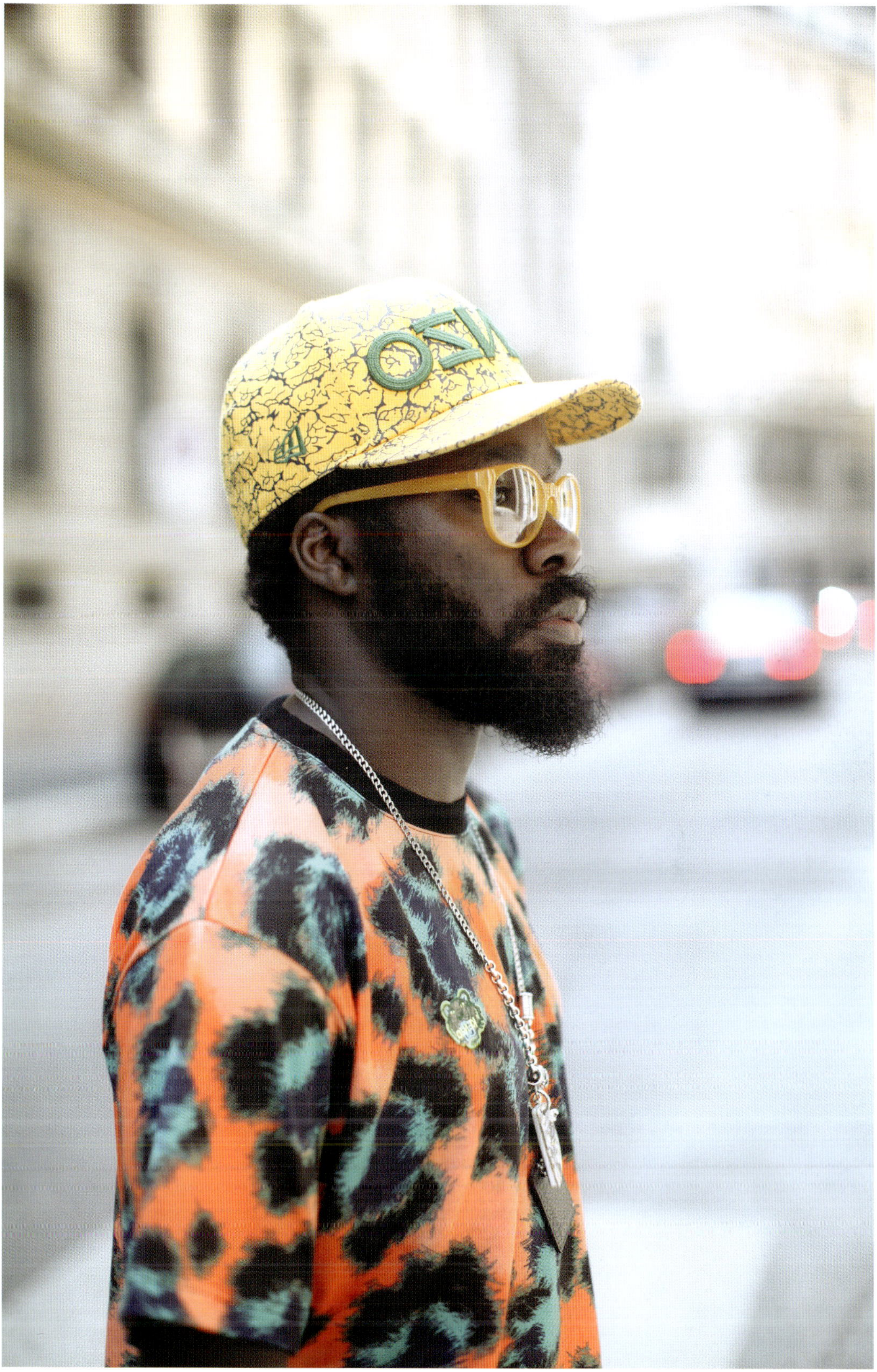

134 • Nzo: Piazza Belgioioso, Milan

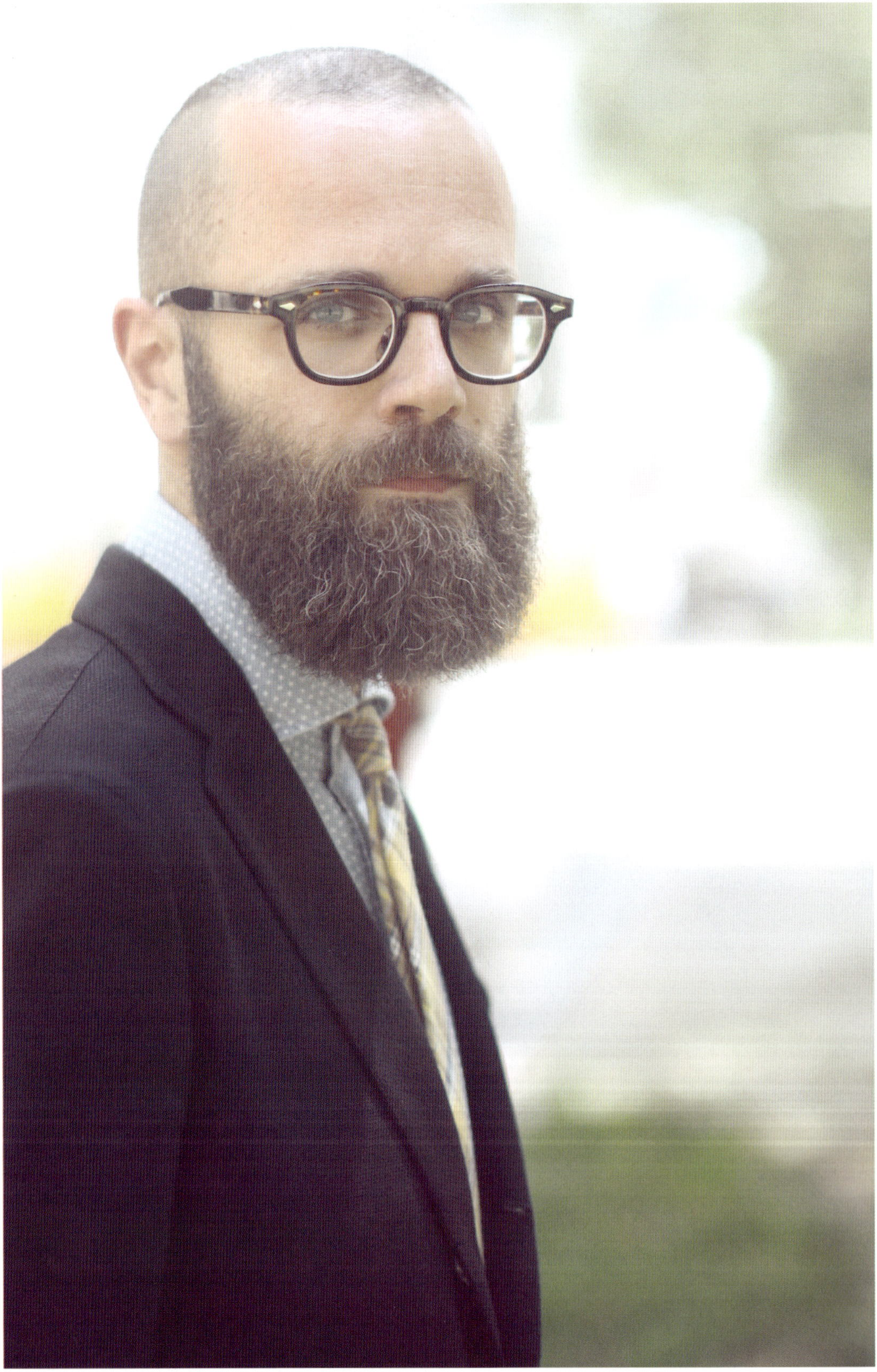

135 • Angelo: Via Generale Mac Mahon, Milan

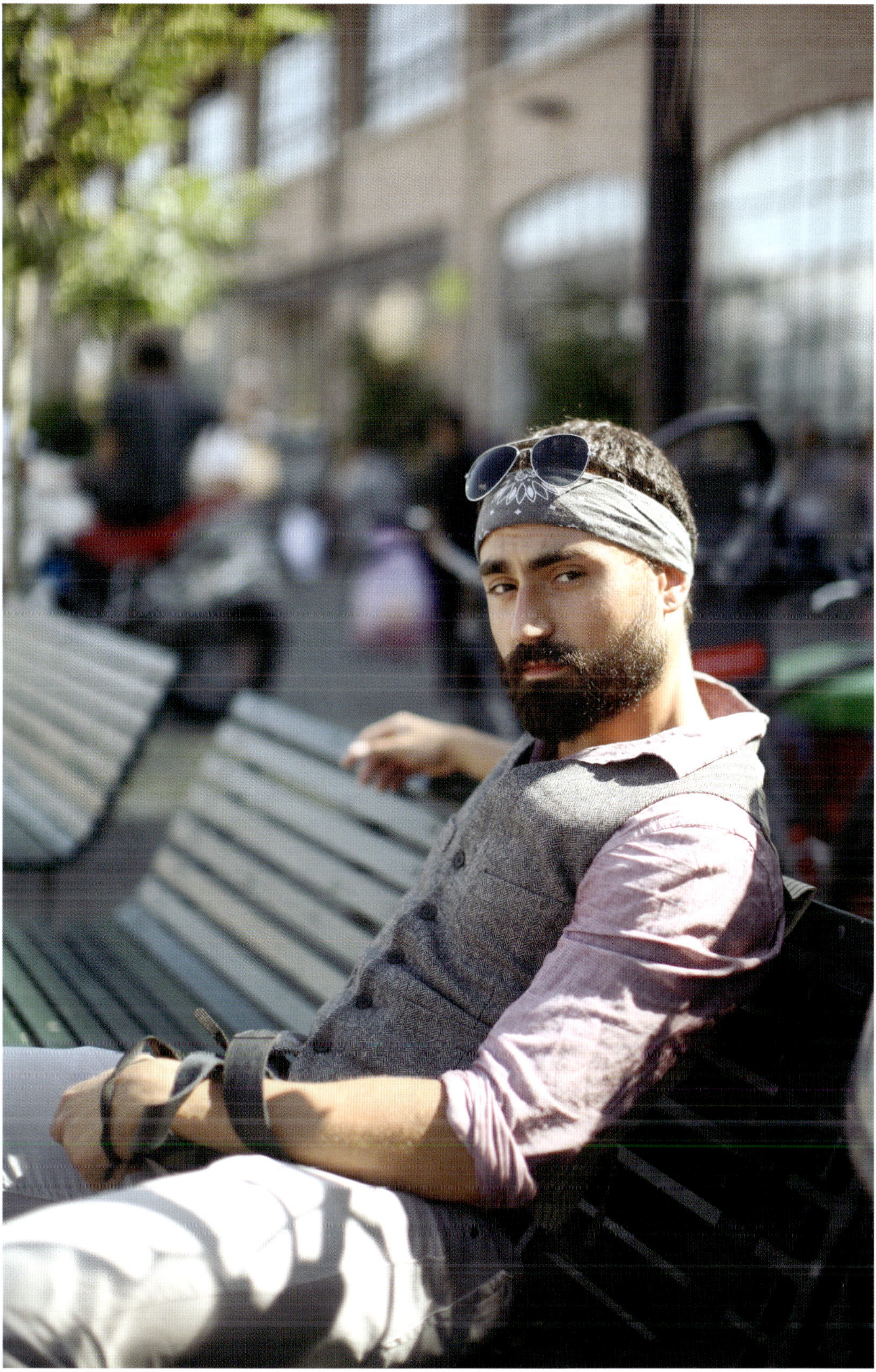

136 • Travis: Via Tortona, Milan

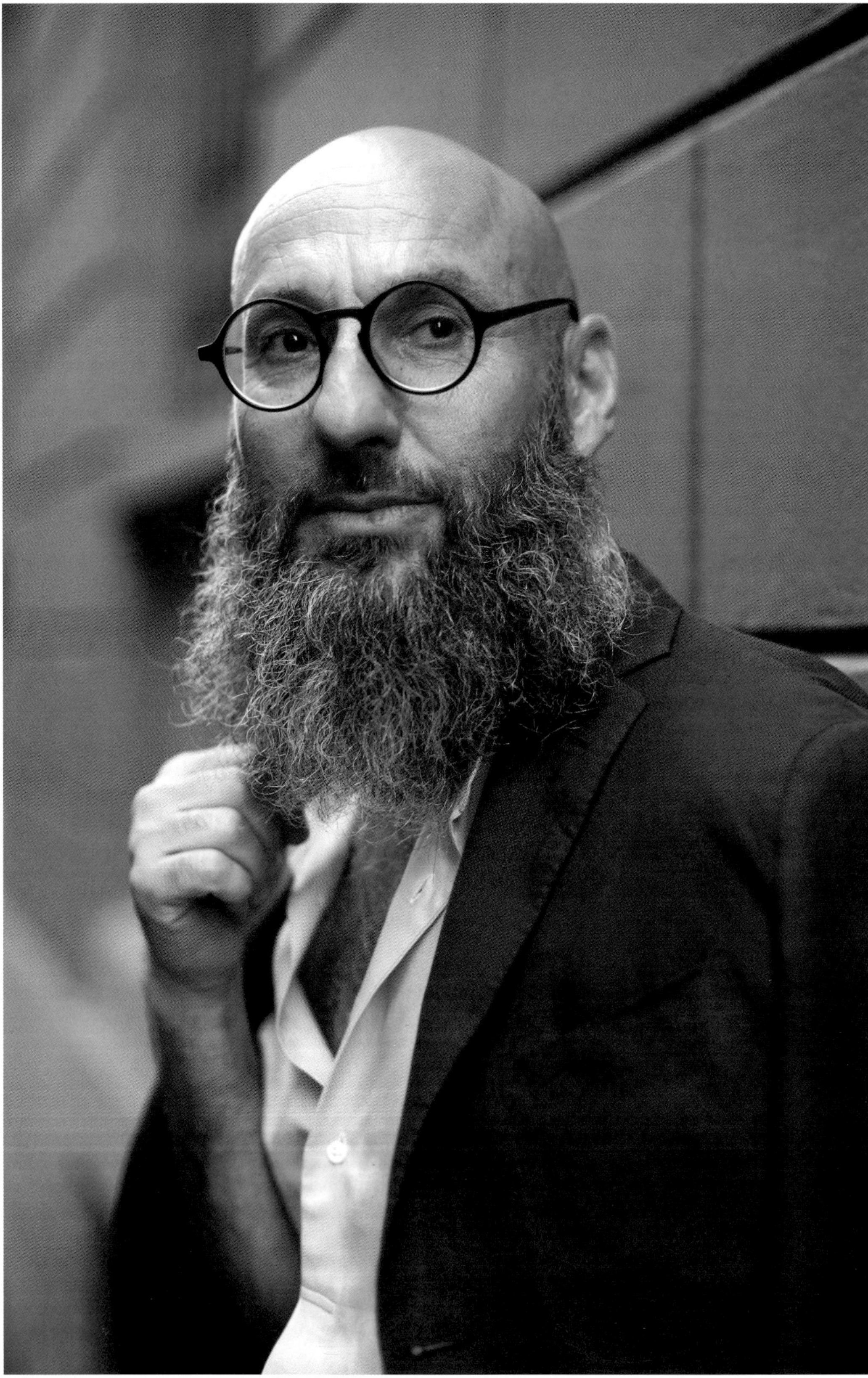

137 • Daniel: Via Armorari, Milan

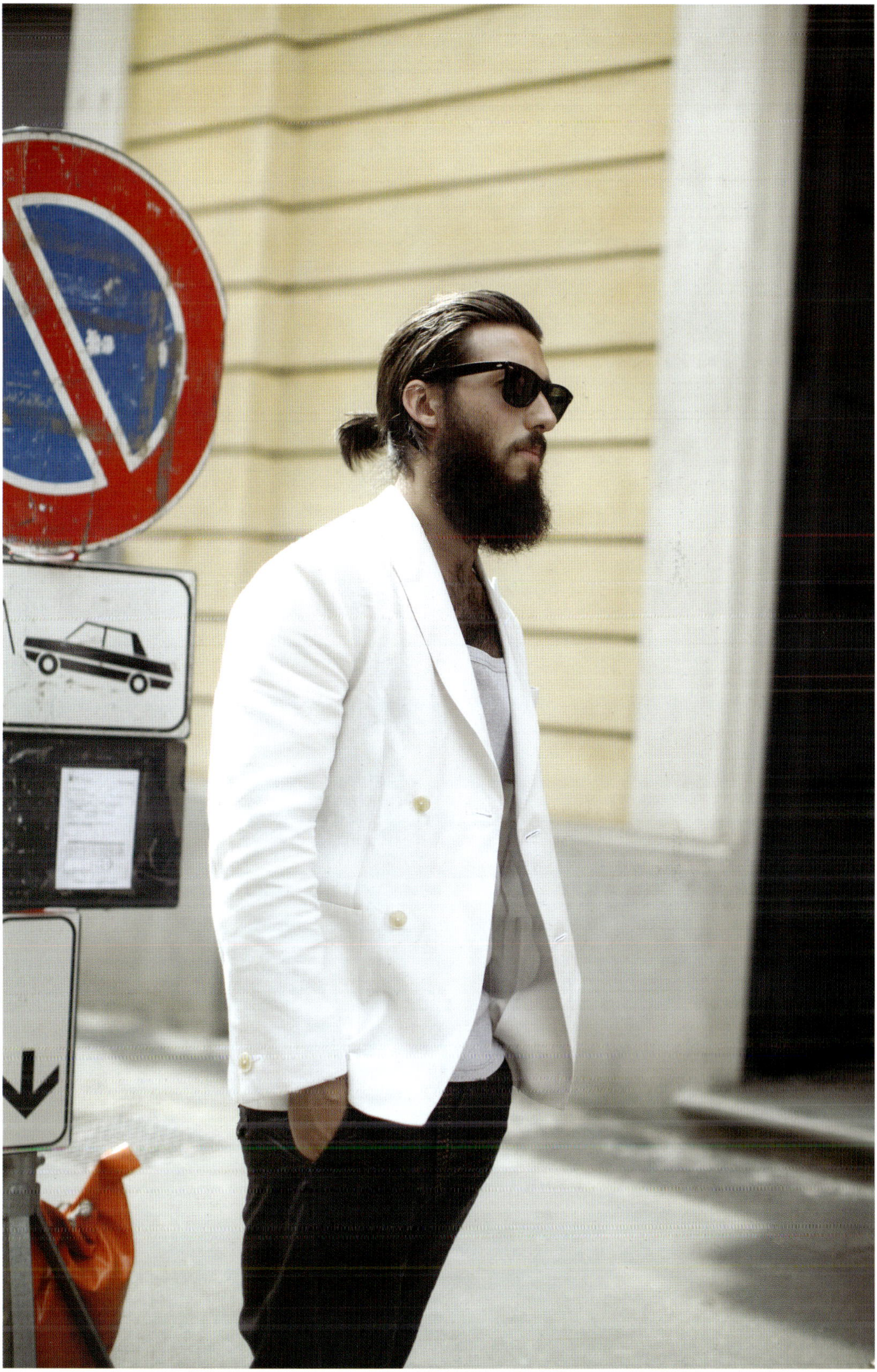

138 • Fabio: Via Fogazzaro, Milan

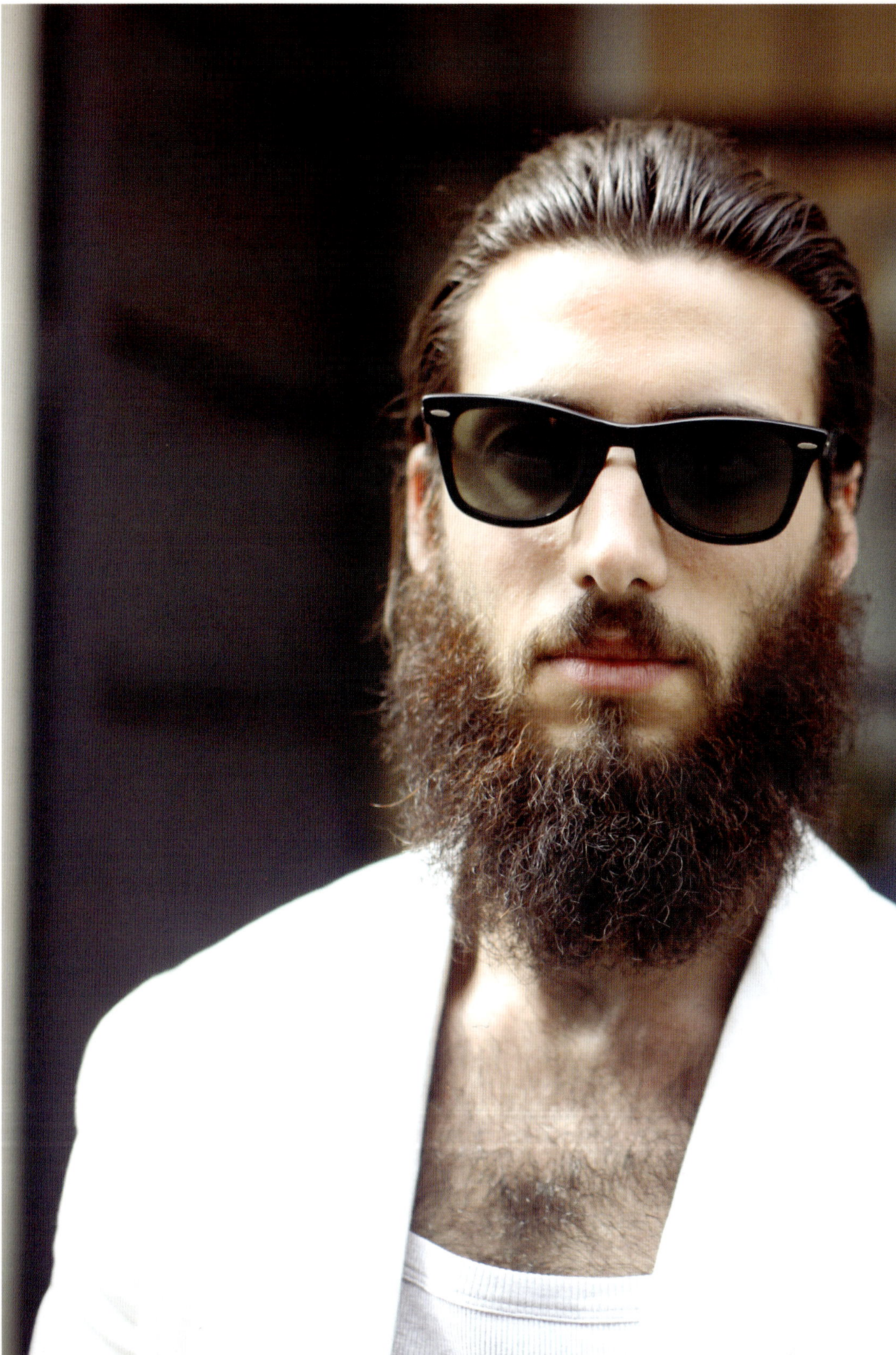

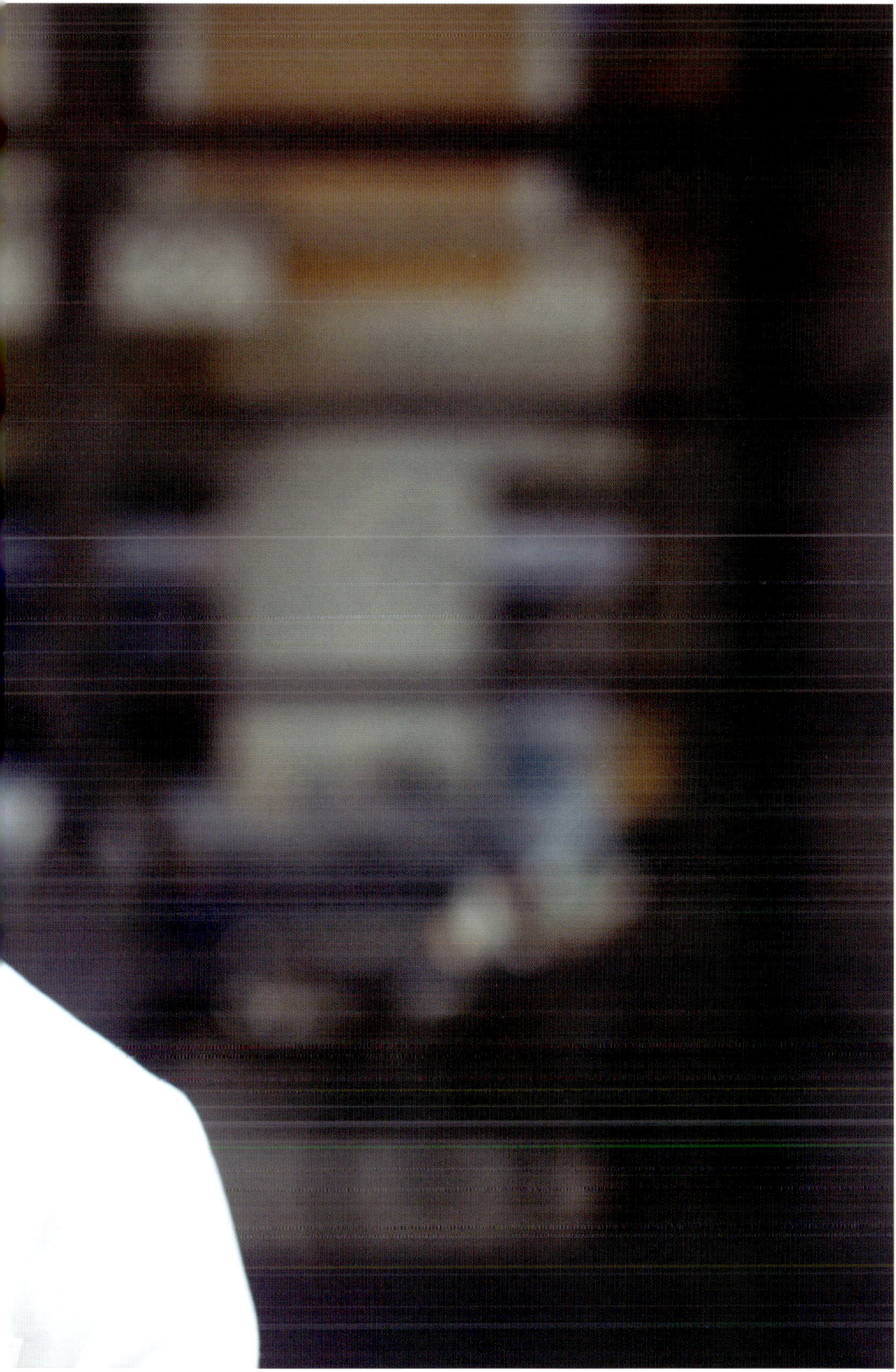

Fabio: Via Fogazzaro, Milan

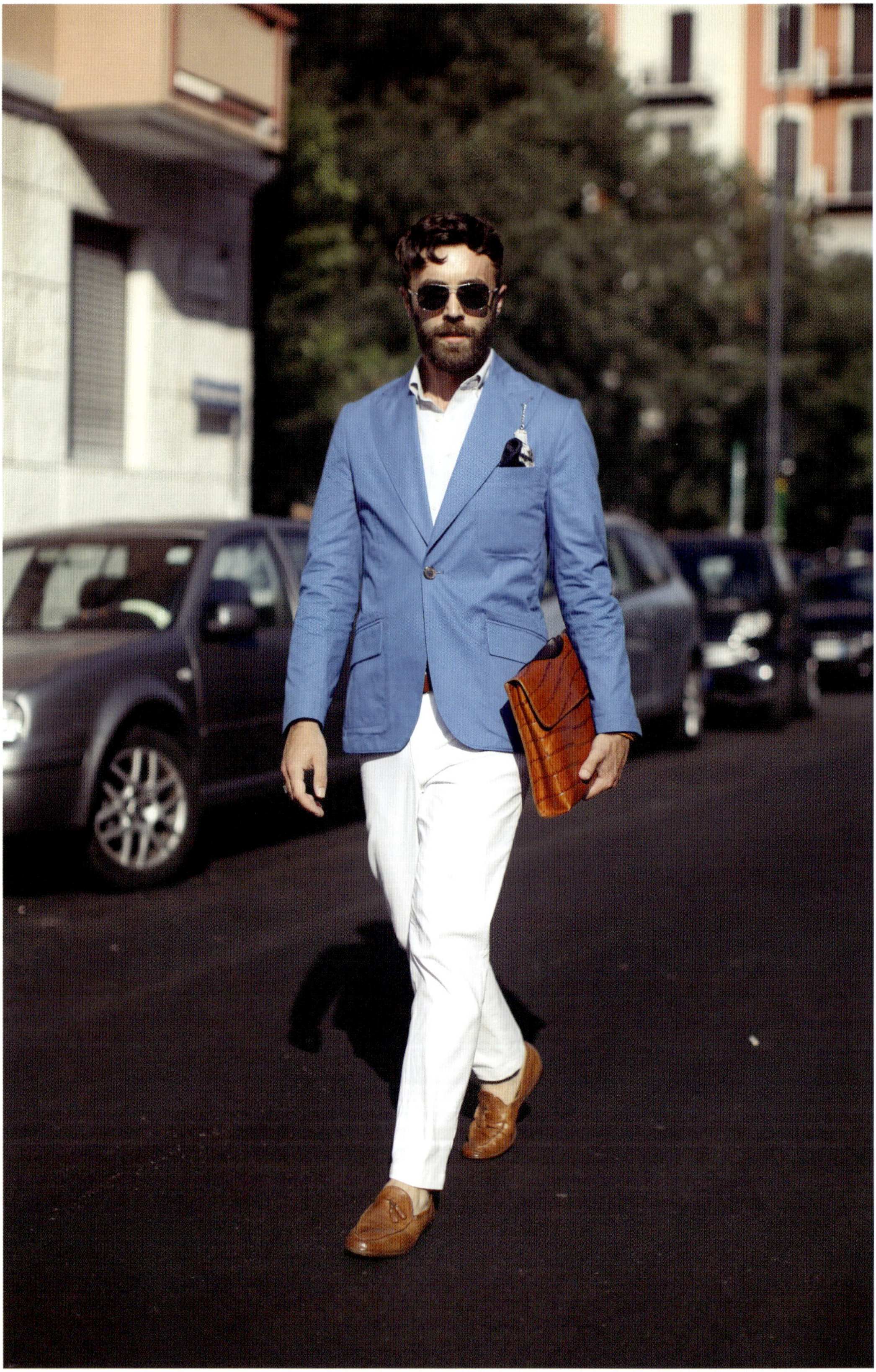

139 • Daniel: Via Fogazzaro, Milan

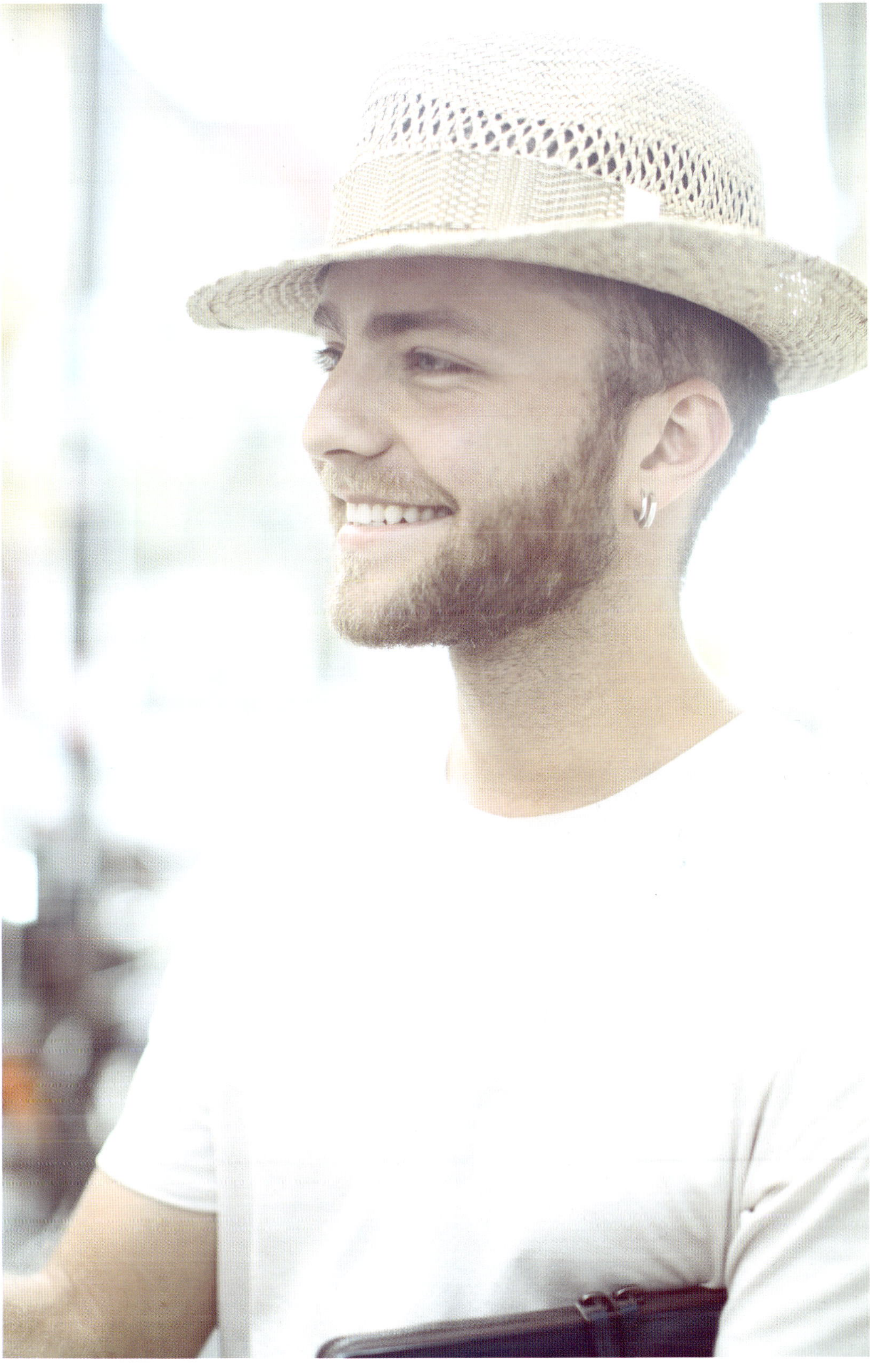

140 • Elissey: Corso Venezia, Milan

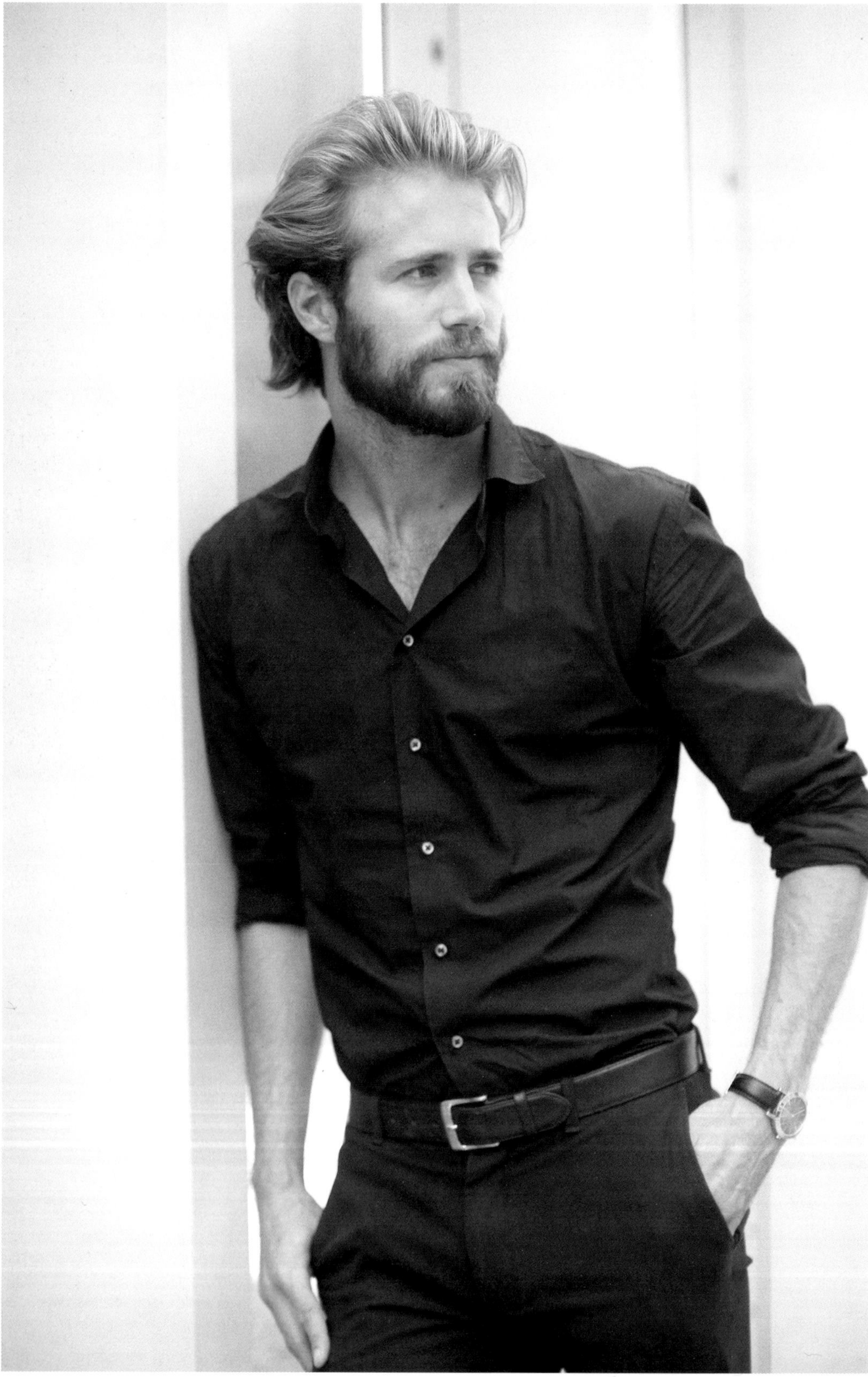

141 • Tom: Via Spartaco, Milan

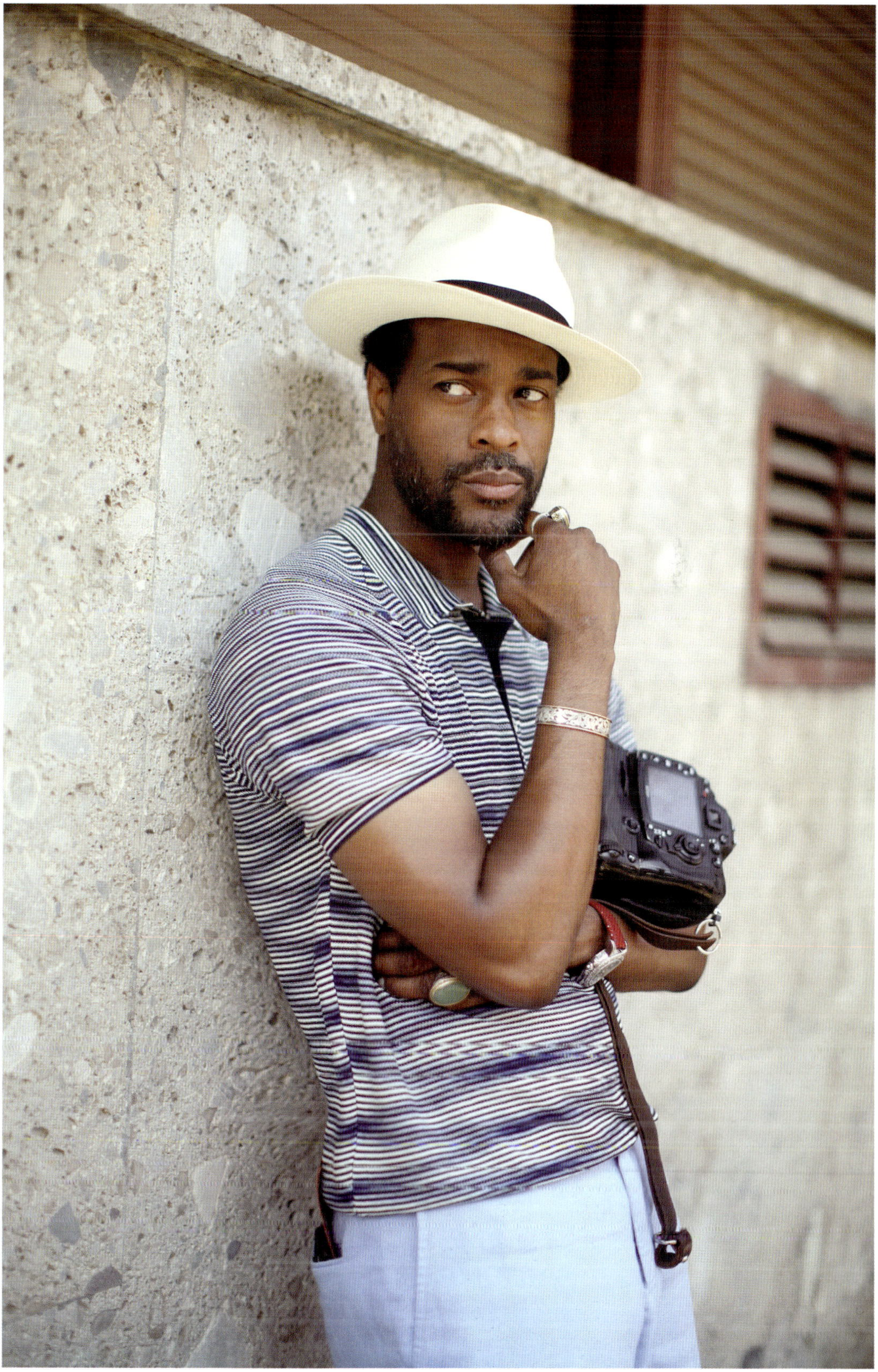

 Guerre: Via Emilio Morosini, Milan

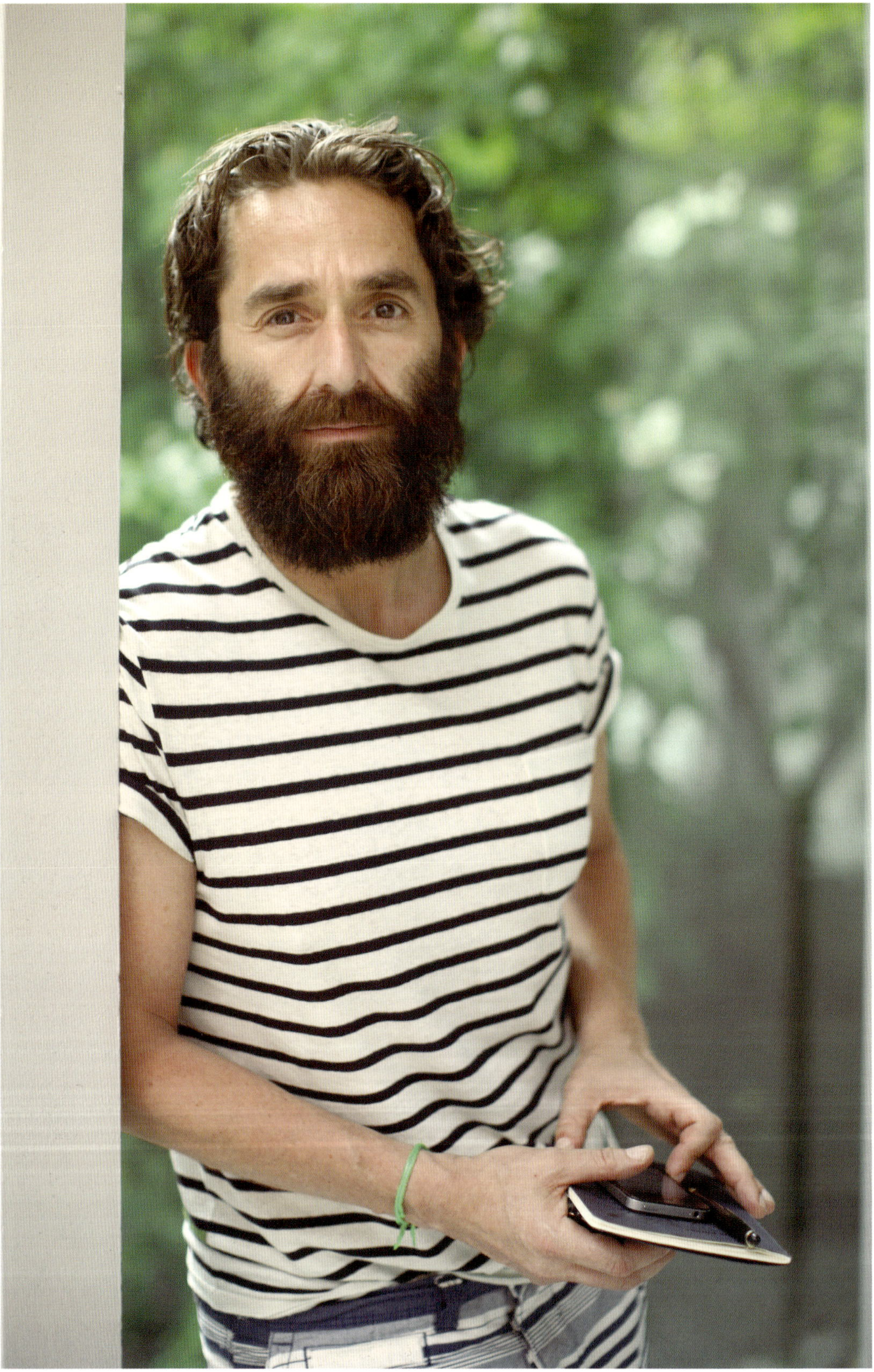

143 • Yilmaz: Via Pier Lombardo, Milan

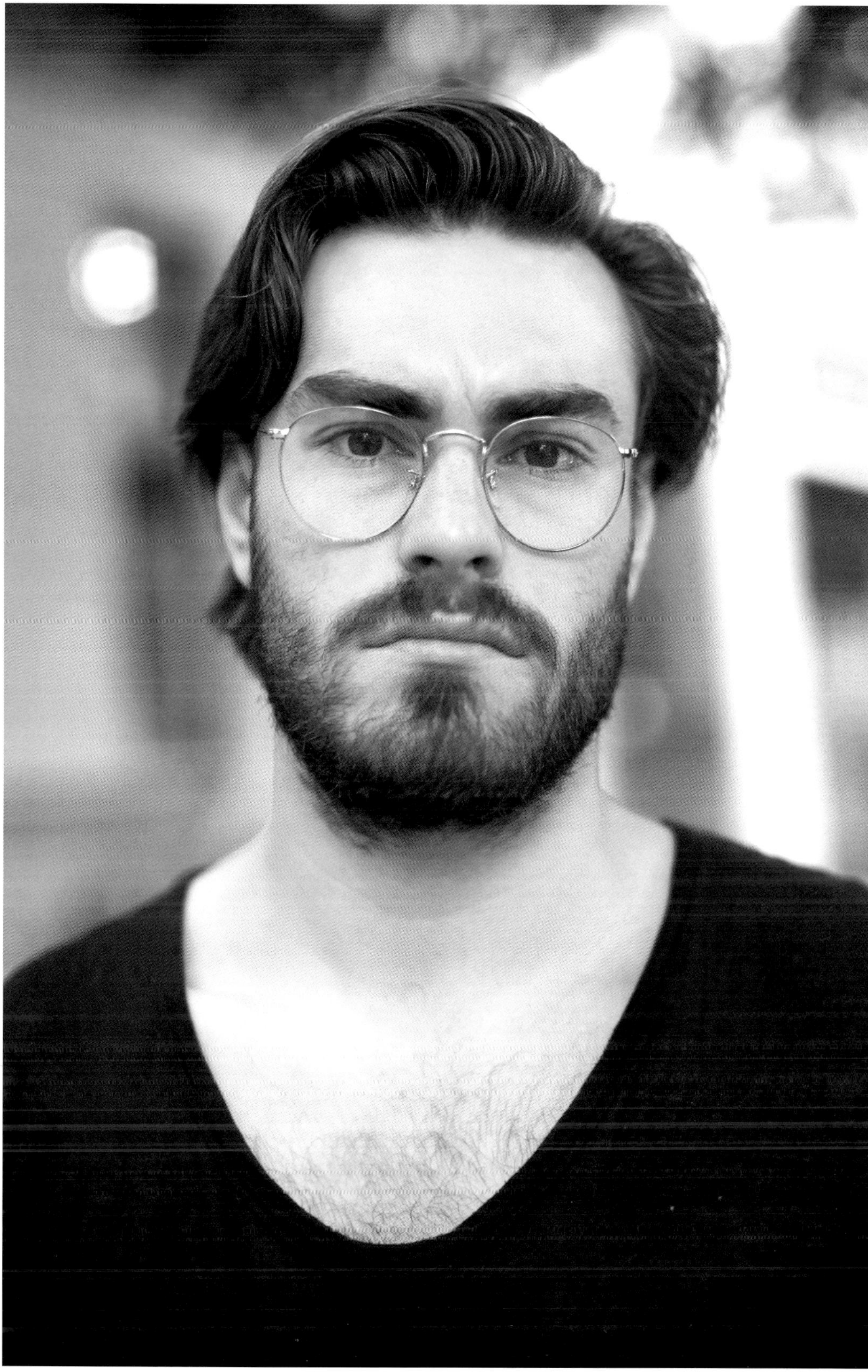

144 • Reidar: Gartenstraße, Berlin

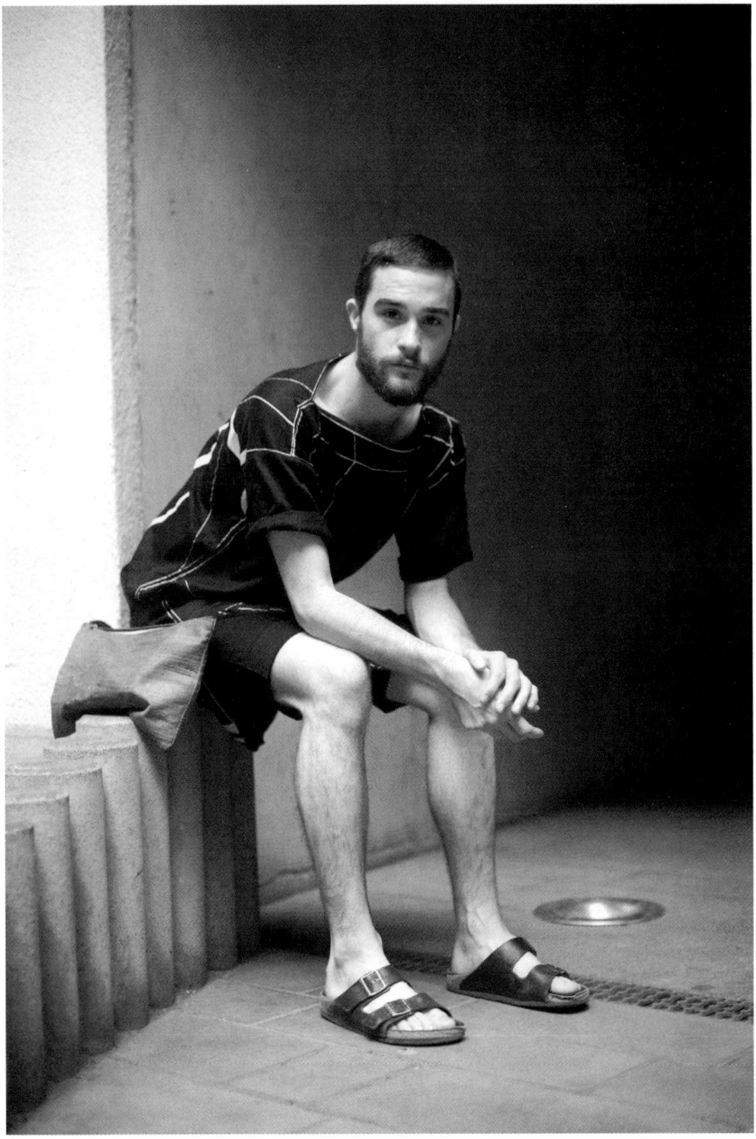

A beard for me means something to play with my look, but its not a statement. I use my wardrobe to express a mood and I can do it with a beard too. The beard makes men look more more appealing. I started to grow my beard since hair could grow from my face. First I did it to look more manly and now I don't see going back! Last winter, I shaved my hair to 1mm and had the longest beard. The biggest compliment for me is when people think I am Israeli or Spanish.

As women are becoming more and more powerful, the traditional 'strong gender' loses more of its role...the last thing society can't take is the need of a beard. There are studies which show that men in higher position get taken more seriously with a beard than without.

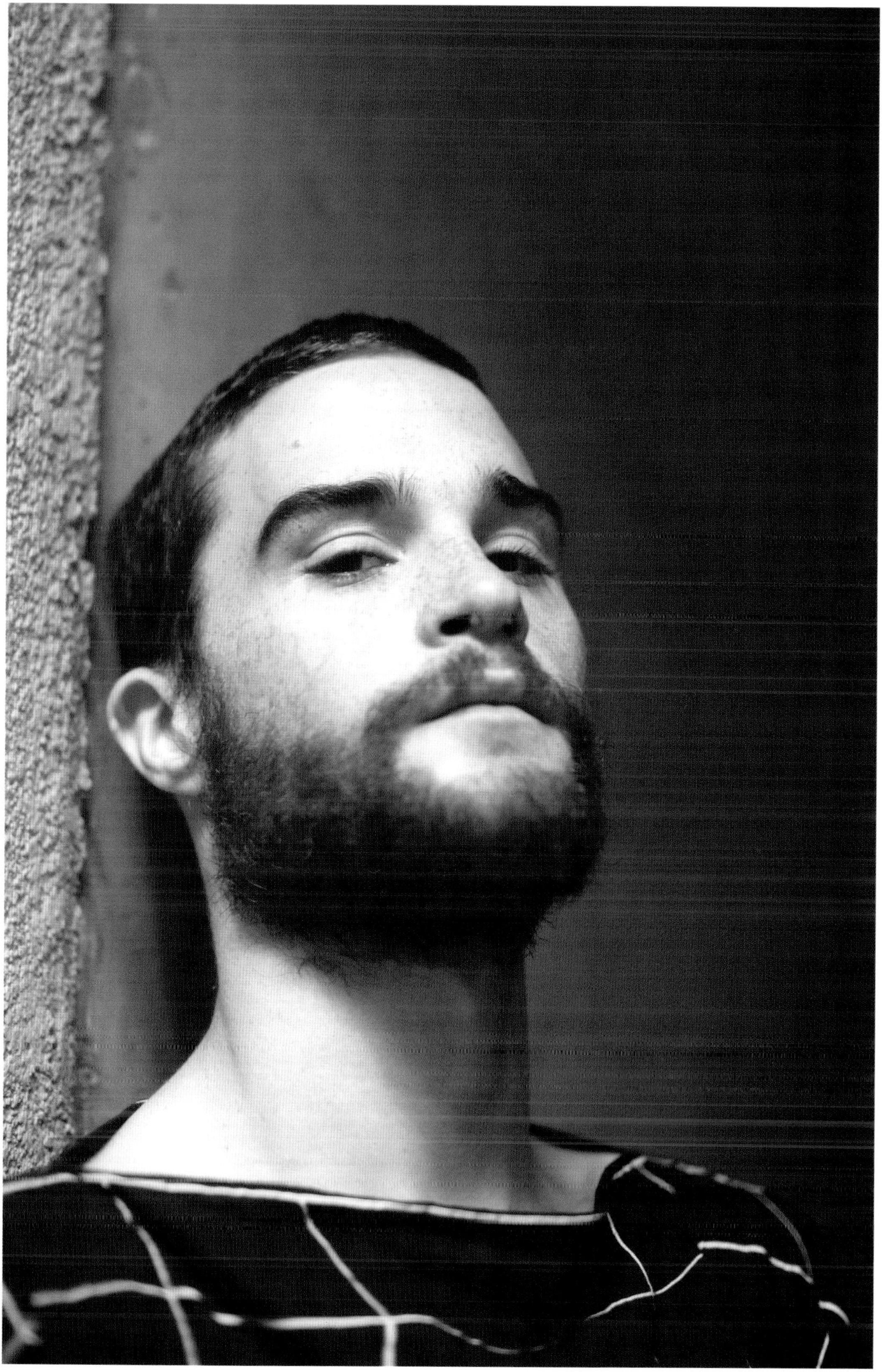

145 • Aleksander: Münzstraße, Berlin

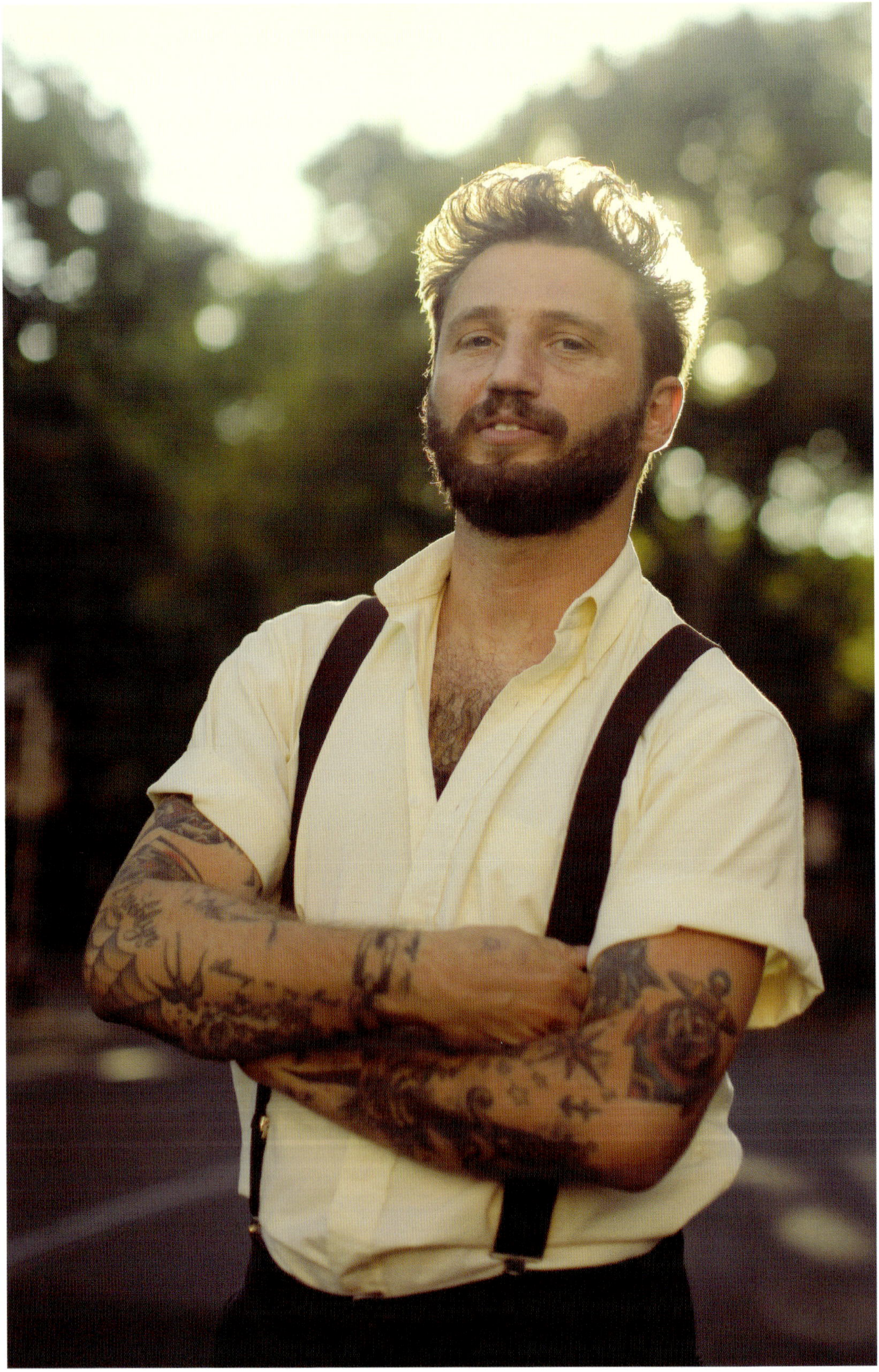

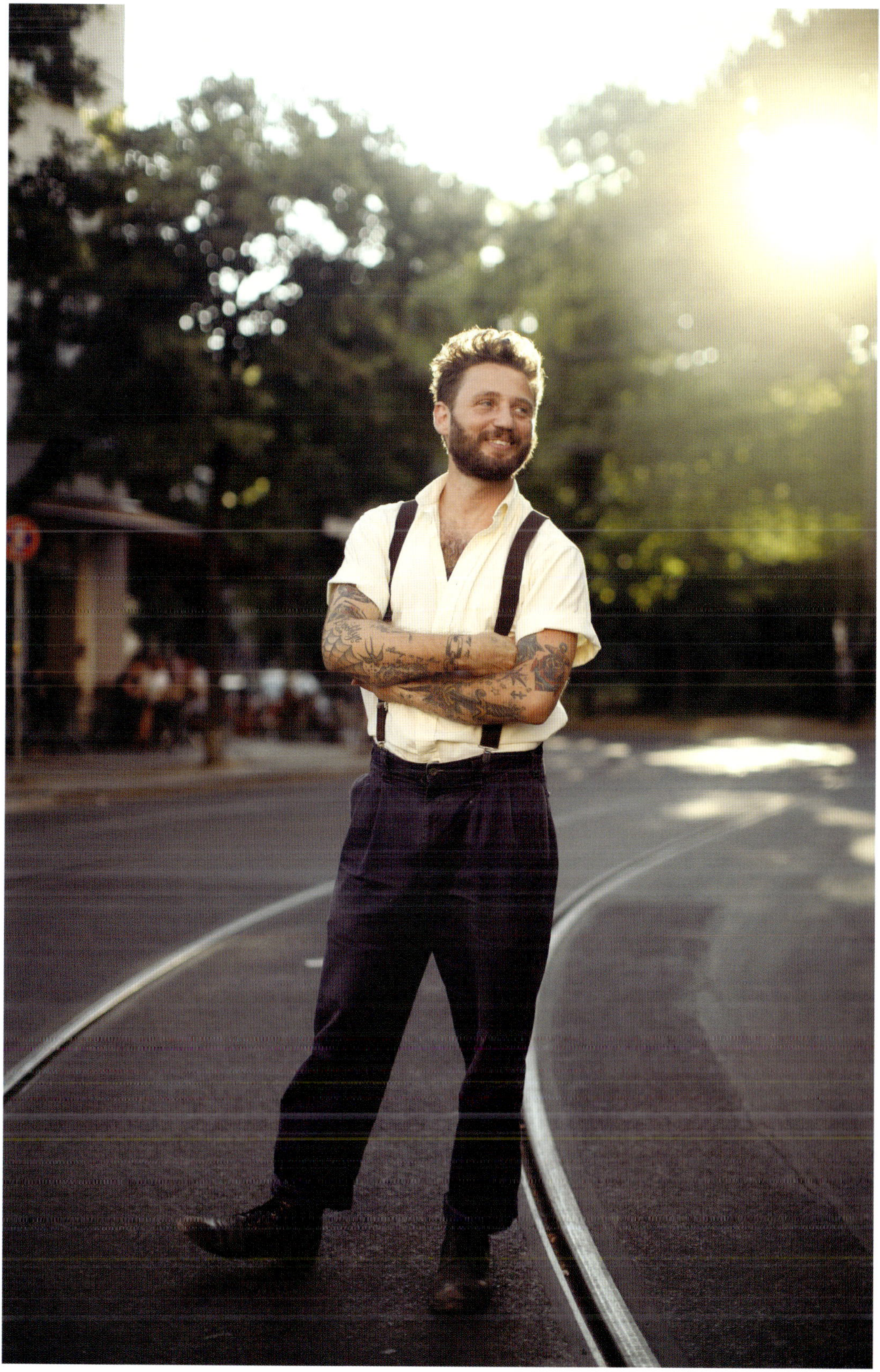

146 • Marco: Kastanienallee, Berlin

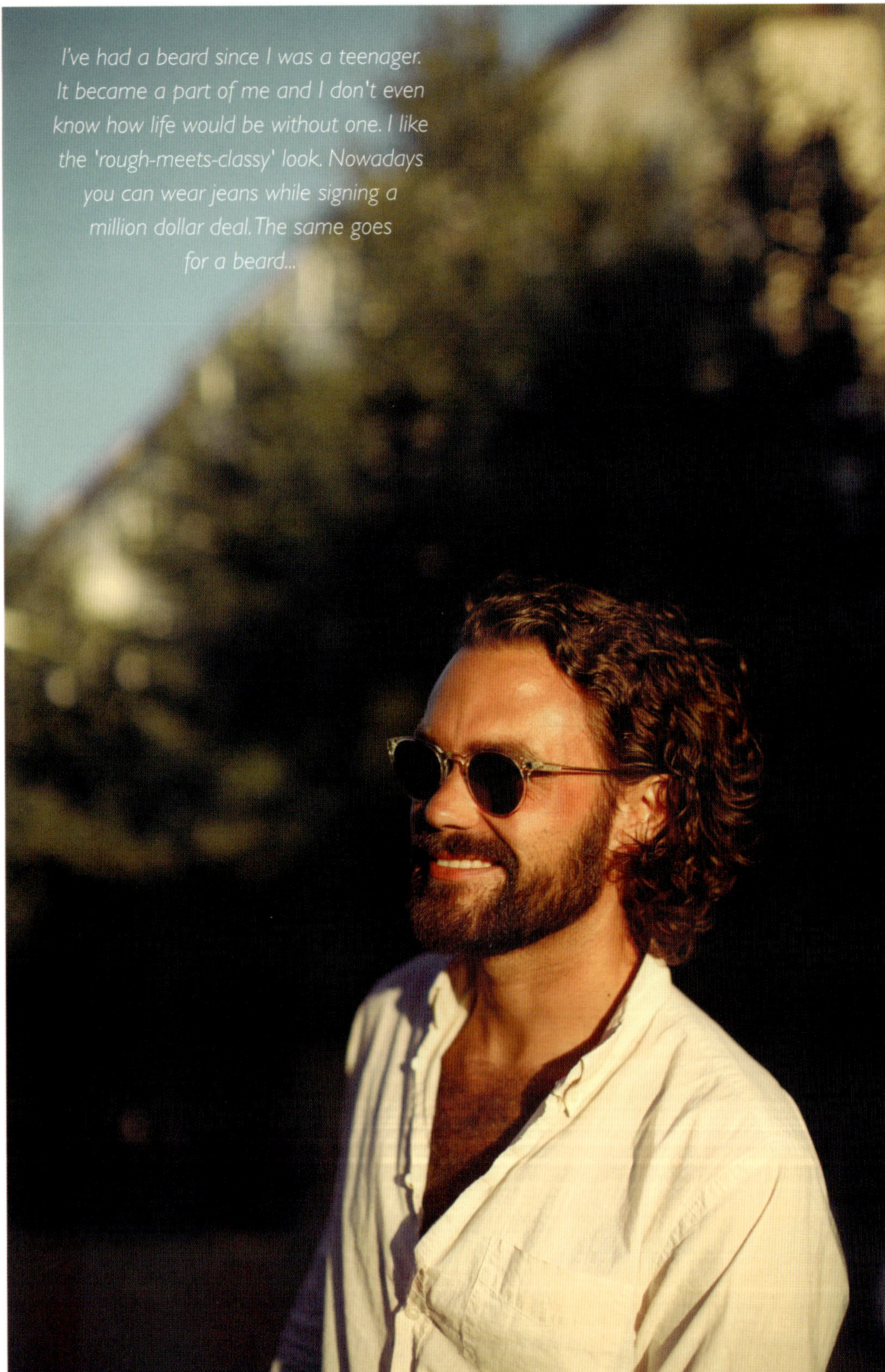

 • Dominik: Torstraße, Berlin

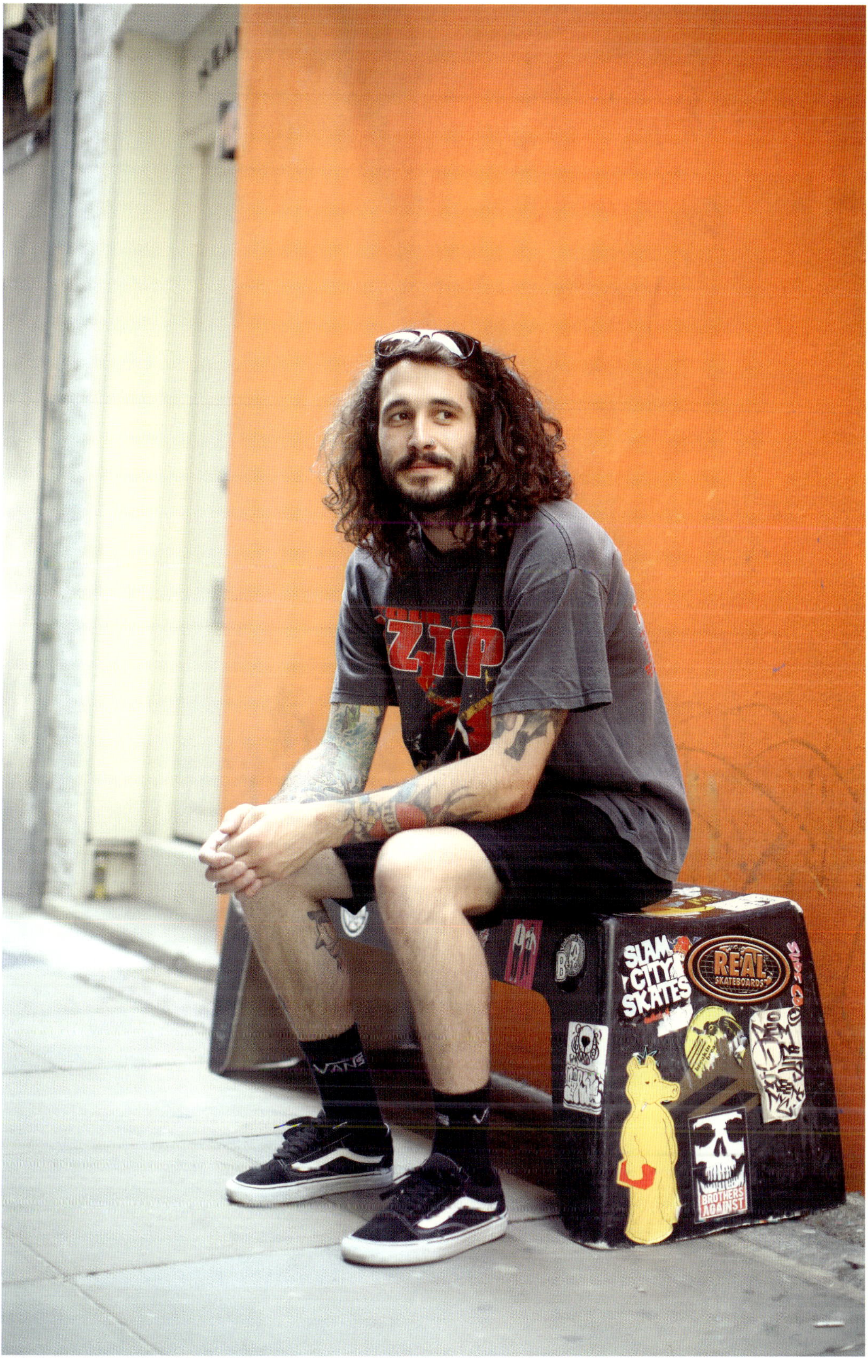

148 • Luke: Neals Yard, London

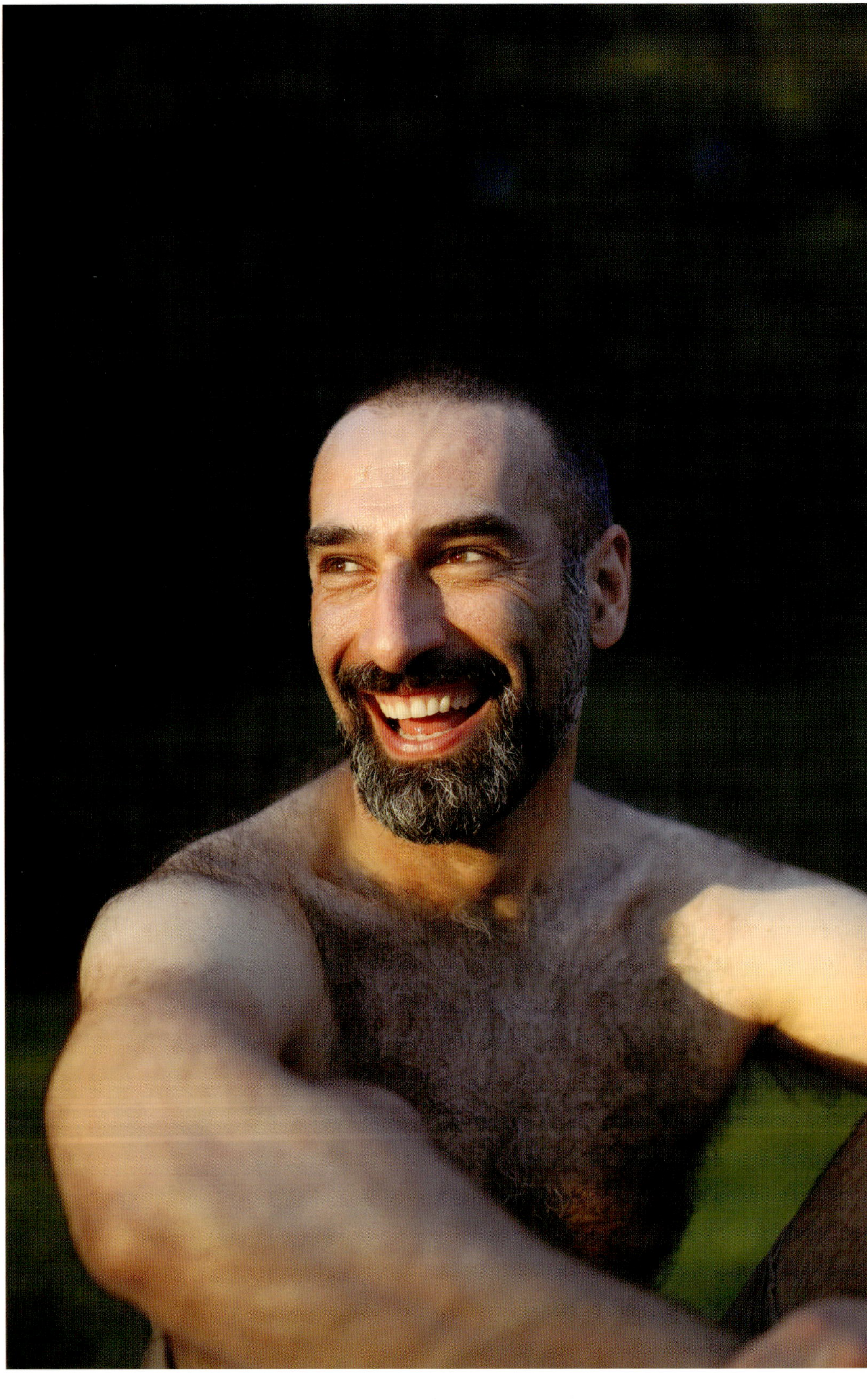

Ten years ago I spent a fantastic month in New York City. I forgot to take my razor and decided to let my beard grow. The reactions to it were so great that I decided to keep it. I called it my New York beard. I went back for many more wonderful months in NYC, but since I moved to London I have been influenced by some of the amazing beards out there to let mine grow longer. Now it is a New York beard with a London twist, and I love it.

149 • Nuno: Hampstead Heath, London

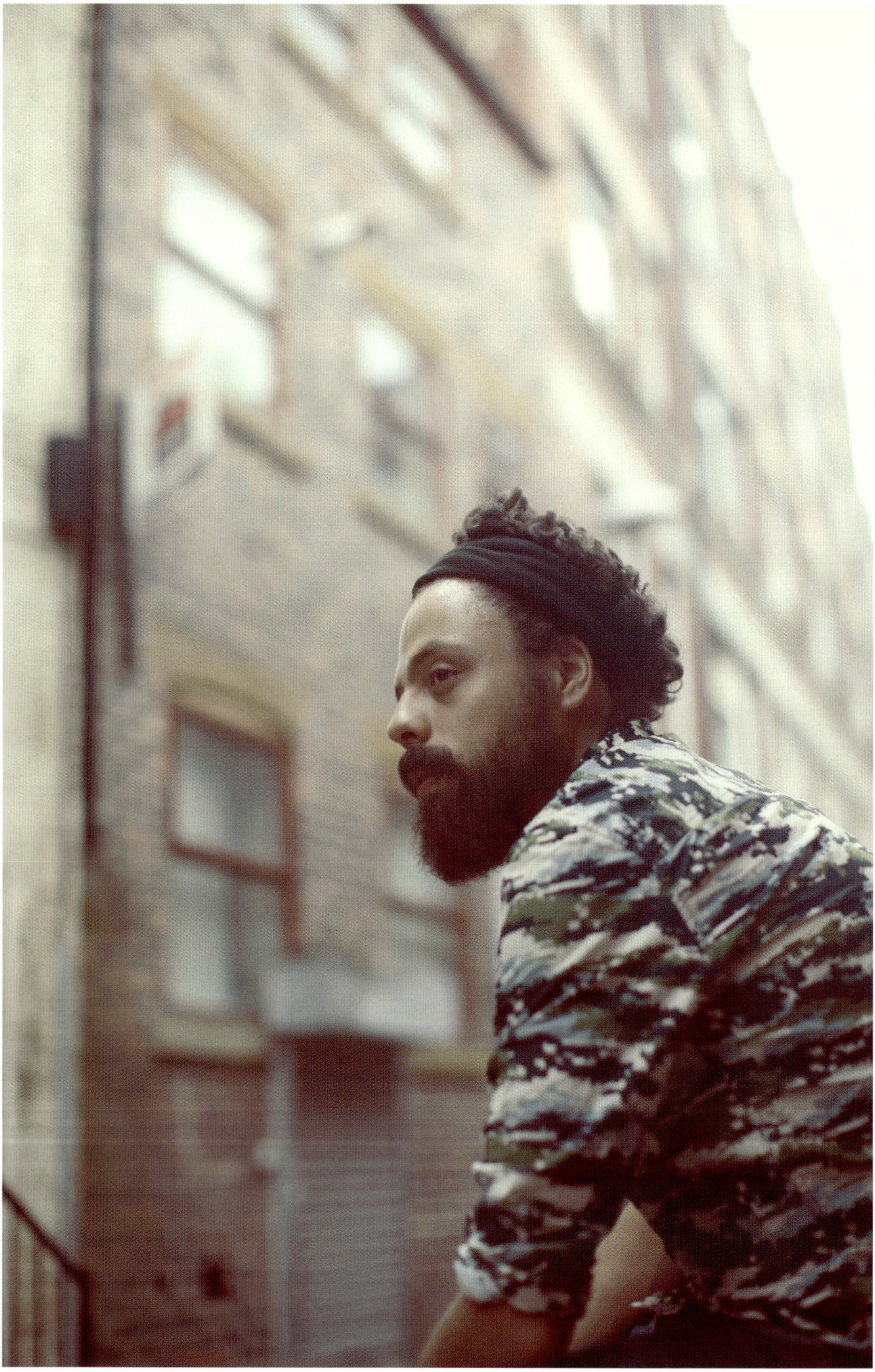

150 • Nathan: Kelvin Street, Manchester

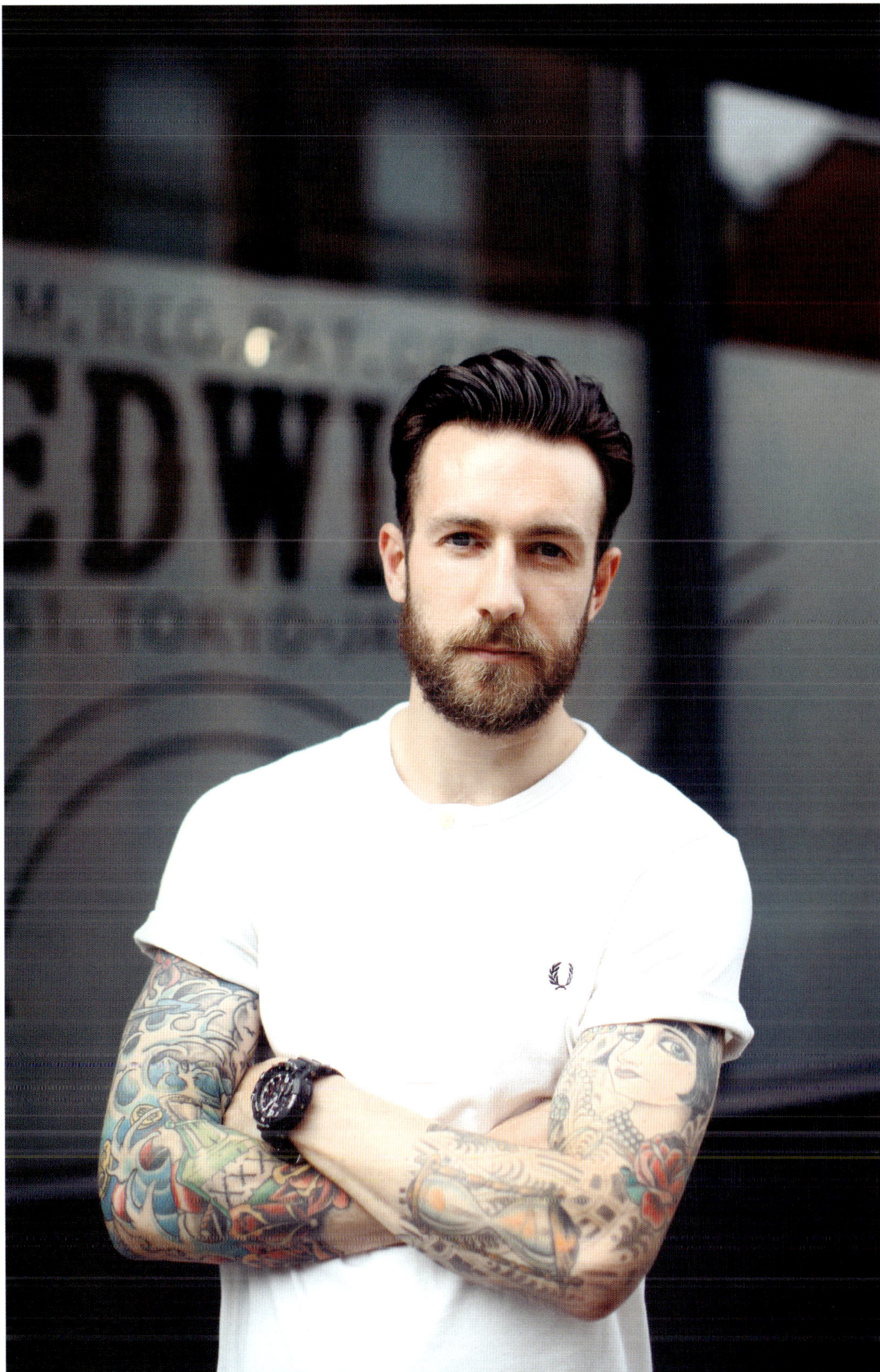

151 • Adam: Thomas Street, Manchester

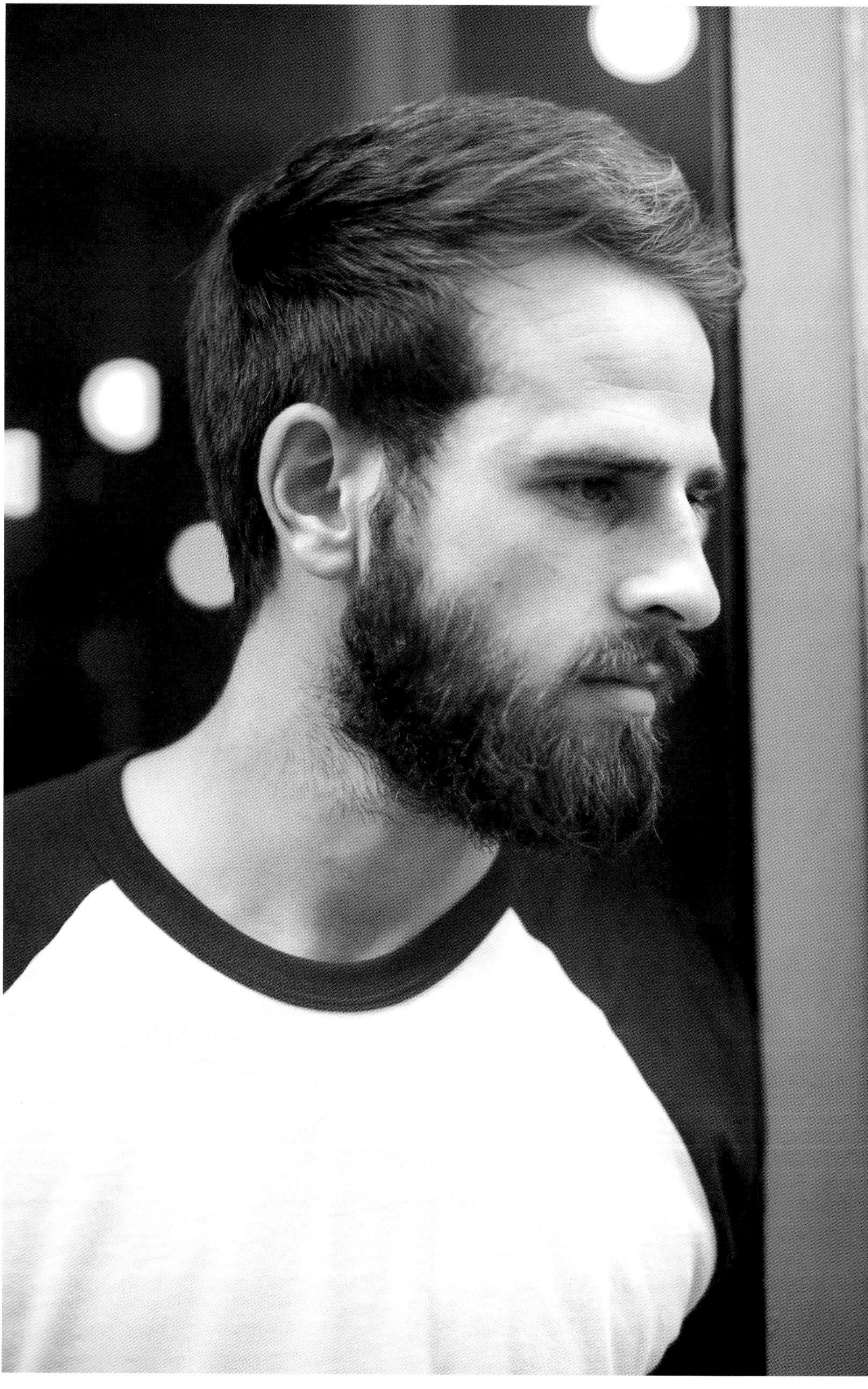

152 • Sam: High Bridge, Newcastle

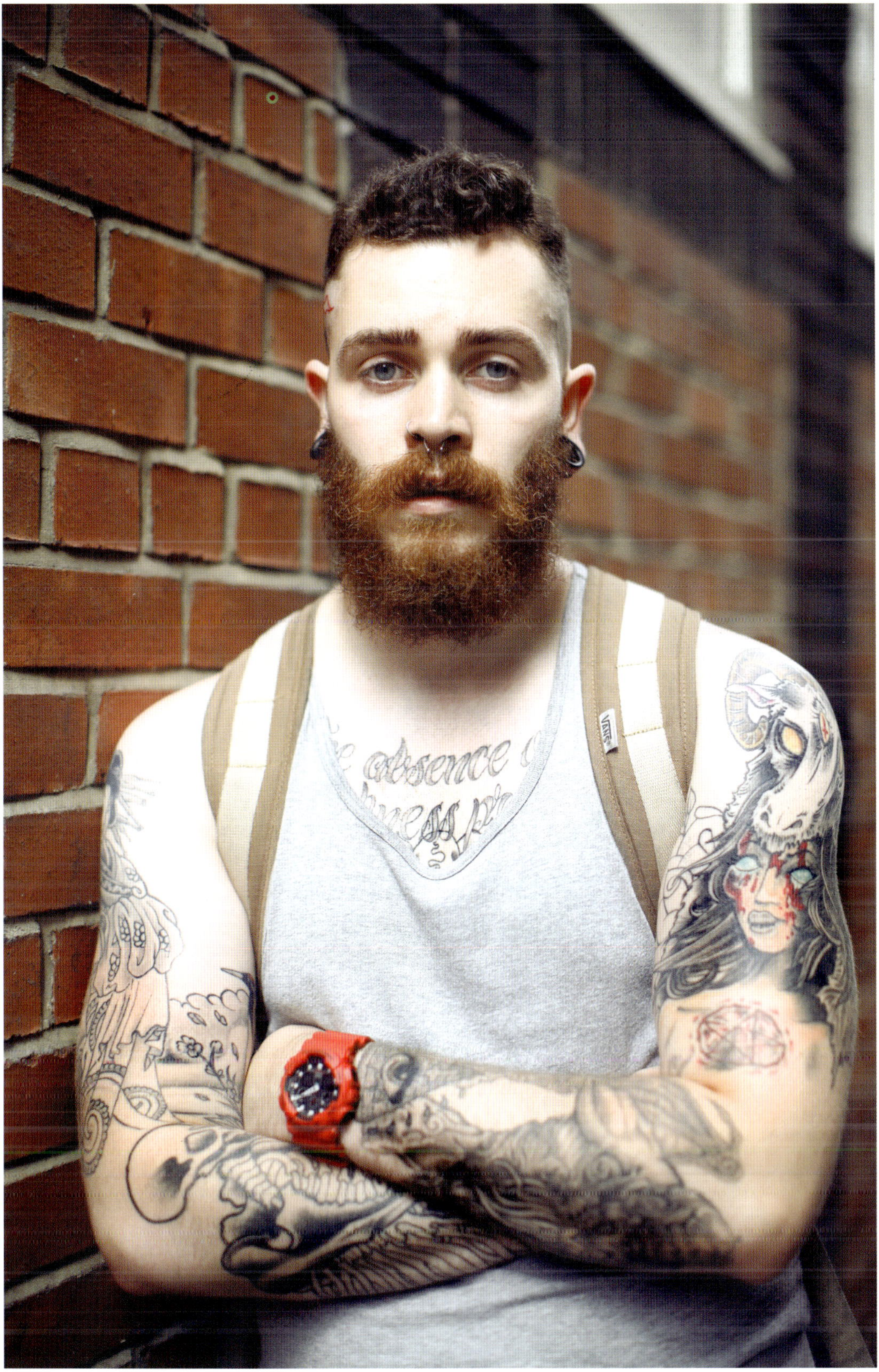

153 • Sam: Lisle Street, Newcastle

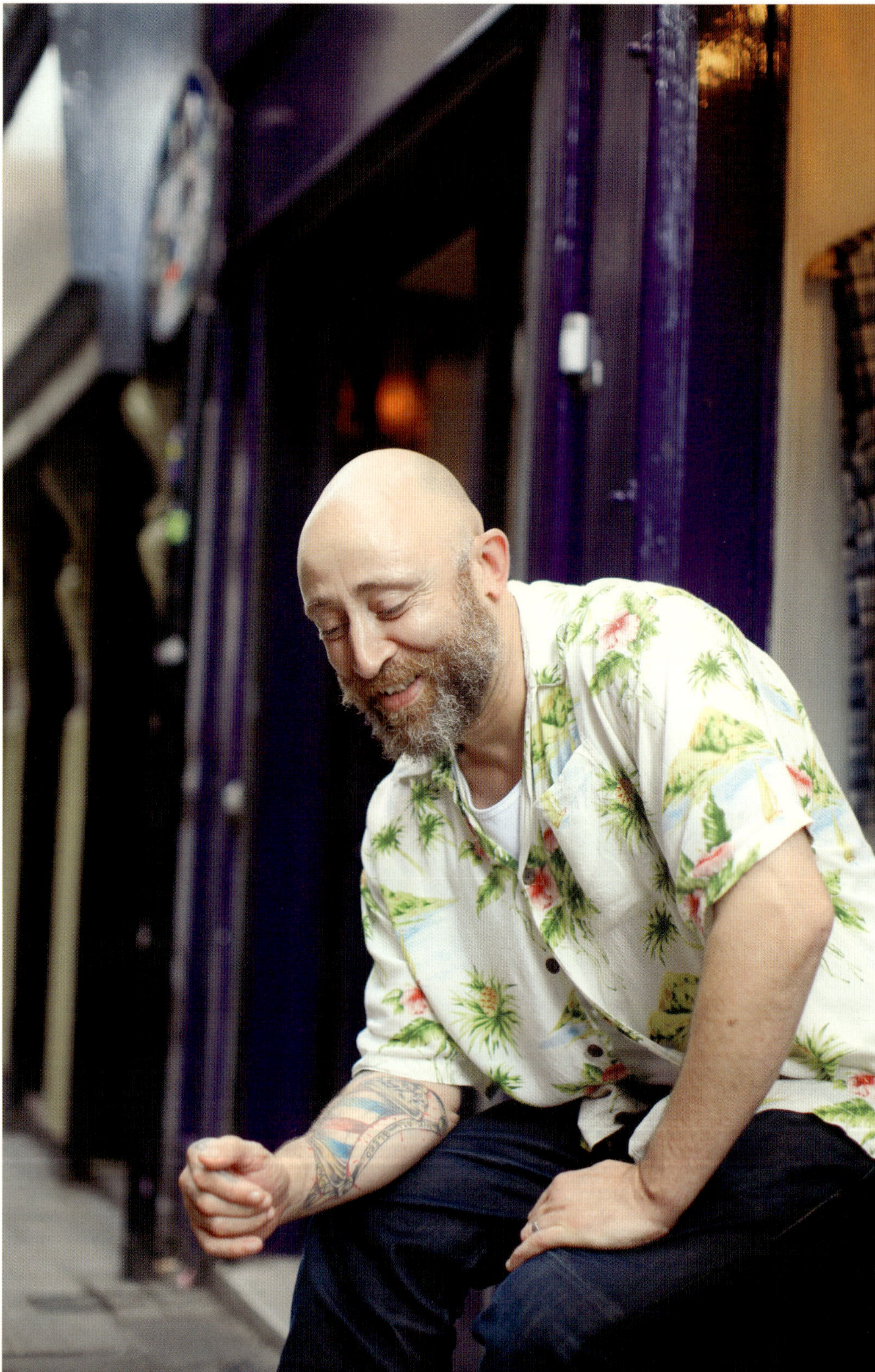

154 • Lloyd: High Bridge, Newcastle

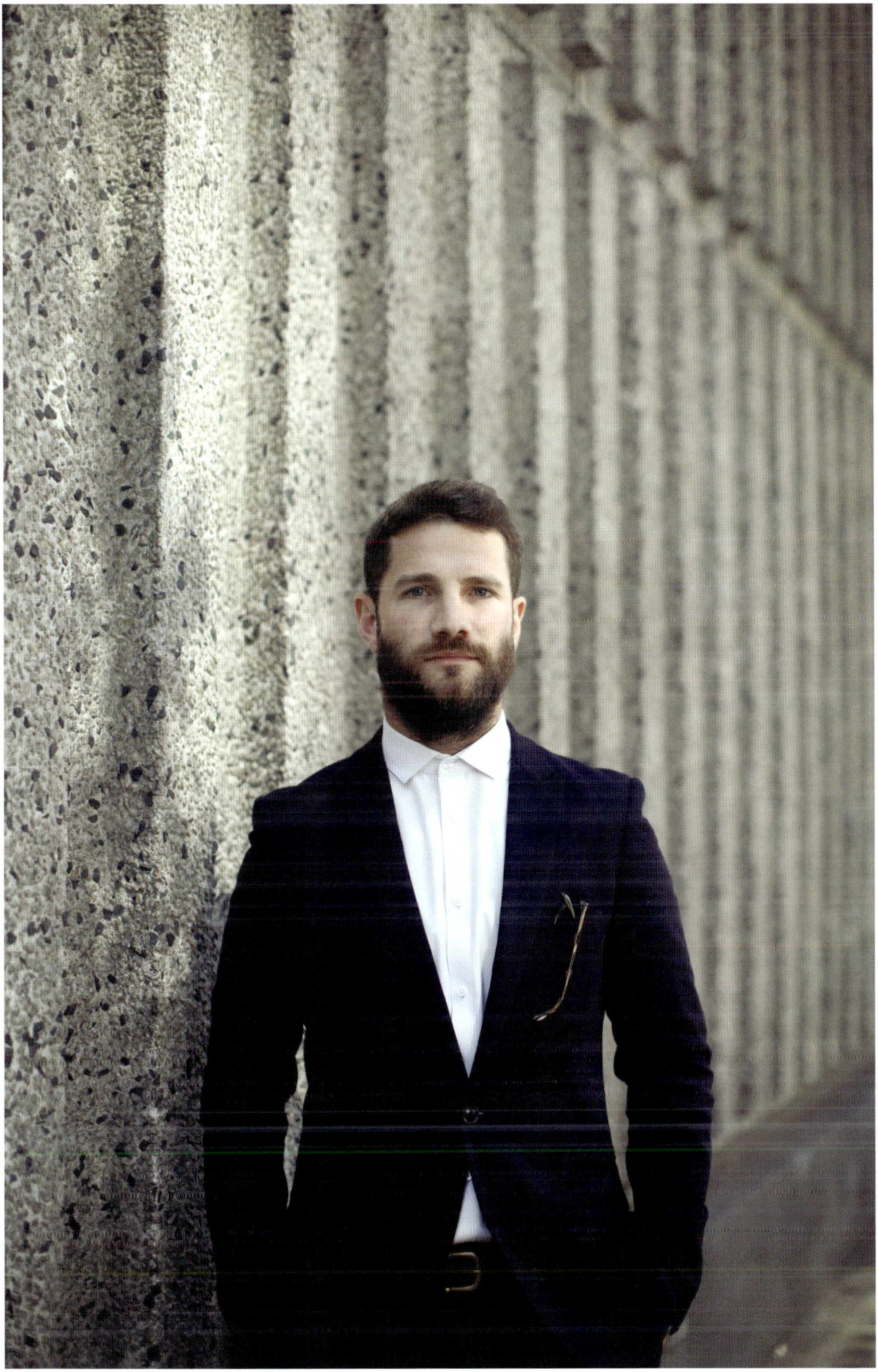

155 • Sam: Marshall Street, London

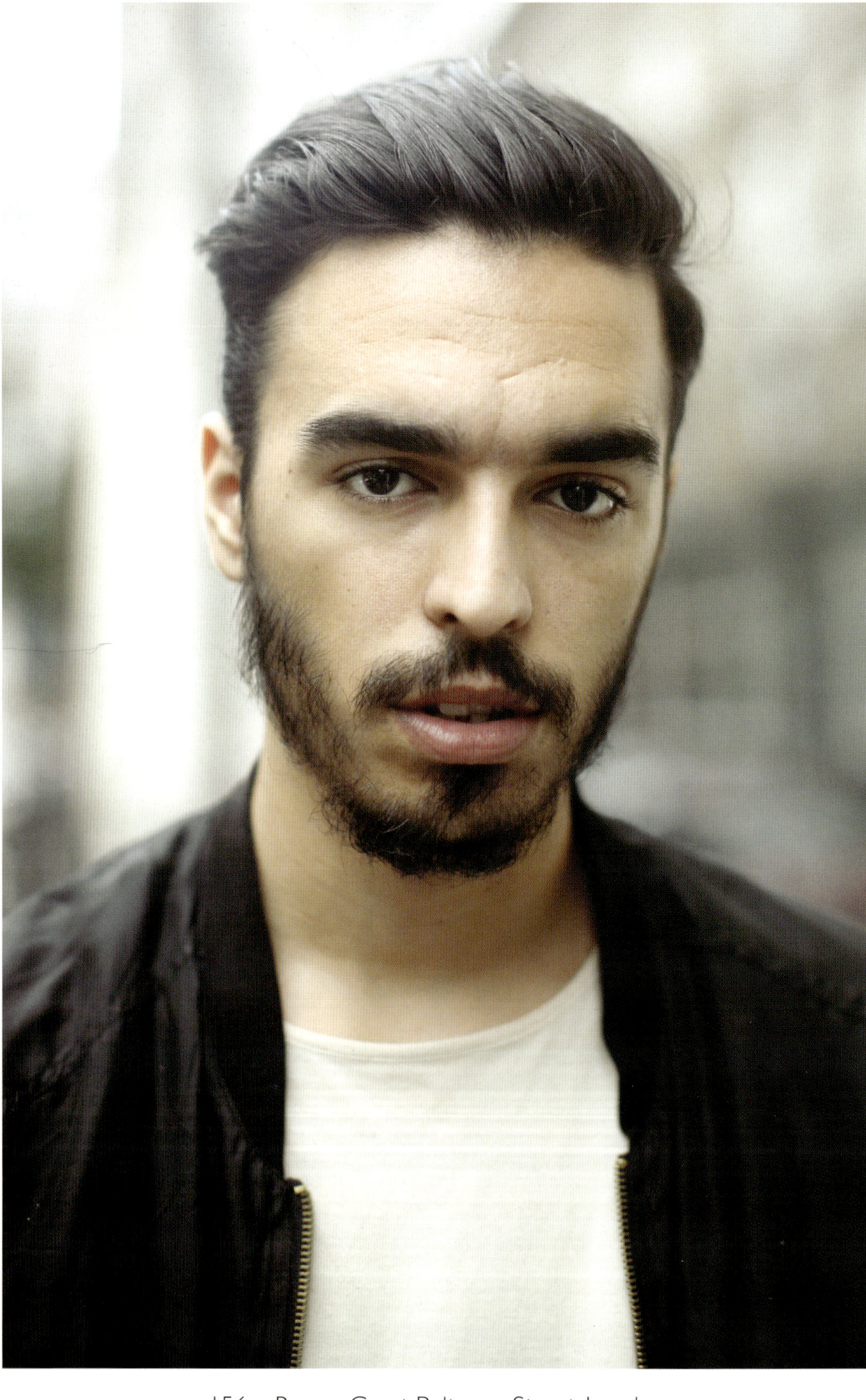

156 • Bruno: Great Pulteney Street, London

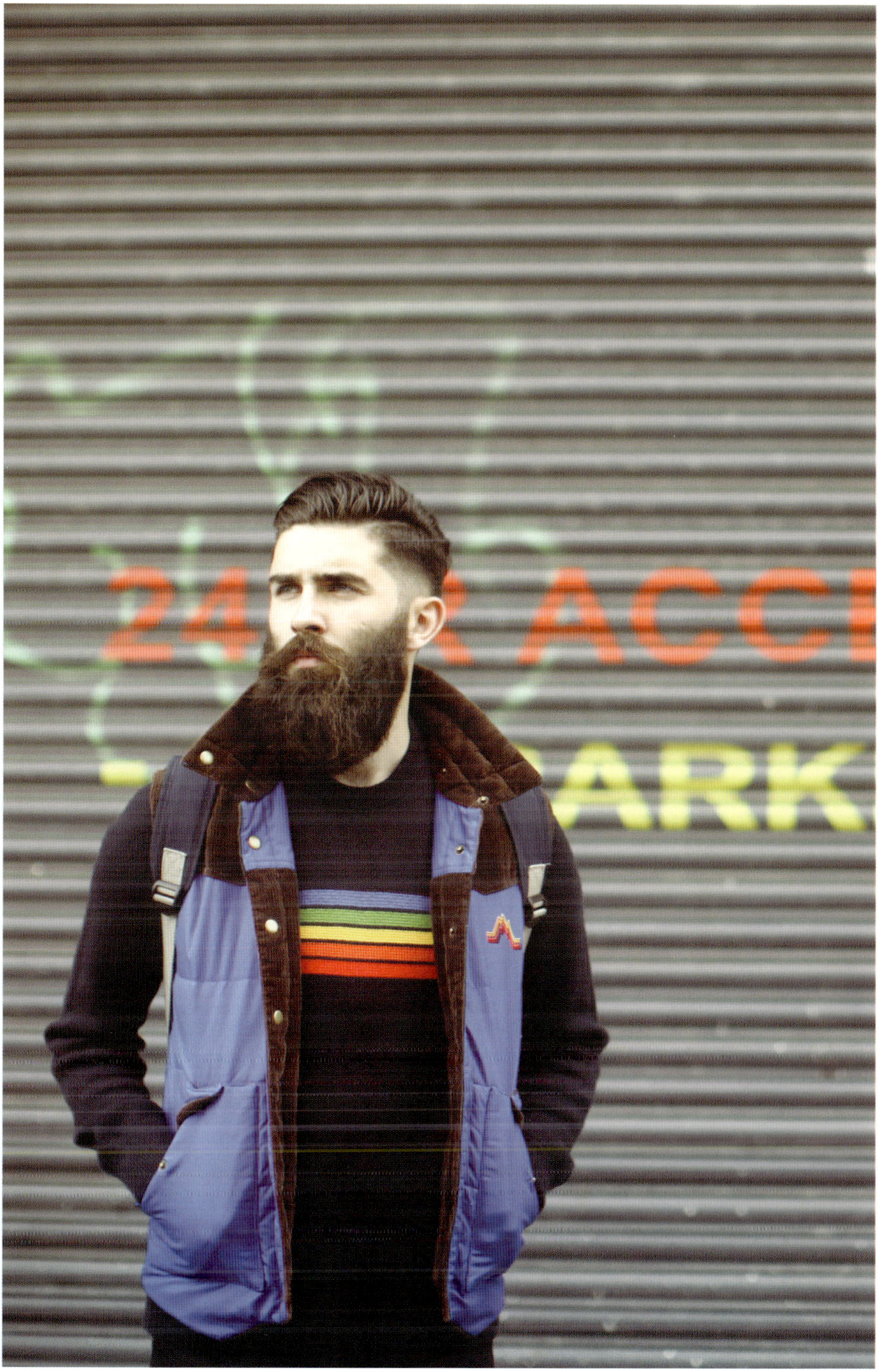

157 • Chris: Wilson Street, Glasgow

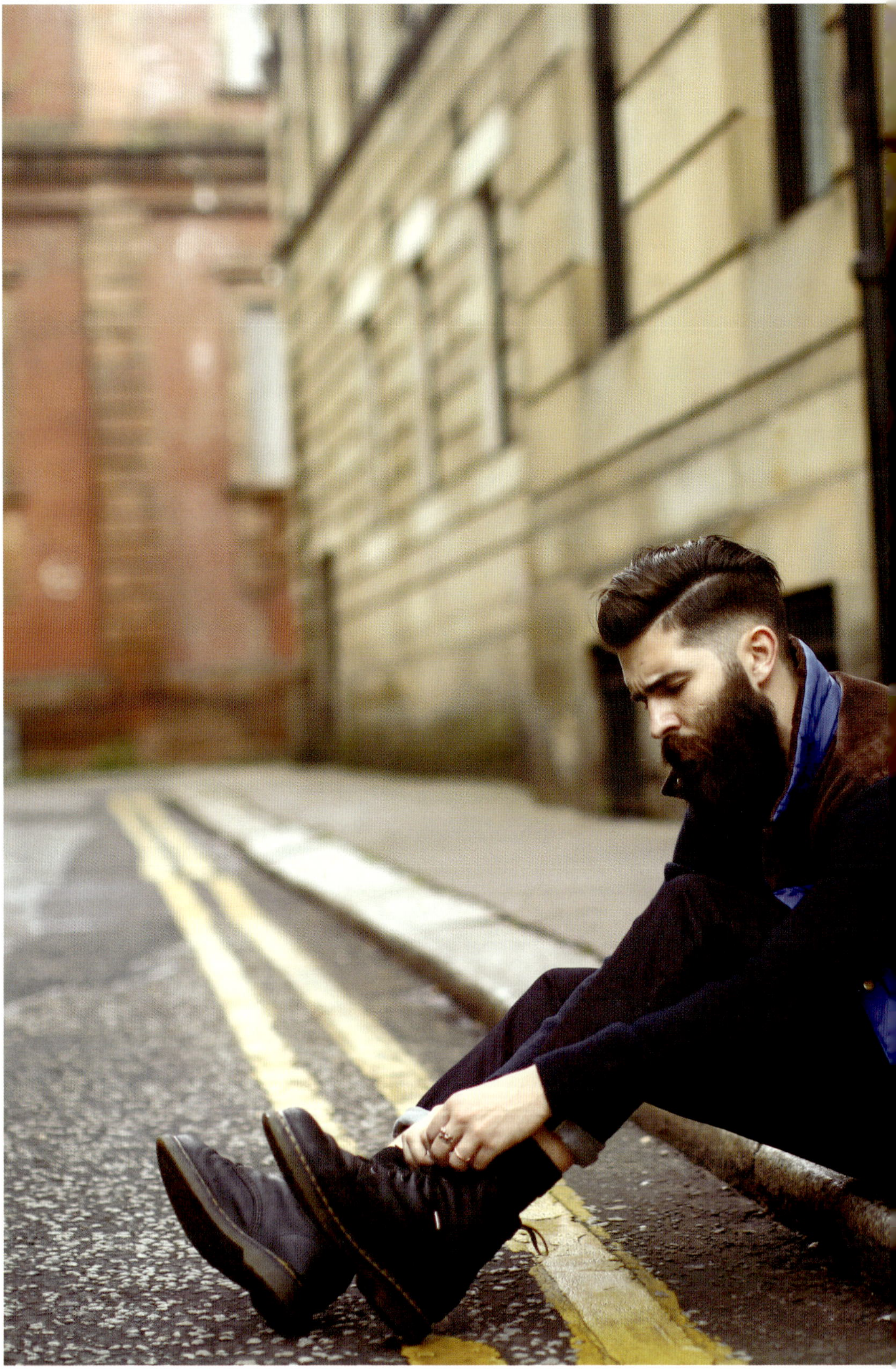

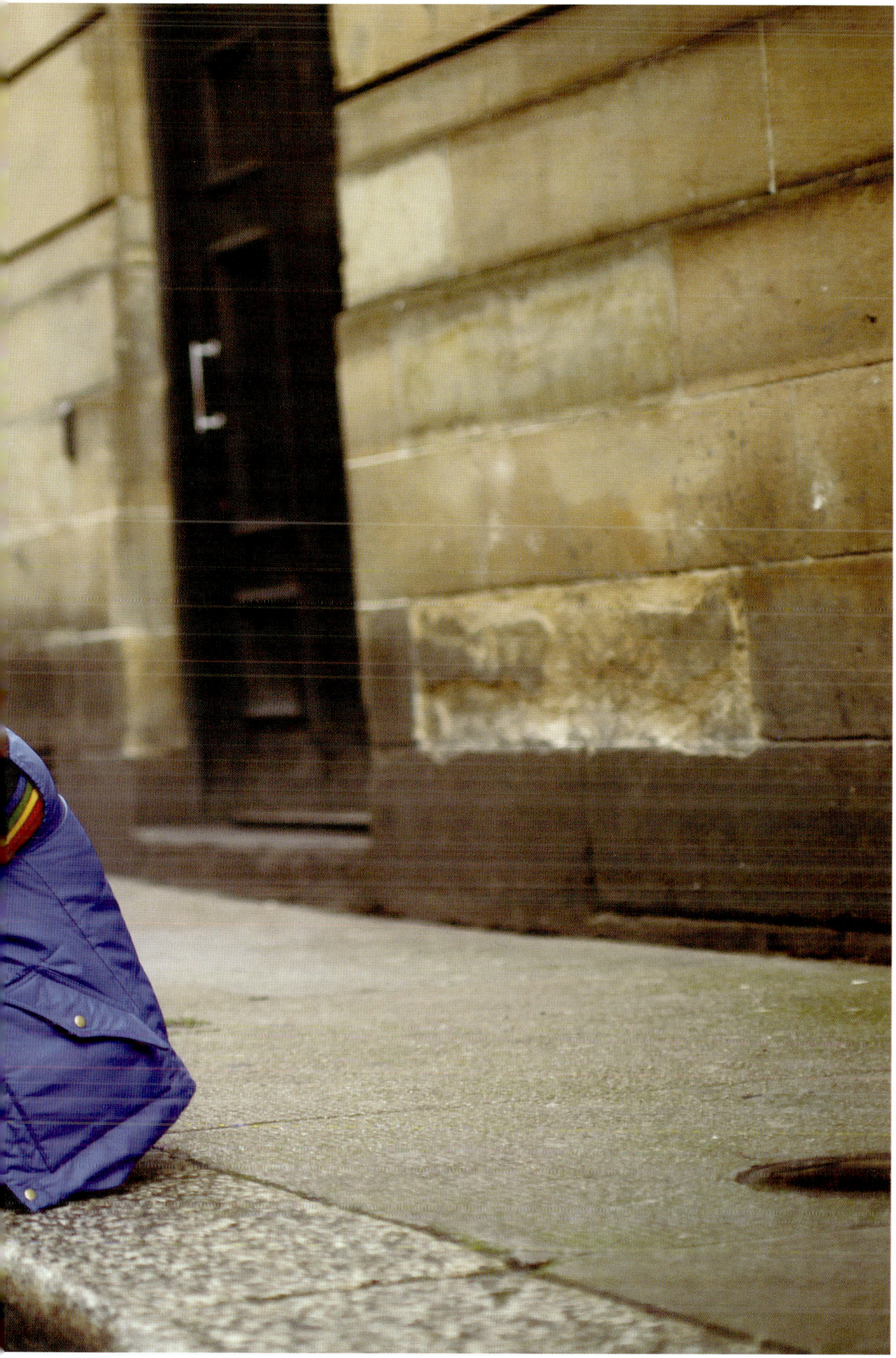

Chris: Wilson Street, Glasgow

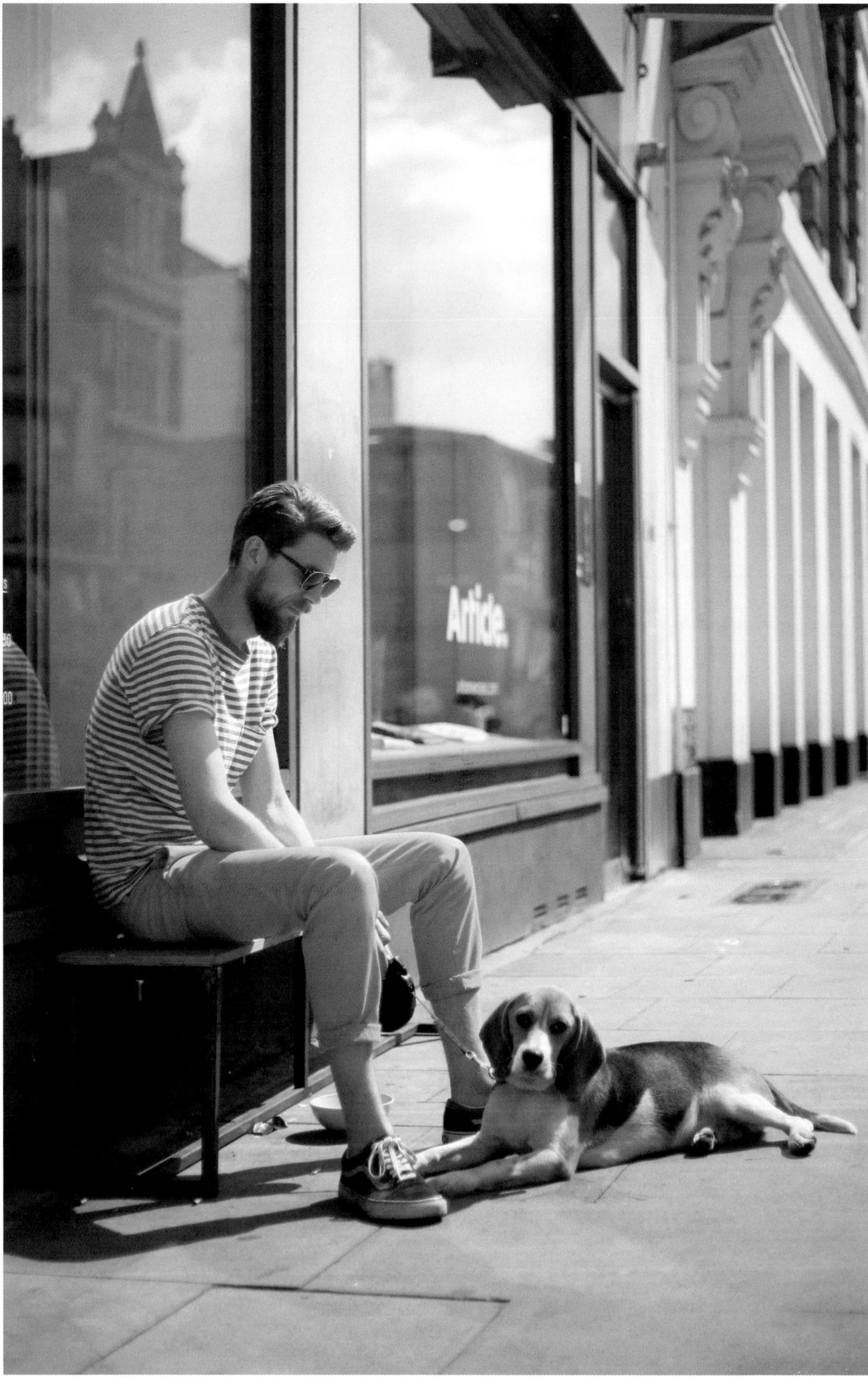

158 • David: Kingsland Road, London

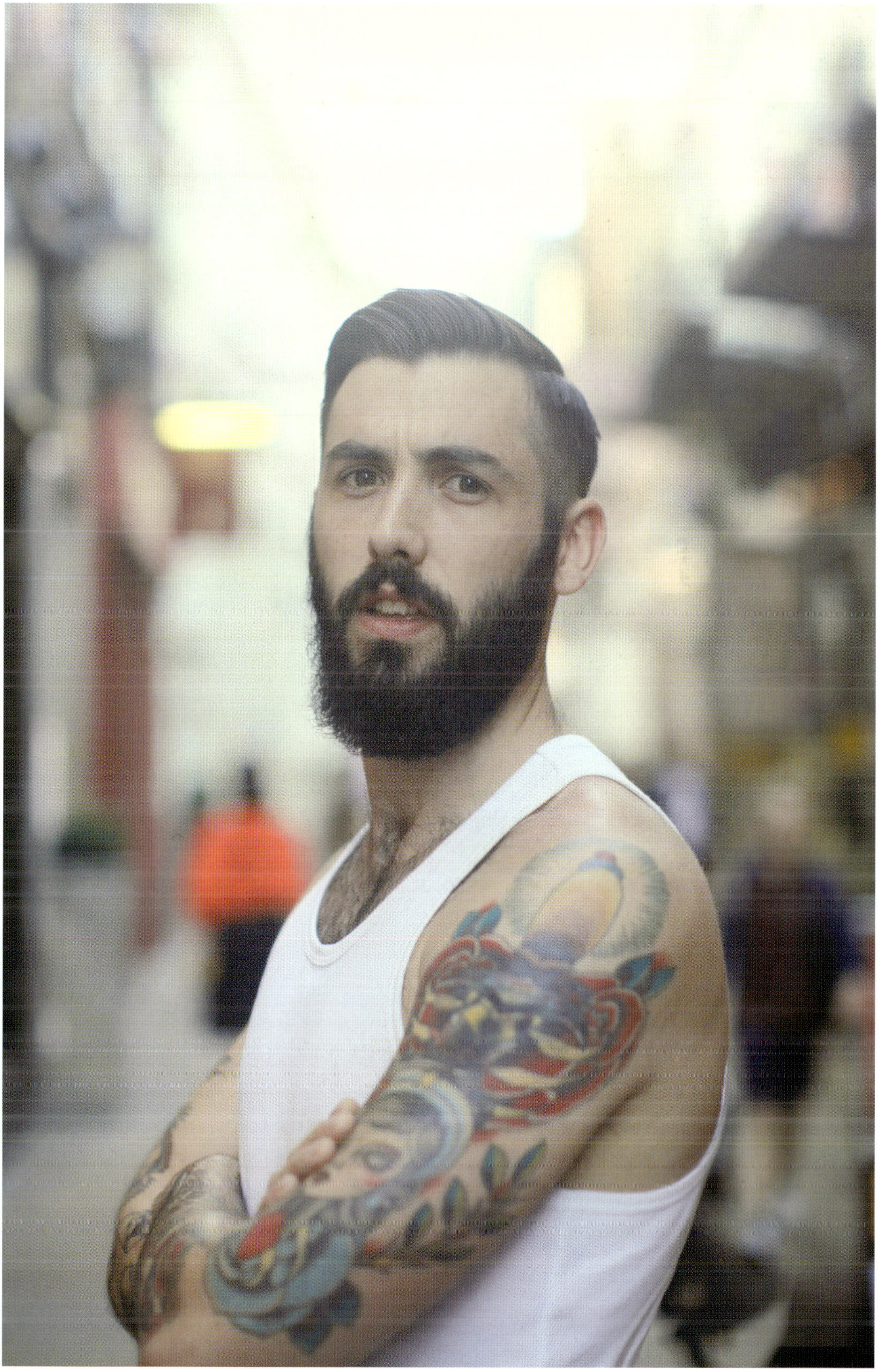

159 • Joey: Gees Court, London

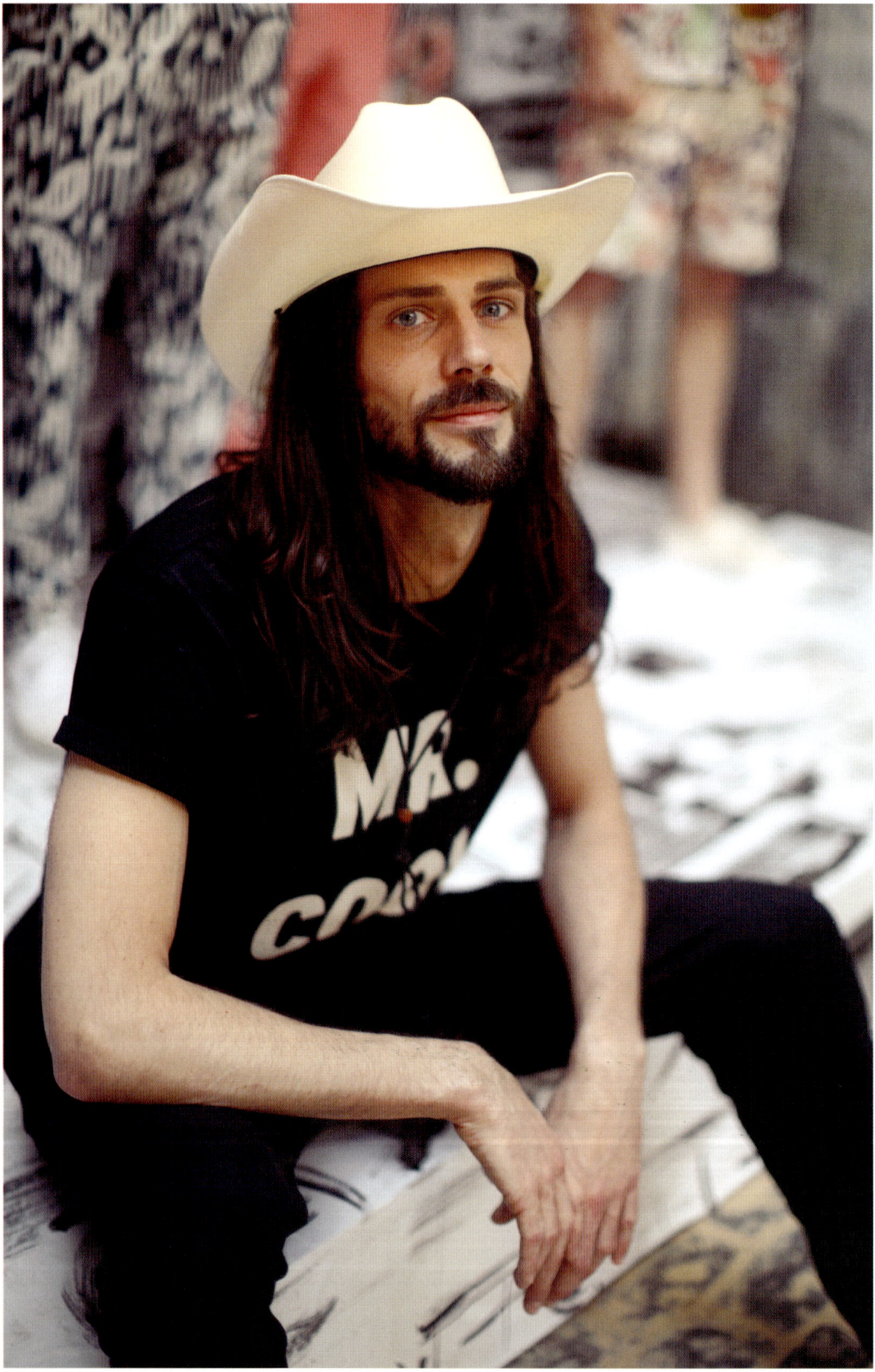

160 • Jimmy: Mercer Street Studios, London

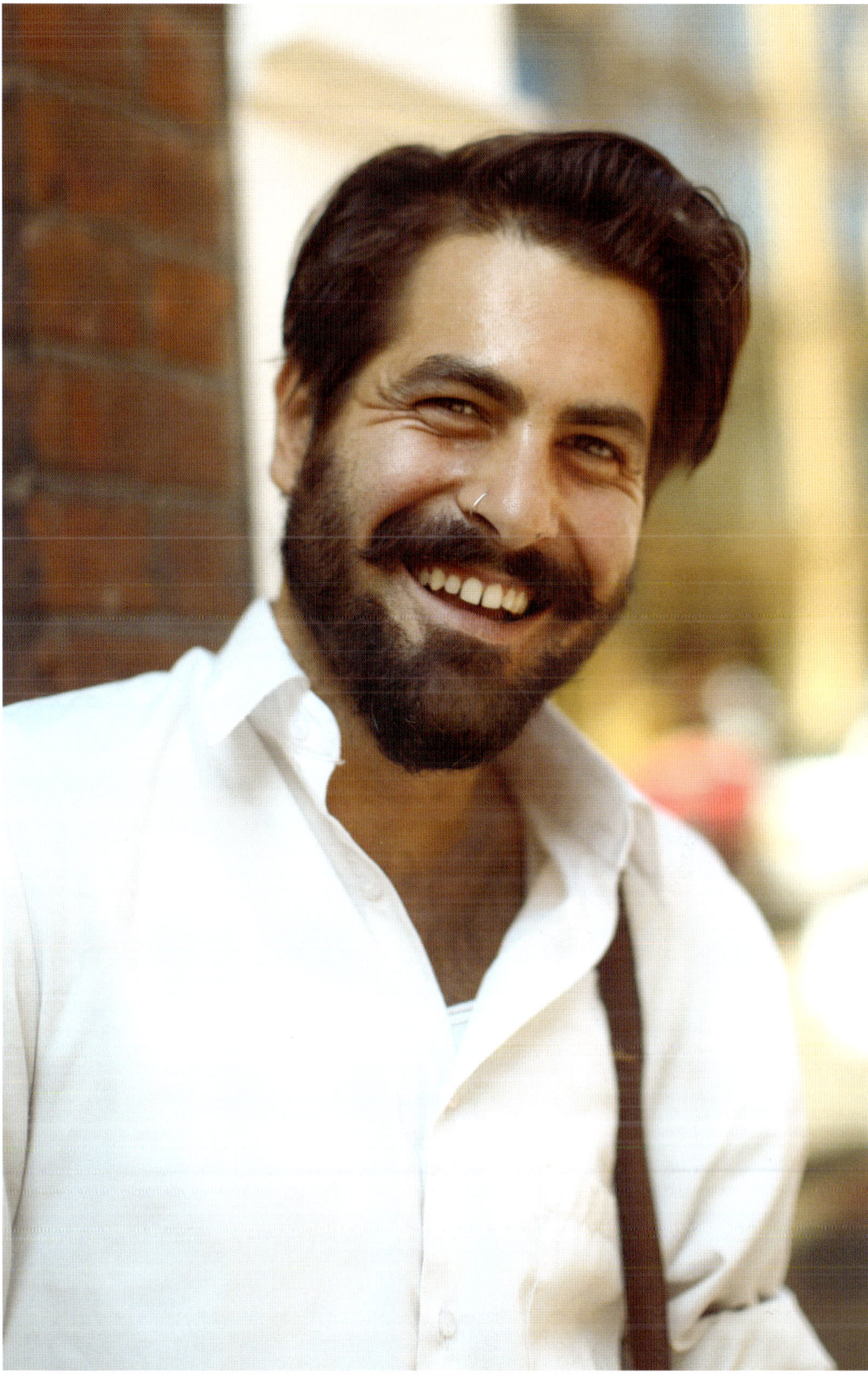

161 • Federico: Long Acre, London

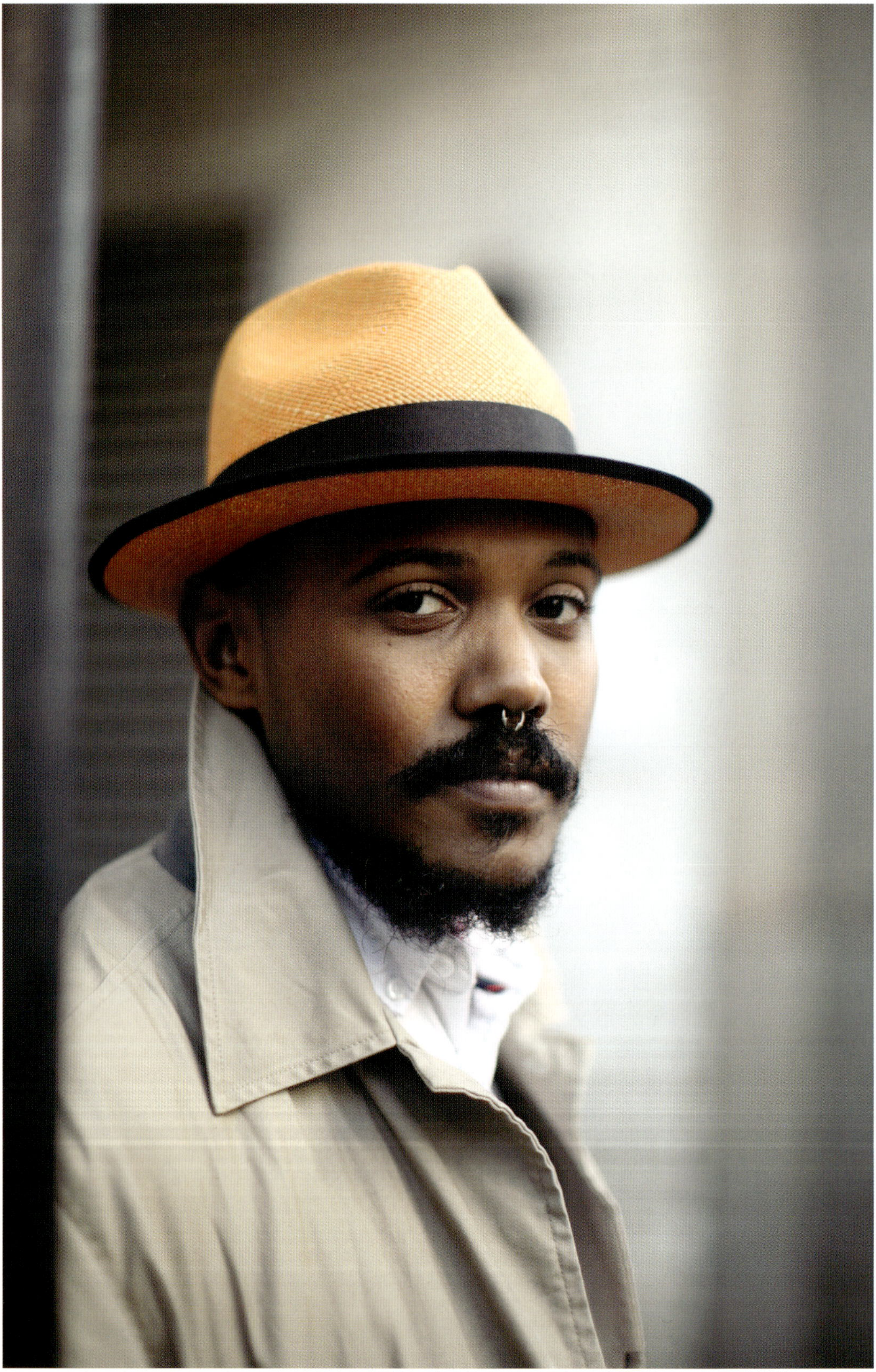

162 • Lee: Wigmore Street, London

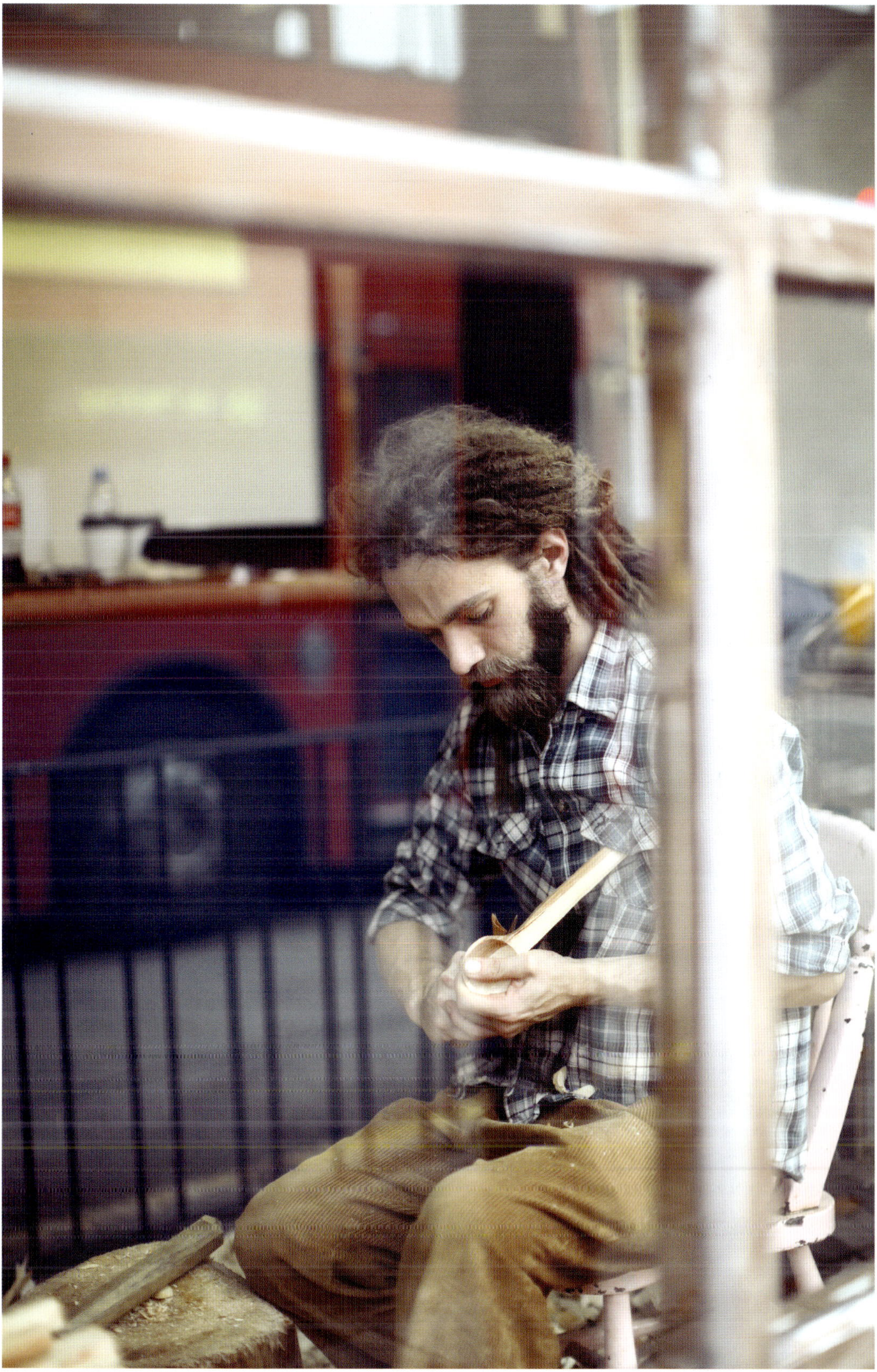

163 • Owen: Hackney Road, London

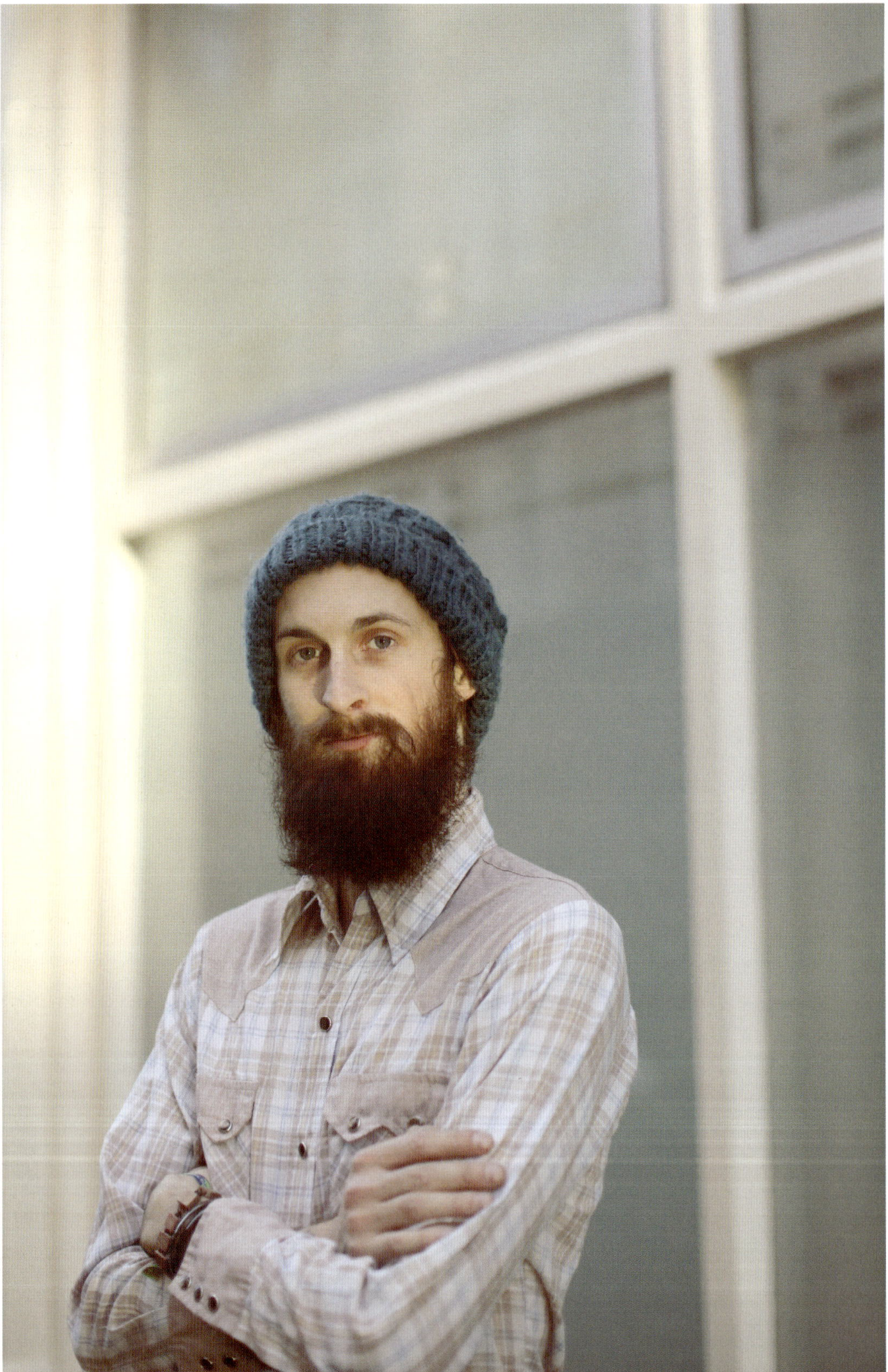

164 • Dan: Great Marlborough Street, London

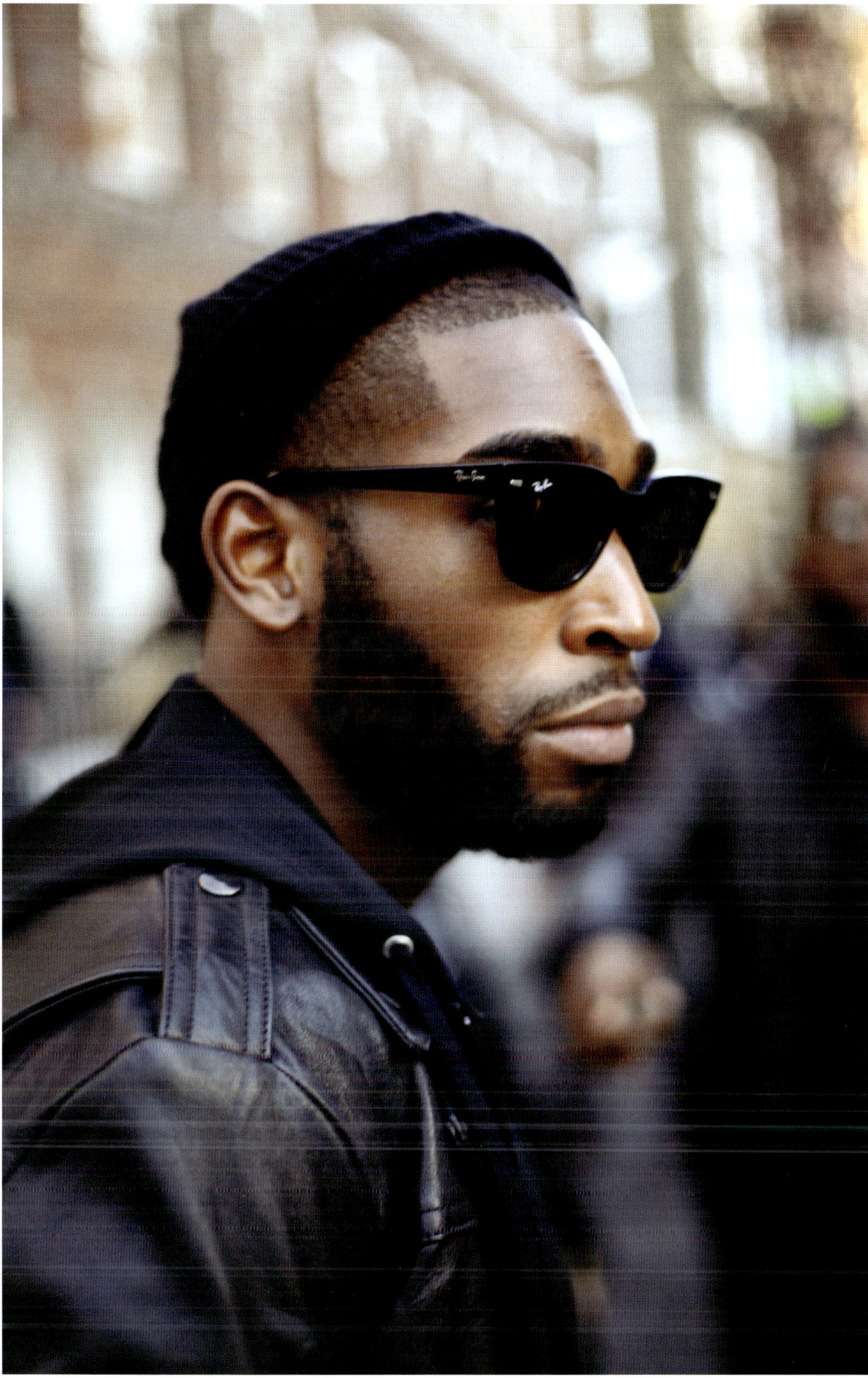

165 • Tinie: Endell Street, London

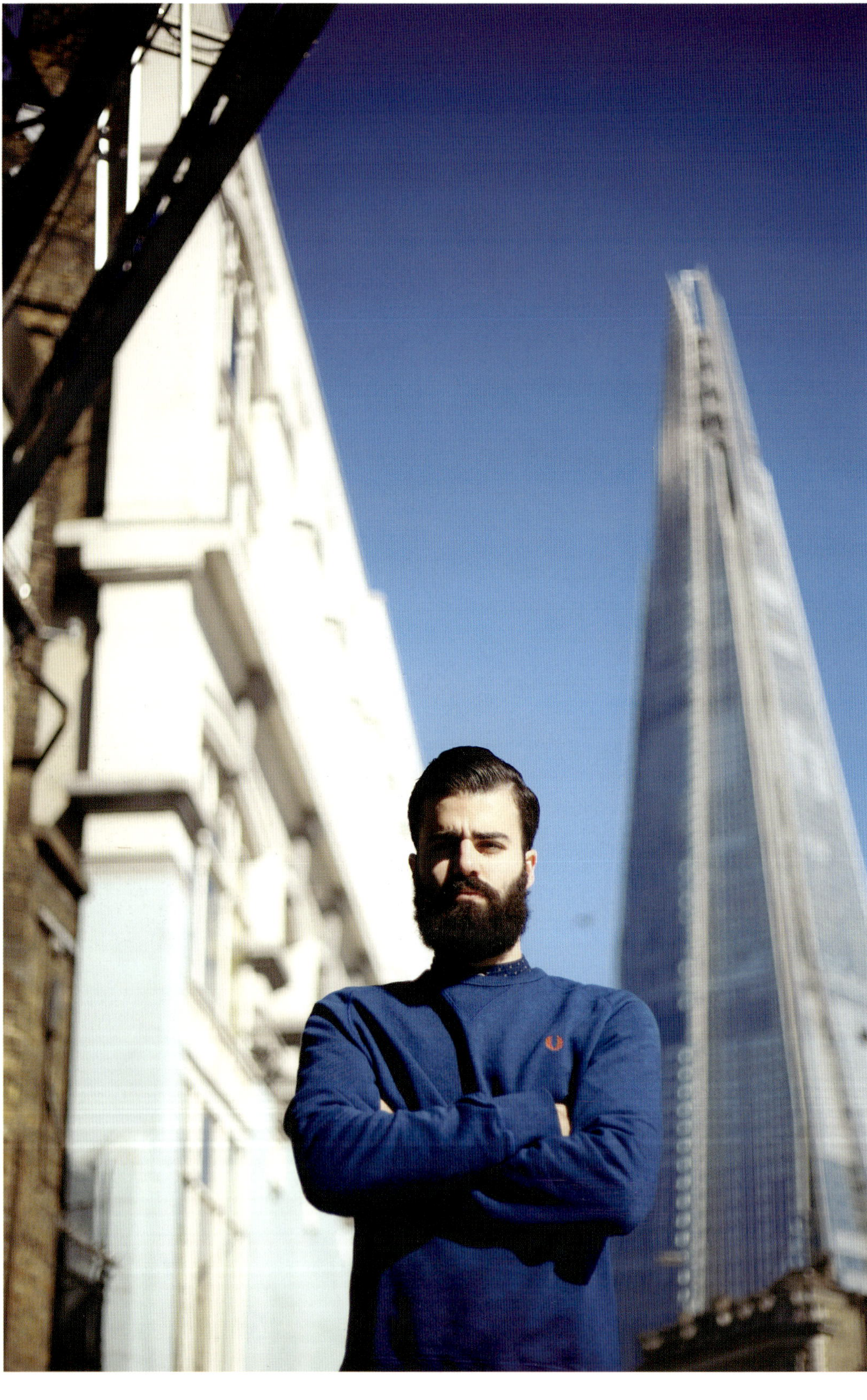

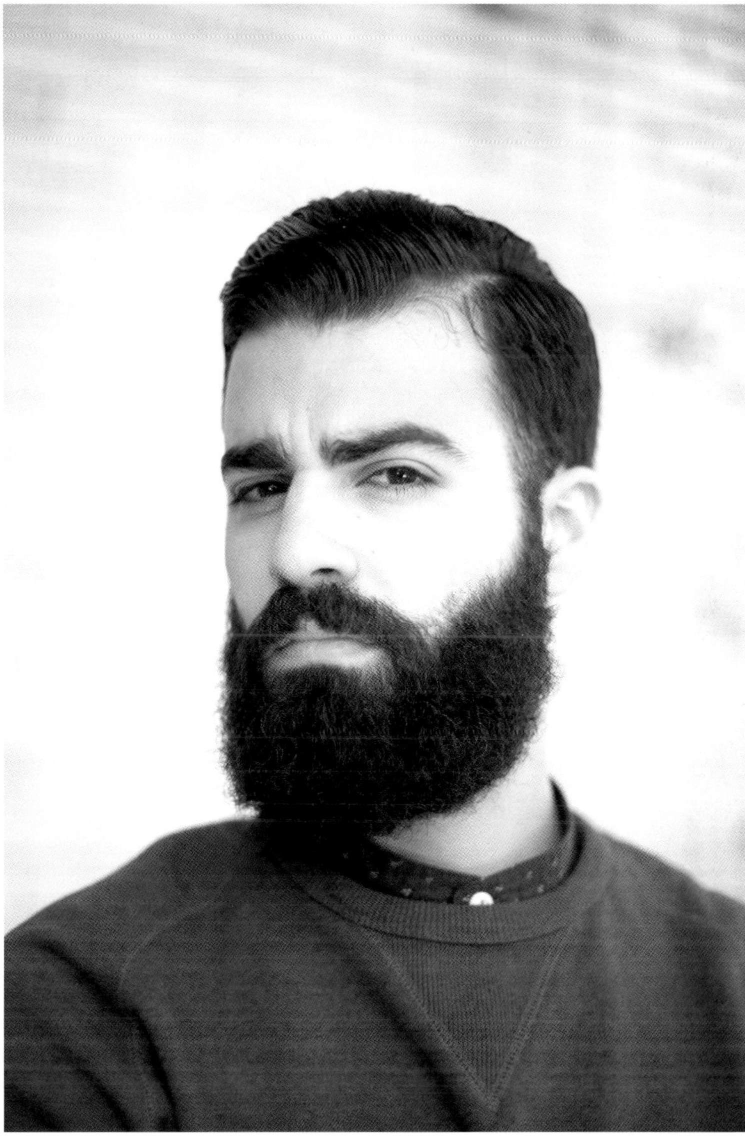

My beard means everything to me. I can't go for a walk down the street without people staring at it, whispering under their breath as I walk past. I get girls coming up to me at the pub asking to touch it constantly, which I find strange and hilarious. It's easier to meet girls with a beard as they are always fascinated by it and it makes a great talking point. I get called Ned Kelly nearly everyday by strangers without fail. The comments are nearly always positive which is nice and I still find the amount of attention it brings a little odd. It's something I'll never be able to get over I think.

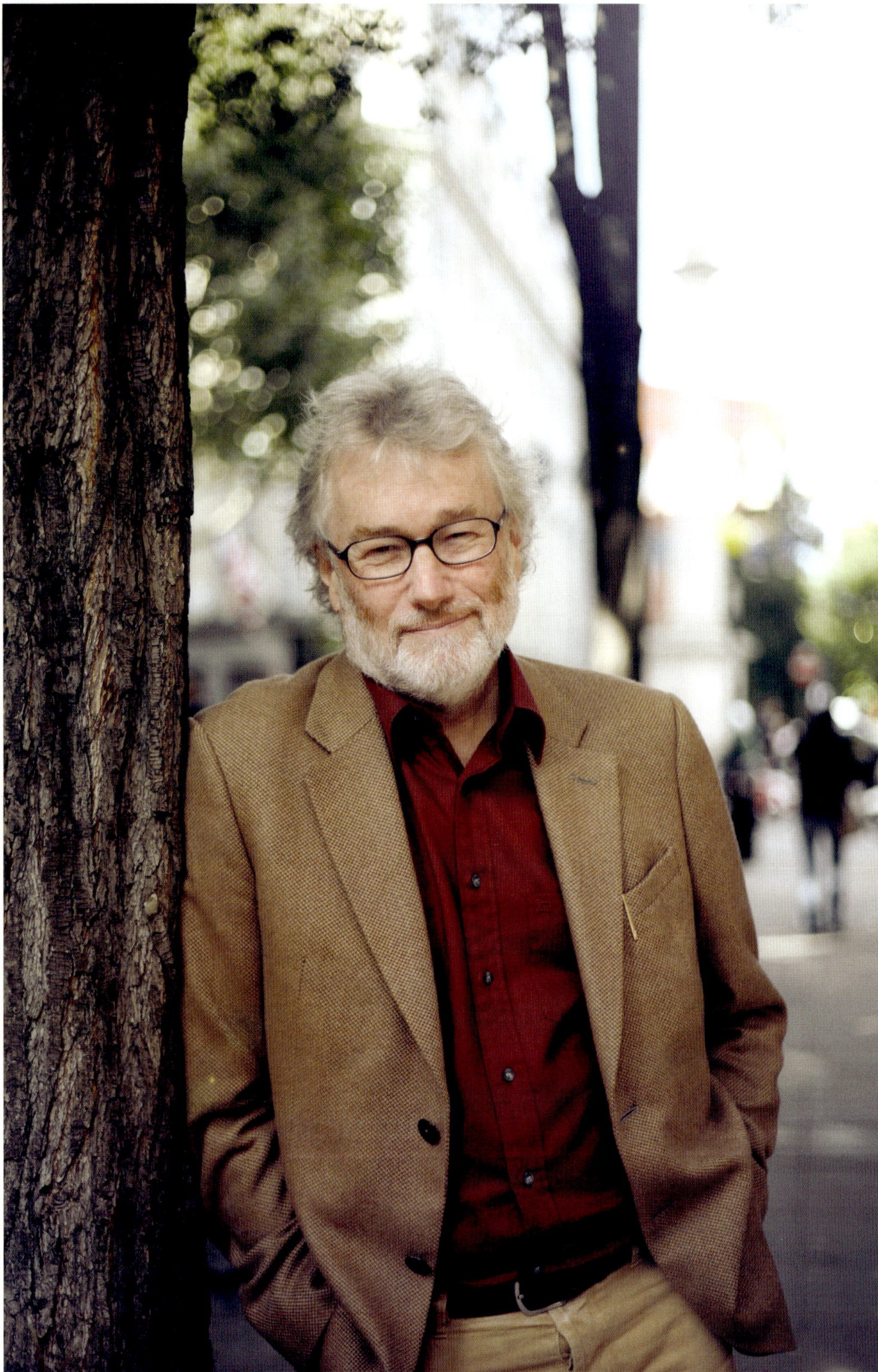

167 • Iain Banks: Monmouth Street, London

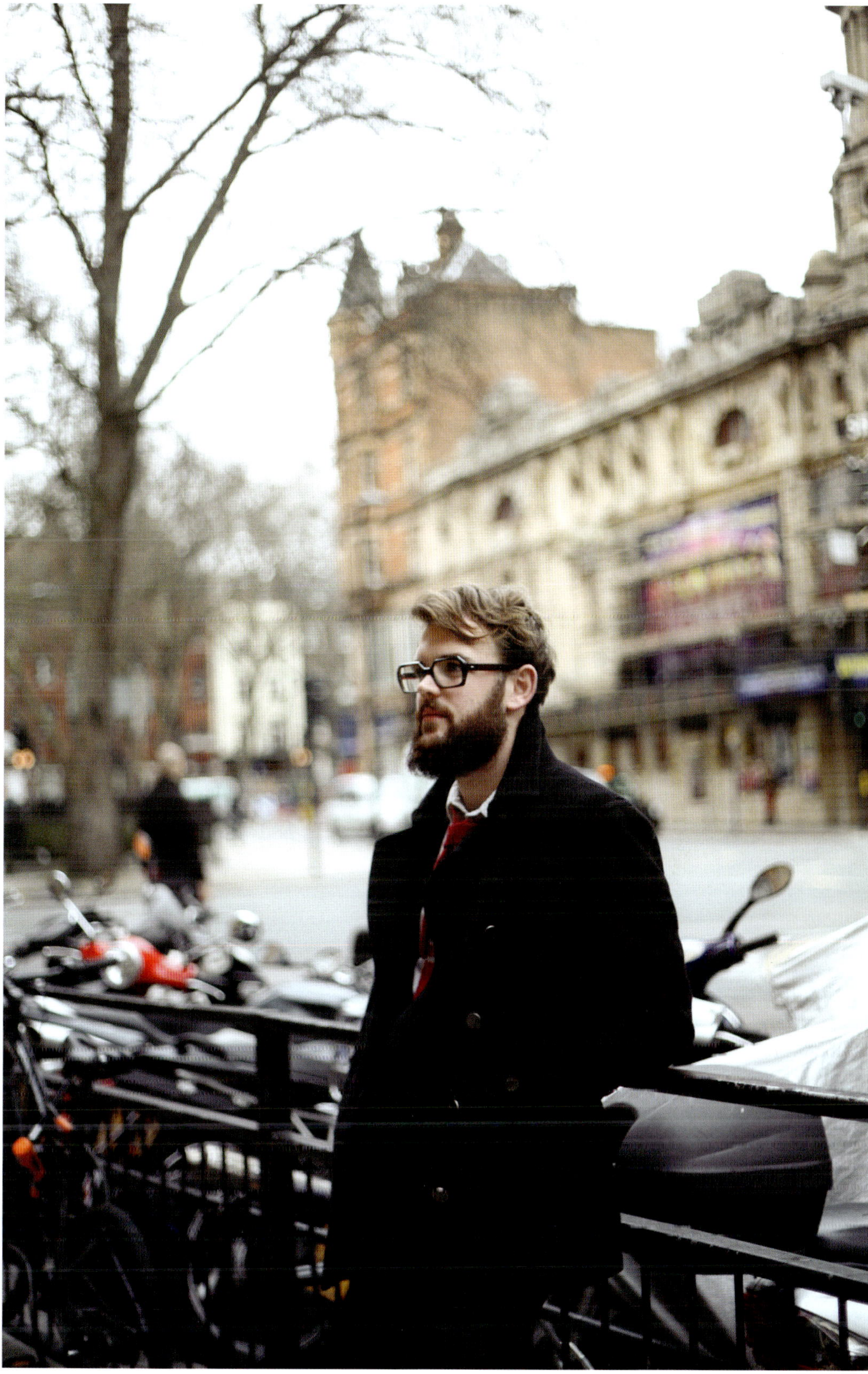

 Josh: High Holborn, London

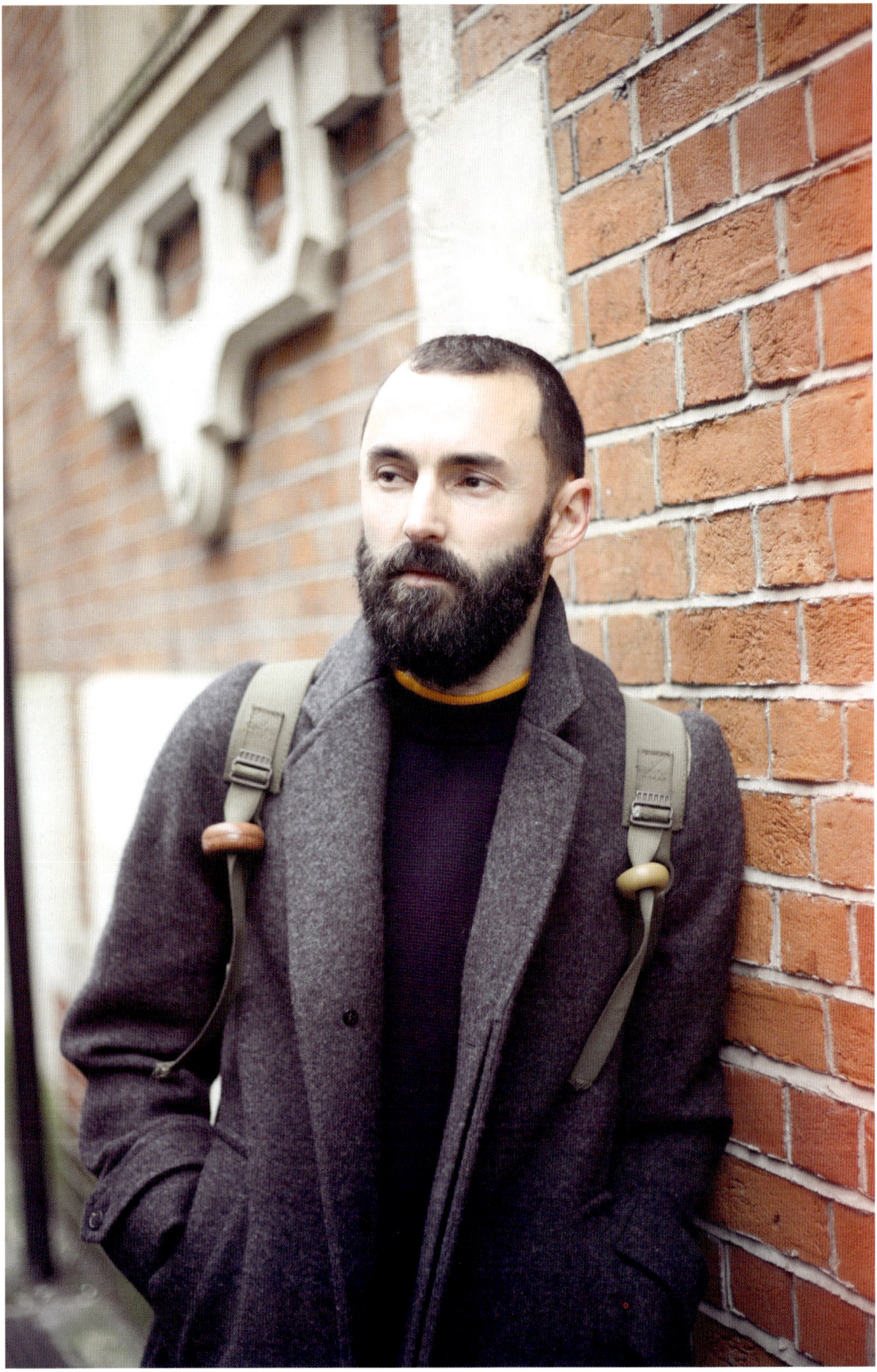

169 • Hugo: Endell Street, London

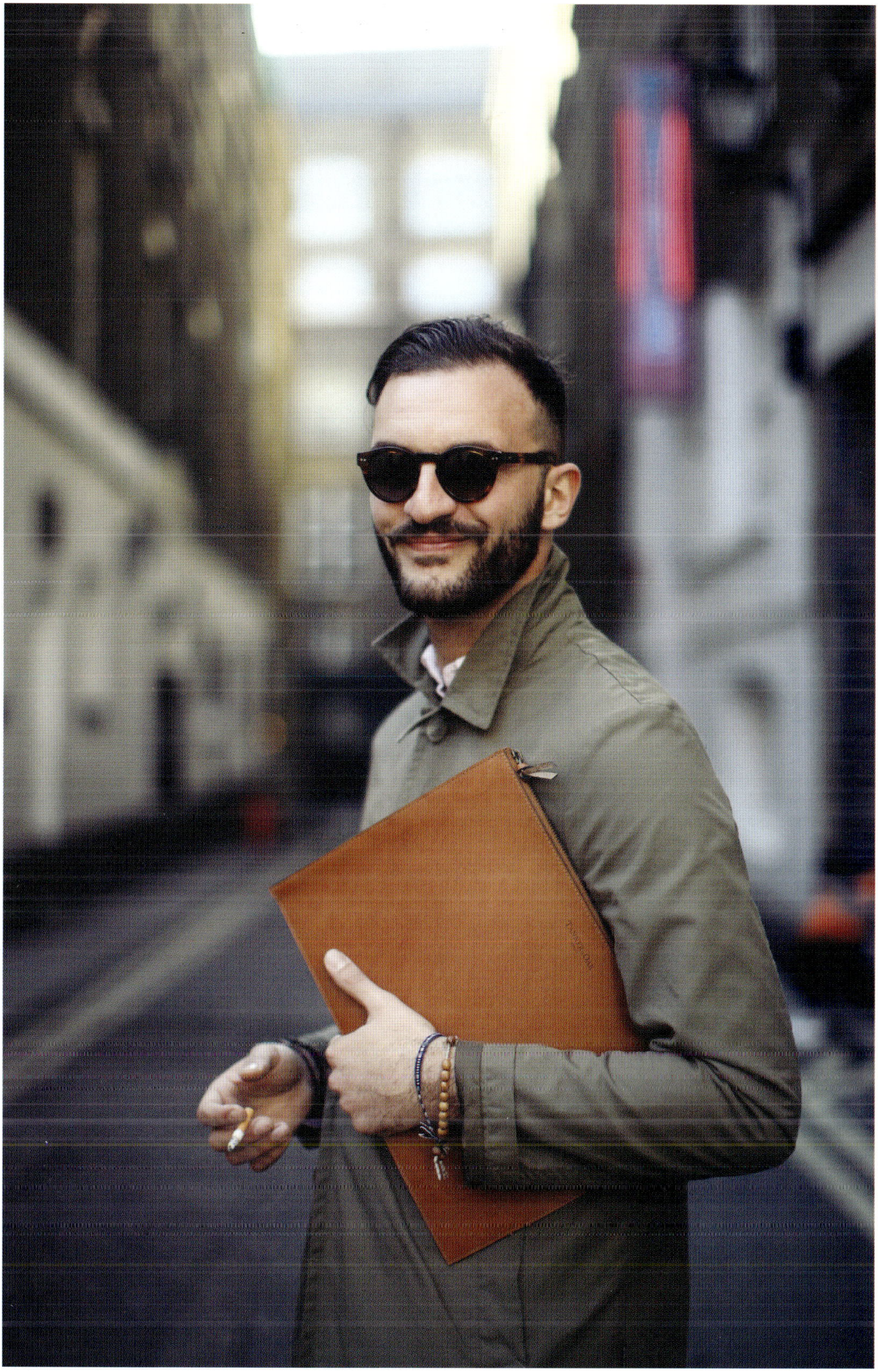

170 • Tee: Mercer Street, London

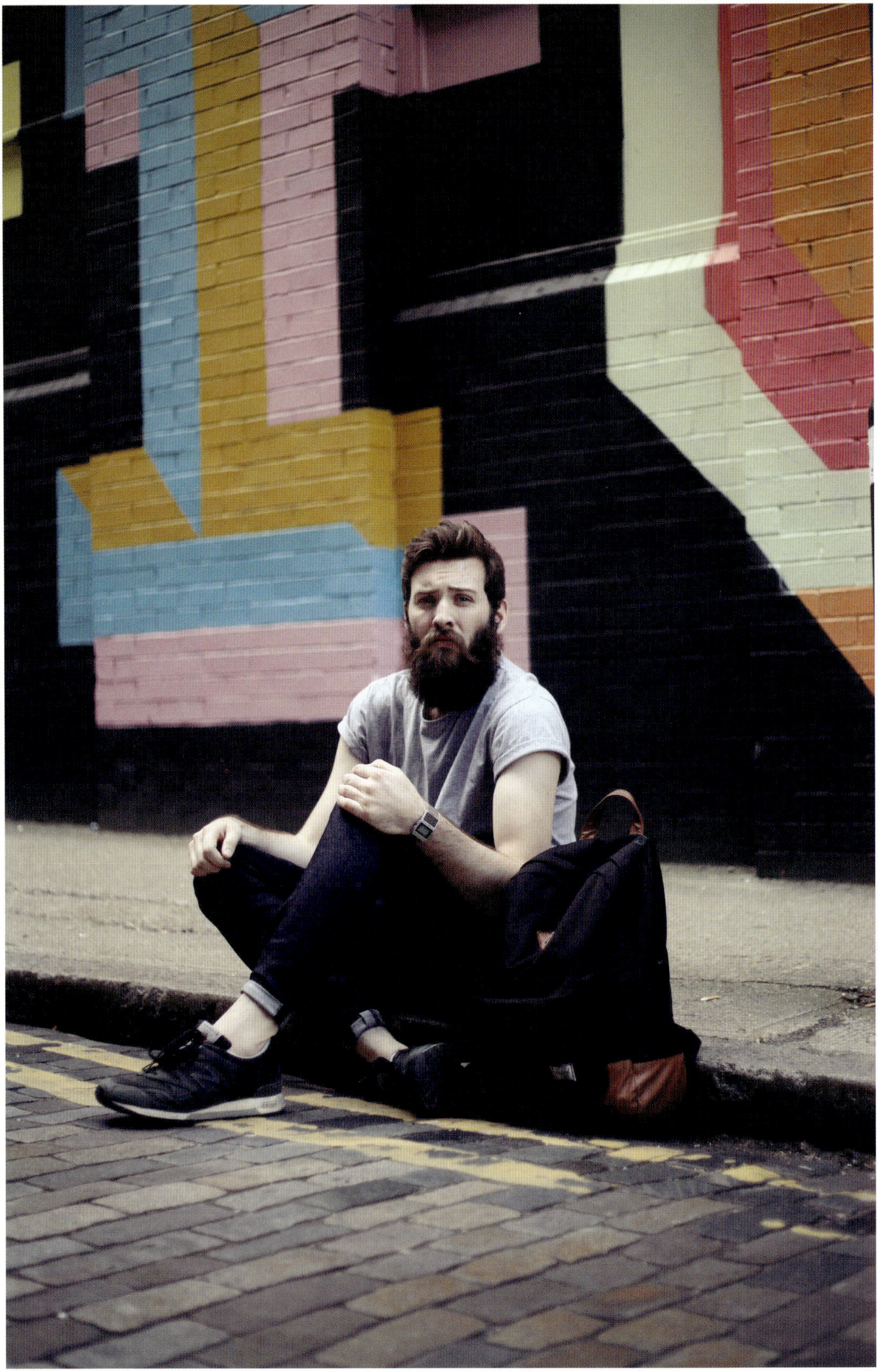

171 • Tim: Ebor Street, London

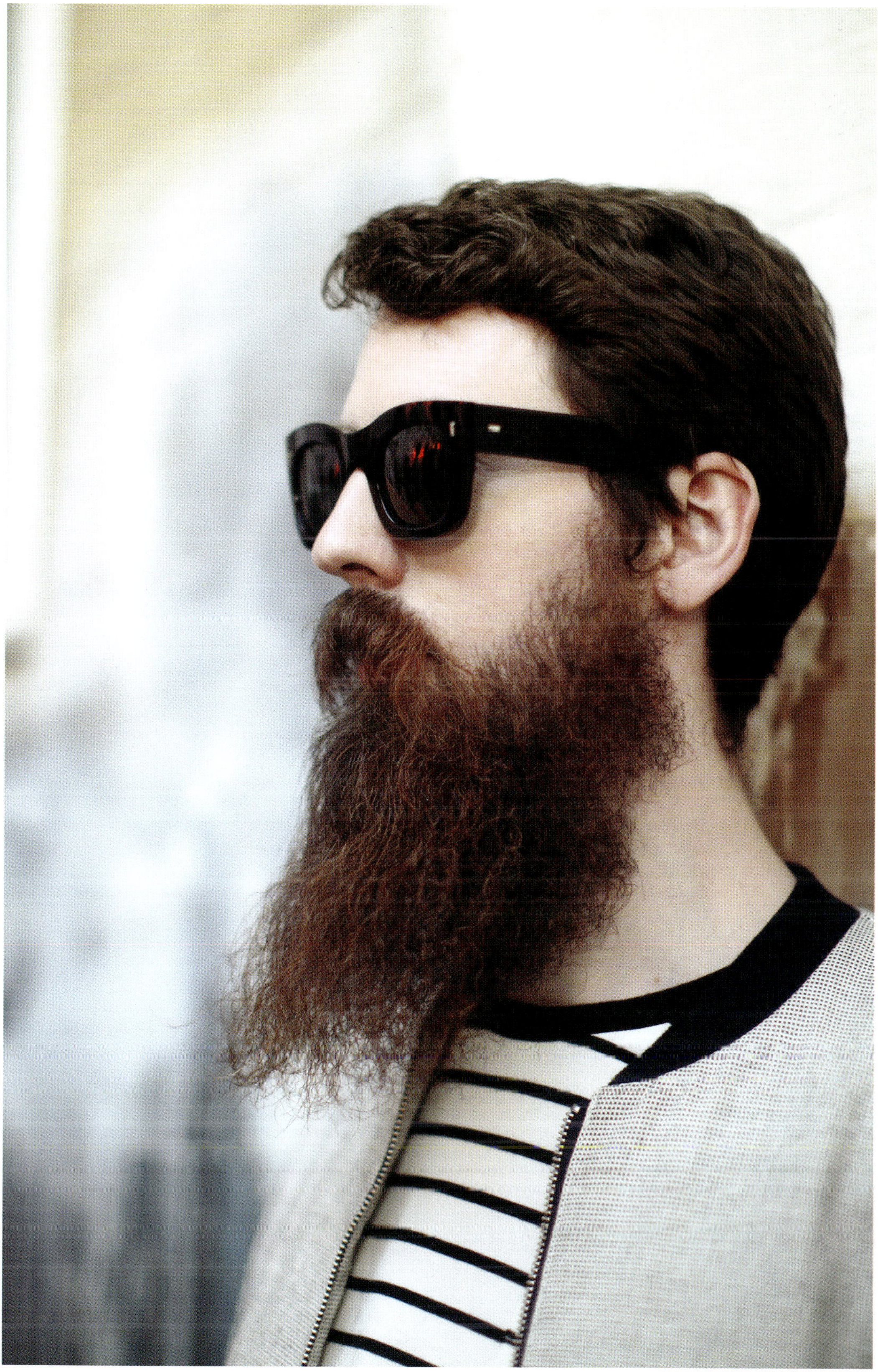

172 • Séamus: Langley Street, London

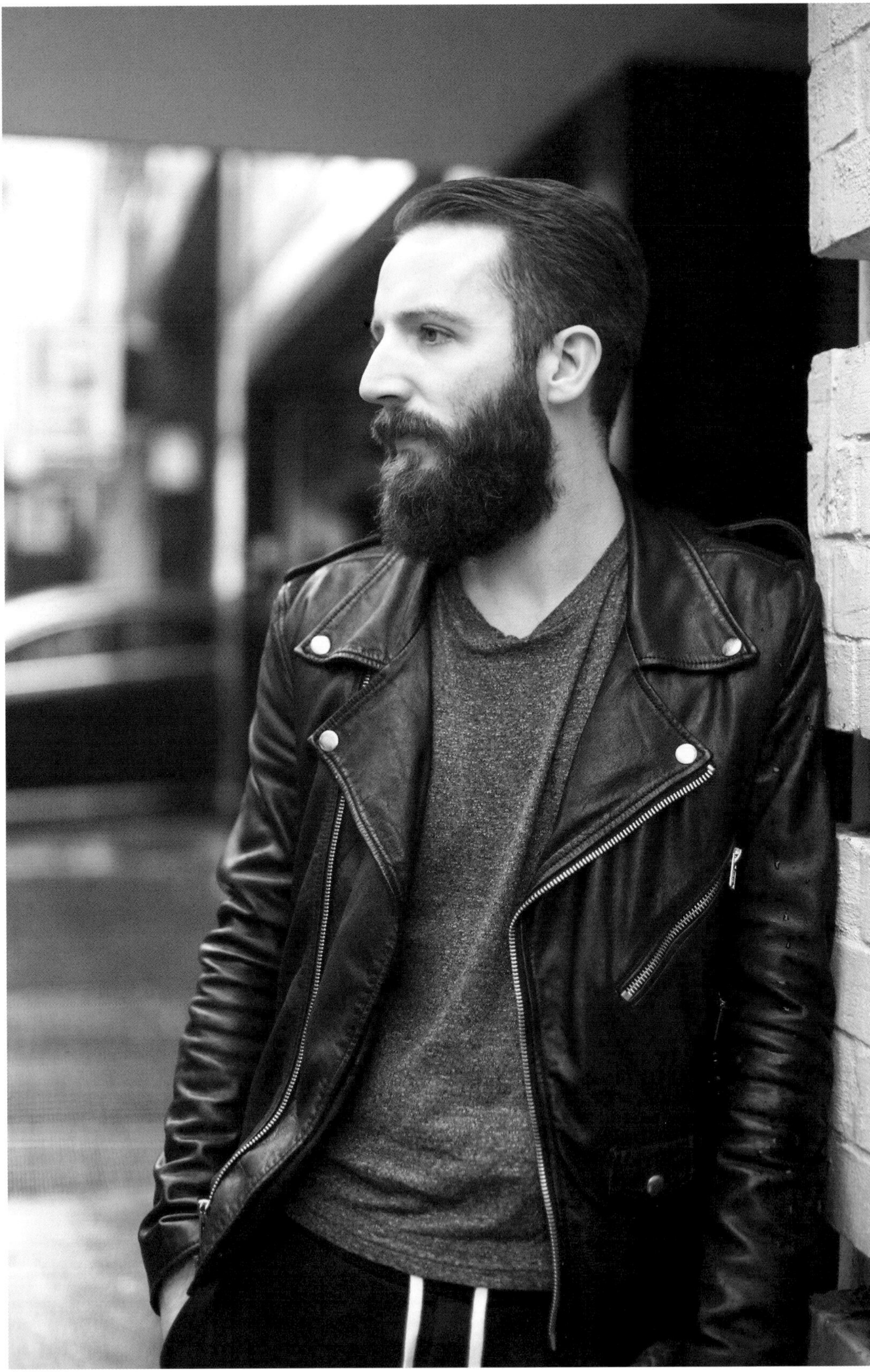

173 • Martin: Marshall Street, London

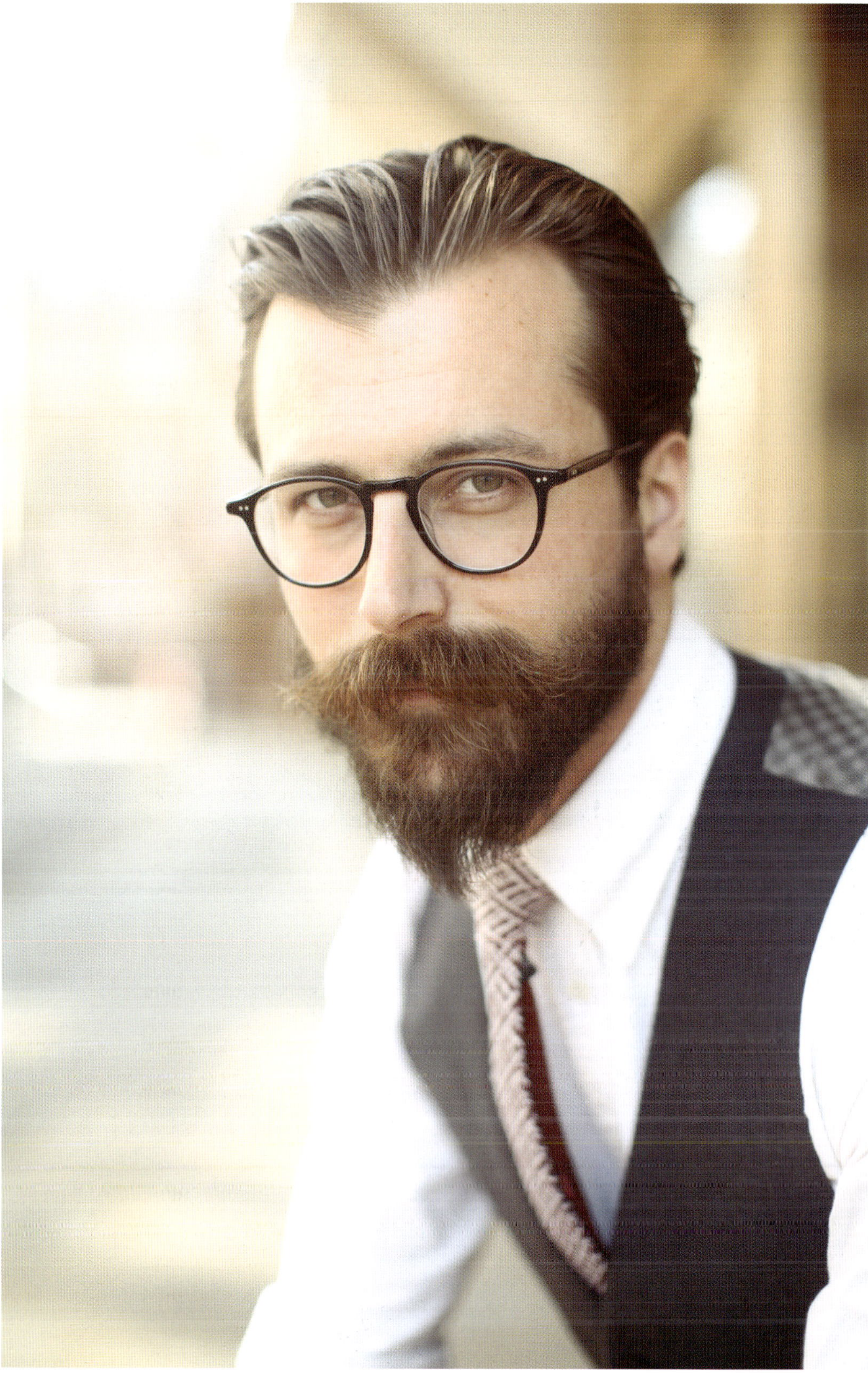

174 • Matteo: Broadwick Street, London

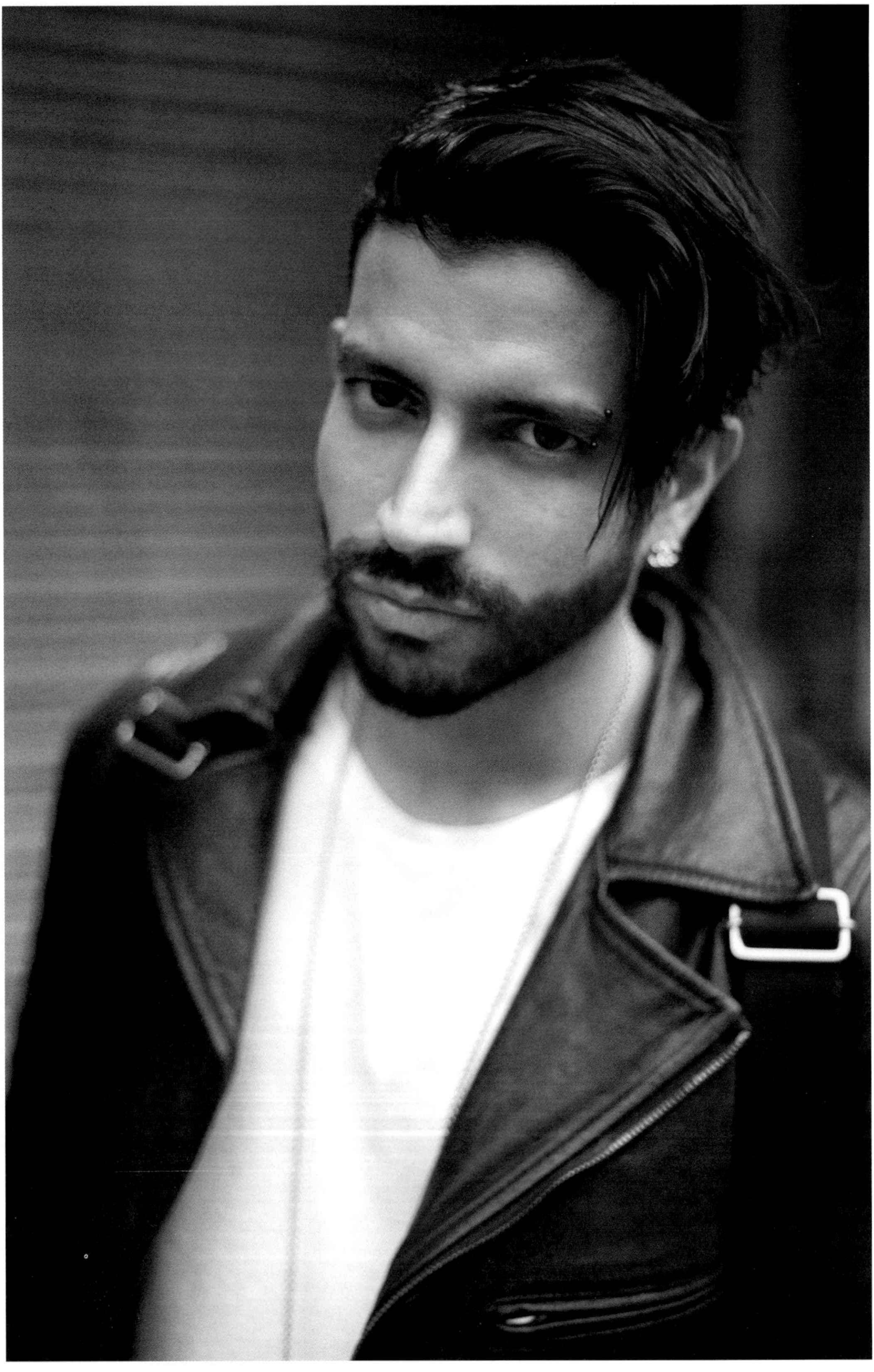

175 • Nik: Endell Street, London

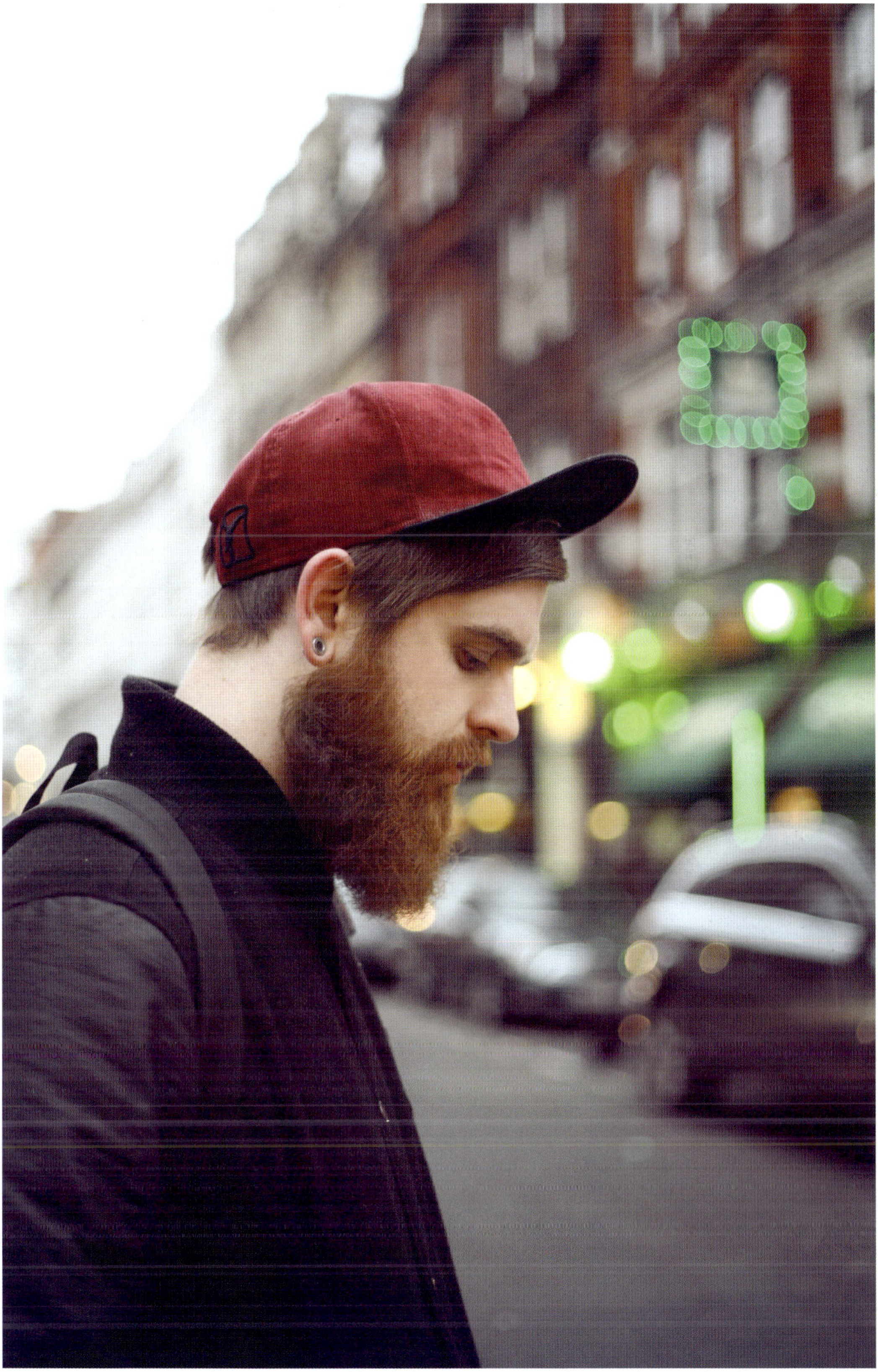

176 • Brendan: Henrietta Street, London

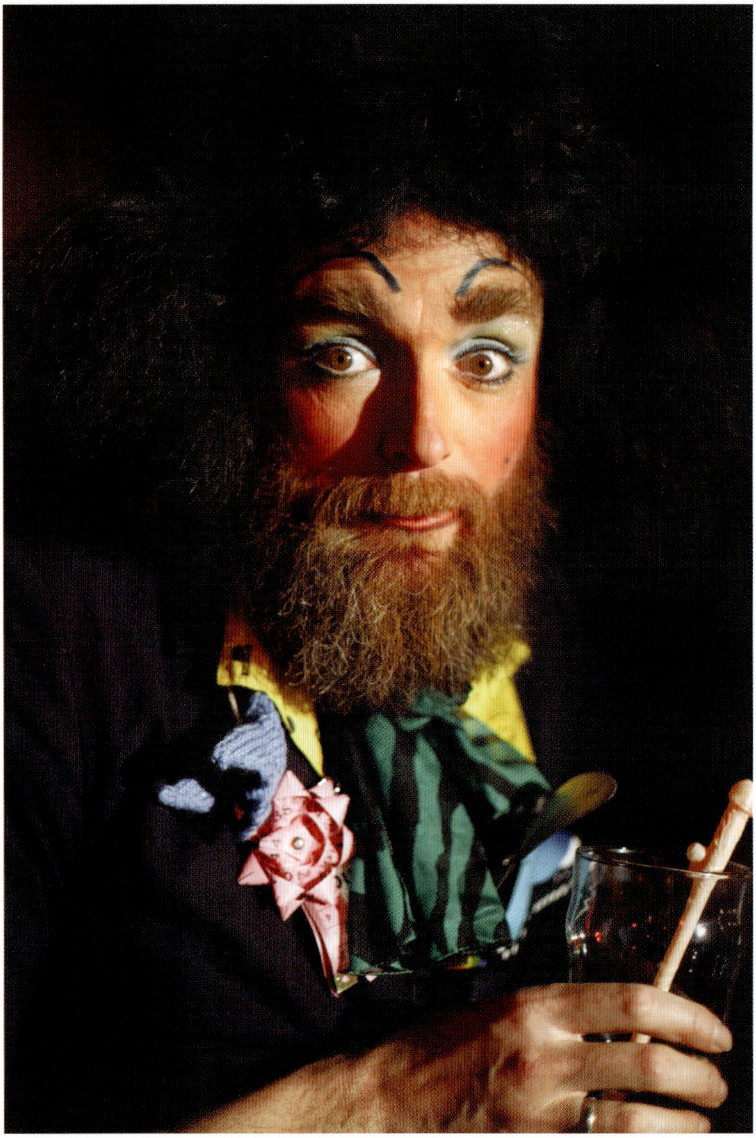

My beard is wonderful. It is at its most wonderful when I'm at my most self-absorbed, lost or in despair - when I forget I have it and someone mentions it. It is a beard of many colours. It's grounding, it's raw, it's a campaign against the tyranny of male grooming products. It's my absolute masculinity. It stops men in their tracks, it's empowering, it's funny. It stops women in their tracks, it's a conversation maker, a peace maker. It is well and truly my best friend and I feel naked and weak without it ... like Samson.

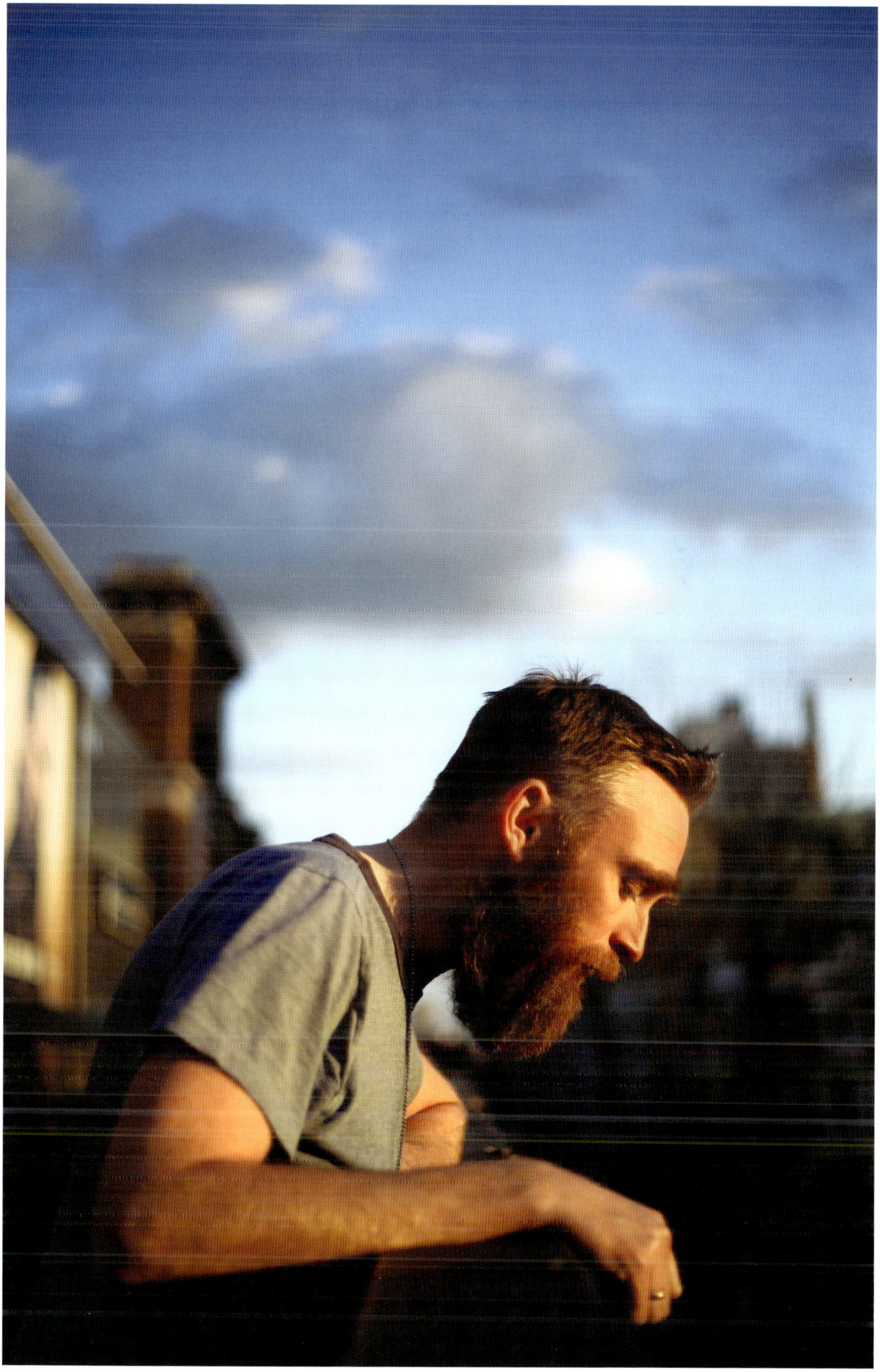

177 • Tim: Vauxhall, London

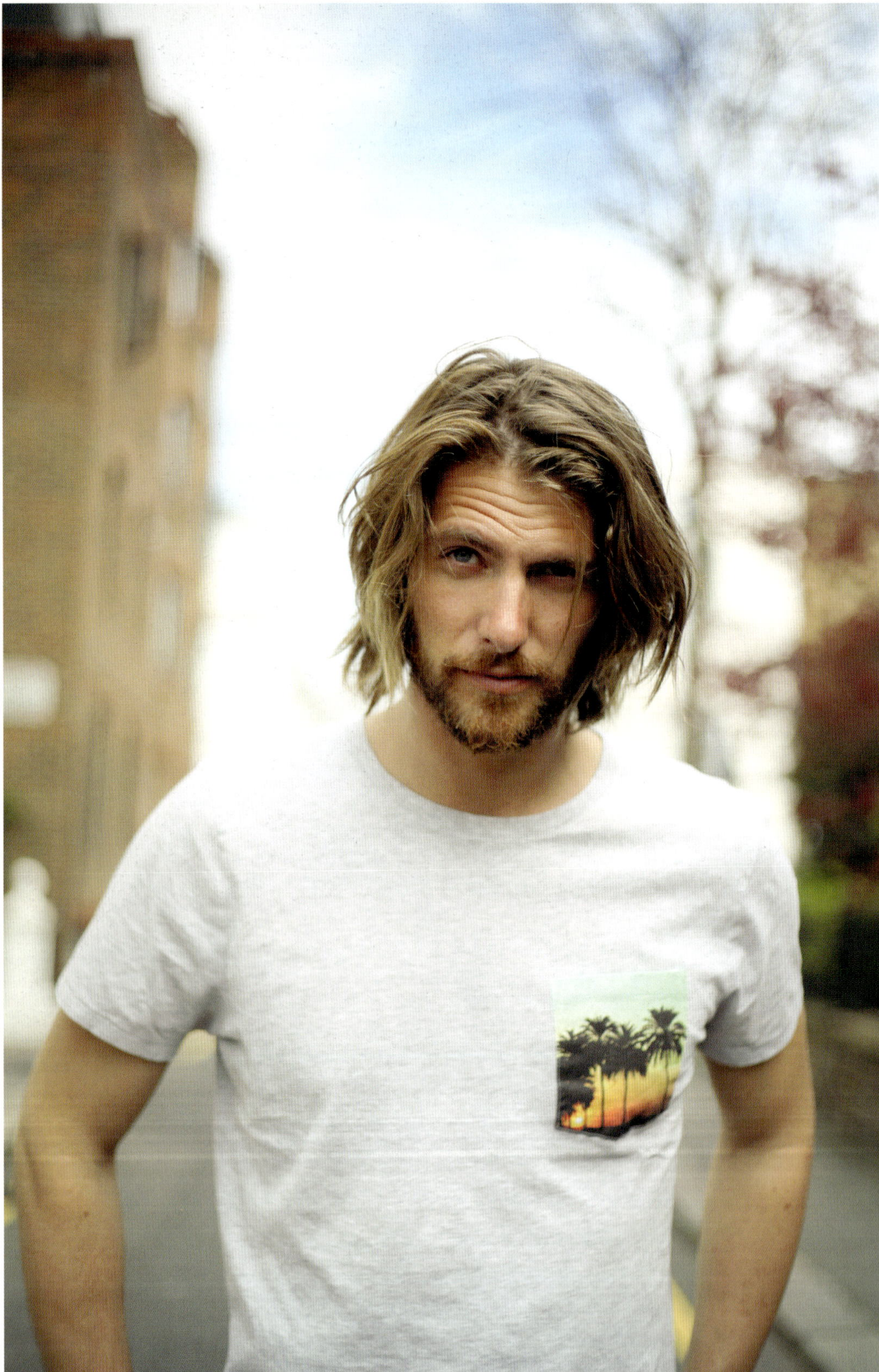

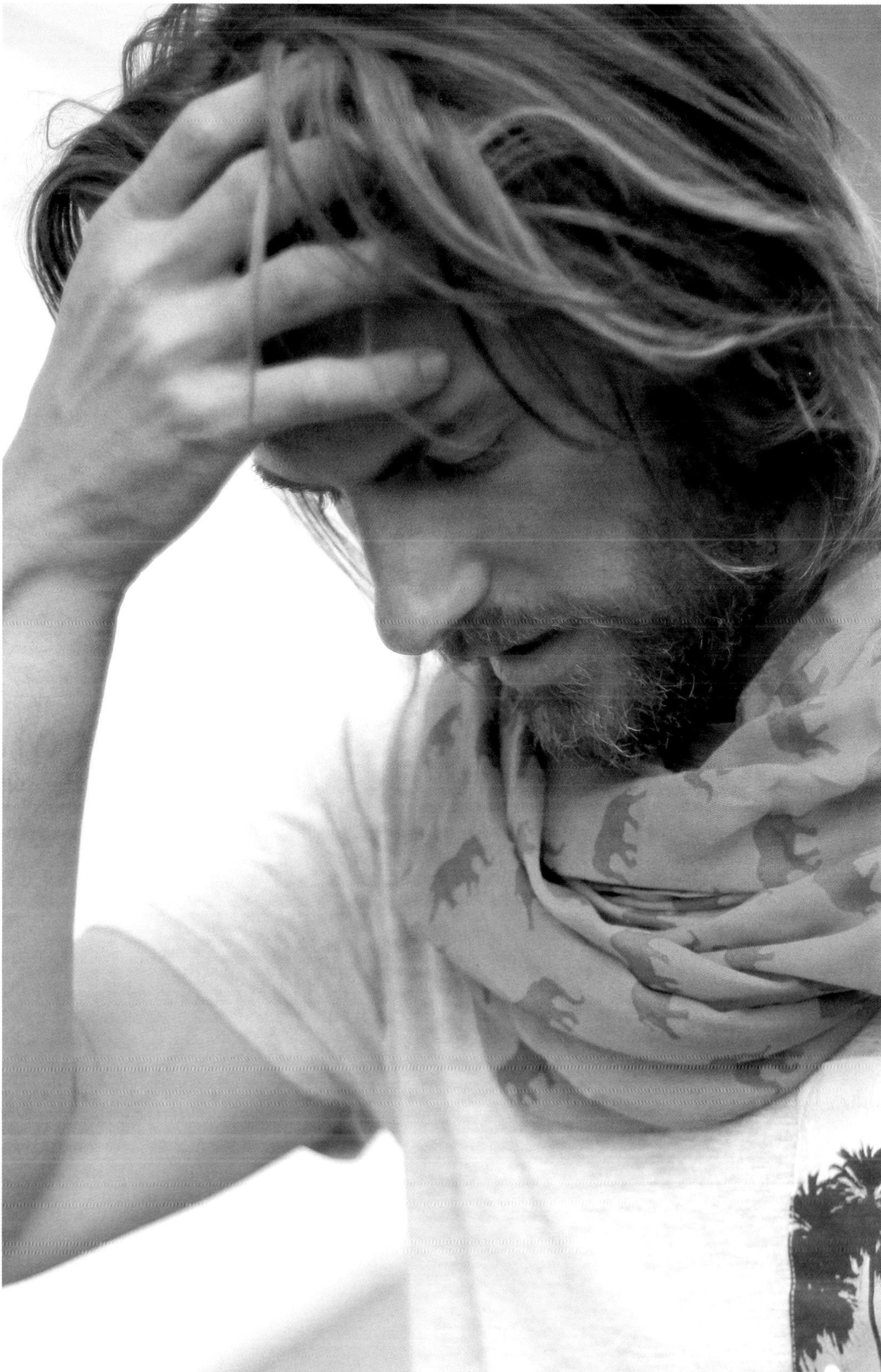

 • James: De Vere Gardens, London

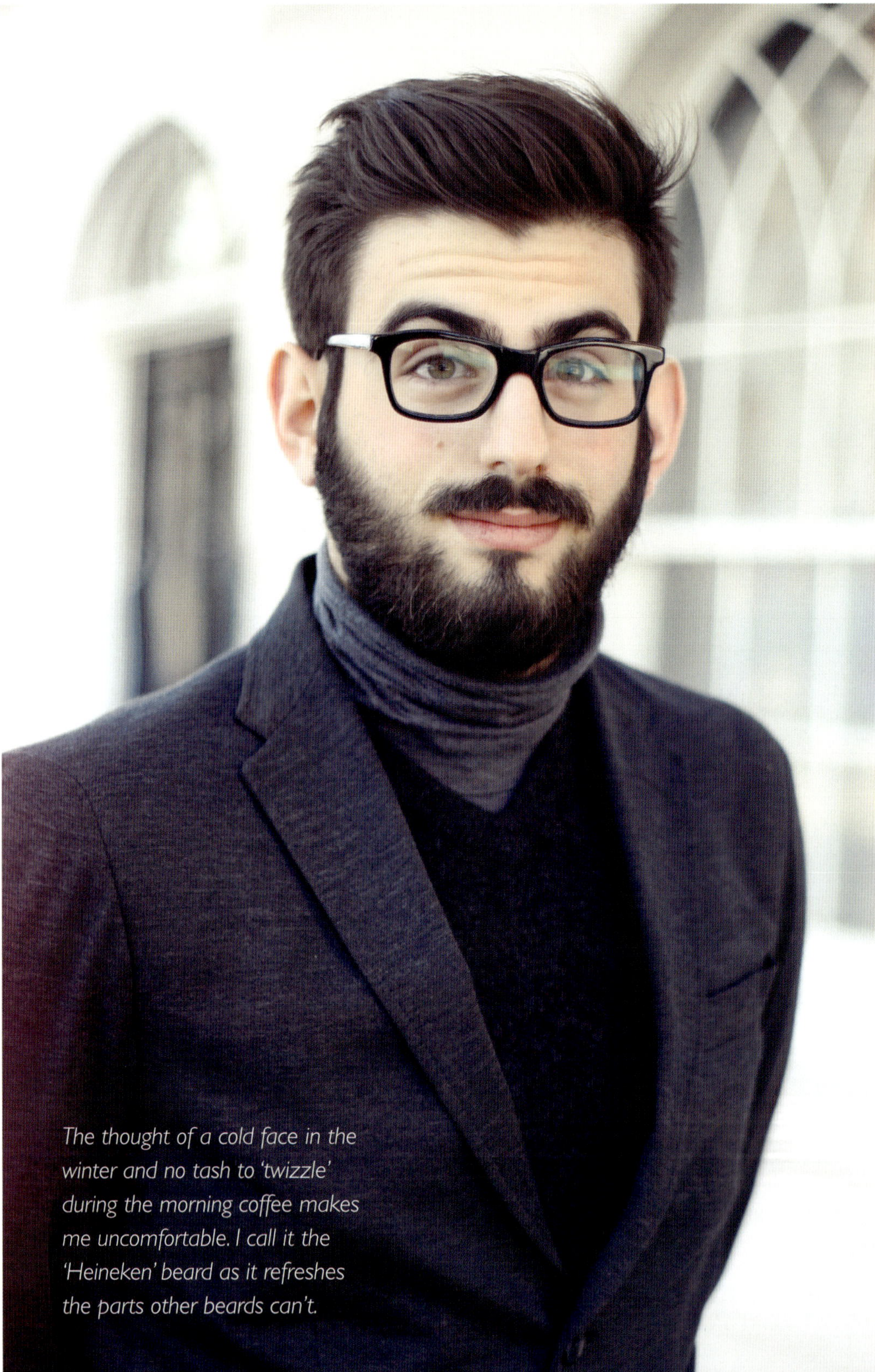

The thought of a cold face in the winter and no tash to 'twizzle' during the morning coffee makes me uncomfortable. I call it the 'Heineken' beard as it refreshes the parts other beards can't.

179 • Denizer: Pratt Street, London

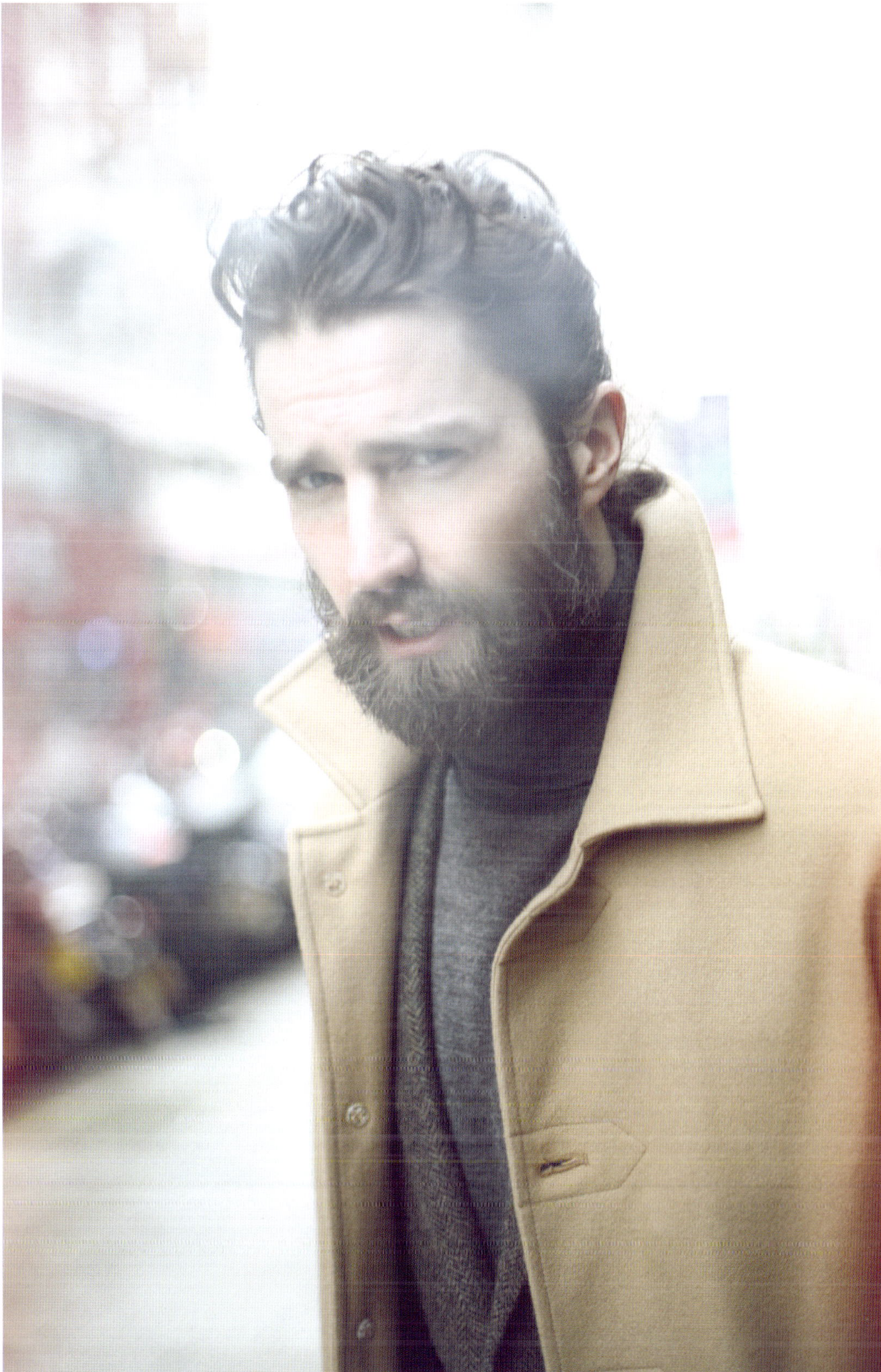

180 • Jack: New Oxford Street, London

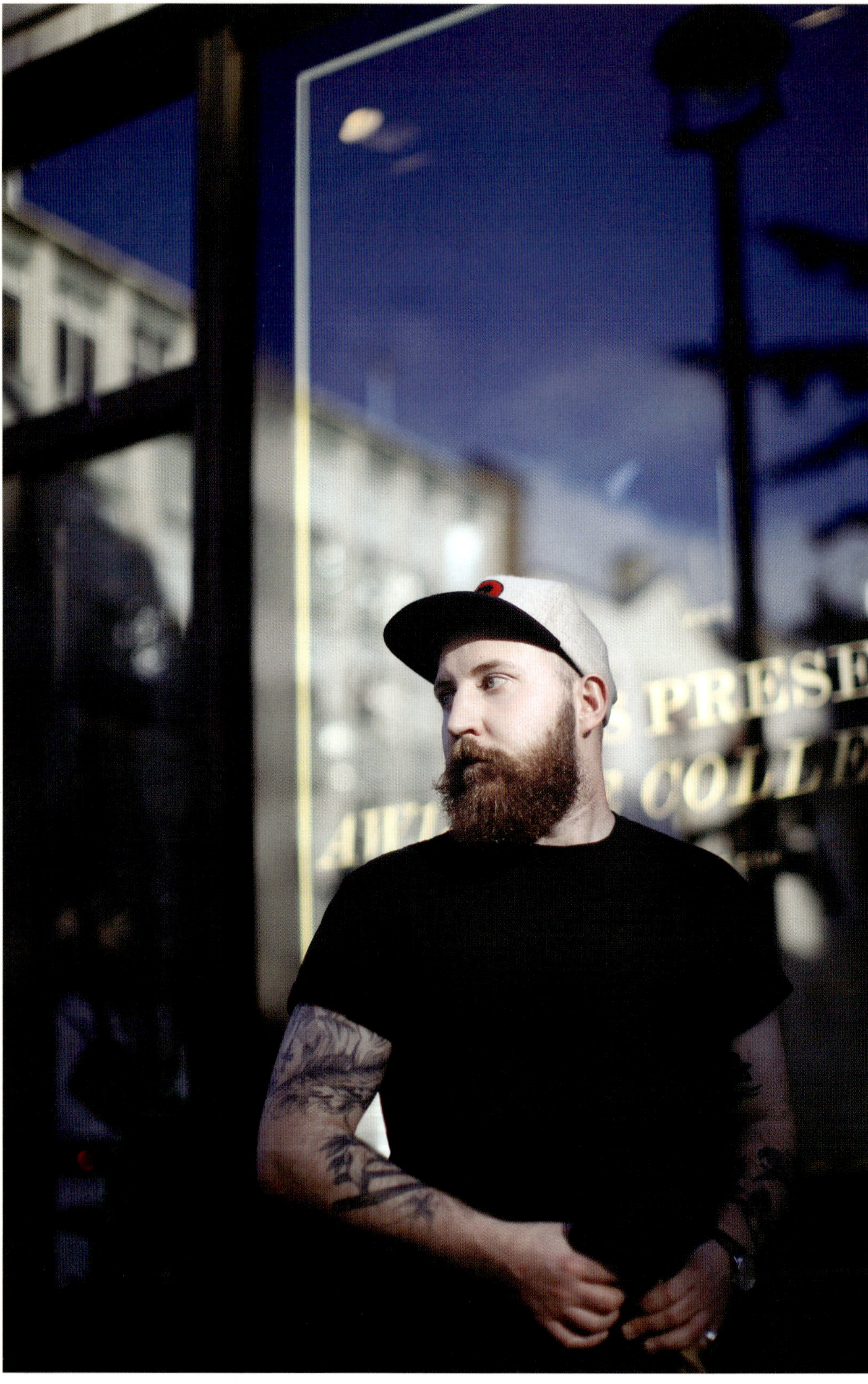

181 • Jamie: Cavendish Place, London

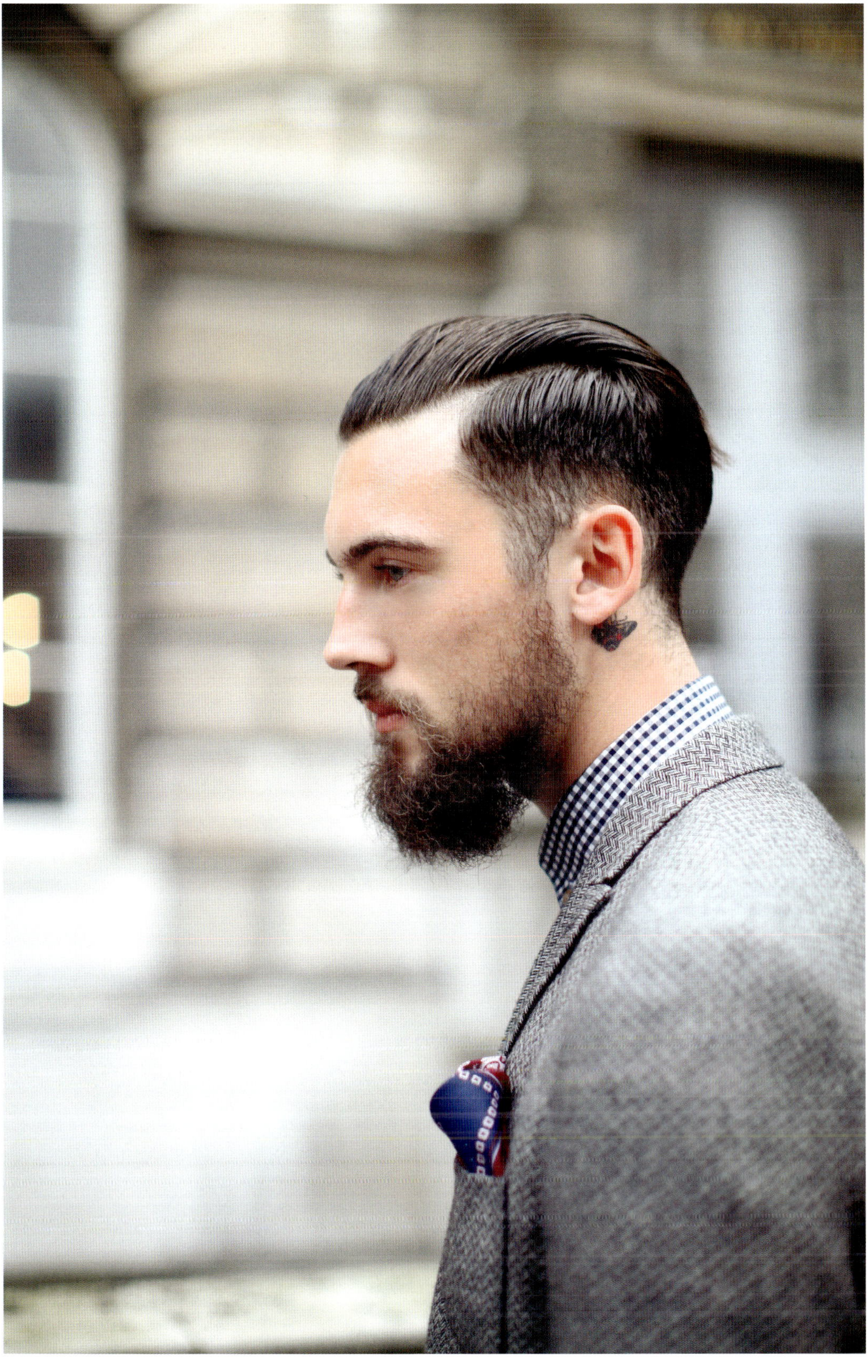

182 • Matt: Somerset House, London

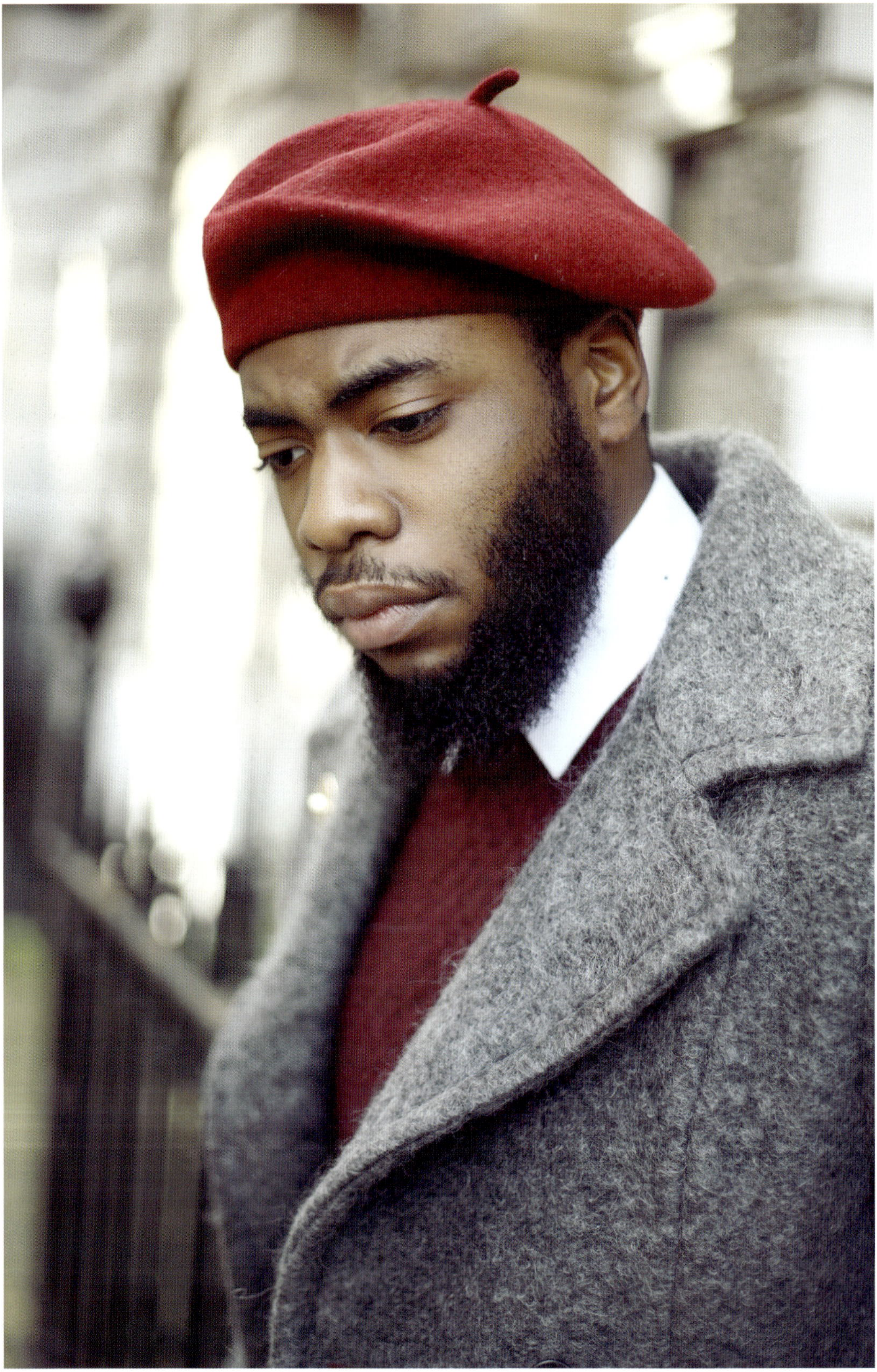

183 • Alain: Somerset House, London

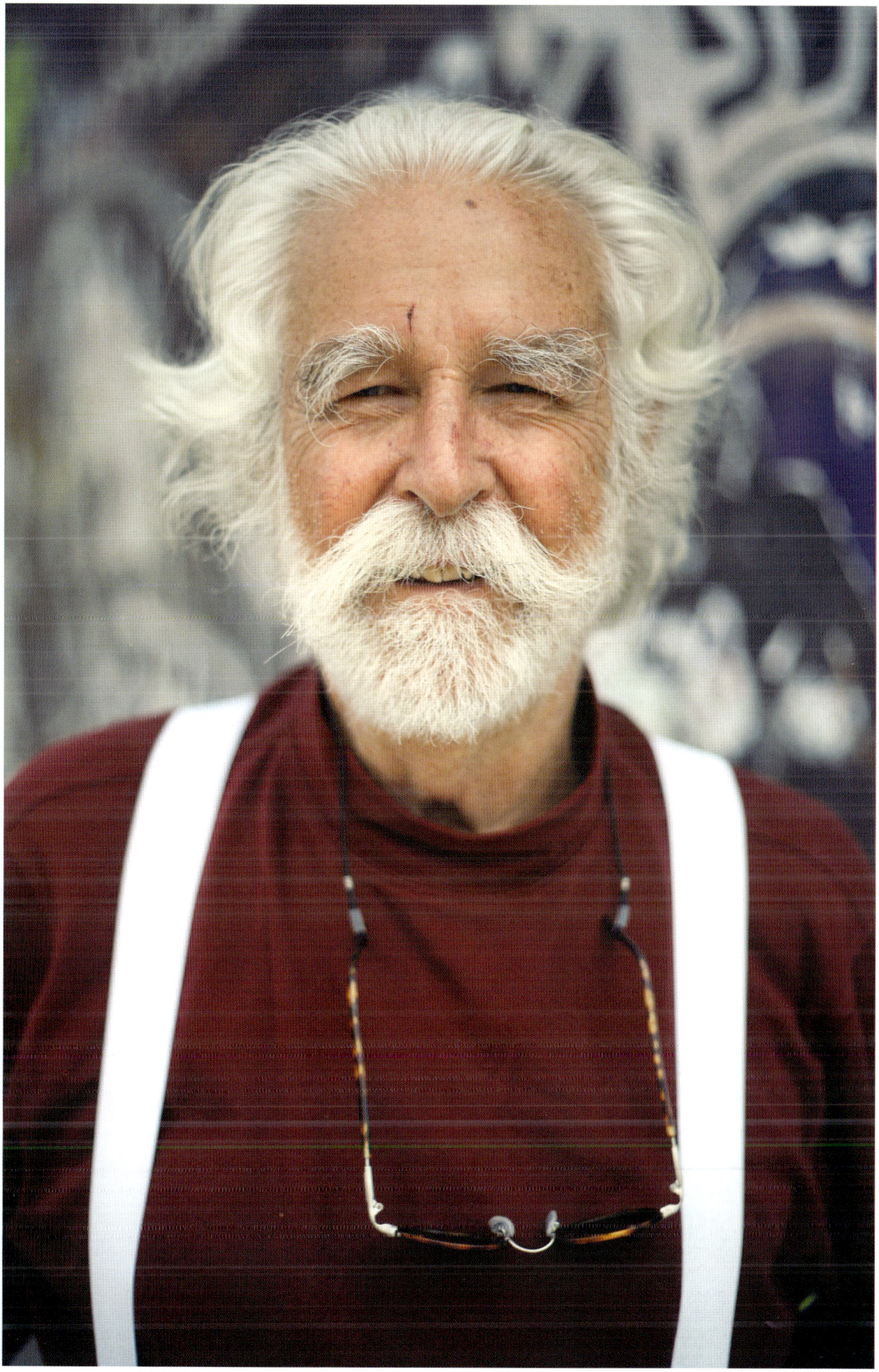

 Bill: Fleur de Lis Street, London

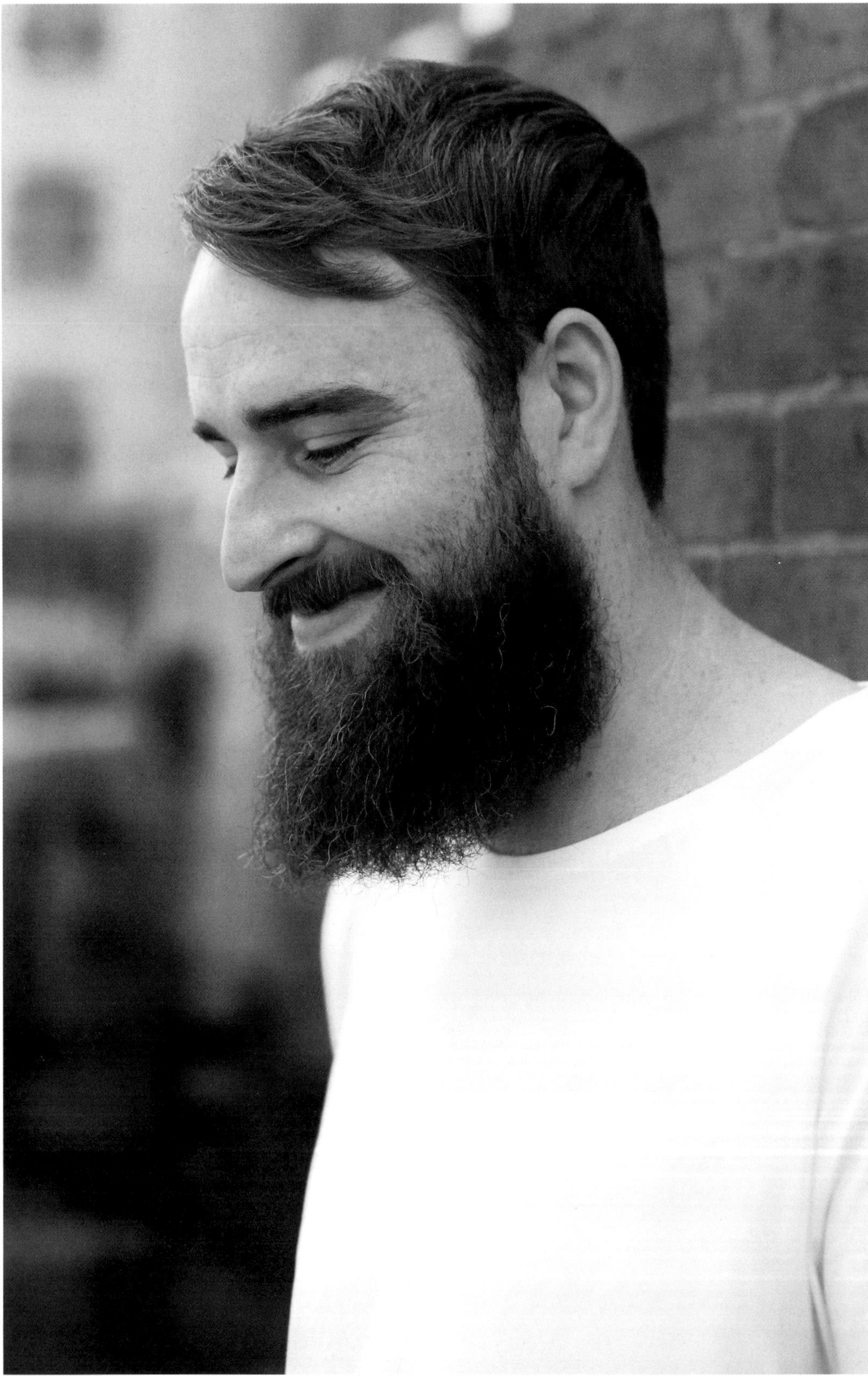

185 • Andrew, Broadwick Street, London

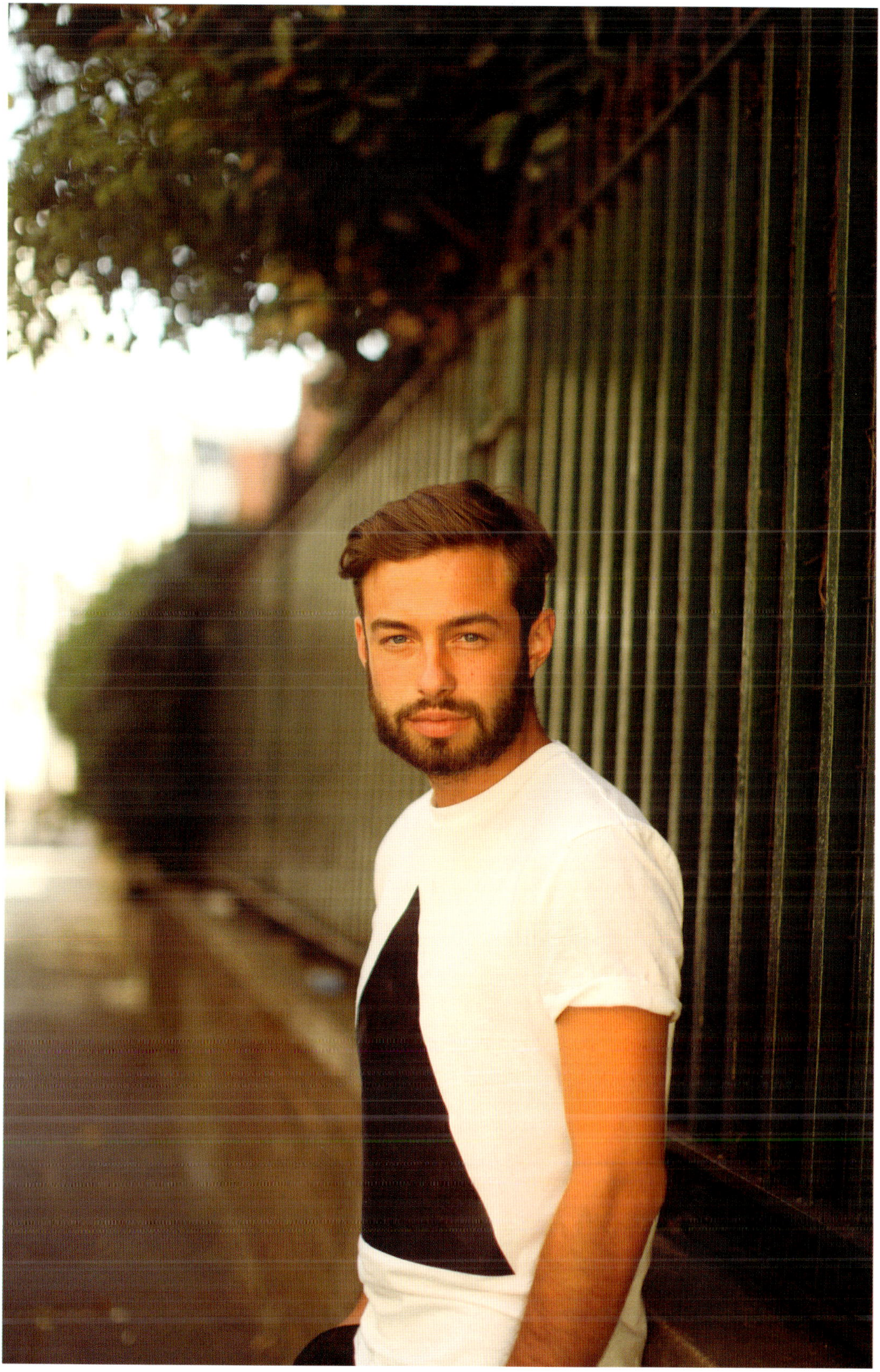

186 • Giammarco: Tower Court, London

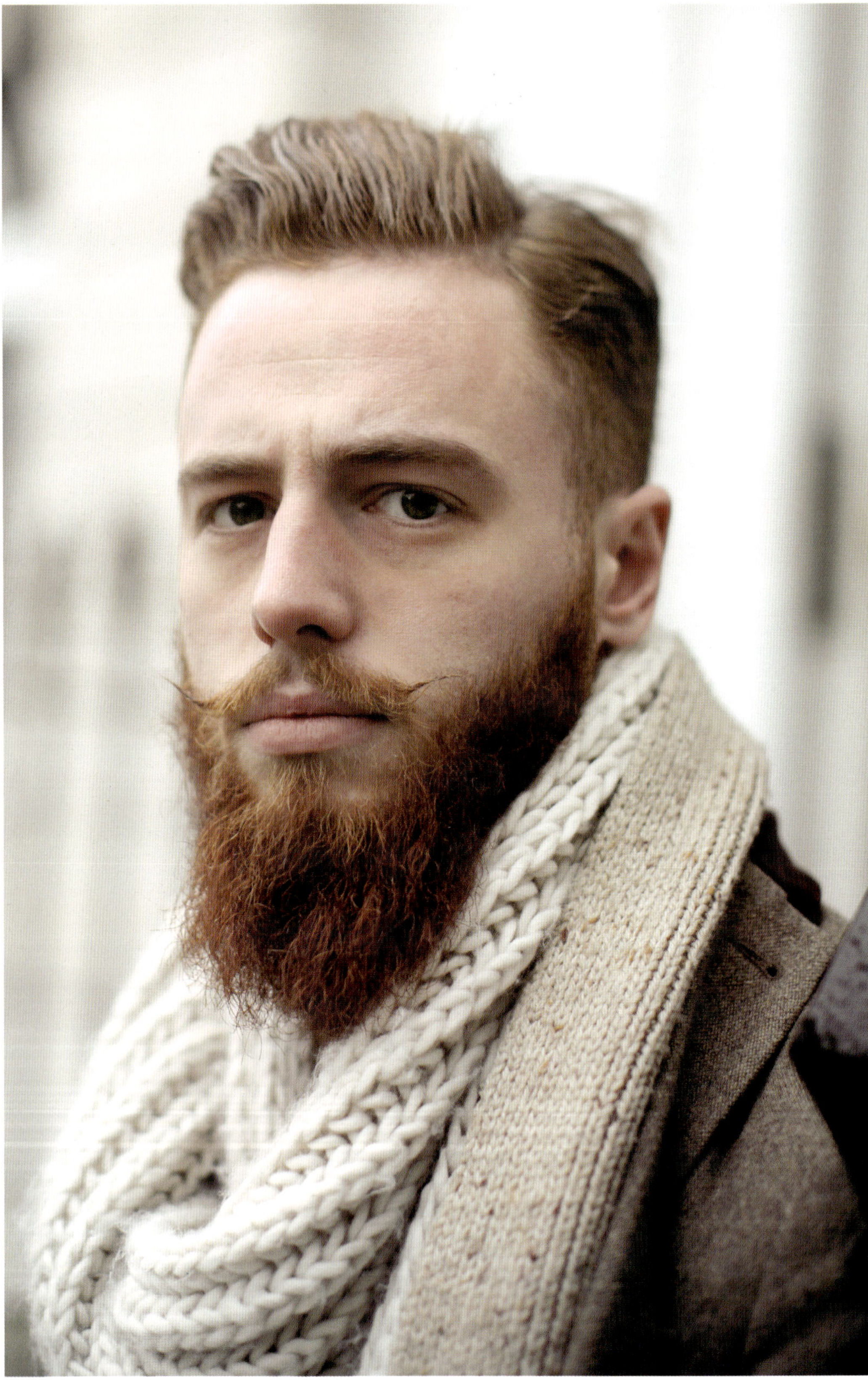

187 • Daniel: Margaret Street, London

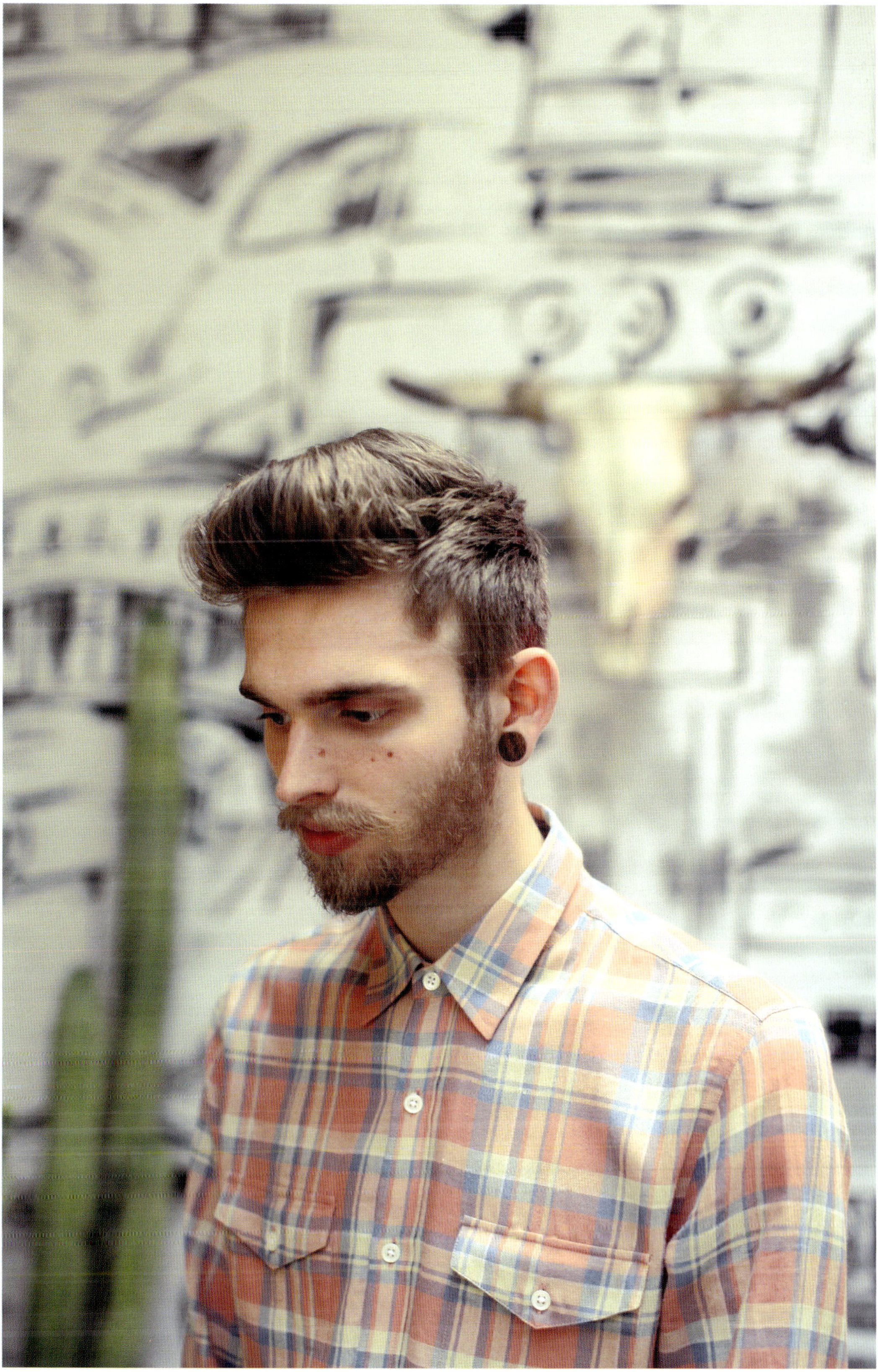

188 • Aaron: Mercer Street Studios, London

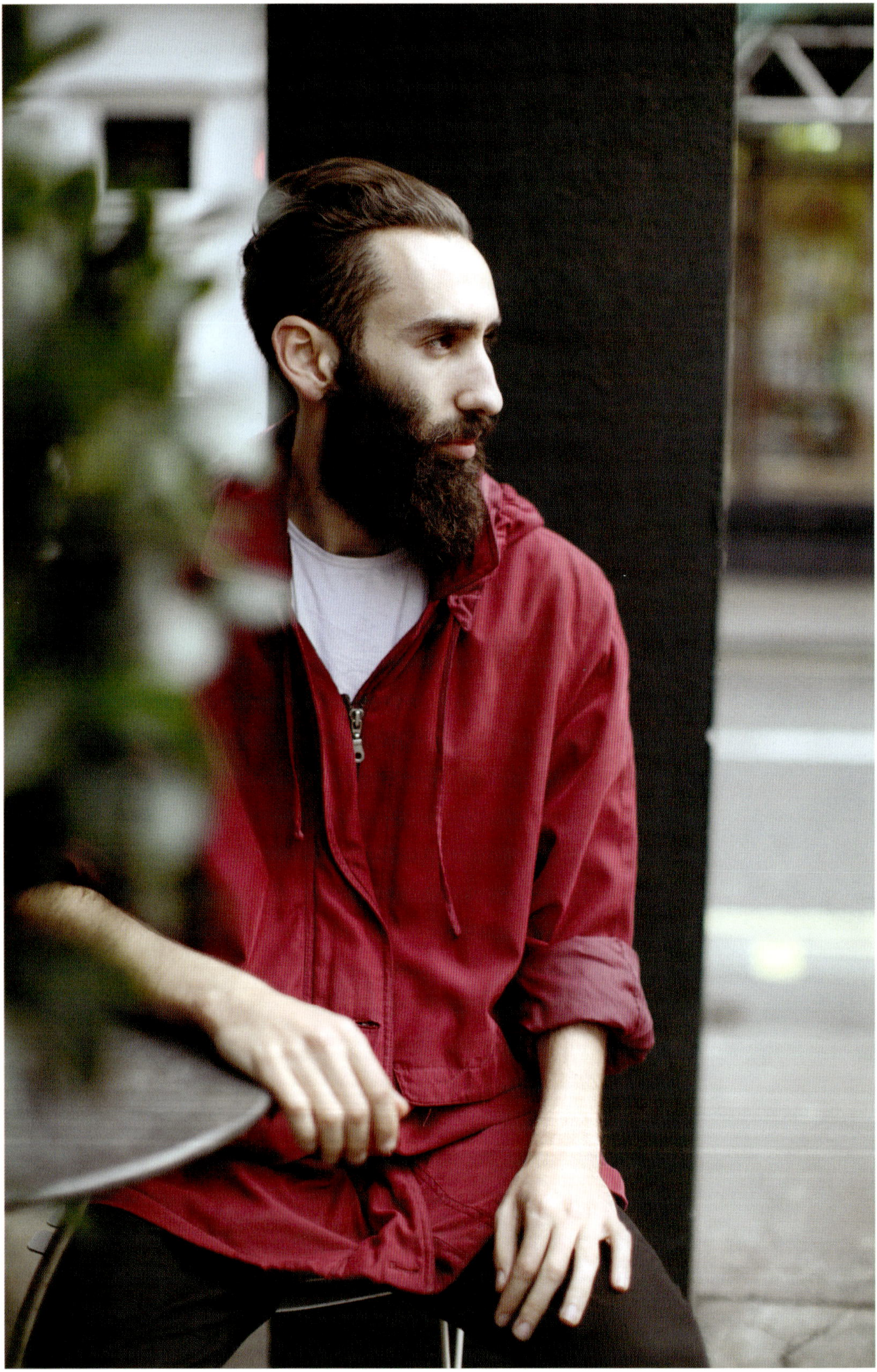

189 • Sergio: Great Pulteney Street, London

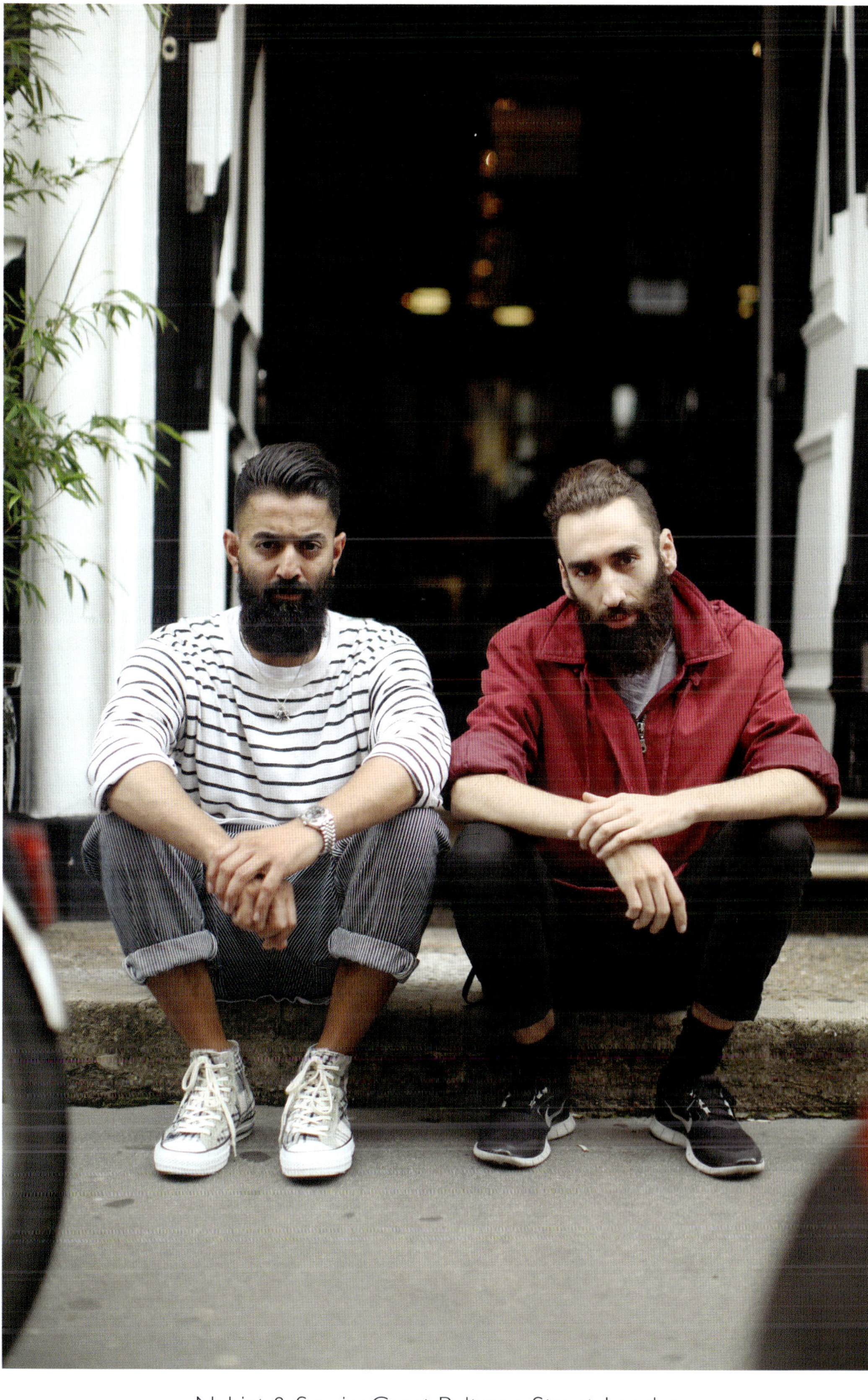

Nehjat & Sergio: Great Pulteney Street, London

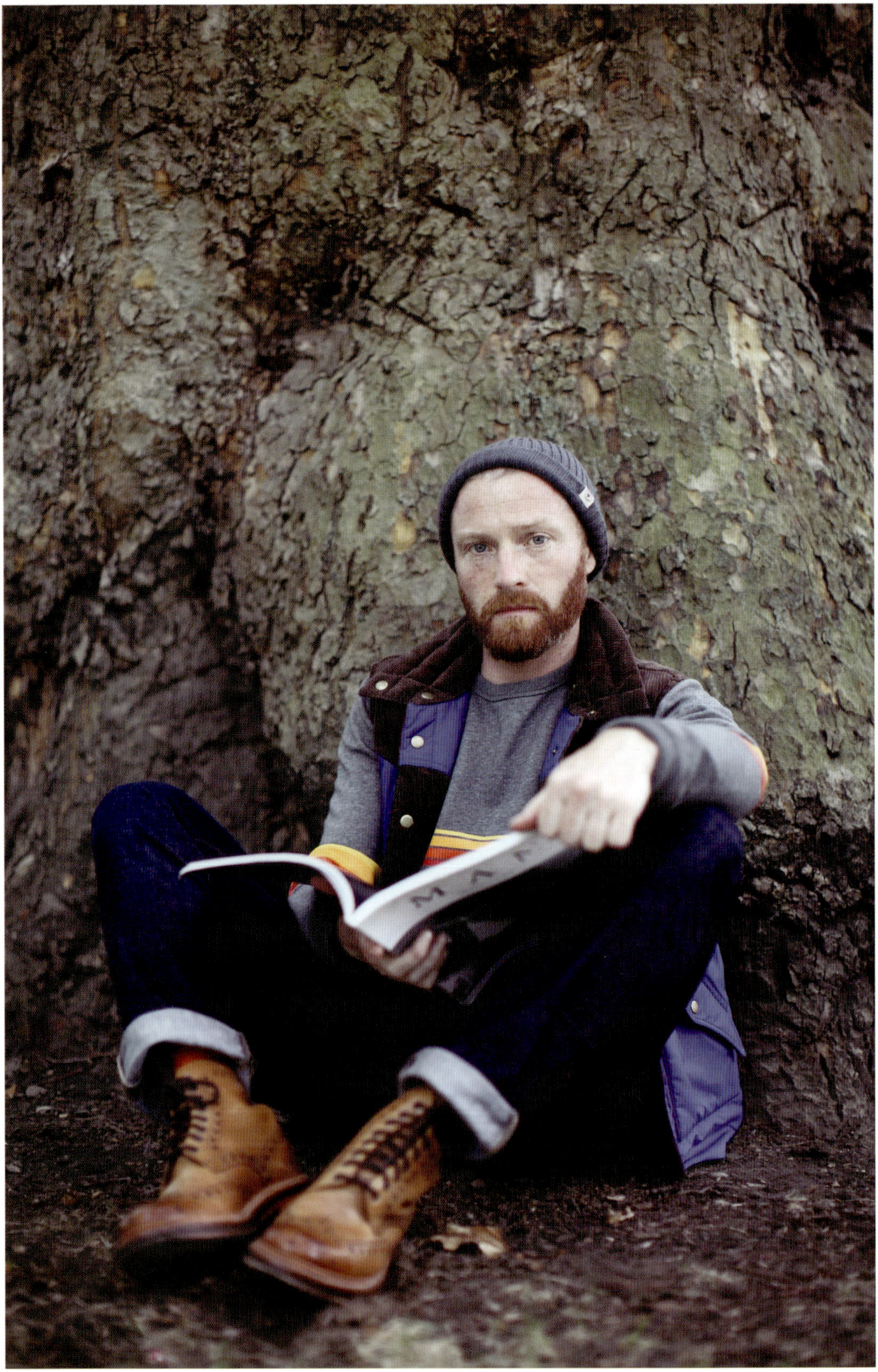

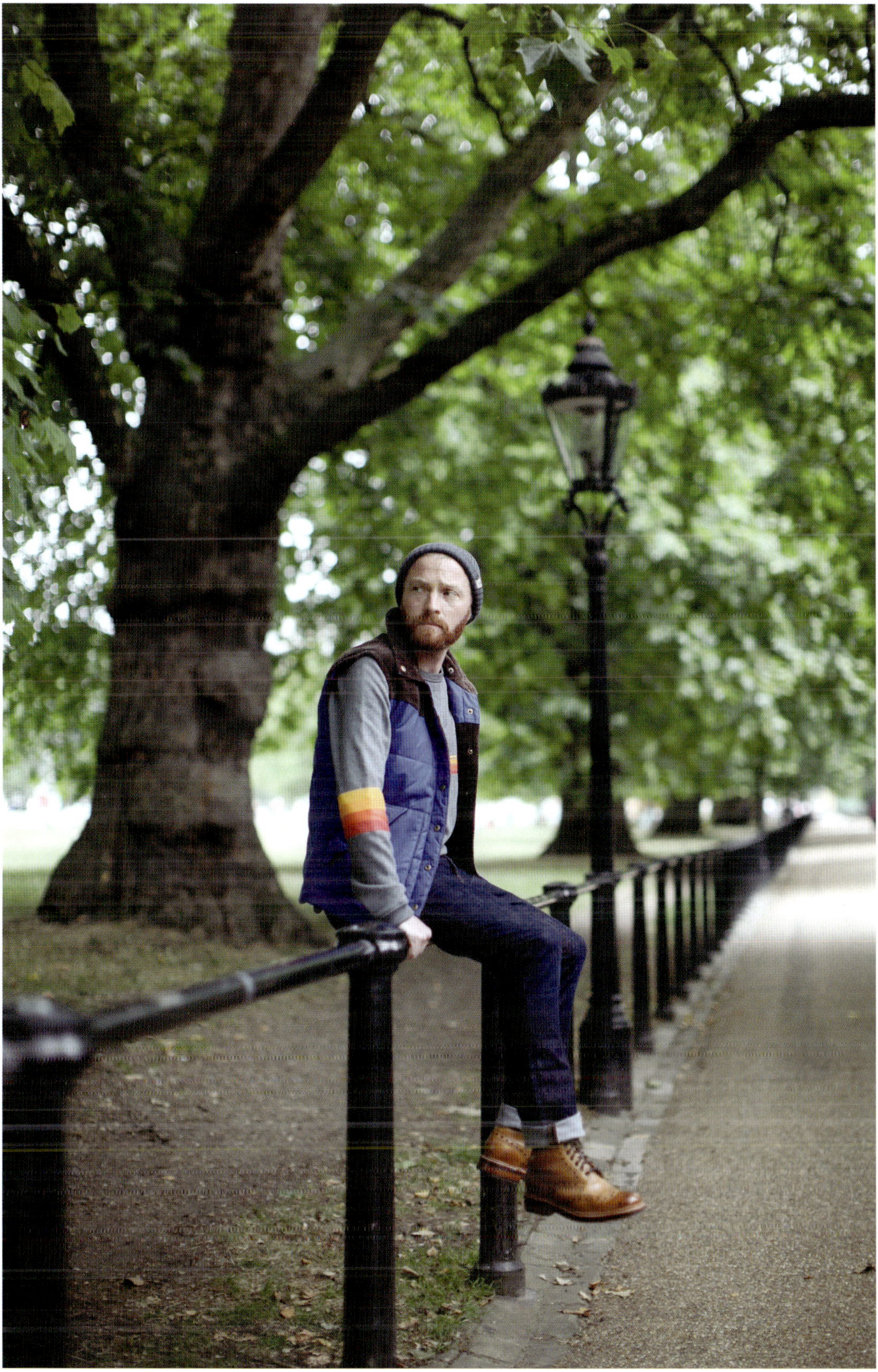

190 • Mark: Green Park, London

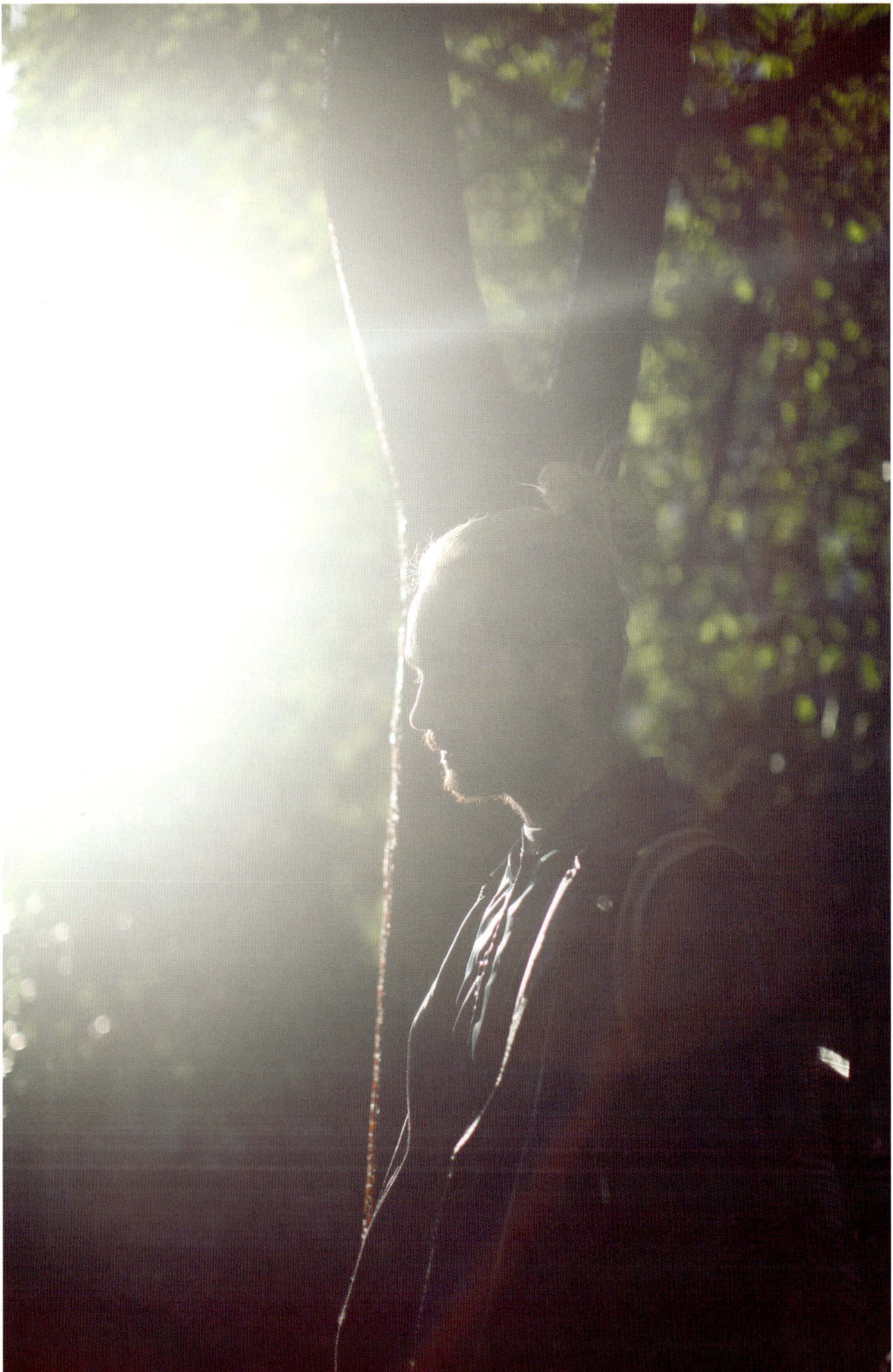

191 • Thomas: Hanover Square, London

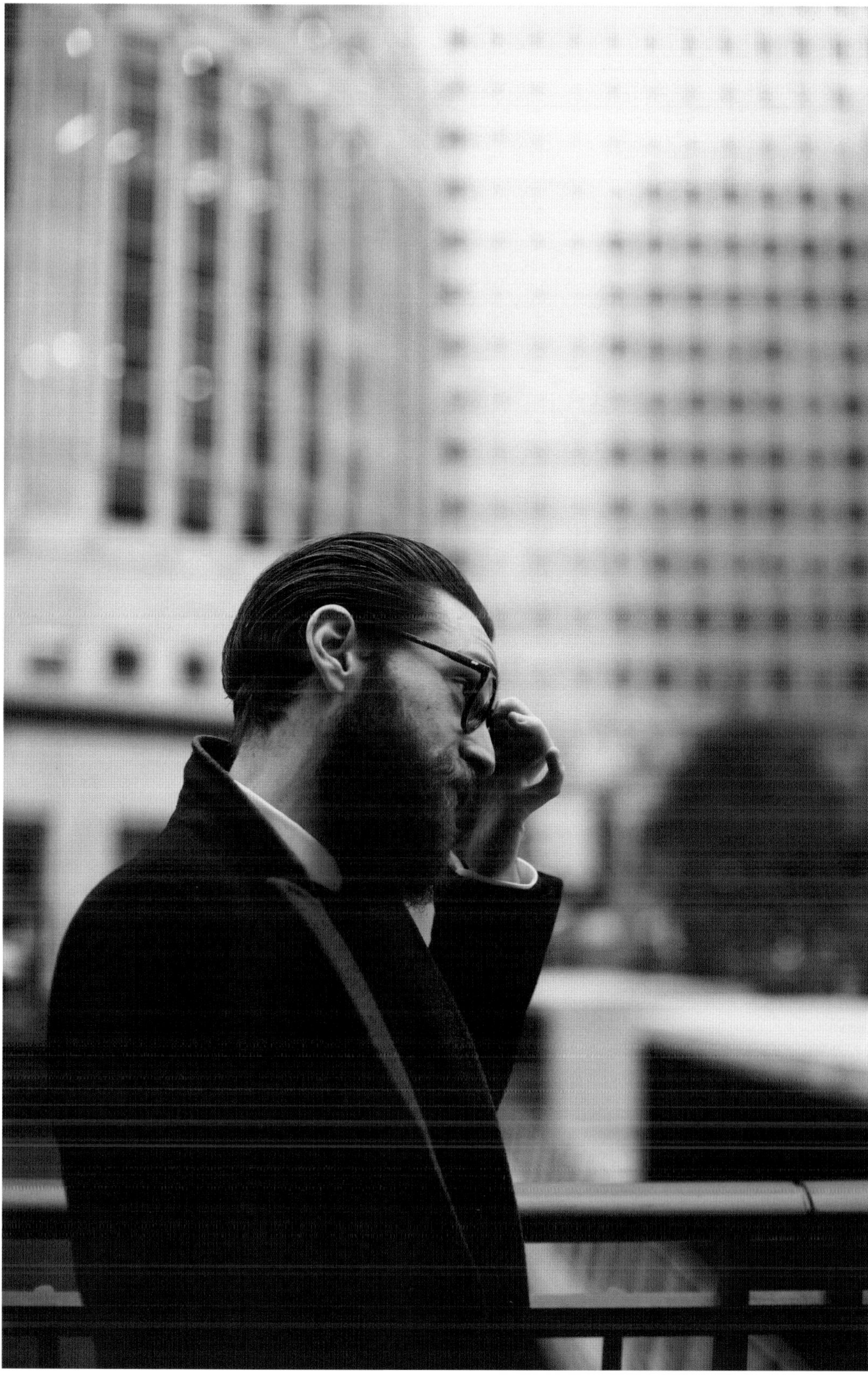

192 • Dominic: CanaryWharf, London

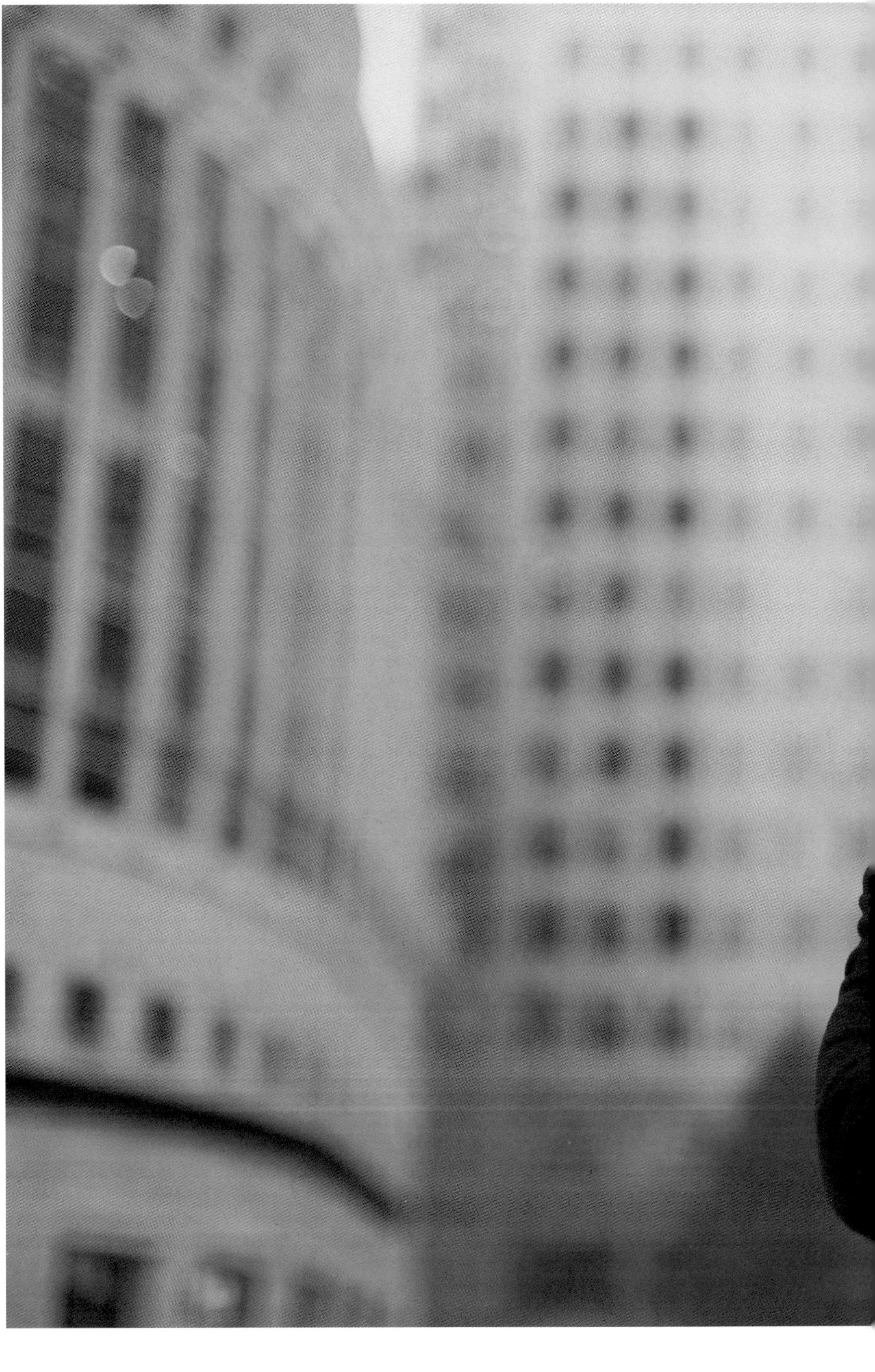

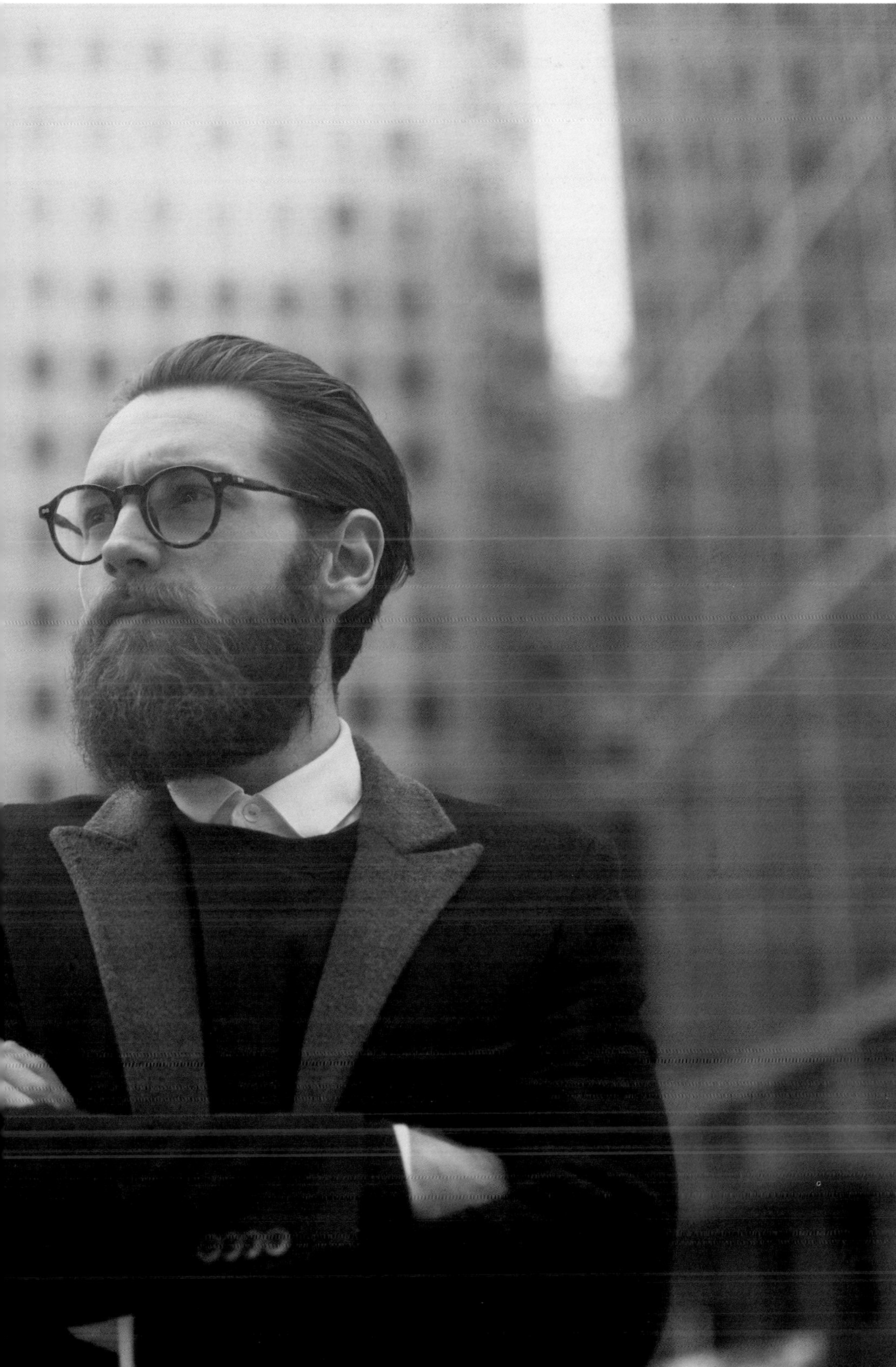

Dominic: Canary Wharf, London

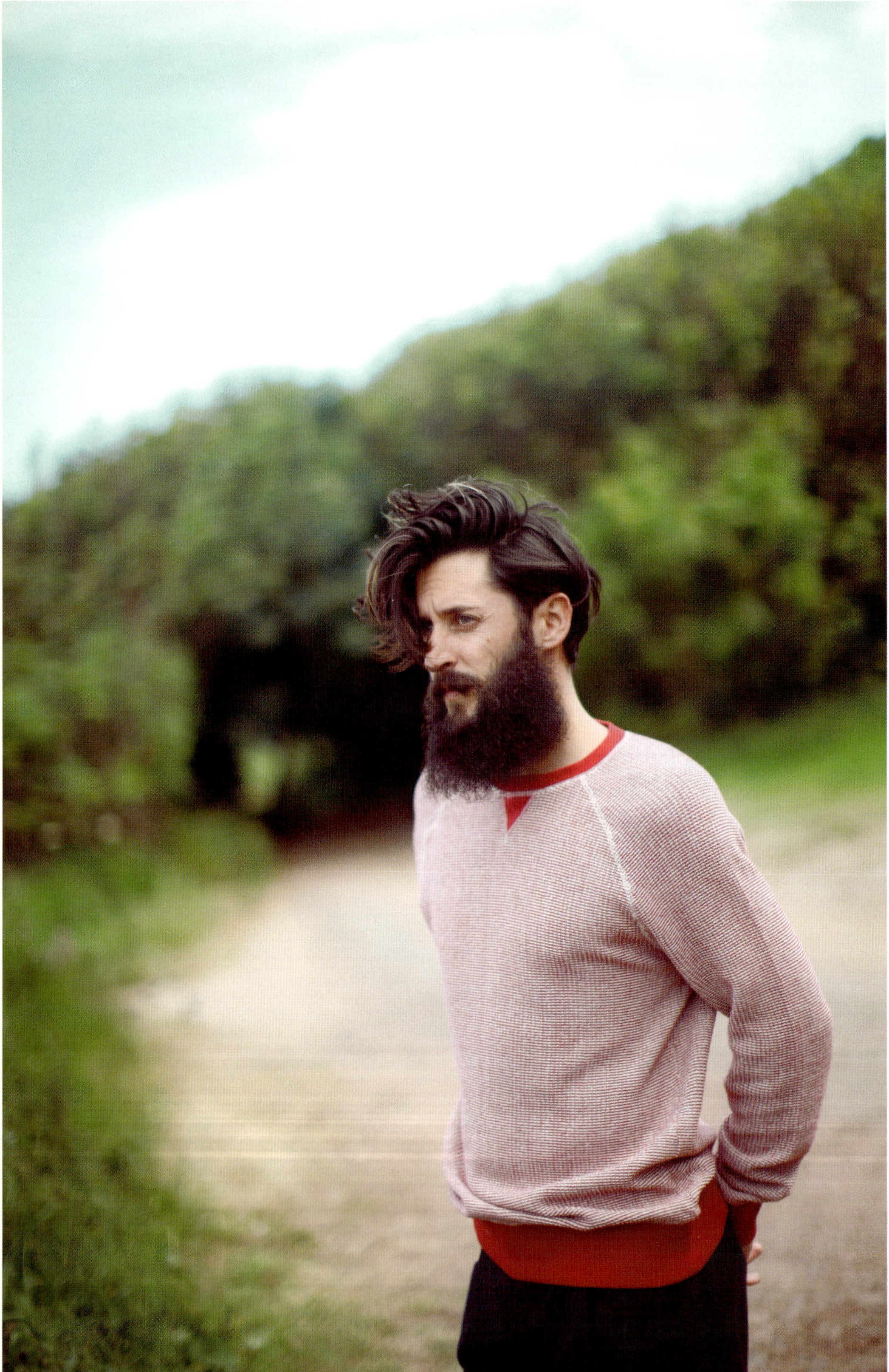

193 • David: Seacliff Beach, North Berwick

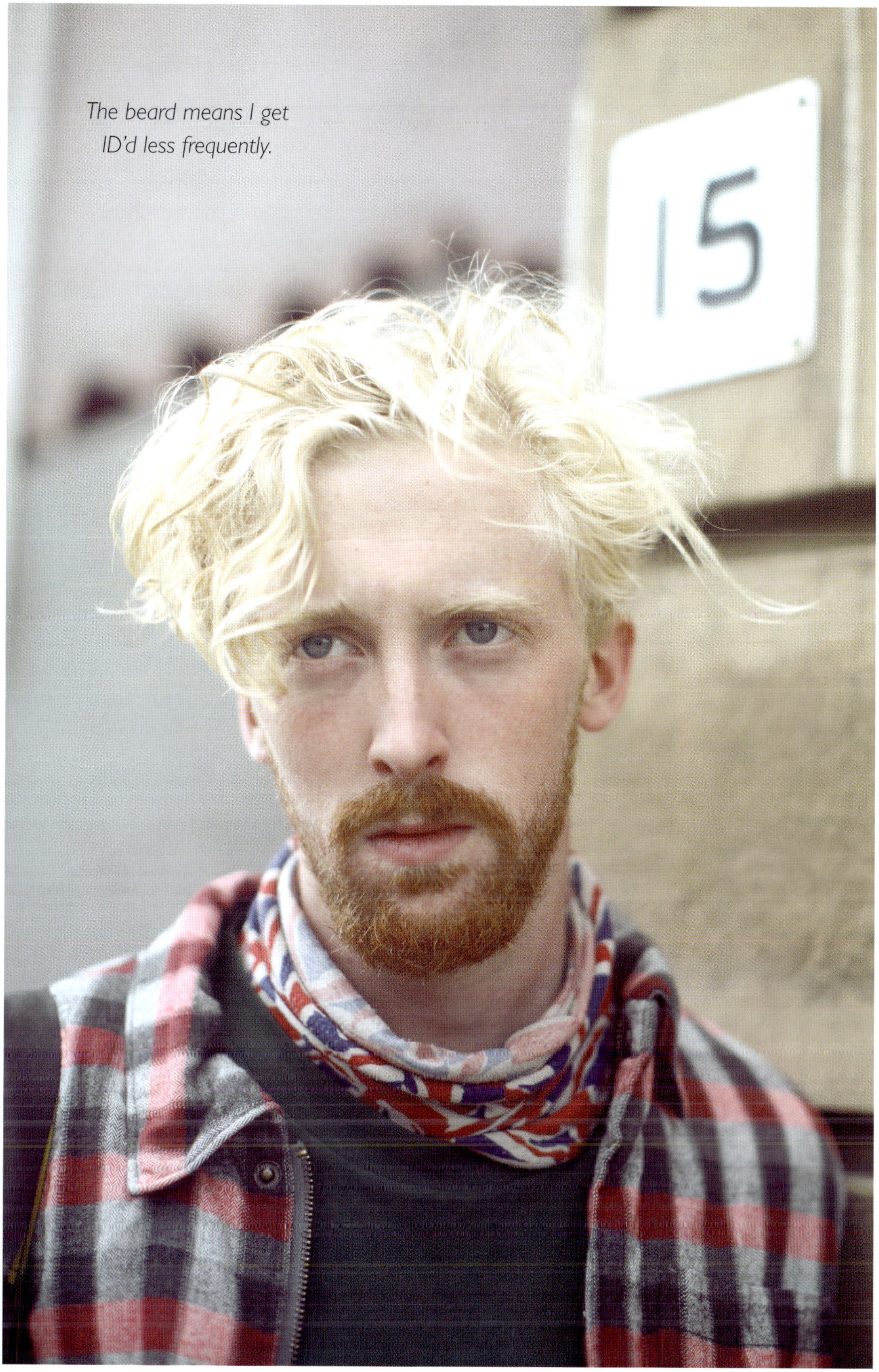

The beard means I get
ID'd less frequently.

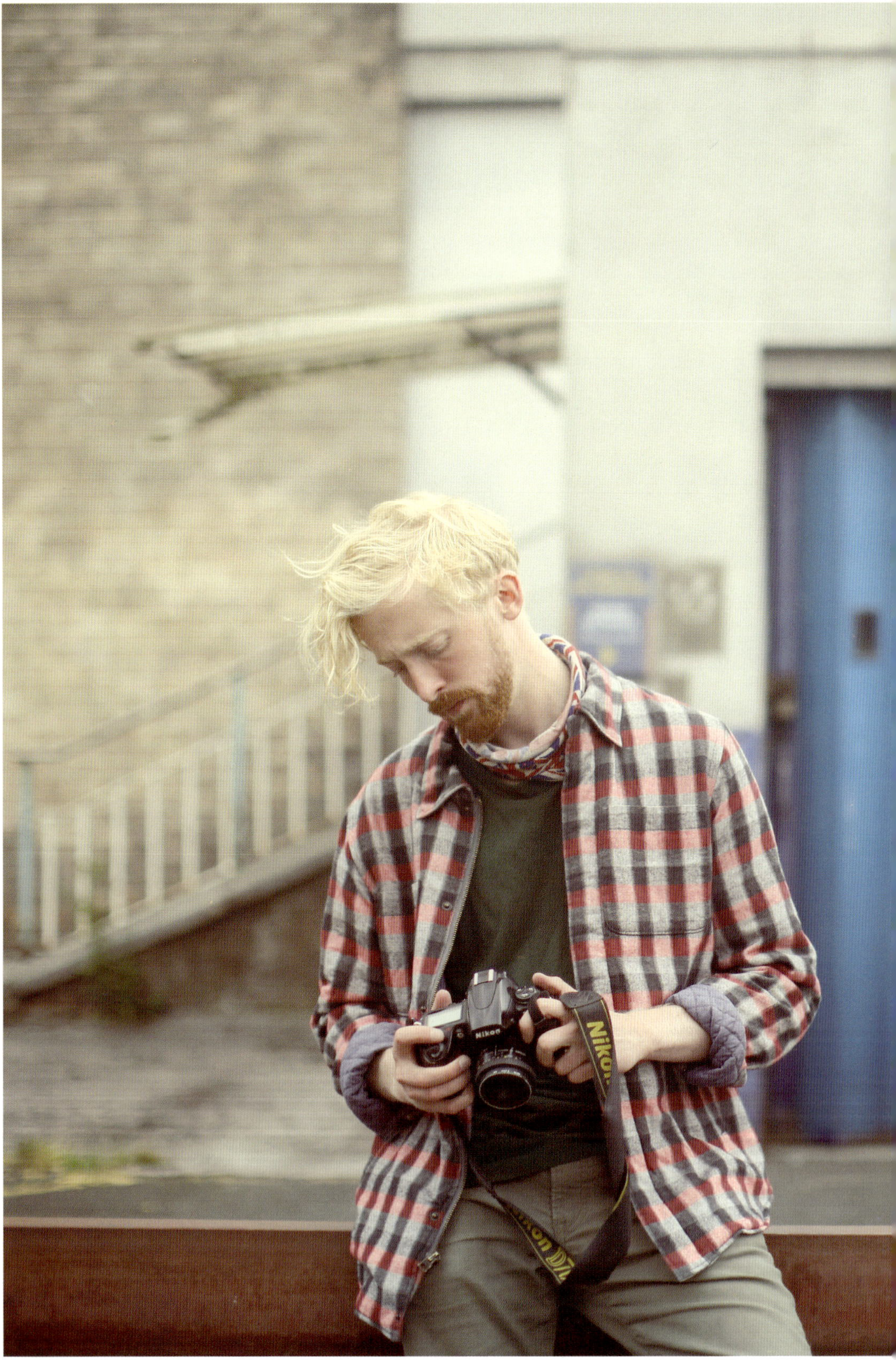
Nikon

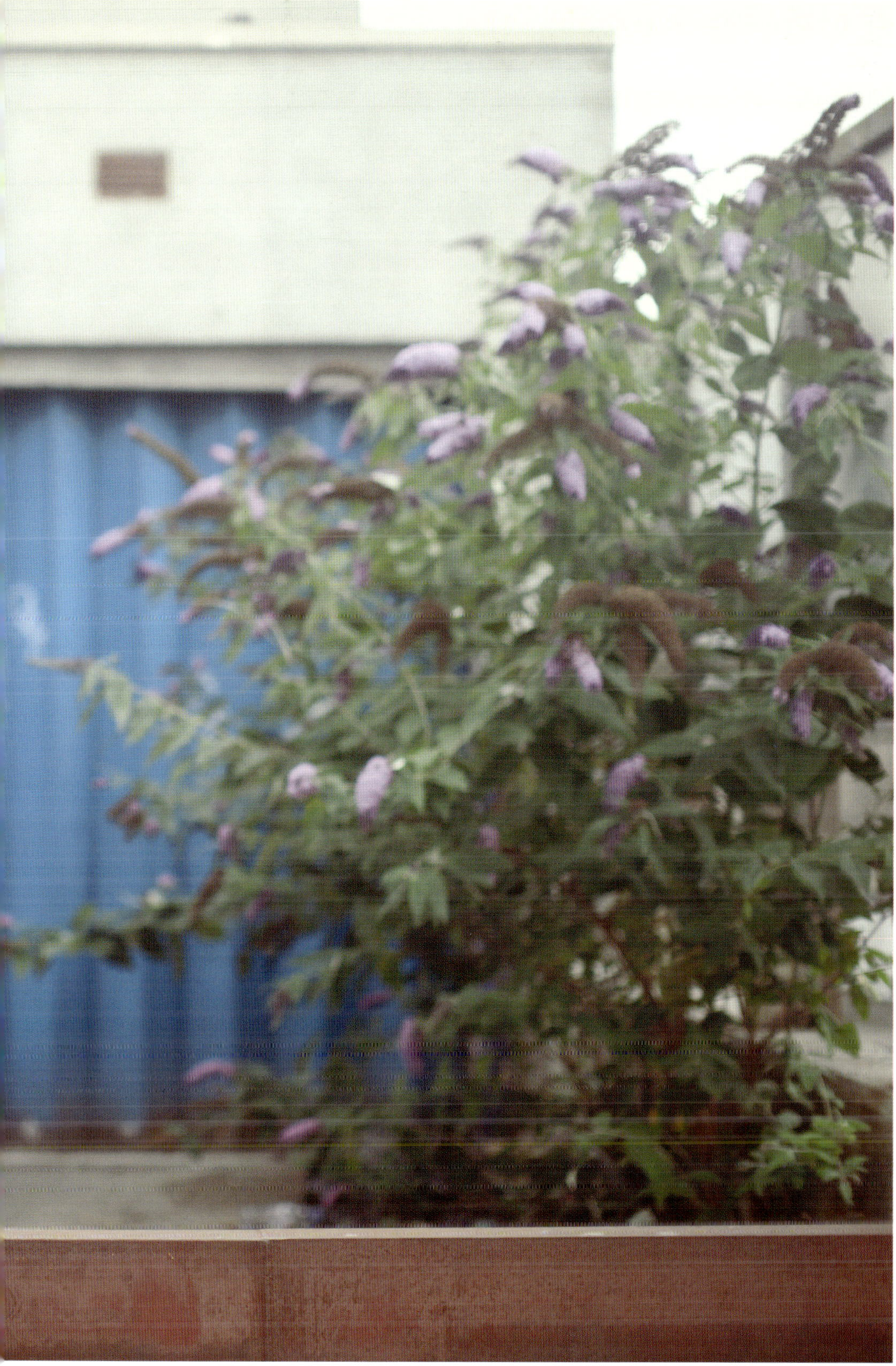

Luke: Dalhousie Street, Glasgow

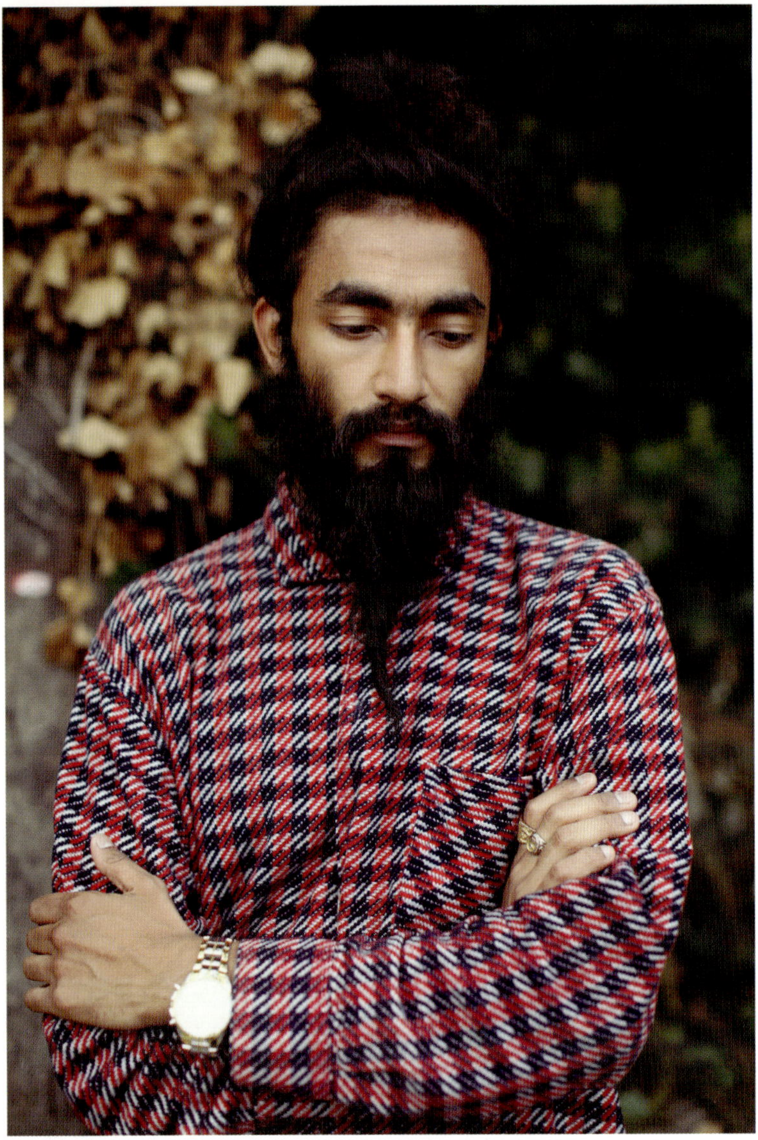

Having lost my father at the age of eighteen, I feel like by wearing a full beard – just like he did – I can pay my respects and remember him in my own personal, private way.

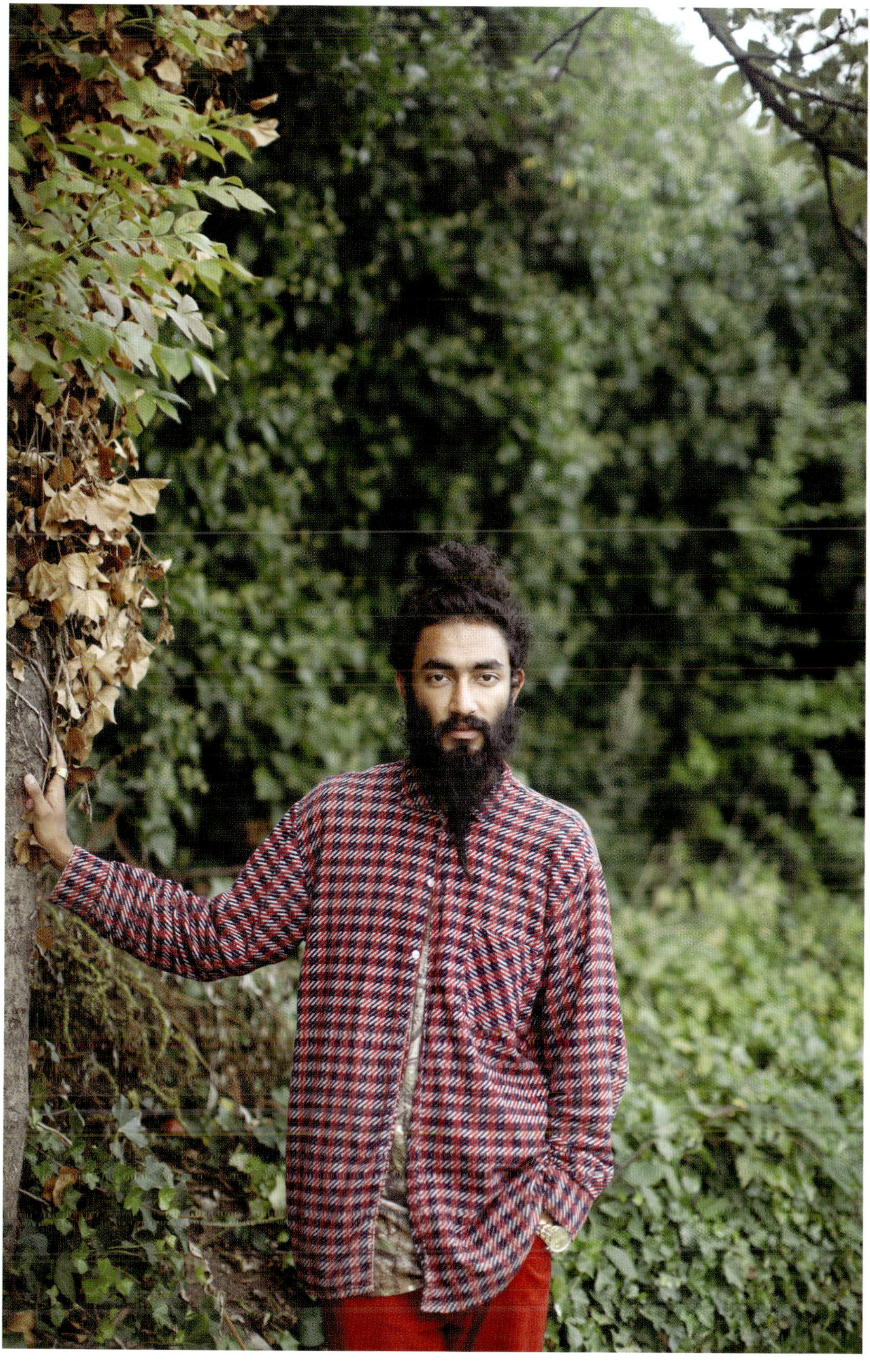

195 • Suren: Grand Union Tow Path, London

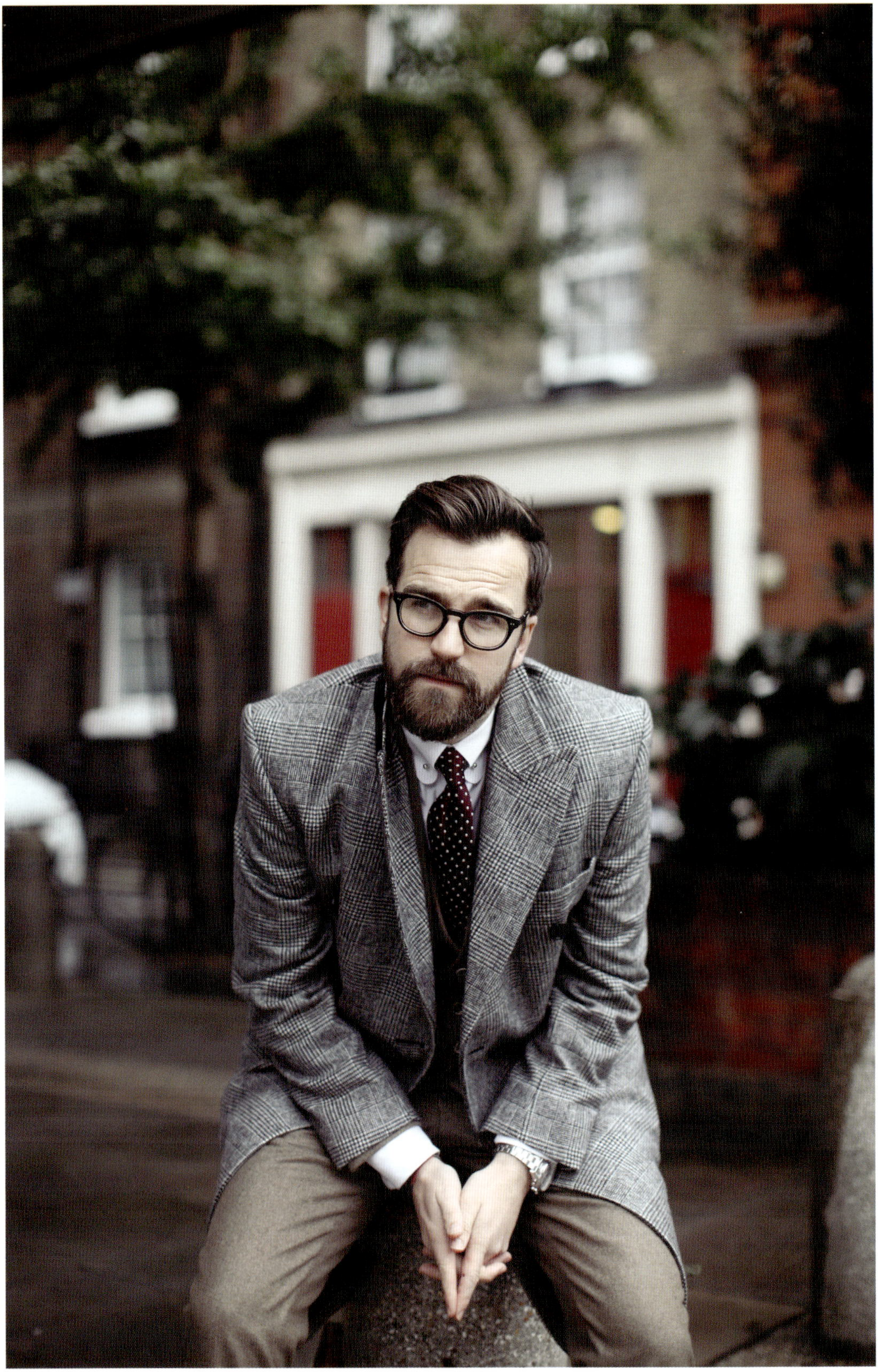

196 • Dan: Lexington Street, London

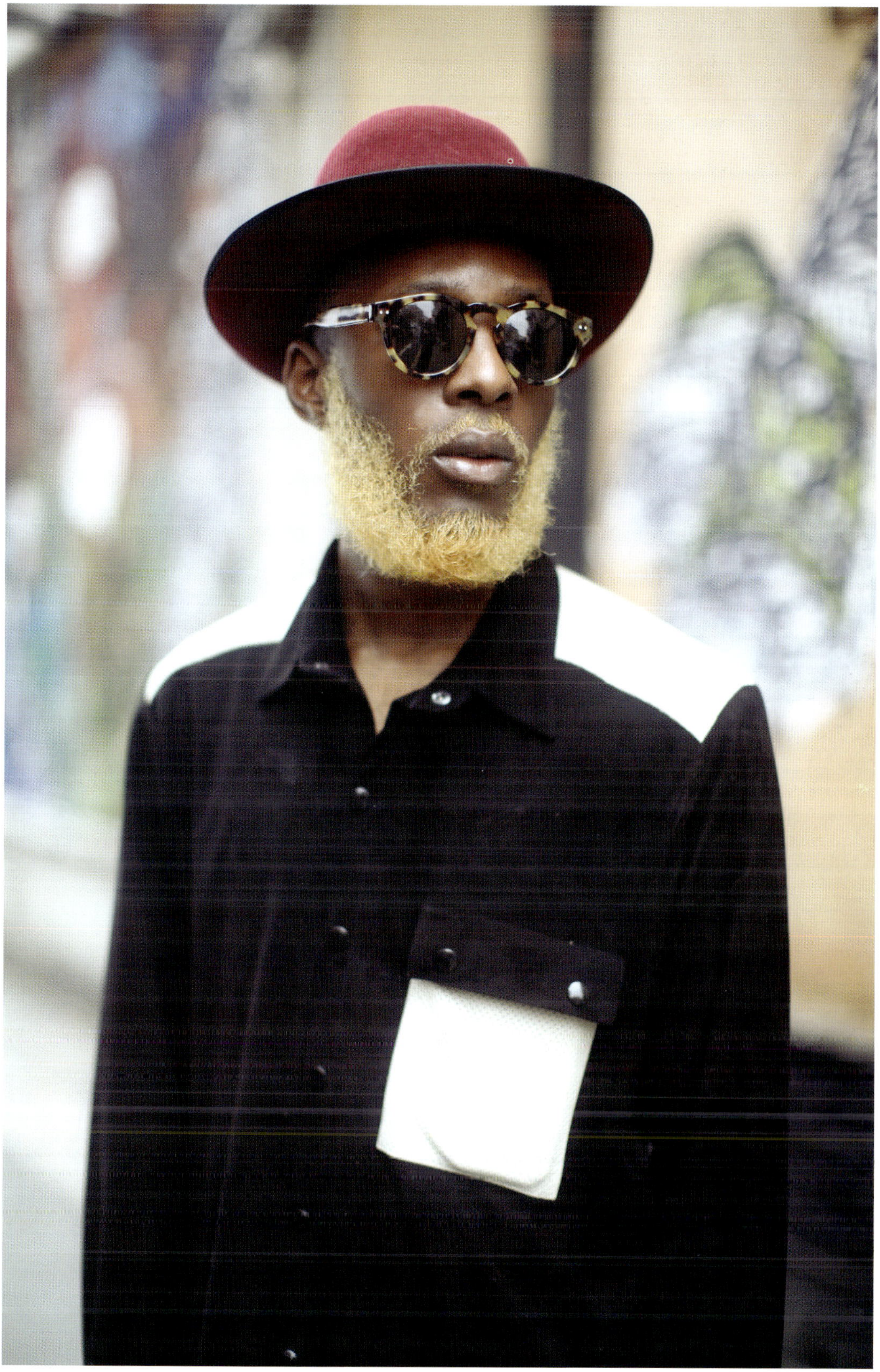

197 • Bevan: Museum Street, London

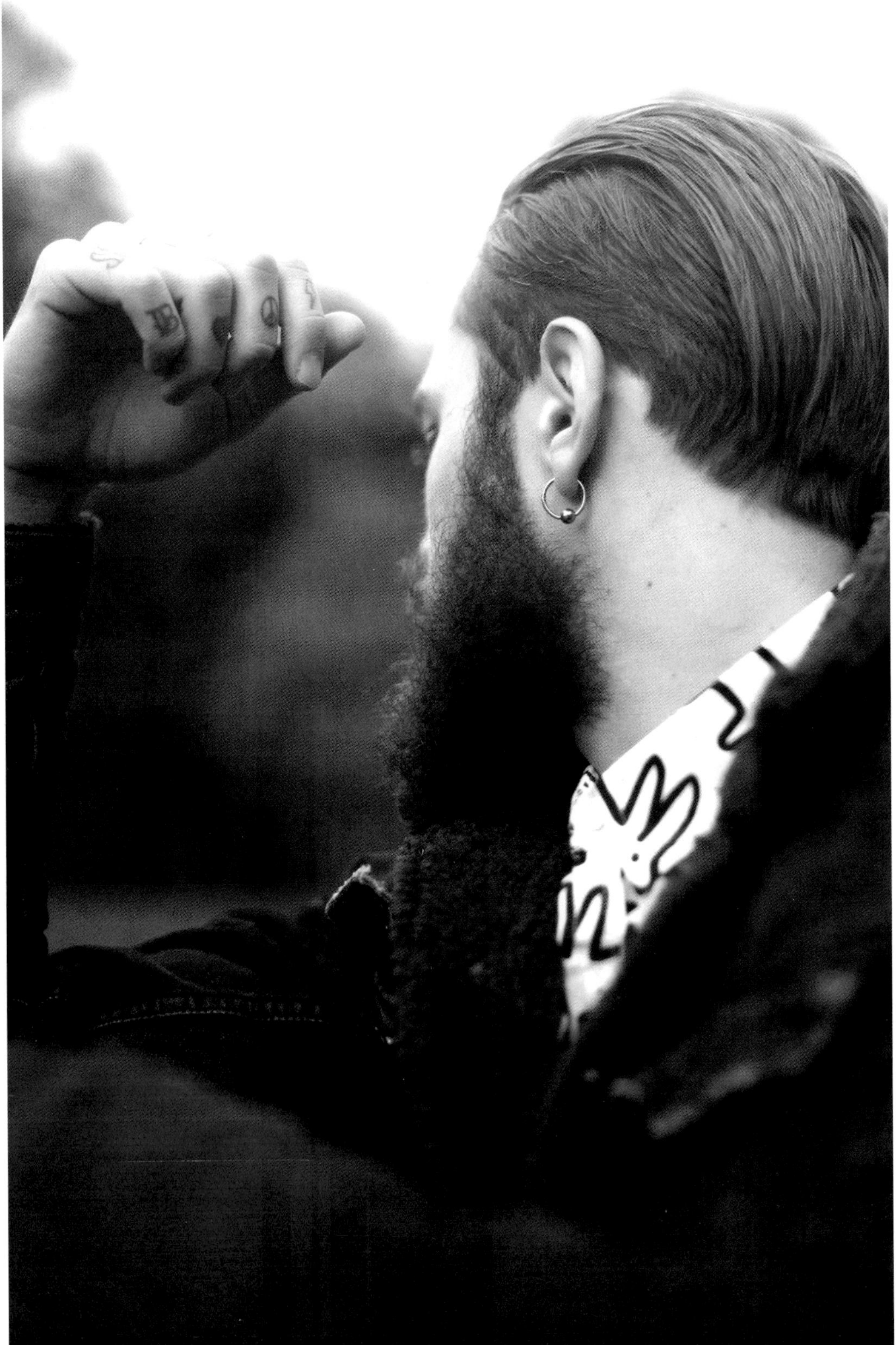

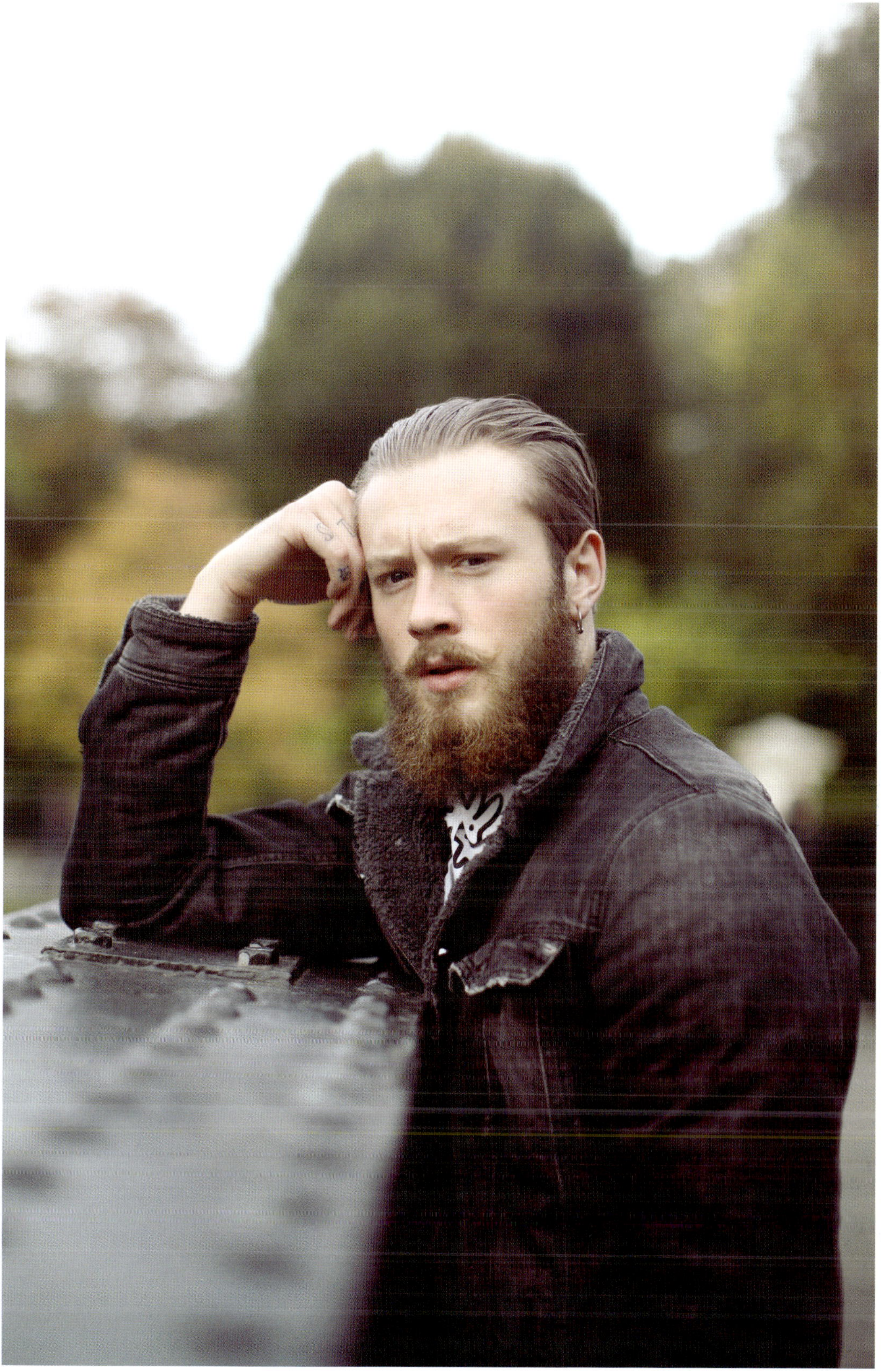

198 • Declan: Regent's Park, London

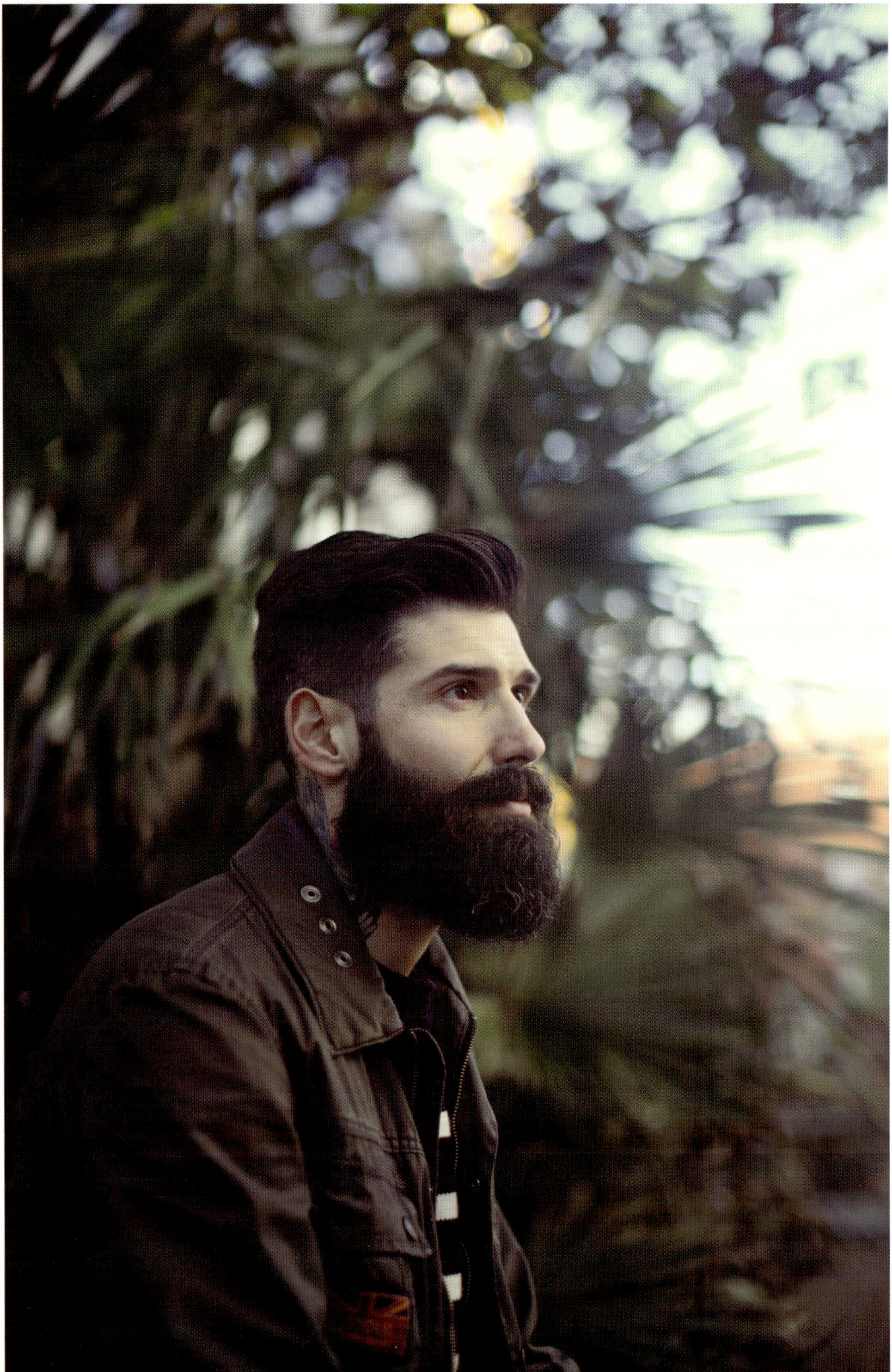

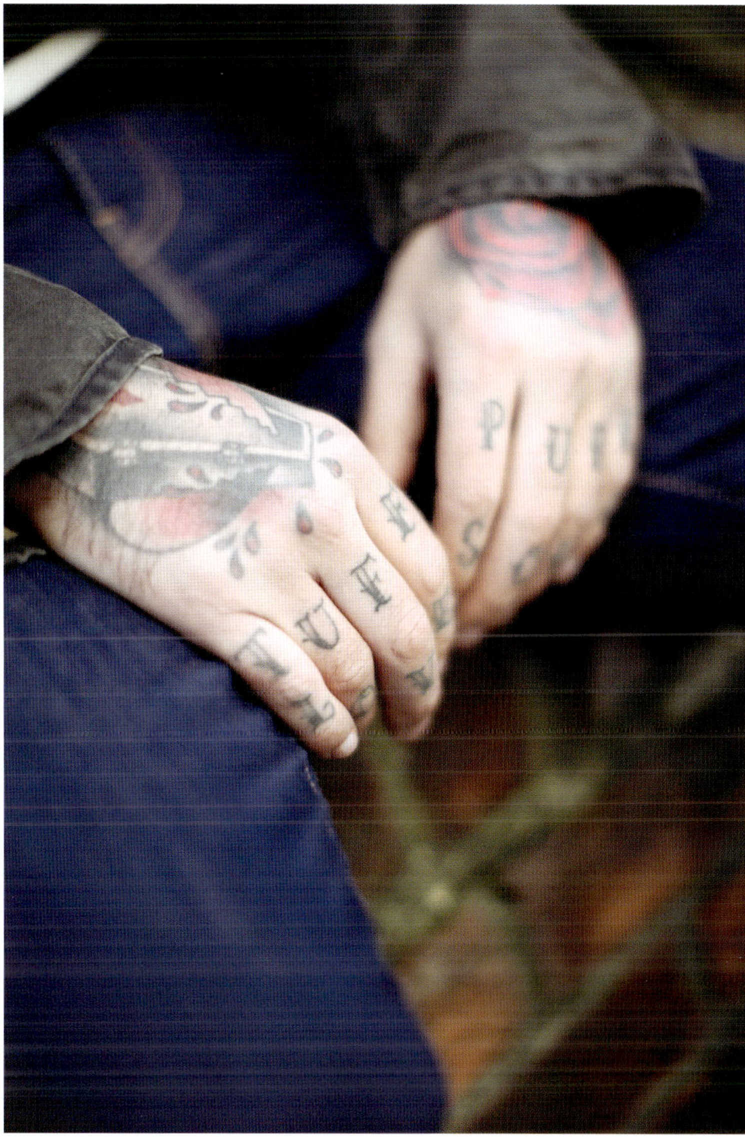

Growing up I was always a big fan of medieval culture & Vikings, and I think from a young age it's been instilled in me that a beard represents strong, powerful men.

To me, it's simple — having a beard is a man thing. It turns heads on the street and I definitely feel more confident with it. I get a lot of people questioning me on my beard and how I keep it looking thick and well maintained — there's a great sense of pride being able to achieve the look I have. Beards sort the men from the boys.

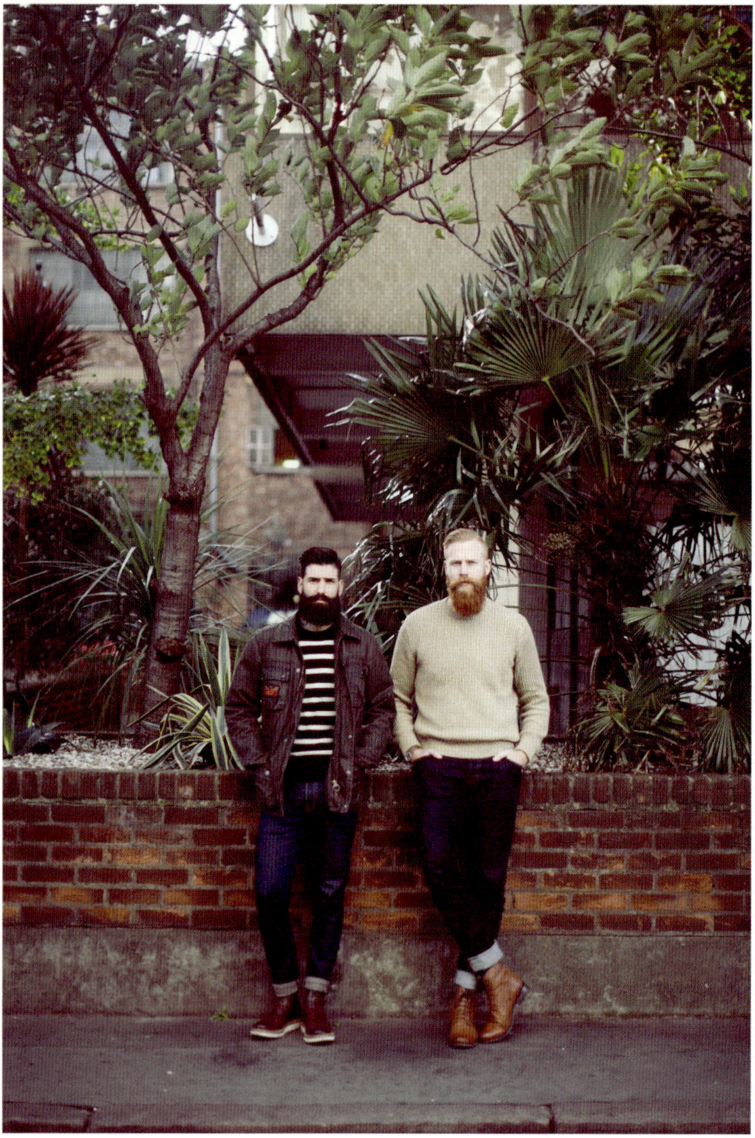

I hear people say that the 'beard trend' will pass and that it'll only been short lived. What these people don't realise is that a strong beard has been the sign of strength, individuality and creativity for many generations past. I didn't grow mine to become part of a trend, but I do find the amount of interest I receive seems to grow directly in proportion to the length of my beard. I've had opportunities, experiences and forged friendships that wouldn't have occurred without it. It's become my identity and I don't anticipate shedding it any time soon, fashion or not!

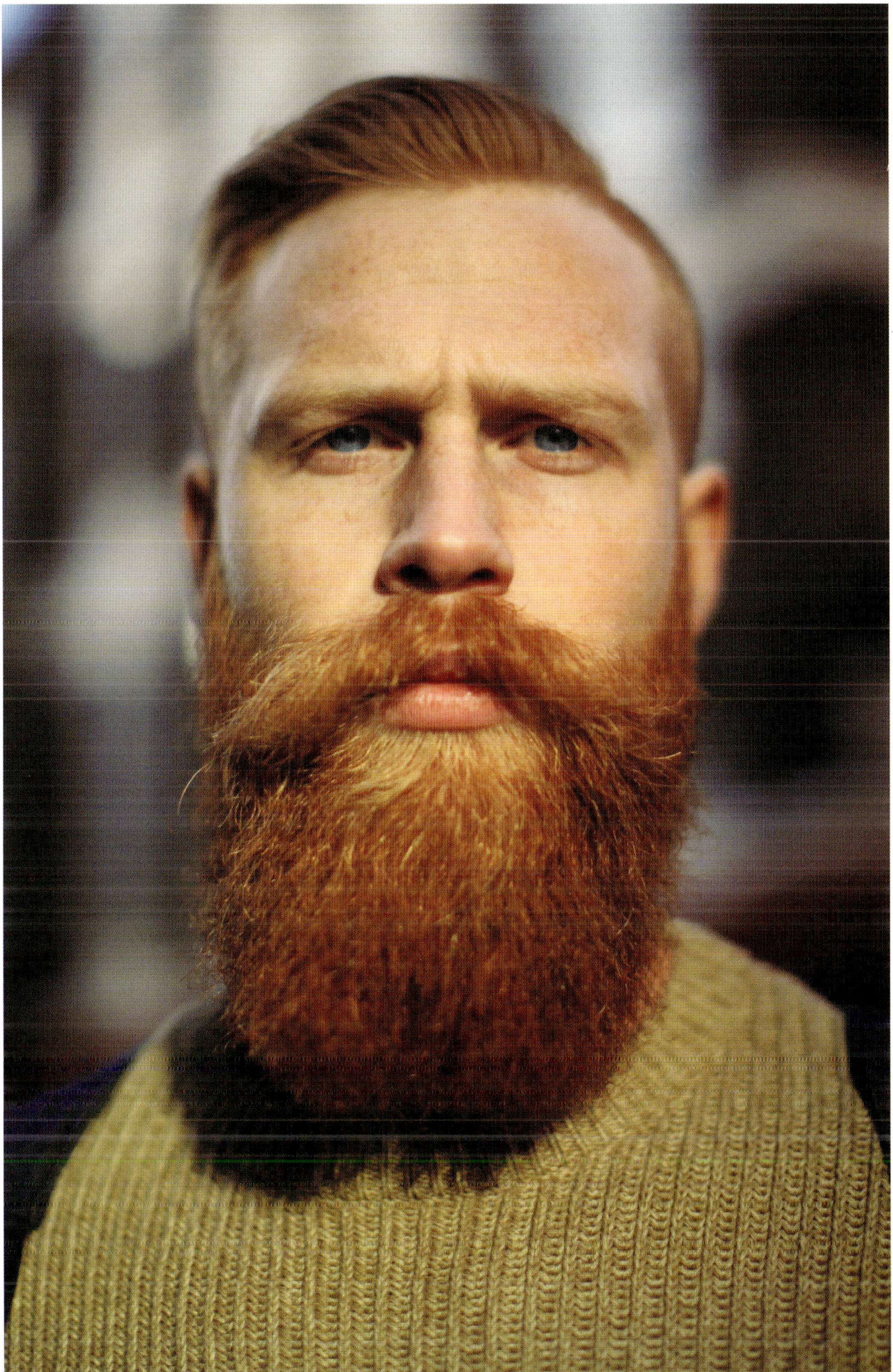

200 • Gwilym: Broadwick Street, London

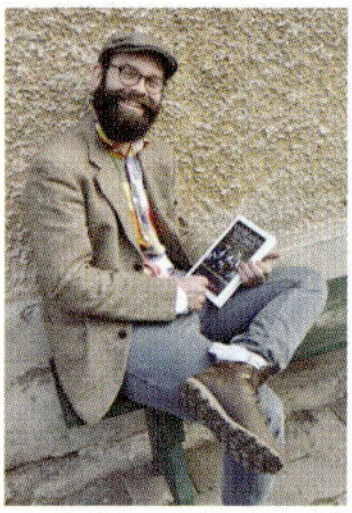

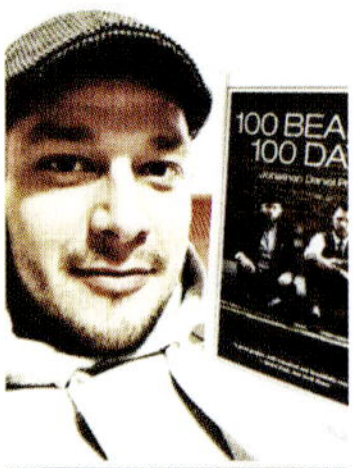

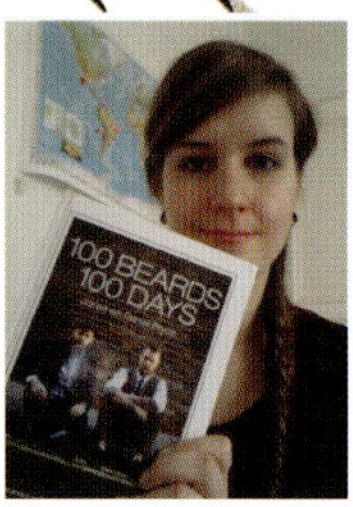

Author Interview

What inspired you to photograph bearded men?

Beards are one of those timeless, fascinating subjects. People of both genders are obsessed with a good beard. I've been photographing style on the street for over 6 years now, so my eyes are tuned into evolving trends. After moving back to the UK from Paris, I became particularly aware of facial hair. Being bearded is ubiquitous in Paris for all age groups and for me this highlighted an evolution in British style. I noticed more and more men were adopting it, so this was really the main spark for the hirsute being the focus of a new documentary project.

Why did you decide to start the project in London when you'd seen so many beards in Paris?

London is an incredible city for diversity and it just felt like the right timing. I'd just won 'Photographer of the Year' at the Scottish Fashion Awards and moved back to the Big Smoke for work. The style in Paris is always chic and the light is perfect for photography but there is a uniformity there. In London the people are as varied as the neighbourhoods so I wanted to take the opportunity to discover new areas. If I were to do a photographic project in Paris over a period of consecutive days, the outcome out be very different from what I've captured here. London is full of colour and grit which makes it a great city to people-watch.

Where did you go looking to find all of your men?

In cities that I know, there are certain areas which are guaranteed to produce great results. I love walking, so took to the streets by foot from east to west, north to south. Of course, every time I passed through Soho, Covent Garden and Shoreditch I always spotted a gentleman with fantastic facial hair, but tried my best to keep it diverse. The central hubs have such high concentrations of people that the power is in the numbers. These are also areas where many artists have studios and creative agencies are based, which makes sense when you consider that many employers still don't allow facial hair at work. Sometimes the best shots come when I'm not looking. I've had many moments sitting in a coffee shop window or reading in the park and having to drop everything and go running when I see a great potential photograph. I actually got thrown out of the British Library on Day 17 when photographing Ali … a long story.

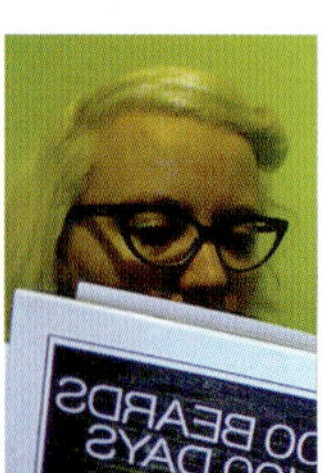

How long did the project take in total?

I first thought of shooting a daily blog of beards in early 2012. It wasn't until July 1st 2012 that I published the first photo on Tumblr. For 100 consecutive days I went into the streets to find a new bearded man to photograph and completed the initial run on October 8th. I published the first book and held the first exhibition in December 2012. The next 100 portraits were completed by October 2013 – a total of 2 years!

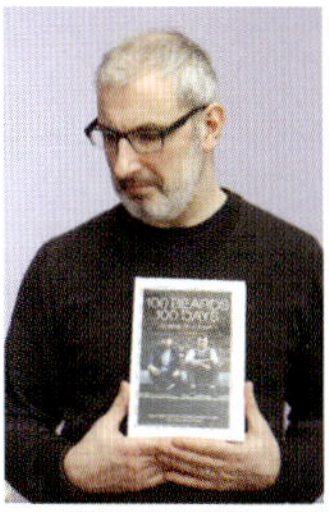

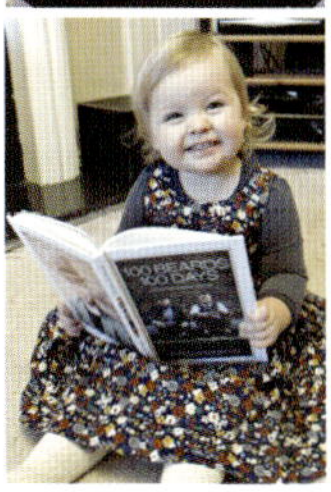

Which beard portraits are your favourite?

It's near impossible to say — each carries a different meaning. It was interesting to speak with people at my exhibitions last year — everyone has their preferences which are always different. As I remember the conversations with each subject, often that influences my opinion on which is the best work. I love Roy in Cecil Court on day 47 for many reasons. Also, Richie Culver on day 99 is a strong image and Suren on day 195 stands out for me. There's something so serene about his presence.

What is your opinion on the beard as a fashion statement?

There's no denying that the beard is a fashion statement. Just looking at the increased use of bearded models in the menswear shows of Milan and Paris over the past few years will prove this. However, there are a core group of beard wearers who don't do it for fashion. It's a way of life or a personal preference. Those men will continue to cultivate a beard when the trend has passed.

Are there any differences in trends for beards in your other destinations compared to London trends?

British style is directly links to street and music culture. I see the rock 'n' roll beard a lot in the UK. There's also a gentlemanly influence here as we do have a tradition of beard-wearing. Paris is more about the 'bobo', the French hipster. Wearing A.P.C., smoking and sipping café créme in a brasserie. In contrast, New York has a greater influence of American biker culture than anywhere else and a history of workwear for men.

Artistically speaking, what did you find most difficult about photographing men with facial hair?

Men are notoriously difficult to photograph on the street because quite often they're too shy. Women tend to be much more open but when I mention the name of the project '*100 beards, 100 days*' it nearly always gets a laugh and then they say 'yes.' About fifty days into it I found, to my surprise, that many of the guys I approached were already fans of the blog, which certainly influenced their reaction. One of my focal points is trying to capture a truly personal moment in the imagery, is a challenge that I feel I overcame with most.

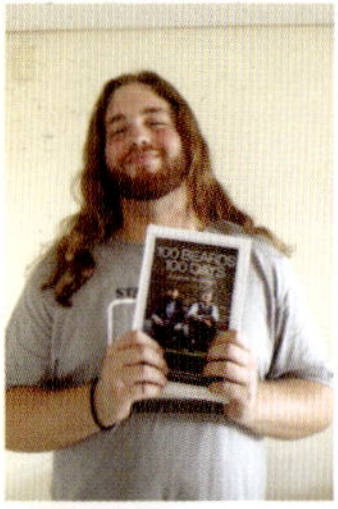

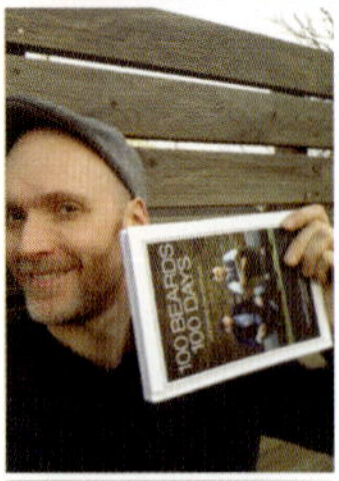

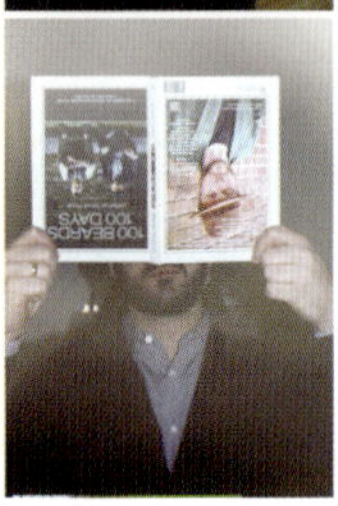

How do these photos differ from your usual street style work?

This project is a lot more about the individual people. I actually discovered a lot about timing, treating my subjects in a new way and also experimenting with light. I intentionally chose beards because they're more intimate than a clothing trend. It was important to come away with a set of portraits capturing a specific group of people in this place and time, and I was conscious of creating a good rapport with the guys, which isn't always possible with street style photography. I'm in touch with quite a few to this day.

With the volume and deadlines involved, how difficult was the process of selection?

I spend anywhere between 5 and 20 minutes per subject, so I can end up with 40 frames — editing is tricky. I spend a lot of time with selections, and sometimes get a second opinion. With nearly every subject there were multiple photographs I loved, and that's part of the reason for having the new book. I wanted to show some out-takes.

The project involved you cultivating your own beard. Why did you do this and who are you're own beard inspirations?

I would never have tried growing my own beard if it weren't for so many people asking me about my facial hair status on Twitter. That, plus I wanted to do something a little different to celebrate day 100 of the blog. I have a wealth of inspiration due to all the guys I photographed. I love Nick Wooster's style and his facial hair is always superb. It was such an honour when he blogged about the 100 Beards project.

Do you have any outtakes that just didn't make the cut?

There were so many photos that didn't make it into the book because I was quite strict about sticking to 200 portraits. It's very tough to narrow to just a single image so I'm glad I had the creative freedom of a book to show off the best as it includes double page spreads and group shots. There's an element of risk with street photography when working solely with natural light – within a minute period it can shift from direct sunlight to thick clouds, then rain. I do enjoy the challenge.

How would you sum them up as a group of subjects?

All of the men I photographed have *panache,* sophistication. And no matter the 'style', I find this refreshingly widespread — in contrast to the media portrayals of men these days. This group has a certain something about them – confidence, self-expression, nuance… signifying, to me at least, a renaissance of much broader proportions.

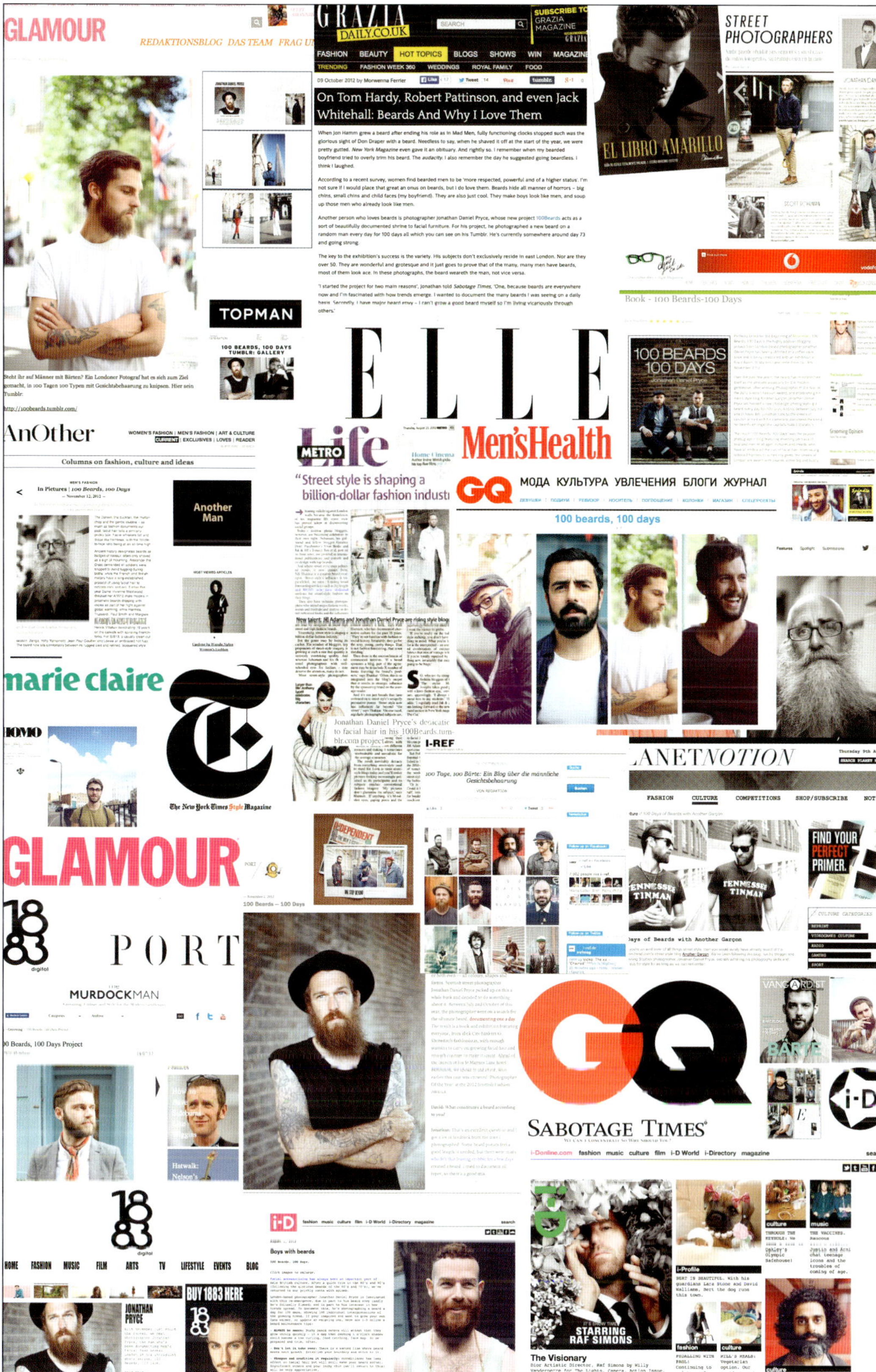

100 beards: IN THE MEDIA

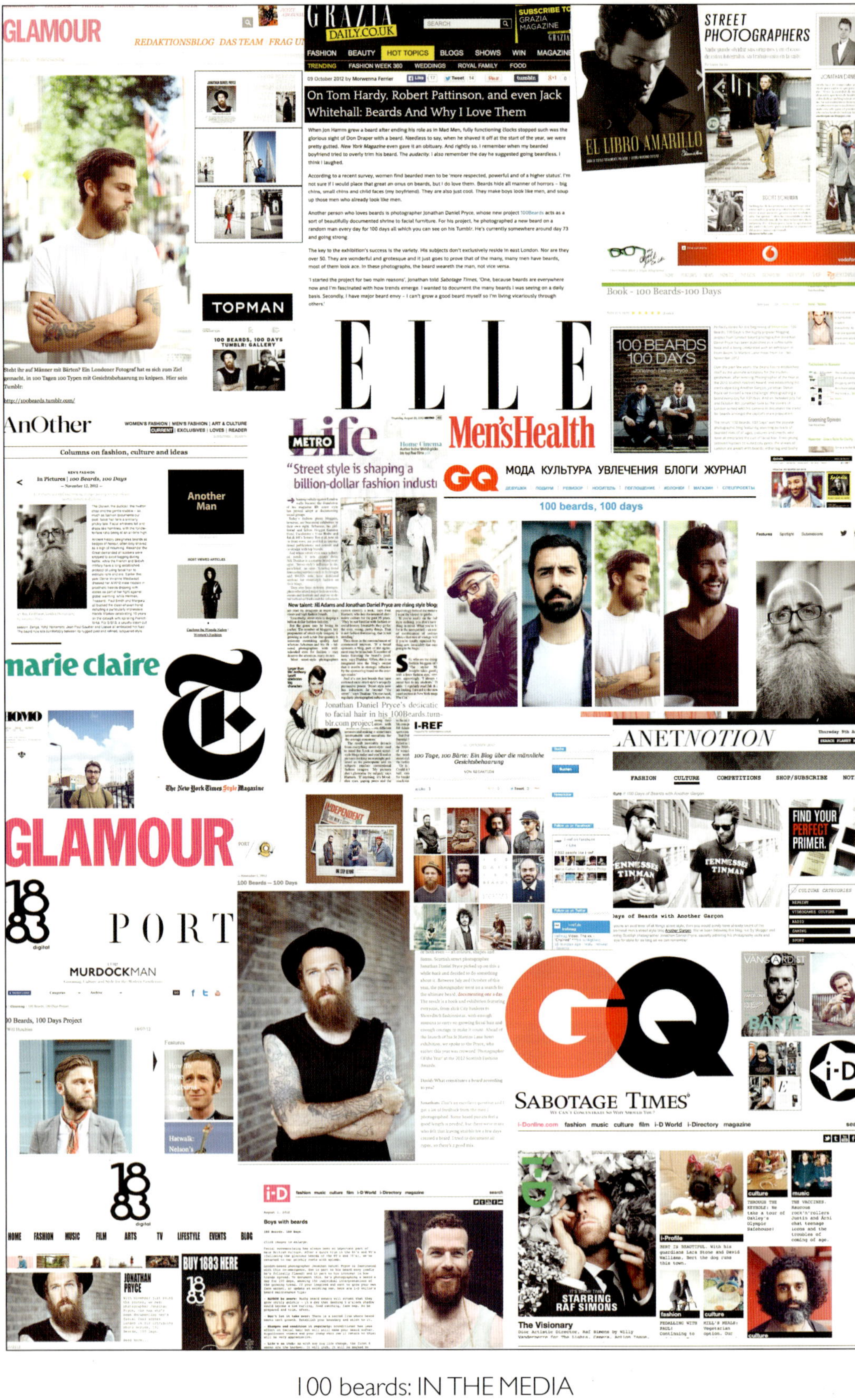

100 beards: IN THE MEDIA